THE ELIZABETHAN TOP TEN

Material Readings in Early Modern Culture

This series provides a forum for studies that consider the material forms of texts as part of an investigation into early modern culture. The editors invite proposals of a multi- or interdisciplinary nature, and particularly welcome proposals that combine archival research with an attention to the theoretical models that might illuminate the reading, writing, and making of texts, as well as projects that take innovative approaches to the study of material texts, both in terms the kinds of primary materials under investigation, and in terms of methodologies. What are the questions that have yet to be asked about writing in its various possible embodied forms? Are there varieties of materiality that are critically neglected? How does form mediate and negotiate content? In what ways do the physical features of texts inform how they are read, interpreted and situated?

Consideration will be given to both monographs and collections of essays. The range of topics covered in this series includes, but is not limited to: History of the book, publishing, the book trade, printing, typography (layout, type, typeface, blank/white space, paratextual apparatus); technologies of the written word: ink, paper, watermarks, pens, presses; surprising or neglected material forms of writing; print culture; manuscript studies; social space, context, location of writing; social signs, cues, codes imbued within the material forms of texts; ownership and the social practices of reading: marginalia, libraries, environments of reading and reception; codicology, palaeography and critical bibliography; production, transmission, distribution and circulation; archiving and the archaeology of knowledge; orality and oral culture; the material text as object or thing.

The Elizabethan Top Ten

Defining Print Popularity in Early Modern England

Edited by

ANDY KESSON
University of Kent, UK

and

EMMA SMITH
Hertford College, Oxford, UK

ASHGATE

Published by
Ashgate Publishing Limited
Wey Court East
Union Road
Farnham
Surrey, GU9 7PT
England

Ashgate Publishing Company
110 Cherry Street
Suite 3-1
Burlington, VT 05401-3818
USA

www.ashgate.com

British Library Cataloguing in Publication Data
The Elizabethan top ten: defining print popularity in early modern England. – (Material readings in early modern culture)
　　1. English literature – Early modern, 1500–1700 – Appreciation. 2. Books and reading – England – History – 16th century. 3. Books and reading – England – History – 17th century. 4. Reading interests – England – History – 16th century. 5. Reading interests – England – History – 17th century.
　　I. Series II. Kesson, Andy. III. Smith, Emma (Emma Josephine)
　　028.9'0942'09031-dc23

The Library of Congress has cataloged the printed edition as follows:
The Elizabethan top ten: defining print popularity in Early Modern England / edited by Andy Kesson and Emma Smith.
　　pages cm. — (Material Readings in Early Modern Culture)
　　Includes bibliographical references and index.
　　ISBN 978-1-4094-4029-1 (hardcover: alk. paper)—ISBN 978-1-4094-4030-7 (ebook)—ISBN 978-1-4724-0587-6 (epub)
　　1. English literature—Early modern, 1500–1700—History and criticism. 2. Popular literature—England—History and criticism. 3. Popular culture and literature—Great Britain—History. 4. Great Britain—History—Elizabeth, 1558–1603. I. Kesson, Andy, editor of compilation. II. Smith, Emma (Emma Josephine) editor of compilation.
　　PR428.P65E45 2013
　　820.9'355—dc23

2012050687

ISBN 9781409440291 (hbk)
ISBN 9781409440307 (ebk)
ISBN 9781472405876 (ebk - ePUB)

Printed in the United Kingdom by Henry Ling Limited, at the Dorset Press, Dorchester, DT1 1HD

for Elizabeth Macfarlane and Jimmy Tucker

Contents

List of Figures

Notes on Contributors

S.K. Barker held postdoctoral research fellowships on the French Vernacular Book Project at the University of St Andrews and on the Renaissance Cultural Crossroads Project, based at the University of Warwick. She is lecturer in European History at the University of Exeter, where her current research focuses on international news in the sixteenth and seventeenth centuries.

Brian Cummings is Anniversary Professor at the University of York in the Department of English and Related Literature. His edition of the *Book of Common Prayer: the Texts of 1549, 1559, and 1662,* appeared with Oxford University Press in 2011. In 2012 he was guest curator of the exhibition 'Royal Devotion: the Monarchy and the Book of Common Prayer' at Lambeth Palace Library in London.

Alan B. Farmer is Associate Professor of English at the Ohio State University. He is co-editor of *Localizing Caroline Drama: Politics and Economics of the Early Modern English Stage, 1625–1642* (Palgrave, 2006) and the co-creator of *DEEP: Database of Early English Playbooks* (<http://deep.sas.upenn.edu>). He is currently working on two book projects: *Playbooks and Newsbooks: The Politics of the Thirty Years' War in England, 1620–1640,* and *Print, Plays, and Popularity in Shakespeare's England* (written with Zachary Lesser).

Lori Anne Ferrell is Professor of Early Modern History and Literature at Claremont Graduate University. She is the author, most recently, of *The Bible and the People* (Yale University Press, 2008) and is currently editing *Vol. XI: Sermons Preached in St Paul's Cathedral, 1623–1625* for *The Oxford Sermons of John Donne.*

Juliet Fleming teaches literary theory and Renaissance literature at New York University. She is the author of *Graffiti and the Writing Arts of Early Modern England* (Reaktion, 2001) and is completing a book on Derrida and the early modern archive.

Andy Kesson is Lecturer in Early Modern Studies at the University of Kent. His first book is *John Lyly and Early Modern Authorship* (Manchester, 2013). He is currently working on a project entitled *Before Shakespeare*, a history of early London commercial theatres, and, with Stephen Purcell, on a project studying early modern playtexts and performance choices.

Peter Kirwan is Lecturer in Shakespeare and Early Modern Drama at the University of Nottingham, and a trustee of the British Shakespeare Association. His research on the *Shakespeare Apocrypha* has appeared in *Shakespeare Quarterly* and

Philological Quarterly, and he is currently working on a monograph on the Shakespeare canon as well as a co-edited collection of essays on Shakespeare and the digital.

Zachary Lesser is Associate Professor of English at the University of Pennsylvania. He is the author of *Renaissance Drama and the Politics of Publication: Readings in the English Book Trade* (Cambridge University Press, 2004), and the co-creator of *DEEP: Database of Early English Playbooks*. Currently he is finishing a book on Q1 *Hamlet* and co-writing a book on print popularity with Alan Farmer.

Lucy Munro is Lecturer in Shakespeare and Early Modern Drama Studies at King's College London. She is the author of *Children of the Queen's Revels: A Jacobean Theatre Repertory* (2005) and *Archaic Style in English Literature, 1590-1674* (2013) and the editor of plays by Shakespeare and Wilkins, Fletcher, Brome and Sharpham. She is currently working on editions of Dekker, Ford and Rowley's *The Witch of Edmonton* and Shirley's *The Gentleman of Venice*.

Beth Quitslund is Associate Professor of English at Ohio University. She is the author of *The Reformation in Rhyme: Sternhold, Hopkins and the English Metrical Psalter, 1547–1603* (Ashgate, 2008) and, with Nicholas Temperley, co-editor of *The Whole Book of Psalms: A Critical Edition of the Texts and Tunes* (forthcoming from the Renaissance English Text Society).

Neil Rhodes is Professor of English Literature and Cultural History at the University of St Andrews and Visiting Professor at the University of Granada. His publications include *Shakespeare and the Origins of English* (Oxford University Press, 2004), and he is Co-General Editor with Andrew Hadfield of the *MHRA Tudor and Stuart Translations*.

Catherine Richardson works on the material experience of daily life in early modern England at the University of Kent. She is author of *Shakespeare and Material Culture* (Oxford University Press, 2011) and *Domestic Life and Domestic Tragedy in Early Modern England: The Material Life of the Household* (Manchester University Press, 2006), editor of *Clothing Culture 1350–1650* (Ashgate, 2004) and (with Tara Hamling) *Everyday Objects: Medieval and Early Modern Material Culture and Its Meanings* (Ashgate, 2009), and is currently writing *A Day at Home in Early Modern England: The Materiality of Domestic Life 1500–1700* for Yale.

Abigail Shinn is a Postdoctoral Research Fellow at the University of York, working on the AHRC project 'Conversion Narratives in Early Modern Europe'. She has previously published work on Edmund Spenser and popular print culture and is currently working on a book project entitled *Tales of Turning: Conversion Narratives in Early Modern England*. Alongside Matthew Dimmock and Andrew Hadfield she is editing the *Ashgate Research Companion to Popular Culture in Early Modern England*.

Emma Smith is Fellow and Tutor in English at Hertford College, University of Oxford. She has published widely on Shakespeare and early modern drama, including most recently an edition of *Five Revenge Plays* (Penguin, 2012) and, with Laurie Maguire, *30 Great Myths about Shakespeare* (Wiley-Blackwell, 2013). She is working on a history of the Shakespeare First Folio.

Helen Smith is Senior Lecturer at the University of York. Her publications include *'Grossly Material Things': Women and Book Production in Early Modern England* (Oxford University Press, 2012) and *Renaissance Paratexts*, co-edited with Louise Wilson (Cambridge University Press, 2011). Helen is Co-Investigator on the AHRC-funded project 'Conversion Narratives in Early Modern Europe', and is currently working on a monograph, provisionally titled *The Life in Things: Matter, Materials, and Objects in Early Modern England*.

Adam Smyth is a Reader in Early Modern Literature at Birkbeck College, London. He is the author of, among other things, *Autobiography in Early Modern England* (Cambridge University Press, 2010), and is currently working on forms of book destruction in the sixteenth and seventeenth centuries.

Louise Wilson is a Leverhulme Early Career Fellow at the University of St Andrews. She is the co-editor (with Helen Smith) of *Renaissance Paratexts* (2011) and has also published on early modern romance readerships, reading practices and print networks. She is currently working on a book on reading for pleasure in early modern England and is editing Anthony Munday's *Palmerin of England* for the *MHRA Tudor and Stuart Translations*.

Introduction:
Towards a Definition of Print Popularity

Andy Kesson and Emma Smith

The Crown of Laurel on Bad Art?

After some months dominated by J.K. Rowling's *Harry Potter* series, *The New York Times Book Review* announced a change in policy for its famous book best-seller listings. Their new list of 'trade paperback fiction … gives more emphasis to the literary novels and short-story collections reviewed so often in our pages'.[1] The aim is clear: to exclude some – in fact, the very top – bestsellers from the best-seller list in order to make space for books whose value was signalled more by their presence in the paper's review pages than by their sales figures alone. Six months later the paper attempted again to explain the rationale for its decision, but served to further confuse the distinction between 'trade' and its tautological formula of 'mass-market' bestsellers. In March 2008 Ian McEwan's novel *Atonement* was in both charts, ranked 8th and 17th, respectively.

'You may still wonder', the paper wrote, 'why we decided to separate the mass-market and trade best-seller lists. The reason is that mass-market books – no surprise – tend to sell in larger numbers than trade. A list based on the number of copies a paperback sells will usually be dominated by mass-market'. One might expect that a list headed 'bestsellers' would indeed register those books that sold the highest number of copies, but here this is in conflict with a different measurement of value: trade books 'are the novels that reading groups choose and college professors teach'.[2] 'Best-selling' is here in an uneasy relationship with other, less quantifiable indices of value, or, to put it another way, the hyphenated term 'best-selling' is under some strain, as 'best' starts to serve less as an adjectival modifier to 'selling' and more its ideological opposite. Oscar Wilde's aperçu in his 'Lecture to Art Students' seems relevant here: 'popularity is the crown of laurel which the world puts on bad art. Whatever is popular is wrong'.[3]

This uncomfortable compromise between quantitative and qualitative indicators of value is not confined to newspaper bestsellers. Annual lists revealing which authors are most borrowed from UK public libaries, or the metrics by which Top Ten music charts are calculated have been subject to similar caveats and recalibrations, and indeed the BBC felt itself forced to censor its weekly

---

[1]   *The New York Times Book Review*, 23 September 2007.
[2]   Ibid., 16 March 2008.
[3]   Oscar Wilde, *Essays and Lectures* (London: 1909), 201.

chart show in the week of Margaret Thatcher's funeral in 2013.[4] For various reasons, it seems that we want to elide quantitative and qualitative measures. True 'bestsellers' are just slightly regrettable, an attitude perhaps still bearing the residual anxiety of what J.W. Saunders influentially dubbed 'the stigma of print'.[5]. Popularity is itself suspect. We want the best-seller list to be the same as that list authorized by reading groups and college professors, and when it isn't, we tweak the arrangement to get a more satisfactory result.

Saunders identified the stigma of print as a specifically Tudor problem. If methodological and ideological questions dog contemporary best-seller lists, where publication and sales data are relatively robust, they are multiplied when turning to the question of print popularity in the Elizabethan period. This book attempts to raise, rather than elide, the practical and methodological challenges of defining print popularity, and, in particular, the interpretative difficulties for literary critics and cultural historians when our sense of what ought to have been a bestseller – because it is what college professors now teach – turns out not to have been. Our title, 'The Elizabethan Top Ten', is self-consciously anachronistic. We have not, for reasons discussed below, tried to tabulate a 'Top Ten' on print editions alone (although if we had, the *Book of Common Prayer*, discussed in Brian Cummings's chapter, and Sternhold and Hopkins's psalm translations, discussed in Beth Quitslund's, would have been there). Rather, we have invited contributors to our Top Ten to either propose a particular popularity case study within a genre – sermons or plays, for instance – or survey a particular aspect of the print market, with an eye to how their focus might form a local contribution to broader issues about writing, publishing and consuming print in the early modern period.

We actively encourage disagreements about what has been left out. We'd be delighted, for instance, if someone angrily proposed another sermon in place of *The Trumpet of the Soule*: for all the recent revival in sermon studies in the past decade, no sustained 'top ten'–type argument has broken out. We haven't got a section on ballads, for instance, despite Adam Fox's startling estimate that 'three or four million broadside ballads were printed in the second half of the sixteenth century alone'.[6] We might have included something else on the range of ephemeral literature, including chapbooks, playbills and forms: Juliet Fleming uncovers early wallpaper as an unexpected representative of this wide and diverse category. We chose to take Shakespeare as our example of literary canonization because the stakes are so high for our own contemporary disciplinary practice: the case of John Lyly, whose 11 print works went through at least 46 editions in

---

    [4]   BBC News Entertainment & Arts, 'Ding Dong! The Witch is Dead enters chart at two', http://www.bbc.co.uk/news/entertainment-arts-22145306 (accessed 24.04.13).

    [5]   J.W. Saunders, 'The Stigma of Print: A Note on the Social Bases of Tudor Poetry', *Essays in Criticism* 1 (1951): 139–64.

    [6]   Adam Fox, *Oral and Literate Culture in England, 1500–1700* (Oxford: 2000), p. 15. On ballad popularity see Tessa Watt, *Cheap Print and Popular Piety, 1550–1640* (Cambridge: 1991).

60 years, might have given a different shape to the story. Above all, our aim has been to stimulate debate, including disagreement. Our contributors seek to further a dialogue about notions of popularity and about the relative roles of quantitative and qualitative methodologies for judging and interrogating popularity in the past. This volume brings together book history and literary criticism not merely to nominate or enumerate bestsellers, nor even to problematize them, but rather to try to understand their hold on the market, and with that, the gap between our own literary assessments and those of the past we seek to understand.

'A Pop-holy generation'

Popularity in the early modern period has prompted extensive discussion, not least because the word itself was highly topical in the last decade of Elizabeth's reign. The exorcist or spiritual healer John Darrell was well placed to experience and contribute to the evils of popular opinion at this time. In 1597 Darrell became mixed up in a notorious case of possession and exorcism in which several people were arrested as witches. Initially a scandal limited to Nottingham, the case was retried in London and the resulting controversy produced at least 12 books in as many months. Darrell replied to his very public condemnation by likening the ongoing debate to the massacre of Protestants in 1570s Paris, caused by the 'credulous popularitie of that countrie'.[7] The 'poore weomen and sily multitude [of France], neuer requyringe nor examining the matter any farther, fell straight to a kinde of hissing & clapping their hands'. This instinctive, thoughtless mob, defined by their poverty and gender, reminded Darrell of the credulous popularity he now found himself confronting: 'Now even thus good reader', he explained, 'fareth it with me at this instant'. His good-intentioned part in an exorcism (as he saw it) had brought him the most negative kind of popularity, and those who engaged in his public demolition were as bad as a murderous Catholic rabble. Indeed, Paris's Catholic authorities are described as 'that deuoute and Pop-holy generation': originally a late medieval phrase for sham piety, 'Pop-holy' became a particularly useful term for denouncing Roman Catholicism in Reformation England. Darrell's elision of the early modern Pop(e) and the 'credulous popularitie' of this 'generation' allows us to see the ways that popularity and religious and political sectarianism fused together in early modern England.

If popularity can sometimes be a negative term in modern discourse, it is a downright seditious one in the early modern period. It is a definitively Elizabethan word, coming into use through Elizabeth's reign to designate a dangerous privileging of ordinary people, an emergent democratization of thought, speech and action. As William Cornwallis put it in 1601, 'Princes hate competitors, and popularitie in subiects seemes to bandy with the Prince in power, of which if Princes be suspitious, and carefully remoue the cause of their suspition, they are

---

[7]   John Darrel[l], *A Detection of that Sinnful, Shamful, Lying, and Ridiculous Discours, of Samuel Harshnet* (London: 1600), sig. A1.

not to bee blamed'.[8] Popularity is suspicious and seditious, a mechanism for power on the part of the apparently powerless. As Cornwallis explained elsewhere, in an essay 'On popularitie':

> the cunning of Popularitie, is like that of Iuglers, the cunningest of which can cast mists before mens eyes, but here is their neerest resemblance, Iuglers trickes goe most inuisibly by Candle light; men popular, with those heads that come no neerer the strength of vnderstanding, then candle light the light of the sunne[.][9]

The earliest use of the term in English appears to be in William Bavand's 1559 translation of Joannes Ferrarius Montanus's *De republica bene instituenda*, addressed directly to Elizabeth. Less than one year into her reign, she is warned of magistrates that 'pretende a colour of popularitie and gentlenesse', which 'be onely cautelles and mistes', 'entrapmentes, to bryng soche as beleue the same into the snare, and daunger of their liues'. 'Besides this', Bavand continues, 'Cato Vticensis was wounte to saie, that there was nothyng so hurtfull, nothyng so vnconstaunt, as was the peoples fauour, thenheritaunce wherof was ever pernicious to their posteritie'.[10] 'Popularity', then, was a term equivalent with Elizabeth's reign, designating the views of the people, views which were intrinsically and paradoxically dangerous to the people.

Ten years later, Thomas Norton blamed the Northern Rebellion on 'popularities and hanginges by the vayne ayre', which 'are not auancementes but precipitations' to 'raise' great men's minds 'to a wrong way of climing'.[11] By 1579, the word was being casually listed amongst inauspicious semantic company, when John Jones counselled 'Rulers, Potentates, Prelates and Preachers' to avoid 'popularitie, mutinie and sedition'.[12] This helps to explain why Francis Bacon would describe Essex's rebellion in 1601 in terms of his 'points of popularitie which euery man tooke notice and note of, as his affable gestures, open doores, making his table and his bed so popularly places of audience to suters'. This double kind of popularism was 'either the qualities of a nature disposed to disloyaltie, or the beginnings and conceptions of that which afterwards grewe to shape and forme': attempted regicide.[13] The people's thoughts were considered to be anti-establishment at a time when the establishment defined itself by its ability to keep the people safe.

---

[8]   William Cornwallis, *Discourses upon Seneca the Tragedian* (London: 1601), sig. F1.

[9]   William Cornwallis, *Essayes* (London: 1600–1601), Essay 30, sigs. S3–S3v.

[10]   *A Woorke of Ioannes Ferrarius Montanus, Touchynge the Good Orderynge of a Common Weale* (London: 1559), fols. 171–171v.

[11]   Thomas Norton, *A Warning Agaynst the Dangerous Practises of Papistes and Specially the Parteners of the Late Rebellion* (London: 1569), sigs. G4v–H1.

[12]   John Jones, *The Arte and Science of Preseruing Bodie and Soule in Healthe, Wisedome, and Catholike Religion* (London: 1579), sig. N2.

[13]   Francis Bacon, *A Declaration of the Practices & Treasons Attempted and Committed by Robert late Earle of Essex* (London: 1601), sig. Bi.

When early modern scholars employ the term 'popular', however, they often have very different kinds of popularity in mind. Peter Burke has recently defined popular culture as 'the culture of the non-elite – in a negative way as unofficial culture, the culture of the non-elite, the "subordinate classes" as the Italian Marxist Antonio Gramsci famously called them'. Burke further defines the non-elite's 'most prominent' members as 'craftsmen and peasants'.[14] Mary Ellen Lamb illustrates the diversity of the popular by appealing to the 'householder', 'a morris dancer', 'A London laundrymaid of a Calvinist persuasion' and 'boisterous miners from Wales'.[15] These are not quite the Italian women, French Catholics or English mutineers that early modern writers had in mind, and the various groups, real or imagined, which scholars enthusiastically recuperate as popular were perceived by early modern commentators as a terrifying, potentially revolutionary force. Thus the *OED*'s apparently innocuous definition, 'liked or admired by many people', glosses an early modern idea which is threatening, potentially deadly.

As Lamb reminds us, our models for the popular, as with any other form of lived experience and imagined communities, need to acknowledge the contradictory and multiple ways in which people worked. Lamb herself proposes a model of popular culture as 'a simulacrum existing in early modern imaginaries created from cultural materials assembled from various lower status groups'.[16] The current volume continues and challenges many of these debates by pursuing concepts of popularity via the Elizabethan printed forms which appear to have provoked unusual levels of demand, thus apparently inciting but also reflecting forms of popularity.

The idea of popularity has odd and unexpected implications for the canon. Clive Bloom complains that 'the Jacobean period was *the* great period of English literature and thought – the moment when the medieval gave way to the modern', but has been superseded by 'a mythicised Elizabethan golden age … and an equally mythicised era of struggle between king and Parliament'.[17] In this reading, the recent popularity of the Elizabethan period itself (amongst academics and, more widely, in films such as Shekar Kapur's *Elizabeth* [1998]) has had consequences for the way we represent and experience early modern literary history. In the 1980s, scholars of popular culture still felt the need to negotiate their subjects' scholarly worth: John Simons hoped to go 'some way towards establishing the validity of work on popular texts as an aspect of literary criticism rather than of social history', suggesting that, for his readers, the popular was inevitably non-canonical. For Simons, such texts challenge literary criticism's concern with 'the

---

[14]   Peter Burke, *Popular Culture in Early Modern Europe*, 3rd ed. (1978; Farnham: 2009), p. xiii.

[15]   Mary Ellen Lamb, *The Popular Culture of Shakespeare, Spenser and Jonson* (London: 2006), p. 2; p. 10.

[16]   Lamb, *Popular Culture*, p. 2.

[17]   Clive Bloom (ed.), *Jacobean Poetry and Prose: Rhetoric, Representation and the Popular Imagination* (Basingstoke: 1988), p. 1.

evaluation of what is perceived as "best" in the range of literary production' by confirming that the canon 'represents the cultural interests of dominant social groups'. Texts excluded from this canon go further by offering 'a breach of the protocols of periodisation' (between medieval and Renaissance, in the first instance) and provocatively refuse to demonstrate 'the vision of smooth and harmonious social development' represented by 'a notion of the Renaissance which runs from Sidney and Spenser to Milton via Donne'.[18] Our Top Ten chapters do not construct a narrative of development, nor even a counter-canon. Instead, our case studies toggle between Franco Moretti's 'distant reading', which uses quantified data to provide 'abstract models for literary history', and the old disciplinary procedure of 'close reading', in which the specific instantiation of the literary is irreducible and unreplicable. Martin Mueller's concept of 'scalable reading' is apposite.[19] The chapters attempt to individualize those processes of book history which can flatten out specifics via quantitative rather than qualitative approaches.[20]

But, as Simons also points out, drama represents a potentially 'anomalous case', since it possesses the curious property of being, as Raymond Williams puts it, 'linguistically co-extensive with the whole range of its society'.[21] We might add that it fulfils Tessa Watts's definition of popularity as that which blends the literate with other forms of media.[22] Once plays were printed, they became available to readers who didn't or couldn't go to the theatre, and could be read in a variety of theatrical and non-theatrical ways. Historians of eighteenth-century books on acting theory have argued for 'the importance of recognizing publications about acting as a crucial part of the period's cultural imagination, one that engaged the audience well beyond that immediately involved with theatre and that was implicated with a broad variety of political, aesthetic and literary discourses and practices'.[23] Like these later publications connected with the theatre, Elizabethan playtexts began to establish a stable market, ensuring that plays could be read well beyond the theatre by a wide readership as a means to connect with contemporary political and social debate. Indeed, early modern drama has been at the epicentre of current discussions of print popularity, and the much-cited disagreement between Peter Blayney, Alan Farmer and Zachary Lesser stands behind much of the debate in this book.

---

[18]   John Simons, 'Open and closed books: a semiotic approach to the history of Elizabethan and Jacobean popular romance', in Bloom, *Jacobean Poetry and Prose*, p. 22; p. 9.

[19]   Martin Mueller, 'Scalable Reading' at https://scalablereading.northwestern.edu/.

[20]   Franco Moretti, *Graphs, Maps, Trees: Abstract Models for Literary History* (London: 2005), p. 1.

[21]   Simons, 'Open and closed books', p. 9.

[22]   Watts, *Cheap Print*, p. 7.

[23]   Lisa Zunshine (ed.), *Acting Theory and the English Stage, 1700–1830*, vol. I (London: 2009), p. xvi.

In 1997, Peter Blayney claimed that 'not one in twenty [printed plays] would have paid for itself during its first year', a claim challenged eight years later by Farmer and Lesser arguing that such plays offered 'reasonable profits with unusually low risk' and were therefore excellent investments for stationers.[24] This argument has prompted the current volume's reconsideration of the meanings of popularity as a theoretical and empirical category, the ways in which we measure popularity and the gap between modern canons and the early modern print market. It is not surprising that early modern drama should stimulate such an enquiry, since it is a focus for intense scholarly interest in our own time, appeals to an audience beyond the book and offers various kinds of sensory experience to a heterogeneous mix of consumers.

Even before they reach print, plays represent a challenge to traditional divisions between elite and popular culture. They are both a scripted and an oral form, and therefore available to literate and non-literate audience members alike; they were performed in front of audience members paying different amounts of money and segregated accordingly, but nevertheless gathered together in one building; they were performed across the country, across the capital and at court, as well as in Europe; they were performed by players otherwise defined as vagabonds or common, and available to amateur players to perform. Their very written fabric combines and runs across registers traditionally considered popular or elite, vernacular or learned, as in the famous example when Macbeth tells the audience that his bloody hands will 'The multitudinous seas incarnadine, / Making the green one red' (2.2.62–63). Macbeth's second line translates the first from a Latinate diction to an Anglo-Saxon one, and in so doing may prompt the actor to address each line to different sections of the audience. We might want to ask whether such a moment highlights the inclusive popularity of early modern drama or underlines social segregation.

Stephen Purcell warns against assuming an integral meaning for popularity. '[T]he label implies no shared political standpoint or stylistic features, no distinctive audience demographic, nor any particular measure of commercial success'. But, he suggests, popular theatre is distinguished by a concern to develop a sense of community, especially an unusual or imagined community 'in which the group somehow steps outside of its normal social parameters, and social models alternative to the established order become equally possible'. Thus popular theatre might be theorized as a form 'seeking to affirm and consolidate a communal identity' or 'to disrupt and destabilise that same identity in order to instil a "critical" attitude among that community's individual members'; it may do both of these

---

[24] Peter Blayney, 'The Publication of Playbooks', in John D. Cox and David Scott Kastan (eds), *A New History of Early English Drama* (New York: 1997), p. 389; Alan B. Farmer and Zachary Lesser, 'The Popularity of Playbooks Revisited', *Shakespeare Quarterly* 56: 1 (Spring 2005): 1–32; 28.

things, serving to 'confirm *and* subvert the communal values of its audience'.[25] We might therefore want to think of Darrell's 'Pop-holy generation' of 'credulous popularitie', Cornwallis's worries about popularity bandying with and competing for power or Norton's 'popularities and hanginges by the vayne ayre' in the terms Purcell provides for popular theatre: popularity is that which might either confirm or subvert communal value, or confirm *and* subvert it, remembering that for early modern politics communality itself was viewed suspiciously by those who saw hierarchy, monarchy and patronage as guarantees of social stability.

'We're more popular than Jesus now' (John Lennon, 1966)

Every census of what was published in the Elizabethan period reveals the dominance of religious material in the print marketplace. But despite the much-vaunted (and much-needed) 'turn to religion' in early modern studies during the last two decades, sermons, liturgies, catechisms, prayer books and bibles have been to the question of Elizabethan print popularity what mass-market paperbacks are to the *New York Times Book Review* best-seller lists: something of an embarrassment.[26] As Ian Green points out in his study of print and Protestantism, many attempts to identify early modern bestsellers have, similarly, decided to leave out some or all of this expansive category, in order to bring into prominence works that more closely map onto (or, sometimes, challenge) fields of critical, particularly literary interest. Green's own list, with an exclusive focus on religious bestsellers, sets out a quantitative methodology, including those titles which were reprinted at least five times over a 30-year period: a figure 'low enough to include steady sellers as well as bestsellers, but high enough to eliminate those works which do not appear to have caught the public imagination sufficiently to warrant much more than a couple of editions'.[27] Included among these bestsellers are collected and individual sermons by Henry Smith, Calvin's *The Catechisme or manner to teach children*, Edward Dering's *A Sermon preached before the Quenes Majestie*, and scores of editions of the Bishops' and Geneva Bibles, of *An ABC with a Catechism*, and of the Prayer Book. Some of these books were compulsory, and purchased by churchwardens on behalf of their churches. The Churchwardens' accounts for 1564 in Minchinhampton, Gloucestershire, record a payment of one shilling and threepence for a copy of the official Elizabethan homilies.[28] The publishing history of this book means that it clearly counts as one of Green's bestsellers, but its sales

---

[25]   Stephen Purcell, *Popular Shakespeare: Simulation and Subversion on the Modern Stage* (Basingstoke: 2009), p. 8; pp. 13–14; pp. 15–16 (Purcell's italics).

[26]   Ken Jackson and Arthur F. Marotti, 'The Turn to Religion in Early Modern Studies', *Criticism* 46 (2004): 167–90.

[27]   Ian Green, *Print and Protestantism in Early Modern England* (Oxford: 2000), p. 173.

[28]   William St Clair, *The Reading Nation in the Romantic Period* (Cambridge: 2004), p .459.

are due largely to its status: can we call popular a book that *had* to be bought, even if that compulsion meant large sales over an extended period and extensive exposure to a relatively wide populace?

Religious books did indeed dominate the market. Of the almost 11,000 titles published during Elizabeth's reign, our best estimate is that around 40 percent were in this category, as discussed in the chapters by Lori Anne Ferrell, Brian Cummings and Beth Quitsland, and in Alan Farmer and Zachary Lesser's innovative analysis of the *Short Title Catalogue*.[29] But if we were to take Green's methodology, that five editions over a 30-year period signals a significant intervention into the print market, plenty of more obviously 'literary' titles would also come to the fore. A survey of the ESTC shows that by this measure, literary bestsellers during the second half of the sixteenth century include many works recognized as part of the literary canon of Elizabethan England: poetry, including the works of Wyatt and Surrey in Tottell's *Songes and Sonnettes*, Spenser's *The Shepheardes Calendar*, Golding's translation of Ovid's *Metamorphoses* and Shakespeare's narrative poems *Venus and Adonis* and *The Rape of Lucrece*; prose works, such as Sidney's *The Countess of Pembrokes Arcadia*, Lyly's *Euphues* and its sequel *Euphues and His England*, Lodge's *Rosalynde* and Greene's *Pandosto*; and drama, including Shakespeare's history plays *Richard II* and *Richard III*, Kyd's *The Spanish Tragedy*, Marlowe's *Tamburlaine* and the anonymous *Mucedorus*, discussed by Peter Kirwan in Chapter 14. As Neil Rhodes's chapter shows, the canonization of our uber-Elizabethan, Shakespeare, begins in the late sixteenth century. Farmer and Lesser show us that texts we would now call 'literary' – and therefore give a high status – were a larger part of the late Elizabethan print market. Here popularity – as indicated by the bestseller list – and value – as indicated by presence on college professors' curricula – are often aligned rather than opposing.

Green's quantitative method also prioritizes repeated print editions as the most important metric of popularity. But absence from print need not mean that texts were failures. We know, for instance, that Marlowe's *The Rich Jew of Malta* was a valuable commercial property for Philip Henslowe during the early 1590s – and we know also that the play was not printed until 1633. Here, evidence of popularity from performance and from print pulls in apparently contradictory directions. Likewise, though book historians often characterize a text which is not reprinted as a commercial failure, such a text may simply indicate a book which sold moderately well, or whose publisher became involved in other ventures, or which was inherited by a new publisher with no interest in that genre. Manuscript circulation, of poetry but also of playtexts (such as *A Game at Chesse*) and prose works (such as *A View of the Present State of Ireland*), is an important alternative locus of the popular. We know that some editions of books were apparently read to destruction: survival may be evidence less of popularity than its opposite.

---

[29]   Print numbers from Table 1 in John Barnard and D.F. McKenzie (eds, with the assistance of Maureen Bell), *The Cambridge History of the Book in Britain, Volume IV 1557–1695* (Cambridge: 2002), pp. 779–84.

Alexander Wilkinson's assessment of 'Lost Books Printed in French before 1601' gives survival figures for different genres of between 95 percent (for Heraldic Works) and 41 percent for calendars, almanacs and prognostications.[30] An earlier study of English print by Franklin B. Williams noted that over four thousand *ESTC* titles survive in a single copy, and analyzes the titles listed by the publisher Andrew Maunsell in his *Catalogue of English Printed Books* (1595) to suggest loss rates of around 15 percent of religious titles.[31]

And extreme topicality can mitigate against the longevity required of Green's bestsellers. John Sutherland, writing of twentieth-century bestsellers, proposes the term 'fast-seller' as a preferable label, arguing that the pace, not the ultimate total, of sales best measures the impact of a particular title. For Sutherland, topicality, and consequent transience, are crucial: 'this hand-in-glove quality is inextricably linked with the ephemerality of bestsellerism. A #1 novel may be seen as a successful literary experiment – as short-lived as a camera flash, and as capable of freezing, vividly, its historical moment.'[32] Such ephemeral moments of print popularity are difficult for us to pinpoint, since their manifestations can look to quantitative methodology like print failure. Farmer and Lesser's useful identification of 'structures of popularity' goes some way to rectify this blind spot.

[30 August 1599] 'Wrett of my Common place book'[33]

For some critics, statistics suggest that the vast majority of the people were illiterate, and popularity and print are therefore mutually exclusive. Tessa Watt sensibly suggests that 'in a partially literate society, the most influential media were those which combined print with non-literate forms', such as musical ballads, illustrated books and books for devotion.[34] But we should still ask whether, in an era before mass literacy, any printed text could truly be described as 'popular'. Joad Raymond's intervention is helpful: 'print culture can be described as "popular" not because it is the voice of the people, nor necessarily because it was widely read among the people or reflected their views, but because the people were understood to be involved in the publicity dynamic, the dynamic by which print came to play a part in public life and the political process'.[35] This book explores the ways print, in its content, appearance or placement, addresses itself to and is constructed by

---

[30] Alexander S. Wilkinson, 'Lost Books Printed in French before 1601', *The Library: The Transactions of the Bibliographical Society 10* (2009): 188–205.

[31] Franklin B. Williams, Jr, 'Lost Books of Tudor England', *The Library*, 7th ser. 33 (1978): 1–14.

[32] John Sutherland, *Bestsellers: A Very Short Introduction* (Oxford: 2007), p. 3.

[33] From the diary of Lady Margaret Hoby, quoted by William H. Sherman in *Used Books: Marking Readers in Renaissance England* (Philadelphia: 2008), p. 63.

[34] Watt, *Cheap Print*, p. 7.

[35] Joad Raymond (ed.), *The Oxford History of Popular Print Culture, Vol 1: Cheap Print in Britain and Ireland to 1660* (Oxford: 2011), p. 6.

this sense of the public. Like the contributors to Raymond's recent *Oxford History of Popular Print Culture* (2011), the writers in *The Elizabethan Top Ten* contribute to a reassessment of the role of print in studies of the popular.

Most classic accounts of popular culture disregard print, following Peter Burke's monumental *Popular Culture in Early Modern Europe*, first published in 1978, and prefer the reconstruction of the non-commercial practices of a communal, oral folk culture over the commodified entertainment of a learned elite. Roger Chartier's observation that 'popular culture is a category of the learned', together with Zachary Lesser's recognition that 'the study of popular culture is the desire for popular culture', indicate something of what is at stake in the academy in this aspect of historical recovery.[36] Any attempt to trace the demography of any particular aspect of print culture is beset with methodological and evidential difficulties (and desires). Two aspects of access to print, literacy and cost, are relevant here: both confirm that while 'Early modern England was ... not a society in which an illiterate majority lived without access to print', the extent of both the reading and the customer base was certainly limited.[37]

Stuart Gillespie and Neil Rhodes point out that 'The sixteenth century may have been the first age of print in England, but it was also a time when the majority of people were unable to read'.[38] Accurate assessments of the proportion of the population who could read in this period are hampered by the fact that reading is an activity which need not leave any recoverable traces. Recent studies have, however, emphasized that 'Renaissance readers were not only *allowed* to write notes in and on their books, they were *taught* to do so in school', and the study of readers' marks in particular copies aims to understand this humanist practice.[39] David Cressy's landmark study of literacy in the early modern period 'regards the signatures and marks that men and women made on various documents as the best evidence of literate skills', and uncovers a widely varying picture, in which gender, region, and class all affect writing rates. His estimated literacy rates in 1600 are 30 percent for men and 10 percent for women.[40] But as Cressy admits, reading was taught separately from and prior to writing: John Hart's primer *A methode or*

---

[36]   Roger Chartier, *Forms and Meanings: Texts, Performances and Audiences from Codex to Computer* (Philadelphia: 1995), p. 83; Zachary Lesser, 'Typographic Nostalgia: Playreading, Popularity and the Meanings of Black Letter', in Marta Straznicky (ed.), *The Book of the Play: Playwrights, Stationers, and Readers in Early Modern England* (Amherst: 2006) pp. 99–126; p.100.

[37]   Tim Harris, 'Popular, Plebeian, Culture: Historical Definitions', in Joad Raymond (ed.), *The Oxford History of Popular Print Culture*, p. 55.

[38]   Stuart Gillespie and Neil Rhodes, *Shakespeare and Elizabethan Popular Culture* (London: 2006), p. 9.

[39]   Sherman, *Used Books*, p. 3. See also Lisa Jardine and A.T. Grafton, '"Studied for Action": How Gabriel Harvey read his Livy', *Past and Present* 129 (1990): 3–51 and William H. Sherman, *John Dee: The Politics of Reading and Writing in the English Renaissance* (Amherst: 1995).

[40]   David Cressy, *Literacy and the Social Order: Reading and Writing in Tudor and Stuart England* (Cambridge: 1980), p. 42; p. 177.

comfortable beginning for all unlearned, published in 1570, advised neophytes 'first to learne to reade before they should learne to write, for that it is farre more readie and easie'.[41] Thus marks of writing probably substantially underestimate competence in reading, particularly for women, who are both underrepresented in Cressy's legal documentation and had far less access to the formal education in which writing was taught. Literacy, too, was more than a binary yes (signature) / no (mark), as Adam Fox points out:

> The vast range of capacities and competencies which lay behind the term 'literacy' were as stratified as the social order itself. Many more people could read than could write, while among readers there were some who could manage the printed word but could not always decipher one, or any, of the variety of scripts which characterised contemporary handwriting.[42]

While the argument that some readers were literate only in the more 'basic skill' of reading blackletter or gothic type – used in many reading primers – has undergone some decisive critical modification, it is true that different types of scripts, print and manuscript, were differently legible.[43] Of the best-selling books discussed in this volume, however, it is striking that few are in blackletter, despite Mark Bland's contention that the persistence of blackletter at the end of the sixteenth century 'illustrate[s] how typographic convention might continue older traditions into a period where cultural change had taken place, and must, in part, testify to the status of such books as popular classics'.[44]

The historiography of literacy is itself undergoing important reconceptualization. Heidi Brayman Hackel summarizes some recent developments:

> Scholars have come up with many terms to suggest both the degrees and forms of popular literacy in the early modern period: alphabetic, abecedarian, reading-only, marginal, partial, full, signature, comprehension; delegate, surrogate, artisanal, material, contextual, nonverbal and others. Nowhere, then, does it make more sense to move away from signature literacy as the standard than in studies of popular literacy, which is various and multiple, visible in some formats and media, invisible in others, encompassing many acts and practices. [45]

---

[41]   John Hart, *A methode or comfortable beginning for all unlearned, whereby they may be taught to read English in a very short time, with pleasure* (London: 1570), sig. 4vo.

[42]   Adam Fox, *Oral and Literate Culture*, p. 42.

[43]   Keith Thomas, 'The Meaning of Literacy in Early Modern England', in Gerd Baumann (ed.), *The Written Word: Literacy in Transition* (Oxford: 1986), pp. 97–132; Lesser, 'Typographic Nostalgia'.

[44]   Mark Bland, 'The Appearance of the Text in Early Modern England', *Text: An Interdisciplinary Annual of Textual Studies* 11 (1998): 91–154; 95. On John Wright's use of blackletter as part of the nostalgic popular world evoked by Dekker's play *The Shoemaker's Holiday*, see Lesser, 'Typographic Nostalgia'.

[45]   Heidi Brayman Hackel, 'Popular Literacy and Society', in Raymond, *Oxford History*, p. 97.

Access to print culture – in forms from bills to ballads and from legal writs to romances – was, therefore, probably wider than the estimates of the literacy of the population have suggested, and also less neatly divided between the states of 'literacy' and 'illiteracy'. We know that access to print in this period increasingly included non-readers: as Adam Fox discovers, 'reading aloud helped to draw everyone into the ambit of the written word', and he adduces examples of public and familial reading from bibles to ballads.[46] Both Peter Kirwan's discussion of *Mucedorus* and Lori Anne Ferrell on Henry Smith's sermon oratory discuss the interplay between oral and printed texts and the extent to which print popularity registers, capitalizes on or supersedes the reception of an original performance. We know, too, that the pages of type with which the sixteenth-century print shops were routinely most concerned were what Peter Stallybrass calls 'small jobs' rather than books: books were only one part of a market with a high demand for ephemeral and administrative printed material such as advertisements, playbills, proclamations, licenses, indentures, bonds, petitions, indulgences and oaths.[47] Non-readers could therefore be exposed to printed material and print content in various forms and contexts.

Cost of printed material was one further factor in the extent of 'popular' access to print culture. Tessa Watt observes that, in real terms, books became more affordable during the course of the sixteenth century, as their prices remained steady against a backdrop of rising prices and rising wages.[48] Assessments of dispersed evidence about book prices suggest that they approximated the price set by the Stationers' Company in 1598 as a 'remedy' against 'divers abuses [that] have been of late committed by sundry persons in enhancing the prices of books and selling the same at too high and excessive rates and prices': *viz*, a penny for two sheets.[49] Small pamphlets were, however, proportionately more expensive for their size, and fashionable literary works were more expensive still. Specific prices are hard to come by, but the 1581 edition of Lyly's *Euphues* cost 2s. unbound, Sir Henry Cocke bought a copy of Spenser's *Complaints* in 1590–1591 for 2s. 6d. (a cost of 1.3d per sheet) and the *The Book of Common Prayer* was an early example of price-fixing, stating its maximum permitted prices of 2s. 6d. unbound, 3s. 4d. bound in parchment and 4s. bound in leather.[50]

But the public for print needs to be seen as extending beyond those who actually bought it and into a more heterogeneous, increasingly print-aware culture. As we have seen, estimates of the number of print ballads in circulation in the Elizabethan

---

[46]   Fox, *Oral and Literate Culture*, pp. 37ff.

[47]   Peter Stallybrass, '"Little Jobs": Broadsides and the Printing Revolution', in Sabrina Alcorn Baron, Eric N. Linquist, and Eleanor F. Shevlin (eds), *Agent of Change: Print Culture Studies after Elizabeth L. Eisenstein* (Amherst and Boston: 2007), pp. 315–42.

[48]   Tessa Watt, *Cheap Print*, p. 261.

[49]   Francis R. Johnson, 'Notes on English Retail Book-Prices, 1550–1640', *The Library*, 5th ser., vol. V (1950): 83–112; 84.

[50]   Johnson, 'Notes', pp. 91–92; St Clair, *Reading Nation*, p. 458.

period reach into the millions; religious texts like the *ABC and Catechism* went into scores, perhaps hundreds of editions; almanacs, as Adam Smyth shows here, were printed in the hundreds of thousands. For bibles, prayer books and other state-sponsored religious publications, the Stationers' Company print-run limit of 1,500 – a figure we do not seem to be entirely sure about – was sometimes, perhaps often, suspended, but one important caveat about the reach of specific print titles relates to the number of copies printed. We have little hard evidence about print runs: 106 copies of a 1558 official proclamation on licensing of preachers were printed; during the 1560s official decrees were printed in runs of 20–700, mostly at the lower end. John Dee's *General and rare memorials pertaining to the art of navigation* (1577) was printed in a run of 100; a pirated version of *the ABC and catechism* (1581) in a run of 600; Richard Stanyhurst's *The First Foure books of virgil, his Aeneis* (Leiden, 1582) in a run of more than 928; 1,250 copies of a reprint of Bullinger's *Decades*, a compulsory book of sermons, were printed in 1587; the 1595 edition of Foxe's *Book of Martyrs* had a print run of 1,200–1,350.[51] And although press run for particular print artefacts is not the only indicator of 'popularity', it does suggest which works were already, or anticipated to be, commercially successful and which had relatively widespread penetration.

We can see that numbers here vary widely, but even at the upper end of the range they remain small, particularly when set against, for example, the capacities of the theatres or the expected crowd at a sermon; on the other hand, we do not know how many people might encounter any one copy of a book. In their contributions to the current volume, Helen Smith cites Gabriel Harvey's habit of signing his books 'et amicorum' and Abigail Shinn discusses Harvey swapping books with Spenser. The study of popularity needs to incorporate a study of human networks and the reception and ongoing use of books, as well as their publication and distribution.

The Elizabethan Top Ten

The current book engages with these issues in two sections, one on methodology and the other the Top Ten itself. The first four chapters sketch out the conceptual and evidential issues associated with popularity. Thus Alan Farmer and Zachary Lesser open our discussion by investigating and interrogating how the *English Short Title Catalogue* represents popularity within the early modern book trade. They provide new categories for a large-scale analysis of the print market, drawing together theoretical, evidentiary and bibliographic themes. Lucy Munro demonstrates how Elizabethan popularity was driven by books first printed before Elizabeth's reign, so that age, paradoxically, offered new possibilities to a print market often criticized for its fixation on newness and novelty. Helen Smith abandons financial concerns entirely, advocating the early modern book as an

---

[51]   St Clair, *Reading Nation*, pp. 462–63.

object of friendship, conviviality and advice. In the final methodological essay, Neil Rhodes revisits Shakespeare's writing career to show how 'the best-selling English author of all time' negotiated ambitions for exclusivity whilst responding to unanticipated levels of popularity amongst his readers. These four chapters offer sustained, different perspectives from which to rethink approaches to popularity.

The second section of the book is the Top Ten: ten short chapters presenting for the case of a particular genre as popular. Our contributors unpack and interrogate assumptions about the popular, decentre narratives about the canon and rediscover an early modern world which looks both oblique and new.

We move from self-writing in almanacs to censored script behind wallpaper, international news to Spenser poems, domestic books to public sermons, psalm books to Munday's serialized stories and from *The Book of Common Prayer* to polar bears at the Stuart court. As explained above, this Top Ten is not intended to be the final word on the most popular kinds of books available to early modern readers. Rather, we offer here a range of current thinking about early modern popularity, bringing together material textual criticism, the history of the book, conceptual frameworks, empirical data and evidence of reading practices, combining book history and literary studies in order to begin a new conversation about the nature of popularity. This is, above all, a book about people – people who produce, consume and love books and the content of books – and seeks to restore a sense of the vitality and radical implications of the Elizabethan 'Pop-holy' generation.

PART 1
Methodologies

Chapter 1
What Is Print Popularity?
A Map of the Elizabethan Book Trade[1]

Alan B. Farmer and Zachary Lesser

The study of popular culture has long been a central aspect of early modern studies, but the definition of *popularity* has remained contested. As Roger Chartier has argued, the search for 'popular culture' may rest on a number of false premises:

> first, that it is possible to establish exclusive relationships between specific cultural forms and particular social groups; second, that the various cultures existing in a given society are sufficiently pure, homogeneous and distinct to permit them to be characterized uniformly and unequivocally; and third, that the category of 'the people' or 'the popular' has sufficient coherence and stability to define a distinct social identity that can be used to organize cultural differences in past ages according to the simple opposition of *populaire* versus *savant*.[2]

These difficulties, of course, should not and have not prevented historians and cultural critics from seeking more subtle methods of reconstructing the popular cultures of early modern England (often now imagined in the plural). From the beginnings of this field in the work of German Romantic historians like Johann Gottfried von Herder, much of the culture of 'the people' has been imagined to be oral, communal, and ritualistic.[3] But the printed book has also played an important role, especially in more recent revisionist studies. These approaches attempt to link the cultural meaning of the word *popular* with its economic meaning of success in the book trade, turning to mass consumption as a guide to popular culture. The difficulty of articulating these two ideas of the popular has often been noted. Most important, since literacy was weighted towards the upper social strata, 'there is no straight equation between "popularity" in numerical terms and print

---

[1] For their helpful comments on earlier drafts of this essay, we would like to thank Tamsin Badcoe, Richard Dutton, Lukas Erne, Harvey Graff, Andy Kesson, Aaron Pratt, Emma Smith, and Peter Stallybrass.

[2] Roger Chartier, *The Cultural Uses of Print in Early Modern France*, trans. Lydia G. Cochrane (Princeton: Princeton UP, 1987), 3.

[3] On the origins of the search for popular culture, see the first chapter, on 'The Discovery of the People', in Peter Burke, *Popular Culture in Early Modern Europe* (New York: Harper, 1978).

for the "popular" classes'.[4] This evidence must therefore be handled carefully, but scholars have nonetheless been eager to assess the relative popularity – that is, economic performance – of different kinds of books in early modern England, because the circulation of print remains one of our best avenues of investigation in this field.[5]

We are primarily interested here in this economic sense of *popularity*. While our findings may well prove useful to studies of popular culture, directly connecting the two understandings of the popular is beyond our scope here.[6] Furthermore, there are a host of reasons to be interested in the economic popularity of different categories of books beyond its use as a possible index to the culture of 'the people', however we might define that ambiguous term. But assessing print popularity presents nearly as many difficulties as the study of popular culture, and it similarly needs to be understood as multiple rather than singular. In this essay, we begin by outlining some of these difficulties and suggesting how we can account for if not entirely resolve them. We then provide the most detailed analysis to date of the various kinds of books offered for sale in early modern bookshops and of their relative proportions in the marketplace of print. Finally, combining this information with other key statistical measurements of the economic success or failure of books, we present a 'map' of the Elizabethan book trade, a guide to the different kinds of print popularity that structured the retail trade. This map, we believe, is fundamental to assessing the popularity of any early modern English book.

---

[4]   Tessa Watt, *Cheap Print and Popular Piety, 1550–1640* (Cambridge: Cambridge UP, 1991), 259.

[5]   As Bob Scribner notes, 'print culture' is not simply 'an indicator or reflector of popular culture, since it is also part of a process of cultural modification', one that 'is wider than print itself'. It is this *process* that Scribner urges us to study, imagining 'popular culture as dynamic, as something not frozen in time but continually changing' and shaped by forces 'from outside and from within itself'. The study of printed matter will play an important role in this process. 'Is a History of Popular Culture Possible?', *History of European Ideas* 10 (1989): 175–91, 180, 186. Watt discusses the use of cheap print in relation to Scribner's model; *Cheap Print*, 2–4. See also Natalie Zemon Davis, 'Printing and the People', in *Society and Culture in Early Modern France* (Stanford: Stanford UP, 1975), 189–226; and Jonathan Barry, 'Literacy and Literature in Popular Culture: Reading and Writing in Historical Perspective', in Tim Harris, ed., *Popular Culture in England, c. 1500–1850* (New York: St Martin's Press, 1995), 69–94.

[6]   One of the challenges in linking these two concepts of popularity is theorizing the relationship between buying books and reading books; some books may have been purchased but not read, some may have been purchased for reasons other than to read them, while other kinds of publications may have been read by many different readers after a single purchase. On this question, and on the importance of distinguishing between different kinds of reading, see Barry, 'Literacy', 82–83. We discuss these and other ways in which the two concepts of popularity might, or might not, intersect in our forthcoming book *Print, Plays, and Popularity in Shakespeare's England*.

***

In scholarly studies of 'popular' books, the sheer number that were printed often does important rhetorical work. Tessa Watt's *Cheap Print and Popular Piety, 1550–1640*, for instance, begins by invoking the massive number of ballads produced in the Elizabethan period: 'There were roughly 3,000 distinct ballads published in the second half of the sixteenth century', and as a result the 'total number of copies would reach between 3 and 4 million'.[7] In her study of the popularity of almanacs, Lauren Kassell estimates that 'at least 160 almanac makers produced 600 works before 1600', and Simon Schaffer adds that this number of titles means that 'hundreds of thousands' of copies 'were sold in the sixteenth century and millions in the seventeenth'.[8] In his bibliography of coranto newsbooks, Folke Dahl suggests that around 400,000 copies of at least 400 editions of these pamphlets were printed in England from 1620 to 1642.[9] Ian Green counts up to 800 catechisms and other catechetical works published in England from 1530 to 1740, either independently or as part of other works, and estimates that somewhere between a quarter of a million and three-quarters of a million copies of *The ABC with the catachisme* alone were printed by the early 1640s.[10] Gerald Hammond calculates that 'over half a million copies [of the Geneva Bible] were sold in the sixteenth century, a figure high enough in proportion to the total population to put into question our assumptions about Elizabethan literacy levels'.[11] Richard Greaves argues that 'sermons were popular' because 'about 1,200 different Elizabethan sermons still exist in print'.[12] In her groundbreaking study of 'popular fiction and its readership in seventeenth-century England', Margaret Spufford found enough printed sheets of chapbooks listed in the probate inventory of a single stationer to produce at a minimum 50,000 books, and at a maximum 190,000.[13]

[7]   Watt, *Cheap Print*, 11.

[8]   Lauren Kassell, 'Almanacs and Prognostications', in Joad Raymond, ed., *The Oxford History of Popular Print Culture, Volume 1: Cheap Print in Britain and Ireland to 1660* (Oxford: Oxford UP, 2011), 436, citing Carroll Camden, Jr., 'Elizabethan Almanacs and Prognostications', *The Library*, 4th series, 12 (1931): 83–108; Simon Schaffer, 'Science', in Raymond, ed., *Oxford History*, 402.

[9]   Folke Dahl, *A Bibliography of English Corantos and Periodical Newsbooks, 1620–1642* (London: Bibliographical Society, 1952), 22.

[10]   Ian Green, *The Christian's ABC: Catechisms and Catechizing in England, c. 1530–1740* (Oxford: Clarendon, 1996), 50–52, 65–66. On the press runs for the *ABC* and primers in Restoration England, see John Barnard, 'The Stationers' Stock 1663/4 to 1705/6: Psalms, Psalters, Primers and ABCs', *The Library*, 6th series, 21 (1999): 370–75.

[11]   Gerald Hammond, 'Translations of the Bible', in Michael Hattaway, ed., *A Companion to English Renaissance Literature and Culture* (Oxford: Blackwell, 2003), 165–75, 166.

[12]   Richard L. Greaves, *Society and Religion in Elizabethan England* (Minneapolis: University of Minnesota Press, 1981), 83.

[13]   Margaret Spufford, *Small Books and Pleasant Histories: Popular Fiction and Its Readership in Seventeenth-Century England* (London: Methuen, 1981), 108.

We can see one of the problems immediately. When scholars cite numbers, they often differ widely on the question of just how many books are needed to add up to 'popularity'. Hence for one scholar, 400 or 600 or 800 editions may indicate a large number, while another points to edition totals in the thousands, and still others emphasize total copies in the hundreds of thousands, or even millions. Part of the issue here is the slide from number of editions to number of copies. Multiplying a given number of editions by the 1,000 or 1,250 copies imagined to be typical of early modern press runs will often produce a large number: 'a crooked Figure may / Attest in little place a Million', and 800 editions will suffice to generate a million copies if multiplied by estimated press runs like these.[14] But we lack enough studies of various kinds of books to know how such a number might compare to others. Nor do we know the actual press runs for the vast majority of editions, and estimates that miss the true (but unknown) figure in even a minor way will produce huge differences when multiplied by the total number of editions. We are on surer ground with numbers of extant editions, but here, too, simply citing this number in isolation can be misleading: since the corpus of extant books listed in the *Short-Title Catalogue* (STC) is large, with over 33,000 editions of nearly 20,000 titles, it will be possible to cite an impressive-sounding number for virtually any sufficiently broad category of book, especially when that number is decontextualized from the total universe of books circulating in the period.[15]

In order to provide this crucial context, therefore, we have categorized every entry in the STC, so that the number of editions of any particular type of book can be compared to various others. As we did so, however, another important caveat that we had considered on a theoretical level became abundantly clear in practice: categorizing books is an inherently critical exercise. Judgment inevitably plays a large role, and no two scholars will categorize every book exactly the same way. How one categorizes will obviously have a significant effect on one's sense of the composition of the book trade. For instance, if one is interested in a broad topic or theme rather than in particularly well-defined formats, such as broadsides, or in types of books as they were marketed within the trade itself, one can find that topic virtually anywhere. Trying to determine the popularity of books about, say,

---

[14] William Shakespeare, *Henry V*, Prologue.15, in *Mr. William Shakespeares Comedies, Histories, & Tragedies* (London, 1623), sig. h1r.

[15] A.W. Pollard and G.R. Redgrave, eds, *A Short-Title Catalogue of Books Printed in England, Scotland, & Ireland and of English Books Printed Abroad, 1475–1640*, 2nd ed., rev. W.A. Jackson, F.S. Ferguson, and Katharine F. Pantzer, 3 vols (London: Bibliographical Society, 1976–1991). We use first editions as a proxy for distinct titles. An edition 'refers to all copies printed from a given setting of type', although exactly how much type needs to be reset to qualify as a new edition, rather than as a variant issue or state of the same edition, is a matter of judgment (G. Thomas Tanselle, 'The Bibliographical Concepts of *Issue* and *State*', *Papers of the Bibliographical Society of America* 69 [1975]: 17–66, 18). In counting editions, we almost always follow the distinctions drawn in the STC (1: xli) between reprint editions, variant issues, and texts that have been altered enough to be considered first editions of a new work.

aristocratic life or trade or women by counting the number of editions that treat these subjects will almost inevitably yield different results from counting editions of genres like almanacs or prose romances. Sermons, ballads, playbooks, law books, and husbandry manuals – to name just a few – could touch on a wide range of subjects, and yet these genres of books were typically advertised differently on their title pages, featured different descriptive terms to appeal to potential customers, and, as we will show, occupied different areas of the 'map' of the early modern book trade. Attempting to account for all topics treated in every book would yield a useful subject index of the STC, but it would undermine the entire point of categorizing books by their genres, since the overlap between topics and genres would be enormous. It is all the more important, therefore, to let early modern publishers themselves guide these critical decisions. In categorizing the STC, our governing principle has been, as much as possible, to allow the material forms given to the books by early modern stationers themselves to determine their classifications. Indications of genre on the title page and other signs of early modern categorizing – such as inclusion in a patent that covered an entire class of books – therefore always carry great weight and are often determinative, although by no means mechanistically so. We have used our own judgment throughout – there is no alternative.

Merely counting the total number of editions of different kinds of books, however, is never sufficient for assessing their economic popularity. Most important, again, is the relevant context for these numbers. Unless we know how they compare to the total number of books published in the entire trade, it will remain obscure whether these figures point towards popularity or unpopularity, economic success or the lack thereof. What we need to know, therefore, is the *market share* of the various categories of books. Market share represents a category of books as a percentage of all the editions in the retail trade; it is derived by dividing the total number of editions in that category by the overall number of editions in the trade. Since the denominator in this calculation has generally been unknown, and since previous efforts at categorizing each item in the STC have been limited to a small set of years or a single year, scholars have not been able to calculate market share.[16] Now that we have categorized the entire STC, we

---

[16]   John Barnard and Maureen Bell provide yearly counts of the STC in Appendix 1, Table 1, in John Barnard and D.F. McKenzie, eds (with the assistance of Maureen Bell), *The Cambridge History of the Book in Britain: Volume IV, 1557–1695* (Cambridge University Press, 2002), 779–84, but these figures include a host of entries that must be excluded in order to generate accurate results: duplicate entries that occur in multiple years in Philip Rider's chronological index in volume 3 of the STC, entries for variant issues or states, and entries for 'non-speculative' items (defined below). Furthermore, the STC does not capture one significant part of the retail trade, imported books in foreign languages; we know that this segment of the trade was important, but we lack precise details about the numbers of particular titles and genres that were sold in British book shops. See Maureen Bell and John Barnard, 'Provisional Count of *STC* Titles 1475–1640', *Publishing History* 31 (1992): 46–66. For other studies that categorize single and multiple years in the STC, see G.B.

can provide the market share of all of our categories of books, not merely for the Elizabethan period or the STC period as a whole, but also within any number of date ranges. Not only did the book trade as a whole expand during the Elizabethan period – the number of publications more than tripled between 1559 and 1602 – but its composition varied.[17] We should therefore be attuned to changes in the popularity of different kinds of books over time.

Turning from raw numbers to market share addresses many of the problems that have bedeviled studies of economic popularity, but others remain. Since we do not know the press runs of most editions, compiling a modern-style 'bestseller list' will never be possible for the early modern period. The best we can generally do is to compare the market shares of different categories *by number of editions*, not number of copies. And even with editions, the evidence is incomplete: we can usually only guess at how many editions of different kinds of books have been completely lost.[18] We can be fairly confident, however, that these 'loss rates' disproportionately affected the shortest items, such as ballads and other broadsides, and those books that were subject to particularly heavy and destructive use, such as schoolbooks.

Both of these complicating factors – varying press runs and loss rates – need to be considered when comparing the market shares of different categories of books, but neither poses a fatal challenge to that project. For one thing, as Peter Blayney has observed, 'although few copies of any one book may survive, the survival rate of *works* is significantly greater'.[19] All that is necessary for an edition to 'survive',

---

Harrison, 'Books and Readers, 1591–4', *The Library*, 4th series, 8 (1927): 273–301; Edith L. Klotz, 'A Subject Analysis of English Imprints for Every Tenth Year from 1480 to 1640', *Huntington Library Quarterly* 1 (1938): 417–19; Judith Simmons, 'Publications of 1623', *The Library*, 5th series, 21 (1966): 207–22; Mark Bland, 'The London Book-Trade in 1600', in David Scott Kastan, ed., *A Companion to Shakespeare* (Oxford: Blackwell, 1999), 450–63; Paul Salzman, *Literary Culture in Jacobean England: Reading 1621* (New York: Palgrave Macmillan, 2002). On imported books, see Julian Roberts, 'The Latin Trade', in Barnard, McKenzie, and Bell, eds, *Cambridge History*, 141–73.

[17]   There are 79 extant speculative publications in the STC from 1559, and 280 from 1602, a difference that works out to an increase of 2 to 3 percent per year. On the difference between 'speculative' and 'non-speculative' publications, see below.

[18]   We can occasionally be more precise about the number of lost editions: some books indicate an edition number on their title pages, allowing us to infer lost editions, although the possibility remains that the edition number is merely an inflated 'puff' to attract customers. With serial newsbooks, however, we can be more certain, and this category of books allows us to theorize the relationship between sheet-length and loss rates in important ways. On loss rates, see Alan B. Farmer, 'Playbooks and the Question of Ephemerality', in Heidi Brayman Hackel, Jesse Lander, and Zachary Lesser, eds, *The Book in History, The Book as History*, forthcoming.

[19]   Peter W.M. Blayney, *The Texts of King Lear and Their Origins, Volume 1: Nicholas Okes and the First Quarto* (Cambridge: Cambridge UP, 1982), 38. He notes, however, that often-reprinted books may be more likely to be missing an entire edition, 'since a contemporary collector will not be very interested in multiple editions of a common work'

for the purposes of our study of market share, is the continued existence of a single copy from an edition. And we know that for most books of more than a few sheets, the loss of all copies of an edition is likely to have been unusual.[20] As for variations in the size of editions, while certain titles covered by Stationers' Company monopolies and other patents could be printed in very large press runs, the vast majority of books were subject to Company regulations prescribing a maximum number of copies in an edition.[21] Therefore, with the exception of patented books like the *ABC*, almanacs, and bibles, most editions would have been printed in runs that did not vary widely. Since we have a fairly good sense of the types of books that, on the one hand, may be more likely to suffer from lost editions and, on the other, were probably printed in significantly higher press runs than usual, we can make allowances for these issues in our understanding of the economic popularity of different categories of books.

When one considers the large number of entries involved, as well as these methodological concerns about loss rates, unknown press runs, and the blurriness of category boundaries, it is not very surprising that no one has yet attempted to categorize the entire STC. The endeavor can seem quixotic. And yet, the recurring scholarly emphasis on the numbers of books in a given genre shows the abiding interest in the topic. Without a full categorization of the STC, many of the questions that continue to intrigue us about print popularity will yield only partial answers at best, and misleading ones at worst. The caveats we have raised should warn readers against reifying the market shares that we present here, based on the STC corpus, into simple 'facts' about Elizabethan print culture. Nevertheless, when used with appropriate attention to the complexities underlying them, these figures will offer the best picture to date of the different kinds of books that made up the retail trade.

---

(39); such losses, however, can sometimes be ascertained from edition statements on title pages. For one of the most incisive studies of loss rates, see Oliver M. Willard, 'The Survival of English Books Printed before 1640: A Theory and Some Illustrations', *The Library,* 4th series, 23 (1942): 171–90.

[20]   Coranto newsbooks, for example, were quartos published in numbered series from 1622 to 1642, with editions typically ranging in length from a half-sheet (4 pages), to two sheets (16 pages), to three or more sheets (24 or more pages). Their loss rates are highest for the shortest editions: those of a half-sheet have a loss rate of 72 percent; those of one to two-and-a-half sheets have a loss rate of 61 percent; and those of three sheets or longer have a loss rate of 32 percent. Other factors surely contributed to these different rates, but even here we see that the difference of only a couple of edition sheets could have a substantial impact on whether all the copies of an edition would be lost. These issues are discussed further in Farmer, 'Playbooks'.

[21]   Edward Arber, ed., *A Transcript of the Registers of the Company of Stationers of London; 1554–1640 A.D.*, 5 vols (London: 1875–1894), 2: 43, 4: 22.

***

How does market share relate to print popularity? The kind of popularity that has interested most scholars is rooted in the demand for books by retail customers. In other words, we are generally more interested in what the large number of early modern book customers wanted to buy than in what the relatively small number of early modern stationers wanted to publish. Market share tells us directly about the latter but only indirectly about the former. Of course, since one would assume that publishers would not produce a large number of books of a kind that their customers were not buying, market share does offer a reasonable indication of demand among retail customers. And yet, we should be wary of too quickly assuming that supply and demand were smoothly correlated and that, therefore, a higher market share necessarily indicates greater demand. Some kinds of books may have been abundant for other reasons. Royal proclamations, for instance, were frequently printed in order to enforce monarchical authority, but these editions were usually not purchased by customers in retail shops but, rather, pasted on posts and otherwise used to publicize the royal will.[22] The numerous editions of Oxford and Cambridge act verses and theses were likewise not printed to fulfil the demand of eager book-buyers; they were given out as part of academic ceremonies. Proclamations, act verses and theses, commercial advertisements, and numerous other entries in the STC are what we call 'non-speculative' items, which did not form part of the retail trade. Of course, non-speculative material could be central to a variety of scholarly investigations into early modern print culture, but it provides no insight into the kind of economic popularity that has interested most scholars and that we address here. We therefore exclude these non-speculative editions from all of our calculations.

Other types of books may have been *more* in demand with retail customers than their market share indicates. Not all kinds of 'copy' were equally available to publishers: even if customers wanted to buy many more of a particular genre than its market share suggests, these books may simply not have been available for publication. As we have argued elsewhere, plays from the professional theaters (both indoor and outdoor) offer one such example: there was a limited number of these plays available to publishers, not necessarily because theatrical companies were always reluctant to turn over their scripts (as many scholars used to assert), but simply because for their own reasons these companies were only mounting a small number of new plays each year. There was thus a relatively low upper limit

---

[22] Proclamations were not intended for retail sale, but that does not mean they never could be sold that way. In January 1611, Matthew Law was fined for selling copies in his London bookshop of King James's proclamation dissolving Parliament (STC 8452) before it was officially proclaimed; see W.A. Jackson, ed., *Records of the Court of the Stationers' Company 1602 to 1640* (London: The Bibliographical Society, 1957), 446. On the economics of the printing and distribution of proclamations more generally, see Graham Rees and Maria Wakeley, *Publishing, Politics, and Culture: The King's Printers in the Reign of James I and VI* (Oxford: Oxford UP, 2009), 140–42.

for the publication of plays from the professional stage compared to other kinds of books.[23] In a different way, the royal suppression of news corantos in October 1632 caused the publication of news pamphlets to drop to a very low market share until 1639, even though the demand for this genre of books may not have decreased.

In order to understand print popularity, therefore, we need a more complex and comprehensive view than market share alone can provide. In addition to the total number of editions and the market share of a given kind of book, we should also consider other key indexes of print popularity, including reprint rate (what percentage of first editions in the category were reprinted within 5, 10, or 20 years) and profitability (based on the sheet length of titles in the category, since cost and price tended to vary directly with the amount of paper used to print an edition).[24] And it is just as important to contextualize reprint rates and profitability as it is to contextualize market share and the total number of editions. Without some overall 'benchmark' for reprint rates, it is impossible to know whether the rate for any particular category of books is high or low. To calculate this reprint benchmark, we must again exclude 'non-speculative' publications; the repeated reprinting of a proclamation, for instance, does not indicate that anyone was purchasing it, merely that the government continued to print it for its own reasons. Using the remaining entries in the STC, we can then determine what percentage of all first editions sold well enough to be reprinted.

Of all speculative first editions printed in the Elizabethan period (1559–1602), 22.4 percent were reprinted within 20 years.[25] It was thus the norm in the retail

---

[23]   Alan B. Farmer and Zachary Lesser, 'The Popularity of Playbooks Revisited', *Shakespeare Quarterly* 56 (2005): 1–32, 25–26; see also Farmer and Lesser, 'Structures of Popularity in the Early Modern Book Trade', *Shakespeare Quarterly* 56 (2005): 206–13. This point holds even though most plays performed were never printed. Stationers did not have unrestricted access to each and every example of any type of manuscript, including plays, and we do not know whether the proportion of printed to unprinted plays was higher or lower than the proportions in other genres. The point is that, overall, there were far fewer professional plays written (and performed) than there were most other genres in the STC. We also suspect that at times there were other restrictions on the supply of play scripts to publishers, especially in the period between 1614 and 1628 ('The Popularity of Playbooks', 12).

[24]   The choice of a 20-year window for reprint rates is somewhat arbitrary, of course. The *speed* of reprinting is another important variable that distinguishes the economic performance of different kinds of books. Some books went through multiple editions over a span of decades, while others were reprinted several times within a year or two and never again. This issue is beyond the scope of this essay, but analyzing the corpus of extant editions with this criterion in mind could well yield important results. On this question, see Douglas Bruster, 'Early Modern Best-Sellers and the Matter of Culture', paper presented at the Shakespeare Association of America annual meeting, San Diego, CA, April 2007.

[25]   Since Elizabeth assumed the throne in November of 1558 and died in March of 1603, for our purposes we include only those books printed between 1559 and 1602. In our earlier articles on popularity, we established this benchmark through a statistically significant sample of six widely spread years from 1590 to 1635. Because we were working

book trade for about one in five titles to reach a second edition within 20 years. A category of books with a 20-year reprint rate higher than this benchmark can therefore be said to have done better than average, and since a reprint generally means that the previous edition had sold out, we can often conclude that such a category was in high demand with customers. But reprint rates, too, need to be considered in relation to the entire structure of popularity: some kinds of books, such as serial newsbooks, which were designed to become obsolete after the next number in the series appeared, had low reprint rates for reasons having nothing to do with their popularity. 'Different types of books had different structures of popularity; they sold in different ways and elicited different strategies from publishers', and therefore

> [t]o understand these structures, one must assess all four indices of popularity [total number of editions, market share, reprint rate, and profitability] in relation both to relevant overall markets and to other types of books, because these indices tell different stories, illuminate distinct aspects of popularity, and do not always neatly align, either across classes of books or across time periods for a single class.[26]

One of the obstacles to a full assessment of market share is that, unlike with reprint rates, there is by definition no 'benchmark' that one could use for comparison.[27] It is all the more urgent, therefore, to compare the market shares of a variety of different book categories to get a sense of the range of possibilities. In earlier work, we compared the market shares of playbooks and sermon-books.[28] Here we extend that comparison to cover more than 20 print genres.

We begin by grouping all speculative entries in the STC into six major categories: Religion; Politics and History; Science and Mathematics; School and

---

with a sample, our reprint rate in earlier articles necessarily included a margin of error. The 20-year reprint rate of speculative first editions in our sample was therefore 18.1 percent (± 2.0 percent). Our calculations of the reprint benchmark now include every speculative item in the STC from 1559 to 1602. This reprint rate varies somewhat, though not greatly, over time. From 1603 to 1620, the rate was 20.0 percent, slightly less than for the Elizabethan period. (We do not have the 20-year reprint rate for publications after 1620; the lack of integration between the STC and Wing makes it extremely difficult to track reprints across the divide of 1640/1641.) Likewise, because very few books were first reprinted after more than a decade, the 10-year reprint rate shows the same basic trend: in the Elizabethan period (1559–1602), 18.8 percent of speculative first editions were reprinted; in the Jacobean period (1603–1624), 15.7 percent.

[26]   Farmer and Lesser, 'Structures', 212.

[27]   We do not have space in this essay to address profitability, but like reprint rate (and unlike market share or total number of editions), profitability does have a 'benchmark', namely, the median sheet-count of books printed in a given period. See Farmer and Lesser, 'The Popularity of Playbooks' and 'Structures'. In 'Structures', we explain why the *median* is a more accurate benchmark for profitability than the *average*.

[28]   Farmer and Lesser, 'The Popularity of Playbooks'.

Language Instruction; Poesy and the Arts; and Society and Conduct. Again, these choices necessarily involve critical judgment, and other scholars may prefer other categories, but to us they seemed best able to represent both the range of books published in the period as well as their commonalities. Within each of these major categories, we further sort each book into more specific genres. The category of Religion, for instance, includes genres like bibles and New Testaments, psalm books, catechisms, religious treatises, sermons, and books of prayers and meditations. The category of Politics and History incorporates law, news, travel and political geography, military arts and sciences, trade and economics, political theory, and most other books that treat world events. Within Science and Mathematics, we include almanacs, medicine, husbandry, cookbooks and other books of receipts, works of astronomy, astrology, and cosmography, and most books that treat the physical world. School and Language Instruction includes grammars, dictionaries, handwriting and letter-writing manuals, logic, rhetoric, books by classical authors intended for use in schools, and books advertised for students. Under Poesy and the Arts we group genres such as poetry, plays, ballads, prose fiction and satire, music, and books on the visual arts. Finally, Society and Conduct is the most diffuse category, dealing generally with the conduct of life in a less religious sense, and including moral philosophy, conduct manuals, analyses of social life and social structure, books about hawking, hunting, and games, and descriptions of other secular activities like drinking and smoking.

Furthermore, in order to account for the overlapping interests of genres within these major categories, we have not limited each book to only a single category, unlike many previous attempts at categorization. Rather, we have allowed ourselves the option of placing a book in multiple groups, but with one category always primary. A few examples will demonstrate how this system works. In the early modern period, the distinction between religion and politics was an extremely subtle one, to say the least. Should a petition to the monarch or Parliament on religious questions be categorized under Religion or Politics and History? Our choice here, as elsewhere, has been guided by the form of the book, its title, and its rhetorical situation. We place such petitions in the major category of Politics and History because they aim at political action, whether a royal proclamation or a parliamentary statute, action that happens to deal with religion. But we also include these petitions in the secondary category of Religion due to their prominent concern with that topic. From a different point of view, a book proclaiming the divine right of monarchs by Scriptural exegesis is categorized under Religion because it is primarily a theological treatise that treats a particular political issue, but we also include such a book in Politics given its outright concern with issues of political theory and royal authority. Similarly, any number of topics in the period could be handled in verse form: does Thomas Tusser's *Five Hundred Points of Good Husbandry* belong primarily in Science and Mathematics because of its status as husbandry, or does it belong in Poesy and the Arts since it largely consists of rhyming verse? Since verse is a form without inherent content, when verse seems used in large measure for its mnemonic function, with the emphasis more firmly on the content than the poetry, we have categorized such books primarily under their topics (husbandry, in this case) and secondarily under Poesy and the Arts.

Because a single title can be multiply categorized, when we present data based on *all* of the categories into which the books are sorted, some double-counting is involved and the totals will therefore not add up to 100 percent. But we can always use only the primary categories if we do not want to double-count any titles and want totals to sum to 100 percent. Both ways of picturing the book trade have their own defensible logic, and both enable the kind of comparisons that are necessary to understanding market share, but they tell somewhat different stories. Using multiple categories better acknowledges the fluidity of these categorizations and the critical judgment underlying them; using only primary categories makes market share more readily comprehensible because it is based on the total number of books that were published in a given period.

Despite the inevitable tricky cases, our survey of the entire STC has convinced us that enough books fall clearly into one of these six major categories to justify the effort. Categorizing books may be an inherently critical act, but we do not believe that the degree of judgment involved is so high as to render the results subjective. Scholars may differ on numerous decisions, but it seems to us that such disagreements will generally remain around the margins of what is, after all, a very large corpus of books. If others were to redo the work behind our figures for the market shares of various kinds of books, they would surely arrive at different percentages – but not dramatically different.

The table in Figure 1.1 presents the market shares of each of the six major categories over the Elizabethan period (1559–1602). It is important to remember that all of our market share figures involve *editions*, not individual *copies* of books; since we do not know the press runs of most editions, there is no way to calculate market share by actual copies. We first categorize books by primary categorization only, and then we incorporate secondary categories as well. The two sets of figures do not differ greatly, but the spread between them gives a good indication of the amount of overlap between these genres of books. By definition, each of the six major categories will increase somewhat when secondary classifications are included. But Religion, Politics and History, and Poesy and the Arts increase significantly more than the other three because, as suggested above, these categories had the most porous boundaries in the period and therefore the greatest number of secondary categorizations in our analysis. In order to account for all of these important overlaps, and to avoid reifying distinctions that were far more blurry in reality than they may appear in a table of percentages, for the remainder of this essay we always incorporate both primary and secondary categorizations in our calculations of market share.

Whichever methodology and set of figures we use, the table below confirms something that scholars have long known: in terms of market share and total number of editions, Religion dominated the retail book trade, composing more than two-fifths of that trade. What may be less widely known is that Poesy and the Arts made up another one-fifth to one-quarter, basically the same proportion

Category	Market share by primary category only	Market share by primary and secondary categories
Religion	40.2%	44.7%
Politics and History	20.9%	24.9%
Poesy and the Arts	19.2%	23.1%
Science and Mathematics	9.5%	10.2%
School and Language Instruction	7.5%	8.1%
Society and Conduct	2.7%	3.7%
Total	**100%**	**N/A**

Fig. 1.1   Market shares of the six major categories, 1559–1602

as Politics and History. By comparison with more 'serious' books of religion or politics, scholars have sometimes represented poetry, plays, and other literature as more marginal in the book trade than they actually were. In fact, Poesy and the Arts was one of the major 'lines' in the retail trade. The three other categories together accounted for the remaining fifth of the trade.

The Elizabethan book trade thus had essentially three tiers: the plurality of editions in circulation dealt with Religion; a second tier comprises Politics and History, and Poesy and the Arts; and in the bottom tier, with significantly lower market shares, were Science and Mathematics, School and Language Instruction, and books of Society and Conduct. Loss rates complicate this analysis, though not in any simplistic or obvious way. Since the *ABC* survives in only a few Elizabethan editions, and since other genres as well, such as handwriting manuals, may have been used to destruction, our category of School and Language Instruction surely under-represents the actual number of editions of schoolbooks circulating in the trade.[29] Since some editions of the *ABC* also included a catechism, Religion will also be under-counted in this area; with some prayer books, too, edition statements on title pages suggest that these books have been lost at a higher than usual rate. Similarly, Tessa Watt's estimate of lost Elizabethan ballads suggests that the actual market share of Poesy and the Arts was higher than is reflected in the surviving corpus.[30] Surely there are some lost editions in every major category, but they are

---

[29]   There are only eight extant Elizabethan editions of the *ABC*: four in English, two in Latin and English, one in Irish, and one in Dutch. Clearly, many more editions of this educational staple were actually produced in the period.

[30]   Based on entries in the Stationers' Registers, Watt estimates that only about one in ten sixteenth-century broadside ballad titles survives, the extant first editions of many

likely to have been differentially spread, clustering among certain kinds of books in each of the categories; it is therefore difficult to tell which major category is most affected by loss rates.

The table in Figure 1.1 presents a good sense of the composition of the Elizabethan retail book trade as a whole, but that trade was definitely not static, as can be readily seen by graphing the market shares of the six major categories as they fluctuated over time. Figure 1.2 displays these changing market shares using 10-year running averages, which offers a more comprehensible visualization by smoothing out year-to-year variations.[31] While each category rises and falls somewhat throughout the period, the top three – Religion, Politics and History, and Poesy and the Arts – display far more fluctuation than do the others. This greater variation is due in part to the fact that each of these three categories was far more responsive to topical events than were Science and Mathematics, School and Language Instruction, and Society and Conduct. Each period within Elizabeth's reign can be investigated for the particular constellation of issues driving changes in the book trade. The higher market share of Politics in the early Elizabethan period, for instance, seems to derive in large part from a burst of publications relating to the Scottish succession crisis following the abdication of Mary, Queen of Scots, in 1567, to the Northern Rebellion against Elizabeth in 1569–1570 and to the execution of John Felton. The decline in Politics after 1591, meanwhile, derives entirely from a decrease in the publication of law books and news pamphlets.

We do not have space here to address each of the changes in the market shares of these categories. But we are particularly interested in the transformation that occurred in the last decade of Elizabeth's reign, when the market share of Poesy and the Arts increased dramatically. In this 'late Elizabethan period', publishers brought out books of Poesy and the Arts more often than they ever had before,

---

of which are from the seventeenth century (*Cheap Print*, 141). In the Elizabethan period, there are 145 extant editions of broadside ballads, which translates to a market share of 1.7 percent, but this is surely well below the actual number that were printed. If Watt's estimate is correct and about 3,000 broadside ballad titles were printed, then a bit more than 3,000 editions would have been published once reprints are factored in. This total would result in a market share for ballads of over 26 percent, as well as lower market shares for other types of publications. There are also 81 extant Elizabethan editions of single-leaf verse that are not ballads; if we apply Watt's estimate to these too, the combined market share of single-leaf verse, including both ballads and other poetic forms, would be about 36 percent (over 4,800 total editions). This very high inferred market share of single-leaf verse – which was printed, published, and sold in a fairly different way than most books composed of folded sheets – suggests that one might want to distinguish single-leaf publications in general from other 'books' when thinking about print popularity. We have not done so here, in order to have the broadest possible corpus of publications, although the very high loss rates of these items has in a sense already done much of this work for us.

[31]   Each data point on the graph therefore represents the average market share of that major category over the span of a decade, with the decade moving forward in time by one year in each successive data point.

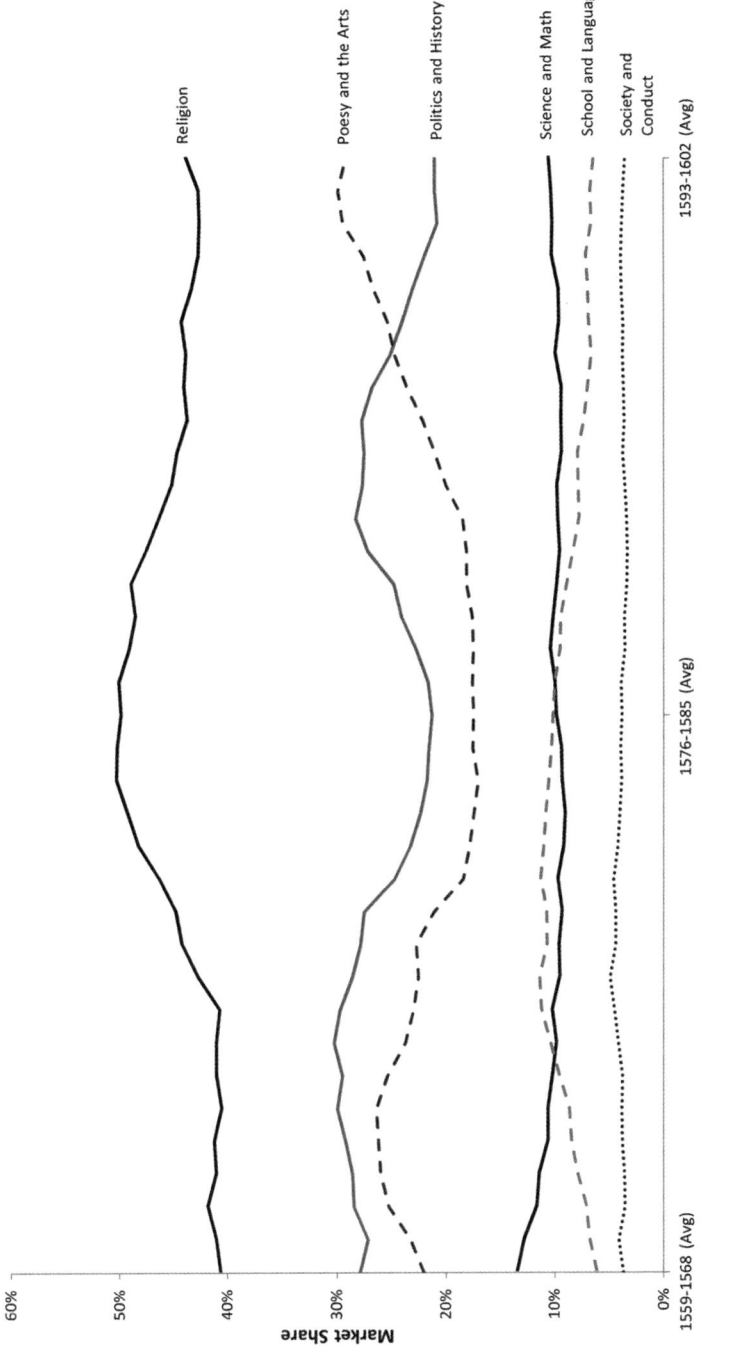

Fig. 1.2   Fluctuations in major categories (10-year running average)

making it the second most populous category in the retail trade as whole. Several factors account for this increase. For one thing, although the London professional theater opened in 1576, plays from the professional stage only began to be published in any real numbers beginning in the early 1590s, and they rapidly became an important segment of the trade. This decade also saw an increase in other forms of poesy that, unlike professional plays, had always been available for publication, including prose satires, prose romances, and books of sonnets and other verse forms.

We examine the late Elizabethan period in more detail later in this essay, but this example highlights that, in order to understand the retail trade, we need not only to follow its changes over time but also to investigate smaller genres than these six major categories. Figure 1.3 does just that for the entire Elizabethan period. We have selected a number of genres within each major category based partly on their prevalence in the book trade, partly on our own interest, and partly on the kinds of books that have been discussed in recent scholarship, including elsewhere in *The Elizabethan Top Ten*.[32] We further subdivide several of these genres into smaller components, giving the figures for each of these along with

---

[32]   As a reminder, Figure 1.3 calculates market shares by including both primary and secondary categorizations. While we have used our own judgment throughout, we have been guided by several scholarly works that include bibliographies of certain genres. For catechisms, Ian Green, *The Christian's ABC*. For schoolbooks of logic and rhetoric, Charles B. Schmitt, *John Case and Aristotelianism in Renaissance England* (Kingston and Montreal: McGill-Queen's UP, 1983); Heinrich F. Plett, *English Renaissance Rhetoric and Poetics: A Systematic Bibliography of Primary and Secondary Sources* (New York: E.J. Brill, 1995); Nancy A. Mace, 'The History of the Grammar Patent, 1547–1602', *Papers of the Bibliographical Society of America* 87 (1993): 419–36; Nancy A. Mace, 'The History of the Grammar Patent from 1620 to 1800 and the Forms of Lily's Latin Grammar', *Papers of the Bibliographical Society of America* 100 (2006): 177–225; and Lawrence D. Green and James J. Murphy, *Renaissance Rhetoric Short-Title Catalogue 1460–1700*, 2nd ed. (Burlington, VT: Ashgate, 2006). For dictionaries, DeWitt T. Starnes, *Renaissance Dictionaries: English-Latin and Latin-English* (Austin: U of Texas P, 1954). For poetry, Lukas Erne and Tamsin Badcoe, 'Shakespeare and the Popularity of Poetry Books in Print, 1583–1622', *Review of English Studies* (forthcoming); Arthur E. Case, *A Bibliography of English Poetical Miscellanies 1521–1750* (Oxford: The Bibliographical Society, 1935 [for 1929]). For prose romances, Paul A. Scanlon, 'A Checklist of Prose Romances in English', *The Library*, 5th series, 33 (1978): 143–52. For bibles and New Testaments, A.S. Herbert, *Historical Catalogue of Printed Editions of the English Bible 1525–1961* (London: British and Foreign Bible Society; New York: American Bible Society, 1968). For Medicine, Paul Slack, 'Mirrors of Health and Treasures of Poor Men: The Uses of the Vernacular Medical Literature of Tudor England', in Charles Webster, ed., *Health, Medicine, and Mortality in the Sixteenth Century* (Cambridge: Cambridge UP, 1979), 237–73. Note that the categories of language instruction and patented schoolbooks have more overlap than others in Figure 1.3 (one-fifth of the editions in each), although there is enough difference between them that we include both separately; as we show below, even given this overlap, the two categories functioned differently in the book trade.

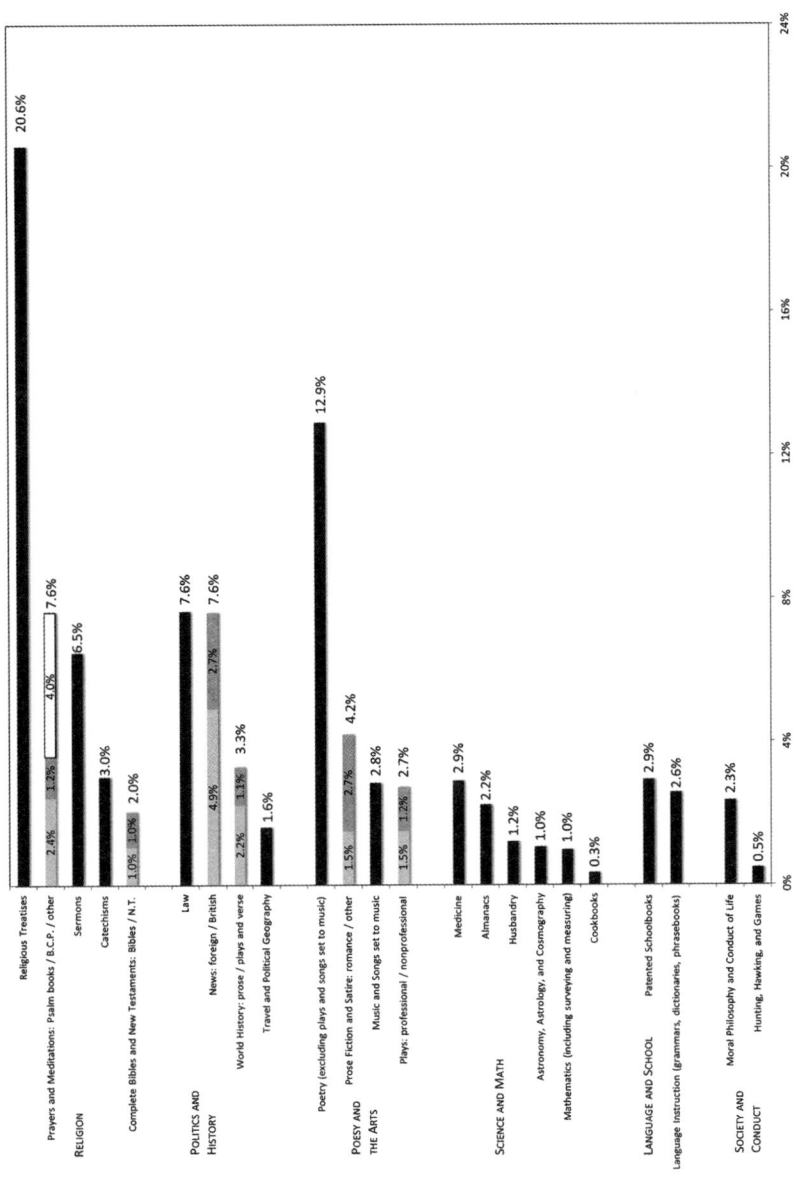

Fig. 1.3   Market shares, 1559–1602

the overall totals. For instance, the different portions of the bar for 'Books of prayers and meditations' (7.6 percent market share total) indicate the market shares of psalm books (2.4 percent) and the *Book of Common Prayer* (1.2 percent), along with all 'other' books of prayers and meditations (4.0 percent). The market share of bibles and New Testaments is 2.0 percent, composed equally of the two components, and so forth.[33]

By far the largest single genre of books in our sample is religious treatises, which alone made up one-fifth of the speculative editions in the STC, about the same market share as three of the six major categories combined (Science and Mathematics, School and Language Instruction, Society and Conduct). The genre of religious treatises encompasses books of polemic and controversy, theology, dialogues, church history, epistles, and a number of other forms of expository prose. Clearly this genre was the backbone of the retail book trade. More surprising may be the genre with the second-highest market share, poetry (12.9 percent). As with religious treatises, this genre comprises a variety of forms, everything from ballads and other verse broadsides to very long books like *The Faerie Queene* and Chaucer's *Workes*. In early modern England, verse was culturally central, used to address a wide range of topics, and it was equally central to print culture. Given that poetry accounts for more than one in ten speculative editions in the STC, early modern publishers must have understood the popularity of verse with their customers.

No other genre in our sample had a market share in the Elizabethan period approaching these two highly prevalent outliers. Indeed, only four others surpassed 5 percent of the retail trade: books of prayers and meditations, law, news, and sermons. Most genres cluster in the range of 2–4 percent market share, including prose fiction and satire, world history, catechisms, medicine, plays, psalm books, and others. At the bottom end of the scale are a number of genres with market shares of less than 2 percent, such as husbandry, mathematics, travel and political geography, and cookbooks. As discussed above, scholarly assessments of print popularity are often suffused with a rhetoric of very large numbers, with common references to hundreds of thousands of copies of certain types of books. But when we situate these books within the retail trade as a whole, a different story emerges: most recognizable genres of books had a market share below 4 percent, a figure that has struck some critics as low but that turns out to be entirely typical.[34] While we have obviously not included every possible genre in Figure 1.3, we have

---

[33] As emphasized earlier, these figures only count extant editions recorded in the STC. Some genres, such as ballads, had a disproportionate number of lost editions, while others, such as almanacs and bibles, were printed in significantly larger press runs than the standard maximum allowed by the Stationers' Company. On the press runs of bibles and New Testaments, see Rees and Wakeley, *Publishing*, 66–92. On almanacs, see Arber, *Transcript*, 2: 43.

[34] Peter W.M. Blayney, 'The Alleged Popularity of Playbooks', *Shakespeare Quarterly* 56 (2005): 33–50; Paul Werstine, 'The Science of Editing', in Andrew Murphy, ed., *A Concise Companion to Shakespeare and the Text* (Oxford: Blackwell, 2007), 109–27.

included all those with the largest market shares in our categorization of the STC; all of our genres not listed in Figure 1.3 have market shares below 3 percent. Any kind of book with a market share of about 4 percent or more, therefore, lies at the higher end of the spectrum.

As we have seen, the book trade underwent something of a transformation in the late Elizabethan period. This period is of particular interest to us as literary critics, and will likely be to many readers, since Poesy and the Arts surpassed Politics and History as the major category with the second-largest market share behind Religion. The decade of the 1590s also saw the first printed editions of much of the poetry and drama that have long been at the center of our canon of Renaissance literature – including works by Sidney, Spenser, Marlowe, Shakespeare, Chapman, Daniel, and others. Figure 1.4 presents a 'before-and-after' picture of the Elizabethan book trade, pivoting around the year 1592. The market shares of many of the 23 genres analyzed above changed very little over the course of the entire Elizabethan period, and so for the sake of clarity we omit these books from the graphs in Figure 1.4.[35] To make the graphs easier to read, we also separate out each of the components of these genres, such as prose romances and professional plays. Since the market share of Sternhold and Hopkins's *Metrical Psalms* did not change, we here exclude that title from the category of music so that the change in the publication of that genre can be more easily seen. Finally, while ballads saw an apparent decline in market share across this divide, this is almost certain to be purely the result of lost editions, and we therefore exclude single-leaf verse and ballads from the category of poetry in order to isolate changes in the publication of books of poetry. Those genres that decreased in the last Elizabethan decade are shaded in gray, and those that increased are in black.[36]

Figure 1.4 makes clear that the increase in Poesy and the Arts in the late Elizabethan period was widely spread: every genre of Poesy that we examined, except for nonprofessional drama, saw an increase in market share. Professional plays are a special case: before 1592, they were virtually nonexistent, with a market share of 0.3 percent. As we discuss elsewhere, for reasons still not entirely clear, plays from the professional stage began to be printed in sizable numbers only in 1594, but publishers quickly brought out more and more of them.[37] In the

---

[35]   The market share of world history did rise in this decade from 2.7 percent to 4.5 percent, but this increase was due entirely to more verse and play histories being published, which are already accounted for in the poetry and professional play categories. The market share of prose histories was essentially unchanged, declining slightly from 2.3 percent to 2.1 percent.

[36]   Because the book trade as a whole was expanding, it is important to remember that a decrease in the market share of a particular genre does not necessarily mean that fewer editions of that genre were being published. In the case of all of the genres in Figure 1.4, the two measures of popularity do, in fact, correlate, but this will not always be the case. Market share tells us about the composition of the trade, but not the total number of editions published.

[37]   See the chapter on the creation of the market for printed professional plays in our forthcoming book, *Print, Plays, and Popularity in Shakespeare's England*.

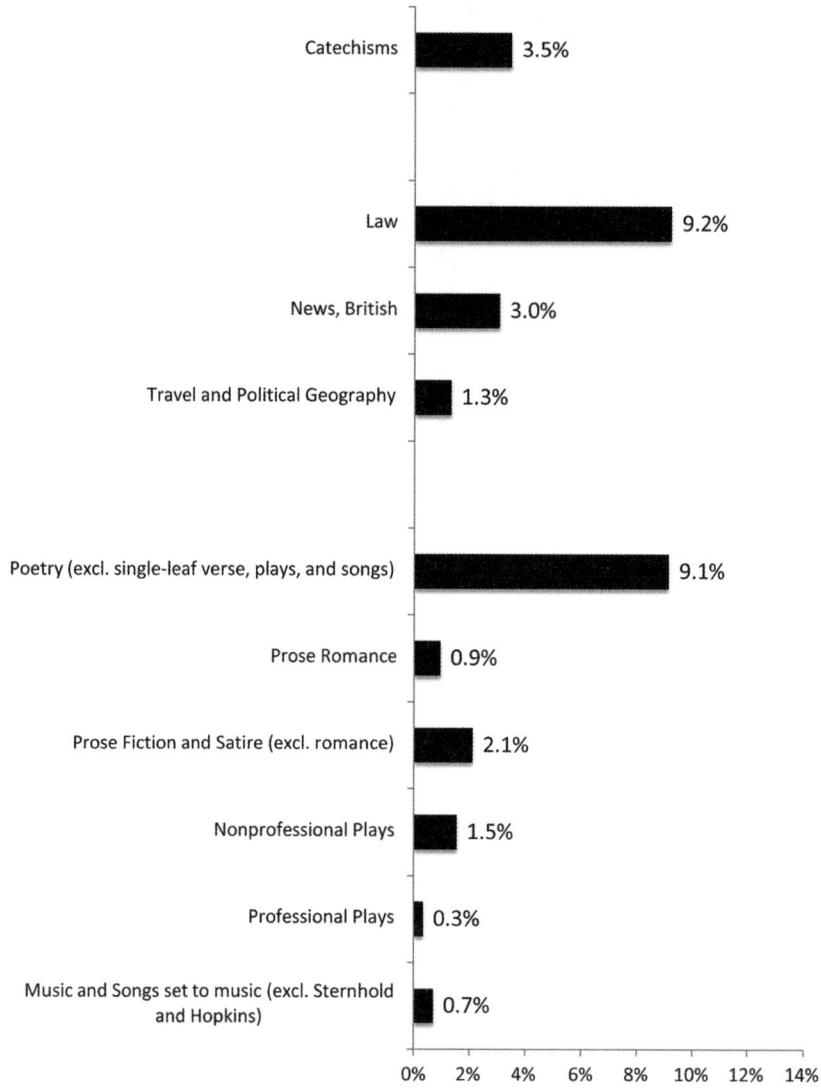

Fig. 1.4a   Market shares, 1559–1591

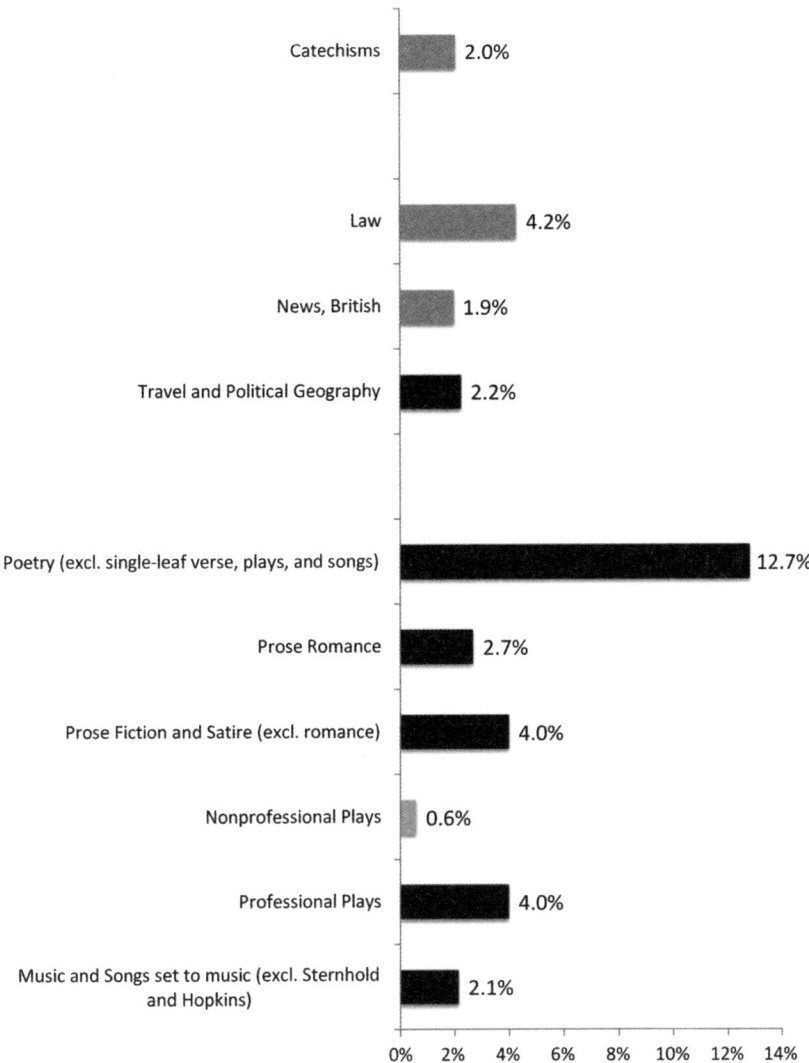

Fig. 1.4b   Market shares, 1592–1602

last decade of Elizabeth's reign, books of professional plays increased to a market share of 4 percent. At that level, while they certainly did not approach the market shares of poetry or religious treatises, professional plays had become a significant part of the retail trade. By contrast, the market share of law books decreased by more than half, a trend that would continue into the seventeenth century: from 1603 to 1620, they had a market share of 3.0 percent, and from 1621 to 1640, 2.0 percent. Law books began the early modern period as one of the most prevalent kinds of books in the retail trade; by the end, they had gradually fallen to the lower end of the scale.

Figures 1.3 and 1.4 need to be used with caution, however; we cannot simply conclude that any category with a longer bar than another was more 'popular' in any absolute sense. As we have argued elsewhere, market share is well suited to answering certain questions about print popularity, although not all of them. Market share can tell us: '*Which books were most prevalent in the book trade as a whole? Which classes of books participated in the greatest number of retail sales transactions? In which classes did publishers invest the most capital and earn the most profits in terms of pounds, shillings, and pence?*' But market share alone cannot answer other crucial questions about popularity, which can only be addressed by looking at reprint rates. Reprint rates 'provide the best available criterion for answering such questions as: *How eager were customers to buy the [different categories of books] that were for sale in bookshops? Was a [particular kind of book] a good publishing investment? Did [it] reliably turn a profit?*'.[38]

Because market share and reprint rates address different aspects of print popularity, the two criteria do not always align neatly. For instance, according to market share, poetry (12.9 percent) massively outperformed medicine (2.9 percent) in the Elizabethan period, and yet first-edition medical books were reprinted 27.6 percent of the time, above the benchmark and twice the reprint rate of poetry (13.8 percent). Likewise, within the genre of world history, prose histories were more than twice as prevalent in the retail trade as verse and dramatic histories (2.2 percent vs 1.1 percent market share), but the poetic forms of history sold out entire editions far more frequently than did those in prose (32.8 percent vs 18.8 percent reprint rate). We see a clear divergence between the two criteria in these cases and numerous others; each criterion tells us something about print popularity, but not quite the same thing.

The explanation for the seeming paradox is that, 'for reasons both cultural and economic, different kinds of books may have sold in different ways, may have had different *structures of popularity*'.[39] News pamphlets and almanacs, for instance, had reprint rates close to zero, but this hardly indicates that they were unsuccessful categories of books. Rather, with genres like these that were highly topical – almanacs on an annual basis, news within a shorter time frame – publishers were seeking to profit from immediate and rapid sales rather than from steady sales of multiple editions over the years. Similarly, but at the opposite end of the spectrum,

---

[38]   Farmer and Lesser, 'Structures', 210, 208.

[39]   Farmer and Lesser, 'The Popularity of Playbooks', 27.

bibles and the *Book of Common Prayer* had extremely high reprint rates (80.0 percent and 75.0 percent, respectively), and yet there were so few first editions in these categories that the reprint rate becomes essentially meaningless. In the Elizabethan period, there were five first editions of complete bibles and four of the *Book of Common Prayer*; in each case, only a single first edition was not reprinted within 20 years.[40] The success of these kinds of books was rooted not in publishers' investment in new titles that might prove popular enough to reprint, but rather in the constant reprinting of a very small number of titles. These two examples represent distinctive niches within the retail book trade: the market for bibles and the *Book of Common Prayer* was narrow (only a few titles) but deep (those few titles were continuously reprinted); the market for news and almanacs was wide (numerous different titles) but shallow (they were almost never reprinted).

As these examples hint, and as more detailed analysis confirms, the economic characteristic that differentiates these niches is the relative weighting of each genre of books towards either new titles or reprints. For any genre of books, we can statistically represent this quality by dividing the number of its first editions by the total of all its editions. The resulting percentage tells us whether the genre was more heavily or more lightly weighted towards new titles. Because they were almost never reprinted, both news and almanacs have a very high 'first-edition weighting' (FEW): among all news pamphlets printed in the Elizabethan period, 92.6 percent were first editions; among almanacs, 89.7 percent. By contrast, the FEWs of bibles (5.5 percent) and the *Book of Common Prayer* (4.0 percent) are the lowest of any of the genres we have examined; virtually all of their editions were reprints. While our earlier work gestured towards these distinctions, it was only after we had categorized the entire STC that we could see just how crucial this economic characteristic is to understanding the diverse structures of popularity in the early modern book trade. The structure of popularity of some kinds of books depended more on new titles, whereas others depended more on reprinting steady sellers.

Most genres, of course, fall somewhere between the two extremes of news and bibles. First-edition weighting allows us to perceive connections among genres at a fundamental economic level that would otherwise remain hidden because the genres differ greatly at the level of content. For instance, sermons (Religion), travel and political geography (Politics and History), professional plays (Poesy and the Arts), medical books (Science and Mathematics), and moral philosophy and conduct (Society and Conduct) fall into five different major categories and would seem to have little in common. But their similar FEWs reveal that they shared a structure of popularity: all of these genres (and several others) depended for their economic success on a high proportion of new titles.

Figure 1.5 graphs the genres we have been studying here according to FEW, revealing that there were four major structures of popularity in the early modern retail book trade, which we name the 'Topical', 'Innovative', 'Mature', and 'Monopolistic' structures. (These structures of popularity segment the marketplace

---

[40]   These were STC 2347, a Welsh bible published in 1588, and STC 16429, a *Book of Common Prayer* in Latin and Greek, published in 1569.

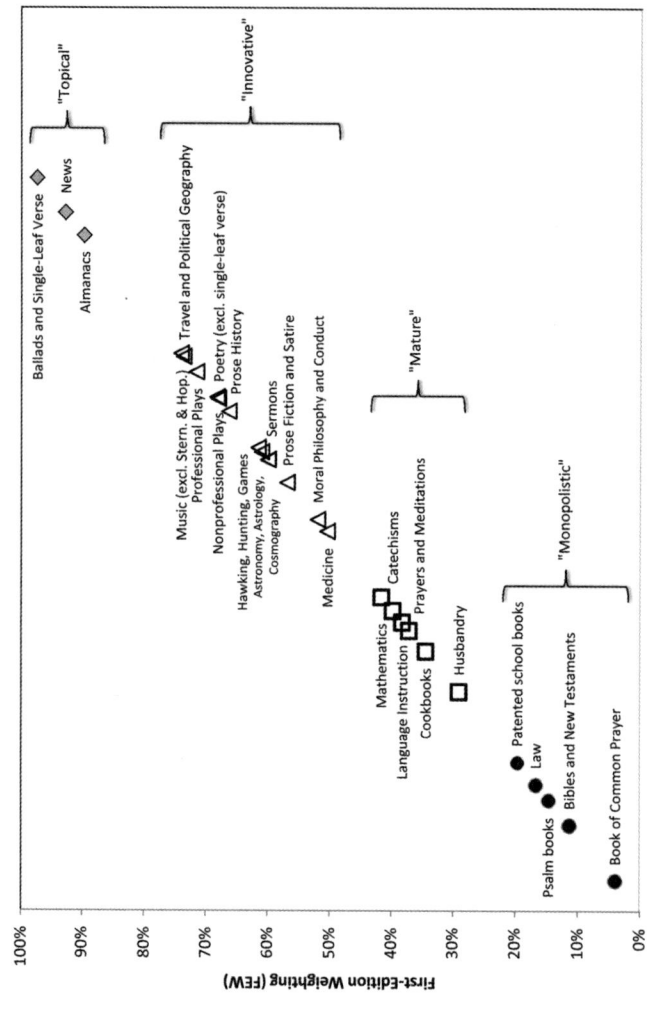

Fig. 1.5   The four structures of popularity

of print by *books*, not by *stationer* or *bookshop*: over their careers, most prolific publishers brought out books in at least three of these segments of the trade, and some in all four, and any retail bookshop would have stocked books from all the segments.) As discussed above, categorizing books is an inherently critical exercise, but one of the most interesting things about FEW is that thinking through this lens can allow economic evidence from the book trade itself to challenge our preconceptions about categories. For instance, if we analyze the category of poetry with this characteristic in mind, we can see that it included two kinds of books that operated somewhat differently on an economic level. Ballads and other single-leaf verses sold far more like news and almanacs, as part of the Topical structure of popularity, than they did like the rest of poetry, an Innovative genre. Partly for this reason, in Figure 1.5 we sometimes subdivide categories that we have previously considered as a whole.

Figure 1.5 thus provides a map of the Elizabethan book trade, organized according to how different types of books sought economic popularity. At the top right of Figure 1.5 are books like ballads, news, and almanacs, with a FEW of 90 percent or above. When publishers brought out books within this Topical structure of popularity, they did not expect to reprint them, nor were reprints central to their success. Nearly all of the books in these genres were new titles, and hence reprint rates are not a good measure of their print popularity. Market share, instead, is their most important index of popularity, supplemented by profitability (most of these items were quite short).

For the Monopolistic segment at the bottom left of Figure 1.5, reprint rates are likewise comparatively unimportant, and market share is ultimately more significant – but for the opposite reason. The books in this structure of popularity had very high reprint rates, but almost no new titles at all. The Monopolistic structure consisted overwhelmingly of reprints of a few select titles, with FEWs ranging from 4 percent to 20 percent. All of the genres in this group were covered by patents or published by the King's Printer, and they were gathered into these patents by powerful stationers precisely because they involved titles that could be successfully reprinted again and again. Bibles, New Testaments, and law books, moreover, were among the longest publications in the book trade and therefore would have generated much higher profits than works in other genres typically did. Monopolistic books varied widely in market share, from law (7.6 percent market share in the Elizabethan period) to psalm books (2.4 percent) to New Testaments (1.0 percent), but these market shares only begin to capture what made them so lucrative to early modern publishers.[41] They were among the safest bets in the trade, guaranteed to earn sizable profits for any stationer fortunate enough to be able to publish them.[42]

---

[41]   On the profitability of bibles and New Testaments, see Rees and Wakeley, *Publishing*, 82–88.

[42]   Almanacs were, of course, a patented genre, but their structure of popularity places them in the Topical rather than the Monopolistic segment of the book trade.

While market share is the more pertinent index of popularity for the Topical and Monopolistic structures, it is also more difficult to apply because these two structures were disproportionately affected by the evidentiary problems of loss rates and variable press runs. Topical books in general tended to be only one to three sheets long and hence much more subject to lost editions, and almanacs, in particular, were also covered by a patent that exempted them from the Company limits on press runs. Most of the Monopolistic books could also be produced in these higher press runs, which means that a category with a low market share in terms of number of editions, such as bibles (1.0 percent) or New Testaments (1.0 percent), would have had a somewhat higher market share if we were able to account for press runs – exactly how much higher is impossible to know, although a reasonable estimate might be three to four times their apparent market share for bibles and New Testaments, and more for almanacs.

The other two structures of popularity lie between these two poles and incorporate a range of genres, from those primarily made up of reprints to those primarily composed of new titles. The Mature segment includes genres with FEWs in the range of 30 percent to 40 percent, meaning that about two-thirds of the books in this structure of popularity were reprints. For a variety of reasons, publishers working in these Mature genres privileged a handful of existing steady sellers rather than consistently looking for new titles that might (but might not) turn into steady sellers. In some of these genres, publishers probably thought it would be difficult for a new title to succeed because of institutional factors: school curricula were highly conservative, for instance, and the chances of a new catechism or math textbook selling well in this area were lower, since books like Calvin's and Nowell's catechisms and Robert Record's *Arithmetic* were already entrenched. Other reasons have more to do with the content of the books than their institutional locations. For example, dictionaries required (according to one author) 'infinit paynes & great charges' to compile, and much of that work would simply duplicate existing scholarship, making new titles costly and risky to produce. Certain dictionaries, therefore, seem to have become established as the standard works.[43] For all of these reasons, authors do not seem to have written many new titles in some of these Mature genres, and publishers seem to have been reluctant to invest in them.

The idea that a few titles provided 'standard' knowledge in a given area may also have been responsible for the low proportion of first editions in husbandry. A number of pre-Elizabethan titles controlled the field: John Fitzherbert's *Boke*

---

[43]   This complaint was from Francis Holyoke, who for this reason was seeking a patent for his additions to John Rider's earlier dictionary, *Bibliotheca Scholastica*; see W.W. Greg, *A Companion to Arber: Being a Calendar of Documents in Edward Arber's* Transcript of the Registers of the Company of Stationers of London 1554–1640 (Oxford: Clarendon, 1967), 318–319; David McKitterick, *A History of Cambridge University Press: Volume 1: Printing and the Book Trade in Cambridge, 1534–1698* (Cambridge: Cambridge UP, 1992), 118–19.

of Husbandry began the period with its fifteenth edition and was reprinted five more times; Tusser's *Points of Good Husbandry* was reprinted 17 times in the Elizabethan period; Thomas Hill's gardening manual was first printed in 1558 and went through seven Elizabethan editions. Tree husbandry saw a succession of standard references, the one superseding the other, in a niche that could generally only sustain a single work at a time: the anonymous *Craft of Grafting and Planting Trees* (1505, c.1518, c.1563, c.1565) was followed by Leonard Mascall's *How to Plant and Graft All Sorts of Trees* (eight editions, 1569–1599) and an anonymous book on *The Orchard and the Garden* (four editions, 1594–1602), then by Arthur Standish's *New Directions* (five editions, 1613–1616) and *A Second Direction* (three editions, 1613–1614), and finally by William Lawson's *New Orchard and Garden* (five editions, 1618–1638). With numerous subjects in husbandry already well served by a few titles from the beginning of the Elizabethan period, new authors, titles, and stationers apparently had a hard time breaking into the market. One author who did was Gervase Markham, who began writing about animal husbandry in the 1590s, and in keeping with the Mature structure of this genre, his books on horses were soon frequently reprinted, while very few other new titles entered the field.

Since the genres in the Mature structure of popularity are already weighted towards reprint editions, the reprint rates of these genres will be somewhat less important as a measure of their popularity than their market share.[44] As the map of the Mature structure of popularity in Figure 1.6 shows, almost all of these genres have reprint rates above the benchmark of 22.4 percent, but since the reprint rate measures the relative success of *first* editions, it does not describe the fundamental economic structure of these genres, which was rooted in later editions. The reprint rate of a genre like prayers and meditations (35.7 percent) is certainly significant, especially when compared that of mathematics (14.3 percent), but even prayers and meditations was weighted towards reprinting established works rather than publishing new ones. This fundamental emphasis on reprinting led to what would seem a paradox if we did not understand the Mature structure of popularity. Generally we would expect the market share of a genre with a higher-than-average reprint rate to increase over time, as publishers realized those books were selling well and therefore sought out new manuscripts to print. But publishers did not act that way towards these Mature genres; rather, they continued their strategy of reprinting the same steady sellers. Thus, even though prayers and meditations had a high reprint rate in the Elizabethan period, this did not lead to an expansion

---

[44] Since the reprint rate measures the percentage of first editions to reach a second, in a genre without a substantial number of first editions, this statistic will not be as meaningful. The very high reprint rate of cookbooks (70 percent), for instance, becomes less important when we realize that there were only 10 first editions in the Elizabethan period, and that the genre as a whole only had a market share of 0.3 percent. But the underlying dynamic of the Mature structure of popularity is not related to the absolute number of first editions in a genre, but to their proportion of the whole.

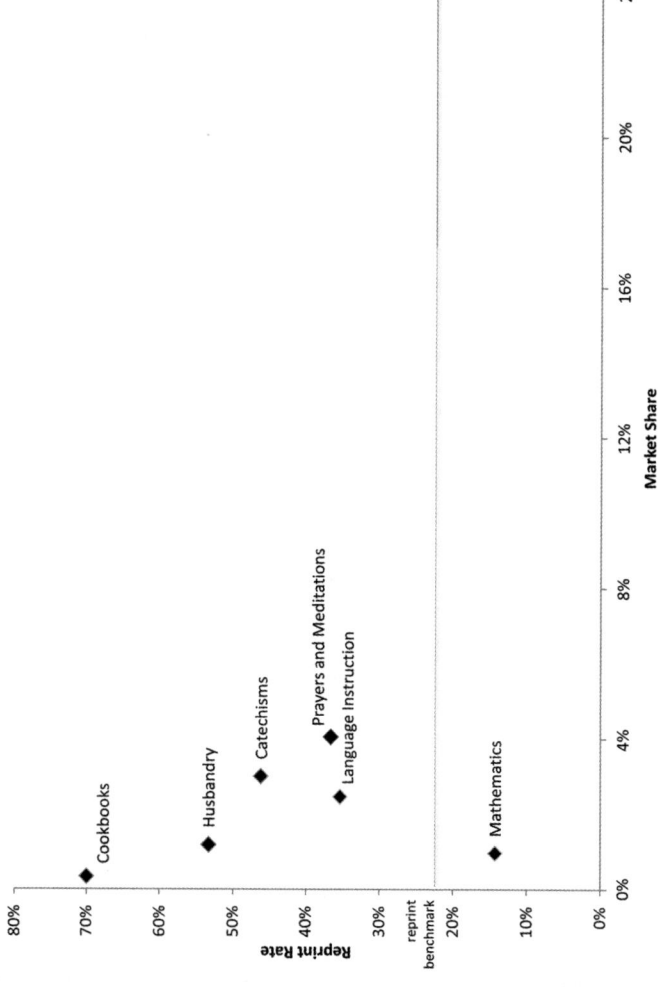

Fig. 1.6   The mature structure of popularity, 1559–1602

in the number of first editions being published in the following decade.[45] While reprint rates in the Mature structure are generally high, these genres had already been winnowed down to the more successful titles, and publishers were not taking many risks on new titles. The print popularity of Mature genres is based on the tried and true, and as a result, their market shares cluster towards the lower end of the spectrum. Once we understand the Mature structure of popularity, what stands out most about prayers and meditations – what indicates its strong popularity as a genre – is not its high reprint rate, which is, after all, only in the middle of the pack for Mature genres. Instead, the striking feature of prayers and meditations is its market share, which not only is at the higher end in general but also far outpaces the other genres in the Mature structure of popularity.

Since the Mature segment included numerous steady sellers that had already proven themselves over the years, it could be a relatively safe and lucrative area of the trade; any publisher would have wanted the rights to print a book like Tusser's *Points of Good Husbandry* or Mascall's *How to Plant and Graft All Sorts of Trees*, with their recurrent reprints. The same was true to an even greater degree in the Monopolistic segment, which included genres that were virtually guaranteed to turn a profit. But not all stationers could work in these two segments of the market, and breaking into them was difficult if one was not already on the inside. Patents largely excluded all but the most powerful stationers from publishing any new titles in the Monopolistic genres. The Mature segment also included some patents for catechisms and for books of prayers and meditations, but for the most part in this segment, the restrictions were economic, not legal.[46] As we have seen, the Mature genres relied on frequently reprinted, well established titles that were, of course, already protected by the Company's right to copy: the same structure of popularity that made it safe and lucrative to publish these old 'standards' thereby also made stationers more cautious in publishing new titles. The one aspect of the Mature segment was entirely related to and dependent on the other.

---

[45]   From 1592 to 1602, there were 38 first editions of prayers and meditations, an average of 3.5 per year; from 1603 to 1613, there were 41 first editions, an average of 3.7. The difference is not statistically significant, as shown by the fact that the Jacobean first editions actually represent a lower overall market share, since the retail trade in general was expanding. In other words, there is no evidence that publishers responded to the high reprint rate of prayers and meditations by seeking to publish first editions more frequently than they had been.

[46]   For the patents governing books of prayers and meditations and of catechisms, see Appendices A–E in volume 3 of the STC (197–202). In line with the tendency of Mature genres to narrow to a select group of steady sellers, when Gervase Markham became too effusive on the subject of the diseases and cures of various farm animals, the Stationers' Company convinced him to accept an unusual agreement not to write any more books on this topic. This regulatory arrangement restricted the supply of new works by this one prolific author and created a *de facto* monopoly in this subfield of animal husbandry for the stationers who already owned the rights to his titles. See Arber, *Transcript*, 3: 679.

Both the Monopolistic and Mature segments of the retail trade were captured by a relatively small group of stationers with powerful family and patronage connections, and not surprisingly, many of these books would ultimately be gathered into the English Stock, the most important publishing monopoly of the early Stuart period.[47] But while these two segments were lucrative for those lucky stationers who controlled them, they were also fairly small in terms of the numbers of both genres and total editions. The largest single segment of the retail trade was the Innovative one. Most genres fall into this area, and in the Elizabethan period it composed more than half of all the editions in the STC, more than the other three structures combined.[48] The Innovative segment was therefore at the heart of the early modern book trade. Even accounting for loss rates and the higher press runs of some patented books, we can be sure that a Londoner browsing through the bookshops around St. Paul's would have seen more of these books than those in the Monopolistic or Mature segments.

These Innovative genres were more wide open and easier for publishers to break into: they were made up primarily of new titles, with FEWs ranging from 50 percent to 80 percent. When publishers worked in this segment of the book trade, in other words, they frequently chose to invest in first editions of new works rather than relying more on reprints of older titles. This is not to say that publishers were averse to reprinting titles in these Innovative genres, far from it: unlike in the Topical segment, if an edition in these genres sold out, its publisher was very likely to reprint it. Reprint editions not only earned higher profits than first editions on a copy-for-copy basis, but they were already proven titles that themselves had very high reprint rates; once a book was successful, the odds of its being reprinted yet again went up substantially.[49] The point is that overall, the reprint editions in the Innovative genres were not the kind of steady-selling, 'standard' titles that discouraged the publication of new works.

As a result, unlike in the Mature structure of popularity, when an Innovative genre proved to be in high demand with readers – as evidenced by a high reprint rate – publishers typically responded by expanding the genre into more and more new titles. Thus, while the high reprint rate of prayers and meditations did not lead to this sort of expansion, the frequent reprinting of both professional plays (41.8 percent) and sermons (29.5 percent) in the late Elizabethan period did lead to more new titles being published, beginning around 1600 for professional plays

---

[47]   On the significance of family connections in the early modern English book trade, see John Barnard, 'Politics, Profits and ?Idealism: John Norton, the Stationers' Company and Sir Thomas Bodley', *Bodleian Library Record* 17 (2002): 385–408.

[48]   If we could account for loss rates and variability in press runs, we would almost certainly find that the Innovative structure made up fewer than half of the books in the retail trade in reality, but even here it would almost certainly make up a plurality of the trade in books – that is, excluding single-leaf verse.

[49]   See Farmer and Lesser, 'The Popularity of Playbooks', 20.

and 1606 for sermons.[50] Although this reaction was not inevitable or universal, the Innovative segment was generally more responsive to reprint rates, which will therefore be more significant in our assessments of print popularity in this segment than in the other three. More significant, but not completely determinative – market share matters here as well. The huge market share of religious treatises clearly signals that it was a successful and popular genre, even though its reprint rate did not exceed the overall benchmark.

First-edition weighting thus defines the four large structures of popularity in the retail book trade and serves to sort genres of books into those segments. The divisions between the Topical, Innovative, Mature, and Monopolistic structures were generally stable, but not completely impermeable, and genres of books did occasionally move between them. The category of prose fiction and satire offers an illustrative counter-example to the cases of professional plays and sermons. Like those genres, prose fiction expanded following a period of success: from 1559 to 1591, 48.1 percent of first editions sold well enough to warrant a reprint, and in the ensuing decade (1592–1602), publishers tripled the number of first editions they brought out each year. But what happened next is more surprising: the genre retained its relatively high reprint rate, but in the seventeenth century stationers began to move away from publishing first editions. Instead, they relied more on reprinting old titles; as a result, the FEW of prose fiction and satire gradually declined, ultimately landing it in the Mature segment of the trade. By the Caroline period, the genre more resembled the category of prayers and meditation than that of poetry, with an increasing emphasis on old, tried-and-true standards like Lyly's *Euphues*, Greene's *Pandosto*, Lodge's *Rosalynde*, and Sidney's *Arcadia*. However, even though genres thus could shift from one structure of popularity to another, particularly between the Mature and Innovative, by the Elizabethan period the book trade was well enough established that such movement was rare.

With this understanding of the four major structures of popularity in the retail book trade, how might we assess the relative popularity of the different genres of books within those structures? The key theoretical point to emphasize is that comparisons *across* different segments risk ignoring a fundamental aspect of the early modern book trade and can therefore be misleading. For instance, the reprint rate of Elizabethan books of prayers and meditations (excluding psalms and the

---

[50] For the rhythm of playbook publication, see Farmer and Lesser, 'The Popularity of Playbooks', 6–13. Sermons averaged 12.5 first editions per year from 1591 to 1600, which increased to 13.6 from 1601 to 1605, and then jumped to 30.0 from 1606 to 1610. Of course, publishers at the time would not have known any of these figures – for reprint rates, total first editions, market share, or first-edition weighting – and yet the evidence suggests that they did respond to the *effects* of these statistics in the book trade. Given the size of the retail book trade, both numerically and geographically, it seems that London stationers had a reasonably good sense of how different kinds of books were selling and that they acted on that information. In general, we believe that reprint rates and market shares offer the best proxies available for the kinds of information that stationers might have had about how well or poorly editions in different genres were selling.

Book of Common Prayer) was essentially the same as the category of moral philosophy and conduct (35.7 percent vs 32.1 percent), but its market share was nearly double (4.0 percent vs 2.3 percent). It would therefore seem reasonable to conclude that prayers and meditations were more popular than moral philosophy and conduct, since one key index is higher while the other is basically the same.

The problem with this reasoning is that it reifies the market shares and reprint rates of these genres without considering the different ways in which they sold: one was a Mature genre and the other Innovative; stationers and book-buyers focused more on reprints in one genre, more on new titles in the other. Each genre ended up having the market share and reprint rate that it did in part *because* of its particular structure of popularity. The key indices of popularity, in other words, exist in an inextricable, dialectical relationship with the four segments of the retail trade. As we noted above, stationers responded to higher than average reprint rates in different ways when deciding to publish books in the Mature and Innovative segments – either by sticking with older steady sellers in the Mature structure or by seeking out more and more new titles in the Innovative. The elevated reprint rate of prayers and meditations was thus partly the result of this more cautious approach to publication. New works in Mature genres benefitted both from the general popularity of older works in that genre and from having relatively fewer other new titles with which to compete for readers. So while more editions of prayers and meditations were published than of moral philosophy and conduct, the former genre was also less open to new titles, less open to expansion, and less dynamic in the book trade.

With these issues in mind, we cannot assume that a Mature genre would have had the same high reprint rate or the same market share had it sold according to the logic of the Innovative structure of popularity; its market share as well would almost certainly have been different. Indeed, we cannot assume that the reprint rate and market share of any genre would have been the same if it had sold within one of the other segments of the trade, for these statistical measures of popularity were, in part, the products of the particular structure of popularity of the genre. When assessing print popularity, we must take into account *how* genres sold and the underlying structures that governed stationers' choices about which books to publish. And we must be careful to treat statistical measures of popularity, such as market share and reprint rate, not as stable 'facts' but rather as dynamic processes resulting from the web of connections between any genre and the larger segment of the retail trade in which it participated.

Comparisons across different structures of popularity must therefore be quite nuanced to avoid this problem of reification. This is not to say, however, that comparisons within the *same* segment of the trade will be simple or mechanistic. The seeming paradox identified earlier – in which the categories of poetry and medicine each seems more 'popular' than the other, but according to different criteria – can now be seen to occur entirely *within* the Innovative segment. Such comparisons still require critical judgment, but they have the benefit of following, rather than resisting, the underlying logic of the book trade itself. We close this essay by examining the Innovative structure of popularity in more detail: which books found print popularity in this largest segment of the retail trade?

Figure 1.7 maps the Innovative genres in the late Elizabethan period (1592–1602), when Poesy and the Arts overtook Politics and History as the second-largest major category of books. All of the genres in Poesy and the Arts followed the Innovative structure of popularity in this period.[51] As usual, the category of religious treatises stands out for its extremely high market share, more than one-fifth of the entire retail trade, with a reprint rate almost exactly at the benchmark.[52] Poetry (excluding single-leaf verse) also represented a large portion of the market (12.7 percent), with a reprint rate slightly below the benchmark. By far the most successful genre in terms of reprint rate, at nearly double the benchmark, was professional plays, while sermons, prose fiction, and music also did better than average. Each of these six genres, four of them varieties of Poesy and the Arts, was clearly selling well in the late Elizabethan period, with all except music also having a market share towards the higher end of the spectrum – or, in the case of religious treatises, the highest market share.

If we insist on asking which of these six genres was the *most* popular overall, there will be no simple answer. True, in some cases the evidence is clear: if we compare two genres in the same segment of the retail trade, and one has *both* a higher reprint rate *and* a higher market share than the other, we can usually conclude that it was 'more popular' in that period. On this basis, professional plays were more popular than prose history and more popular than travel and political geography in the late Elizabethan period.[53] But often the picture is murkier than

---

[51] We exclude here Stenhold and Hopkins's *Metrical Psalms* from the category of music for the purposes of determining the structure of popularity that the genre of music followed. If, on the other hand, we want to think of the *Metrical Psalms* as an integral part of the market for music books in the period, the presence of that title will mean that the genre as a whole falls into the Mature structure of popularity during the entire Elizabethan period (1559–1602), since reprints of that 'standard' work outweighed new editions. When the *Metrical Psalms* are included, the resulting first-edition weighting of music ends up at 33.3 percent, instead of 74.0 percent. Either method is defensible. We choose the former here to highlight how music sold in the retail trade apart from this one title, but one could equally argue that music as a whole was a Mature category with a single standard work at its center. For more on music publishing in Elizabethan England, see Mary Chan, 'Music Books', in Barnard, McKenzie, and Bell, eds, *Cambridge History*, 127–37; Peter Le Huray, *Music and the Reformation in England 1549–1660* (New York: Oxford UP, 1967).

[52] Since in the Elizabethan period first editions of religious treatises accounted for 25.0 percent of all speculative first editions in the STC, and in the late Elizabethan period for 23.7 percent, it is worth emphasizing that they were reprinted at almost exactly the benchmark, even when we exclude religious treatises themselves from the corpus that gives us the benchmark. From 1559 to 1602, the reprint rate of religious treatises was 21.6 percent, while that of all other speculative first editions was 22.6 percent.

[53] It is always important to check for statistical significance when comparing genres, most typically by using the chi-square test. On this issue, see Farmer and Lesser, 'Structures'. Furthermore, we would want to ensure that there were not factors external to

this, since the two indices of popularity do not always align in this way. Publishers were bringing out, and customers were buying, more total editions and more individual copies of religious treatises than of any other genre in the period, and significantly more of poetry as well. Religious treatises therefore also accounted for more of the monetary investment and more of the total profits than any other genre. (They also surely accounted for more of the total losses.) On the other hand, a publisher who was deciding to invest in a new title stood a greater chance of seeing that edition sell out and justify a more lucrative reprint edition if he chose to invest in a new professional play rather than a new religious treatise, a new sermon, or a new work of prose fiction or poetry. Readers were eagerly buying up entire editions of professional plays more frequently than editions in other genres, which is why that genre has the highest reprint rate. In absolute terms, of course, more first editions of religious treatises succeeded and were reprinted than in any other genre – but then again, more of them were *not* reprinted than in any other genre. These multiple, equally valid perspectives on print popularity – viewed in terms of absolute numbers and of likelihoods, viewed from the perspective of stationers and of readers, in this particular decade and over longer spans – mean that the question of which genre was 'the most popular' does not have a definitive answer, and is indeed something of a false question.

The difficulty of deciding, in any absolute sense, which of these six popular genres was the *most* popular should not really surprise us if we look again at the map of this segment of the book trade. As Figure 1.7 makes clear, that difficulty results from the very fact that *all* of these genres were popular; all were good investments for stationers in this decade, because all were in demand with book-buyers. Other kinds of books in the Innovative segment fared less well: very few editions were published in the genres of hawking, hunting, and games; astronomy, astrology, and cosmography; and travel and political geography, all of which had market shares at the lower end of the spectrum and reprint rates well below the benchmark. In the late Elizabethan period, at least, these genres seem to have been comparatively unpopular. Especially with travel and political geography, this unpopularity may surprise us, given how much attention that genre has recently received in Renaissance studies and how central it has seemed to early modern English culture. But of course print popularity is only one way of thinking about the centrality or marginality of texts, books, and discourses and is not straightforwardly indicative of which had the most profound cultural effects.

Print popularity is deeply enmeshed in the larger culture, shaping it in complex ways but also being shaped by it. As the broader culture changed, so, too, did the book trade. Figure 1.7 presents a brief snapshot of one segment of that trade, but the popularity of genres waxed and waned over time, with both reprint rates and market shares fluctuating (often in inverse relationship to each other). For a full picture of the popularity of a particular genre, we would want to track it across a

---

the book trade that restricted the supply of any of these genres or otherwise affected their reprint rates or market shares.

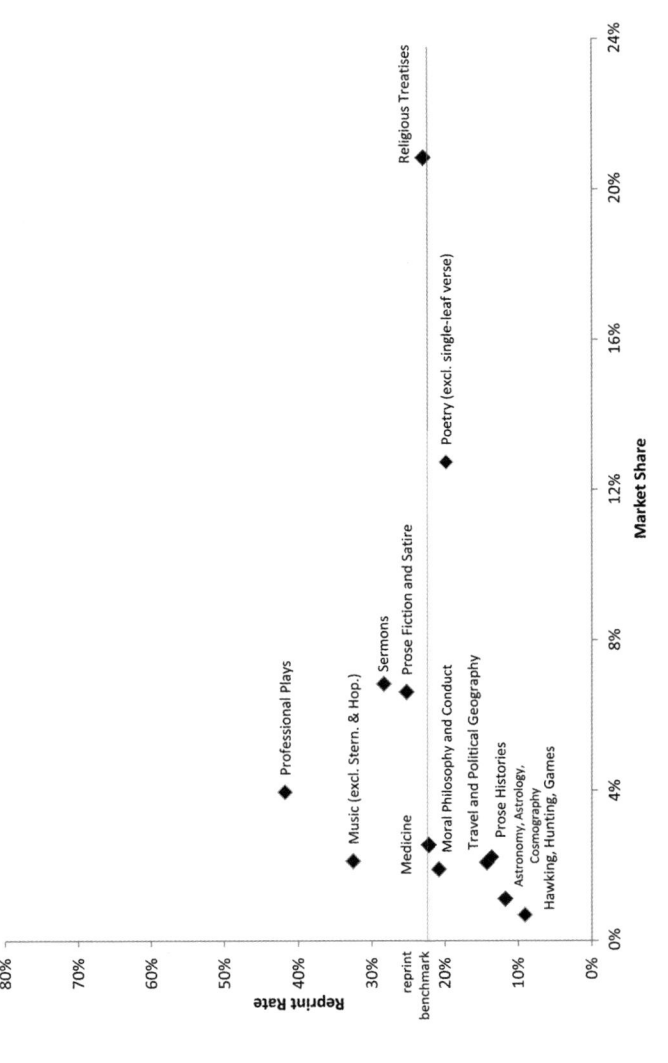

Fig. 1.7   The innovative structure of popularity, 1592–1602

longer span of years and, where possible, to determine the causes underlying its expanding or contracting popularity. Doing so leads us to a host of interesting new questions that we could not have asked before. Why were professional plays almost never printed before the early 1590s, after which they rapidly expanded to 4 percent of the retail book trade? Why did prose fiction and satire shift from an Innovative genre in the Elizabethan period to a Mature one in the Jacobean and Caroline periods? Why did mathematics move in the other direction starting in the 1590s, from a Mature to an Innovative genre, as publishers began to print a wider range of different kinds of math books, compared to their earlier focus on textbooks and standard works of land surveying and measuring? Why did the market share of sermons almost double, from 6.5 percent in the Elizabethan period to 11.9 percent in the Jacobean period? What caused the long, steady decline in the printing of law books over the course of the early modern period? While this essay has relied on statistics to develop economic arguments, these questions and their answers are, in the end, thoroughly cultural.

Chapter 2
'O Read me for I am of Great Antiquity':
Old Books and Elizabethan Popularity

Lucy Munro

In 1563 the publisher John Charlewood issued a small devotional manual called *The Treasure of Gladnesse*. The book was in its own way an Elizabethan best-seller. It appeared in at least 12 editions before 1603; a Norwich bookseller bought 12 copies between July and December 1568, and 11 more in the following year.[1] Other signs of its broad circulation also survive: a sailor named Massey owned it in 1575, Elizabeth Isham mentions in her *Book of Remembrance* that it was sent to her mother by her 'sister Washington', and a Gloucestershire shoemaker and glover listed it in an inventory of his books in 1627.[2] *The Treasure of Gladnesse* also had a wider cultural presence. It features in a list of 'Protestants helpes *for Deuotion, and mat*-ters belonging to the stirring up of the same' in John Brinsley's *The Fourth Part of the True Watch* (1624),[3] and makes an appearance on stage in the first part of Michael Drayton, Richard Hathway, Anthony Munday, and Robert Wilson's *Sir John Oldcastle*, performed by the Admiral's Men in 1599, as one of a set of English – and therefore heretical – books owned by the Lollard martyr Oldcastle: 'Heres the Bible, the testament the Psalmes in meter, / The sickemans salue, the treasure of gladnesse, / And al in English, not so much but the Almanack's English'.[4]

The Treasure of Gladnesse is remarkable, however, not so much for its apparent popularity – many devotional manuals were similarly well known and

---

[1] H.R. Plomer, 'Some Elizabethan Book Sales', *The Library*, 3rd Ser. 7 (1916): 318–29 (320); H.S. Bennett, *English Books and Readers, 1558–1603* (Cambridge: 1965), vol. 2, p. 266.

[2] Pauline Croft, 'Englishmen and the Spanish Inquisition 1558–1625', *English Historical Review* 87 (April 1972): 249–68 (259); on Isham, see the online edition directed by Elizabeth Clarke and Erica Longfellow, http://web.warwick.ac.uk/english/perdita/Isham/bor_p13v.htm (accessed 10 May 2012). The 1627 inventory is discussed in detail in Margaret Spufford, 'The Importance of Religion in the Sixteenth and Seventeenth Centuries', in Margaret Spufford (ed.) *The World of Rural Disssenters, 1520–1725* (Cambridge: 1995), pp. 1–102 (p. 53).

[3] *The Fourth Part of the True Watch Containing Prayers and Teares for the Churches* (London: 1624), sig. V5v.

[4] *The First Part of the True and Honourable Historie, of the Life of Sir Iohn Old-castle, the Good Lord Cobham* (London: 1600), sig. H2r.

widely consumed – but for the fact that this book was old even in 1563. Yet more surprisingly, Charlewood did not attempt to pass the book off as a new work, but foregrounded its antiquity. Its title page claims that it '**semeth by the Copy (beeing a verye litle Manuel, and written in velam) to be made aboue CC. yeres past at the least**' and that '**The coppy hereof is for the antiquity of it, preserued and to be seene in the Printers Hall**' (throughout this essay, in transcriptions of title pages, bold represents blackletter type).[5] Charlewood stresses not only the archaism of the words that he publishes, but the age of the physical artefact, and both of these things help to bolster his claim that the book shows '**howe God in olde time, and not of late only hath ben truly confessed and honored**'. His statement that the manuscript was on display in the Stationers' Company's Hall is presumably accurate; it is not known how long it stayed there, but the claim was still being made on the title page of the 1601 edition, the last extant. Underlining the book's claim to antiquity, this edition mimicked earlier ones and placed the details of its new publisher, James Roberts, in a colophon, a convention which had long since been superseded.

I begin with *The Treasure of Gladnesse* because it crystallizes some of the central issues raised by the fresh publication and active promotion of older texts during the Elizabethan period, and the kinds of popularity that they might pursue or achieve. What, this chapter asks, does it mean to make the implicit or explicit claim, 'O read me for I am of great antiquity', as does the title of another book?[6] My subject here is not, in the main, the circulation of second-hand copies of texts, a subject touched on elsewhere in this collection by Helen Smith.[7] Instead, I am interested in the moments at which publishers made the active decision to reinsert older texts into the Elizabethan book market – to give them a kind of novelty along with their antiquity or to strive to maintain their position as living cultural artefacts. The existence of the second-hand book trade, and the passing down of individual copies of books from generation to generation, must surely have affected the pattern of the publication of new editions of old books, but its commercial pressures and opportunities are not ones that I am able to pursue here.

In some respects, the challenges faced by older texts as they entered the print marketplace were similar to those of their newer counterparts: reaching print in the first place; achieving multiple editions; and reaching a large and sustained readership. They were, however, oddly placed in relation to a literary marketplace

---

[5]   For full details, see Appendix, A4.

[6]   See A21.

[7]   See also Henry Woudhuysen, *Sir Philip Sidney and the Circulation of Manuscripts, 1558–1640* (Oxford: 1996), pp. 50–51; Mark Purcell, 'The Library at Lanhydrock', *Book Collector* 54 (2005): 195–230; Andrew Cambers, *Godly Reading: Print, Manuscript and Puritanism in England, 1580-1720* (Cambridge: 2011). The latter makes a powerful case for the importance of 'the vast body of information that remains to be tapped of the readership, reception and usage of old books' (p. 247).

that often pursued novelty. John Lyly sums up the ephemeral nature of print popularity in the preface to *Euphues*:

> We commonly see the booke that at Christmas lyeth bound on the Stacioners stall, at Easter to be broken in the Haberdasshers shop … It is not straunge when as the greatest wonder lasteth but nyne dayes: That a newe worke should not endure but three monethes. Gentlemen vse bookes, as gentlewomen handle theyr flowres, who in the morning sticke them in their heads, and at night strawe them at their heeles. Cheries be fulsome when they be through rype, bicause they be ple{n}ty, & bookes be stale when they be printed, in that they be common.[8]

If a new book was 'stale' after only three months, or even at the point at which it was printed, older works faced a daunting challenge. Nonetheless, works such as *The Treasure of Gladnesse* suggest that they might provide publishers with specific opportunities and with new ways of reaching readers.

Examining the circulation of old texts also encourages us to reassess some of our preconceptions about Elizabethan taste and literary culture. Continuities between medieval and early modern literary cultures have received valuable attention in the last 20 years from Helen Cooper, Stephanie Trigg, David Matthews, Tim Machan, Siân Echard, Deanne Williams, and others.[9] However, the appearance of fresh editions of older works, and its implications for our understanding of Elizabethan literary culture, has been less extensively studied. Martin Butler's comment on the revival of older plays on the Caroline stage is relevant here: 'By concentrating on those elements in a period which to hindsight appear progressive we subtly but inevitably misrepresent the way things looked to contemporaries'.[10] Moreover, the Elizabethan market for new editions of old books was itself a mixed one, consisting of both long-established favourites and new discoveries. The processes are analogous to those observed by Alan Farmer and Zachary Lesser in the publication of plays in the Caroline period, when select plays reached their 9th, 10th, or even 14th editions, and some publishers set out to create 'undiscovered classics' from unpublished Elizabethan and early Jacobean

---

[8] *Euphues. The Anatomy of Wyt* (London: 1578), sig. A4r.

[9] For representative approaches see Helen Cooper, *The English Romance in Time: Transforming Motifs from Geoffrey of Monmouth to the Death of Shakespeare* (Oxford: 2004); Stephanie Trigg, *Congenial Souls: Reading Chaucer from Medieval to Postmodern* (Minneapolis: 2001), esp. pp. 109–43; Tim William Machan, 'Speght's Works and the Invention of Chaucer', Text 8 (1995), pp. 145–70; Theresa M. Krier, ed., *Refiguring Chaucer in the Renaissance* (Gainesville, FL: 1998), pp. 66–84; David Matthews, 'Public Ambition, Private Desire and the Last Tudor Chaucer', in *Reading the Medieval in Early Modern England*, ed. Gordon McMullan and David Matthews (Cambridge: 2007), pp. 74–88; Siân Echard, *Printing the Middle Ages* (Philadelphia: 2008); Deanne Williams, 'Medievalism in English Renaissance Literature', in *A Companion to Tudor Literature*, ed. Kent Cartwright (Malden, Mass; Oxford: 2010), pp. 213–27; Theresa Coletti and Gail McMurray Gibson, 'The Tudor Origins of Medieval Drama', in Cartwright, ed., *Companion*, pp. 228–45.

[10] Martin Butler, *Theatre and Crisis 1632–1642* (Cambridge: 1984), p. 184.

works.[11] '[T]hese plays,' Farmer and Lesser contend, 'are not merely *older than* but significantly *different from* Caroline plays, and while they may fall short of contemporary drama in the nicety of form and language ... they surpass them in a direct and unrefined style appreciated by numerous playgoers and readers' (34–35; their emphasis). In the Elizabethan period, older works were often similarly valued for their difference from contemporary texts and, significantly, were often marketed precisely on that difference.

In exploring these issues, I first sketch out a general picture of the publication of older texts in the Elizabethan period, highlighting the importance of what Douglas Bruster has termed 'thin description' and discussing the potential impact of recent electronic resources on this area of study. I then examine some of the methodological and terminological problems raised by examining the circulation of older texts, and some of the challenges that publishers faced in presenting this material to their readers. Finally, I look more closely at an intriguing sub-set of older texts: those marketed to readers precisely on the grounds of their antiquity, as were *The Treasure of Gladnesse* and *O Read Me*. Detailed information about 29 of these texts is provided in the Appendix, and I draw on this information in my detailed discussion. Claims to antiquity were used in a range of genres – legal, religious, literary, educational, historical, and political – and in some they are set out in remarkable detail. While some of these texts saw only one edition, others saw 10 or more editions within the Elizabethan period alone, and in some cases the claims made about their antiquity and heritage actually intensify over time. Through these processes, older texts are restored to cultural circulation and become, in their own way, popular.

Thin Description

One approach to the circulation of old texts in the Elizabethan period would be to develop the account of *The Treasure of Gladnesse* with which I began this essay, creating what is often known as 'thick description'. This technique, which uses detailed description of a particular exemplar as the foundation for critical interpretation of a broader phenomenon, has become a predominant technique in literary and, especially, historicist criticism.[12] However, to draw any conclusions

---

[11]   Alan B. Farmer and Zachary Lesser, 'Canons and Classics: Publishing Drama in Caroline England', in *Localizing Caroline Drama: Politics and Economics of the Early Modern English Stage, 1625–1642*, ed. Adam Zucker and Alan B. Farmer (New York: 2006), pp. 17–41 (pp. 32–35).

[12]   The term was adopted by the anthropologist Clifford Geertz from Gilbert Ryle: see Geertz's 'Thick Description: Toward an Interpretive Theory of Culture', in *The Interpretation of Cultures: Selected Essays* (New York: 1973), pp. 3–30. For histories and critiques of 'thick description' in literary studies see Catherine Gallagher and Stephen Greenblatt, *Practicing New Historicism* (Chicago: 2000), esp. pp. 22–31; Douglas Bruster, 'Deep Focus: Toward the Thin Description of Literary Culture', in *Shakespeare and the*

about the popularity of older texts it is necessary to look beyond one example. As part of the research process for this essay I therefore compiled an extensive list of old books published between 1558 and 1603, using the online *English Short Title Catalogue* (*ESTC*) and *Early English Books Online* (*EEBO*), and print resources such as Anthony Francis Allison and D.M. Rogers's *The Contemporary Printed Literature of the English Counter-Reformation Between 1558 and 1640: An Annotated Catalogue*.[13] To a large extent this essay has thus been facilitated by modern electronic resources – it would have been considerably more difficult and time-consuming to draw up such a list using the print *Short Title Catalogue*. However, I do not attempt here to produce a quantitative analysis of the respective popularity of old and new texts, or even to assess fully the relative popularity of old texts in particular genres. Despite the utility of *EEBO* and other resources, there are still lacunae. *EEBO* does not yet include all works listed in *ESTC*, while *ESTC* itself notoriously under-represents Catholic books, many of which were produced on secret and continental presses and written in languages other than English.[14] A full study of the circulation and popularity of old texts would require a much more extensive and refined process of searching and selection.

Acknowledging these limitations, my undertaking here is more impressionistic than definitive. Its methodology is closest to what Douglas Bruster has called 'thin description', a technique which 'first looks to aggregate evidence, to gather available information before coming to any conclusions about the culture toward which that evidence may gesture'.[15] As Raymond Williams notes, 'it is with the discovery of patterns of a characteristic kind that any useful cultural analysis begins, and it is with the relationships between these patterns, which sometimes reveal unexpected identities and correspondences in hitherto separately considered activities, that general cultural analysis is concerned'.[16] Drawing on these concepts, Bruster argues that 'the beginning of cultural analysis resides in *discovering* patterns. ... Where thick description likes to "taste" things and tell stories about them based on a small sample ... thin description seeks to obtain as wide a sampling as possible before making pronouncements about culture'.[17] In this chapter, thin description

---

Question of Culture: Early Modern Literature and the Cultural Turn (New York: 2003), pp. 29–62; Catherine Belsey, 'Historicizing New Historicism', in *Presentist Shakespeares*, ed. Hugh Grady and Terence Hawkes (London: 2007), pp. 27–45.

[13]   See *English Short Title Catalogue* (British Library), <http://estc.bl.uk>; *Early English Books Online* (Chadwyck Healy, 1998–present), <http://eebo.chadwyck.com>; Anthony Francis Allison and D.M. Rogers, *The Contemporary Printed Literature of the English Counter-Reformation Between 1558 and 1640: An Annotated Catalogue*, 2 vols (Aldershot: 1989–1994).

[14]   See 'About EEBO', *Early English Books Online*, <http://eebo.chadwyck.com/about/about.htm> (accessed 12 May 2012); Alison Shell, *Catholicism, Controversy, and the English Literary Imagination, 1558–1660* (Cambridge: 2004), p. 13.

[15]   'Deep Focus', p. 42.

[16]   *The Long Revolution* (London: 1961), p. 63.

[17]   'Deep Focus', p. 48 (emphasis in original).

is a way of approaching the material with fewer preconceptions, allowing patterns to emerge rather than setting out to find particular genres or movements. Sampling as wide a range of older texts as possible, I attempt to draw some broad – albeit provisional – conclusions about their status within Elizabethan literary culture.

Formats and Genres

Over 1,500 older texts were printed between 1558 and 1603, and their range is huge. They encompass many publications that we would now categorize as literary or humanist works. These include texts attributed to major English writers of the middle ages and early Tudor periods (Chaucer, Langland, Lydgate, Malory, Skelton, Thomas More); important pre-Elizabethan collections, such as Tottel's *Songes and Sonettes*, first published in 1557 and reissued regularly until 1587; texts with no named author, many of them romances or comic texts (*Bevis of Hampton*, *Huon of Bordeaux*, *Howleglas*, *A Mery Geste of Robyn Hoode*); texts by continental authors, in both their original languages and translation (Petrarch, Boccaccio, Mantuan, Sebastian Brant, Machiavelli, Ariosto, Erasmus, Castliglione); and texts by classical authors, again in original and in translation (Ovid, Seneca, Terence, Cicero, Plutarch, Virgil, Horace).

Unsurprisingly, religious works are represented in large numbers. These encompass the works of controversialists and martyrs (William Tyndale, Martin Luther, Thomas More, John Fisher, Anne Askew), and of saints, church fathers and Popes (St John Chrysostom, St Augustine, St Gregory of Nazianzus, Popes Innocent III and John XXI), and works of religious comfort and consolation. The latter include medieval and Tudor sermons and devotional manuals such as Thomas Wimbledon's *A Sermon No Lesse Fruitfull then Famous* (published in at least 13 editions by 1603), Hugh Latimer's *Frutefull Sermons* (four editions 1575–1796), and *The Kalender of Shepherdes*, first published in 1503 but still appearing in new editions in the early years of the seventeenth century, despite its apparent incompatibility with the reformed church's strictures.[18]

Early chronicles by writers such as Gildas, Matthew Paris, Geoffrey of Monmouth, Thomas Walsingham, Caradog of Llancarfan, William of Malmesbury, and Henry of Huntingdon appeared alongside and within the work of Tudor historians such as Polydore Vergil, Richard Grafton, John Leland, John Stow, Raphael Holinshed, and Henry Savile.[19] Editions of Anglo-Saxon texts, such as Bede's *Historia ecclesiastica gentis Anglorum* (1565), Ælfric's *Sermo de*

---

[18] On the *Kalender*'s popularity see Bernard Capp, *Astrology and the Popular Press: English Almanacs 1500-1800* (London: 1979), p. 27.

[19] On the persistence of individual historical texts and the chronicle format in general, see Daniel R. Woolf, *Reading History in Early Modern England* (Cambridge: 2000). See also Nicholas Barker, 'Editing the Past: Classical and Historical Scholarship', in *The Cambridge History of the Book in Britain, vol. 4, 1557–1695*, ed. John Barnard and D.F. McKenzie (Cambridge: 2002), pp. 206–27 (esp. pp. 209–12).

sacrificio in die Pascae (?1566), *Archaionomia* (1568), and John Asser's *Ælfredi Regis res gestae* (1574), owed their appearance to religious and legal controversy and to a resurgent interest in England's antiquities.[20] The works of early Tudor humanists and educationalists such as John Colet and William Lily were still appearing in new editions towards the end of Elizabeth's reign, along with reissued or rediscovered scientific and medical texts by writers such as Albertus Magnus, Roger Bacon, George Ripley, Lanfranco of Milan, Paracelsus, and Andrew Borde. Travel narratives included *The Voyage and Travayle, of Syr John Maundevile* (1568); Martin Fernández de Enciso's *A Briefe Description of the Portes, Creekes, Bayes, and Havens, of the Weast India* (1578); and Marco Polo's *Most Noble and Famous Travels* (1579).

Intriguingly, the single largest category appears to be legal material. This includes a long line of collections of medieval and early Tudor laws, published by Richard Tottel between the 1550s and the 1590s. Tottel held patents which gave him the exclusive right to publish common-law books under Edward VI, Mary I, and Elizabeth I, and he published over 100 books in this area.[21] Between them, Tottel and the two other 'great legal-humanist printers', John Rastell and William Rastell, saw to it that 'legal encyclopedias, collections of statutes, reports of cases, and other legal literature circulated in extensive runs never before possible'.[22] In addition to its effects on the legal profession, the publication of medieval laws is striking and potentially suggestive of the ways in which Elizabethan readers responded to or conceptualized the Middle Ages through print. The popular image of Richard III, for instance, might have been the usurping hunchback of

---

[20] For useful accounts see Christopher Hill, *Puritanism and Revolution: Studies in Interpretation of the English Revolution of the 17th Century* (London: 1958), pp. 52–68; Carl T. Berkhout and Milton McC. Gatch, eds., *Anglo-Saxon Scholarship: The First Three Centuries* (Boston: 1982); Allan J. Frantzen, *Desire for Origins: New Language, Old English, and Teaching the Tradition* (New Brunswick and London: 1990), esp. pp. 35–50, pp. 130–167; Timothy Graham, ed., *The Recovery of Old English: Anglo-Saxon Studies in the Sixteenth and Seventeenth Centuries* (Kalamazoo, MI: 2000); Benedict S. Robinson, 'John Foxe and the Anglo-Saxons', in *John Foxe and his World*, ed. Christopher Highley and John N. King (Aldershot: 2001), pp. 54–72; Felicity Heal, 'Appropriating History: Catholic and Protestant Polemics and the National Past', *Huntington Library Quarterly* 68 (2005): 109-32; Christopher Highley, *Catholics Writing the Nation in Early Modern Britain and Ireland* (Oxford: 2008), pp. 84–91.

[21] See Anna Greening, 'Tottel, Richard (b. in or before 1528, d. 1593)', *Oxford Dictionary of National Biography* (Oxford: Oxford University Press, 2004; online edn, May 2009), http://0-www.oxforddnb.com.catalogue.ulrls.lon.ac.uk/view/article/27573 (accessed 12 May 2012). On the wider context of legal publishing, see J.H. Baker, 'English Law Books and Legal Publishing', in *The Cambridge History of the Book*, ed. Barnard and McKenzie, pp. 474–503.

[22] Andrew Zurcher, *Shakespeare and Law* (London: 2010), p. 29.

More or Shakespeare, but he also appeared on the Elizabethan book stall as a maker of laws.[23]

Some works or genres appear to be strongly associated with individual editors or publishers. As we have seen, Tottel published a string of common-law books, while William Copland published romances and jests in the 1550s and 1560s; John Stow was responsible for editions of Leland, Chaucer, Skelton, and other medieval and early Tudor authors. John Day printed the editions of Anglo-Saxon texts sponsored by Archbishop Parker in the 1560s and 1570s, while John Charlewood either printed or published a number of works that made claims to antiquity on their title pages, such as *The Treasure of Gladnesse*, later editions of *A Sermon No Lesse Fruteful then Famous*, *A Knowledge for Kings* (1576), and Walter Lynne's *A Most Necessarie Treatise* (1588). The publication of other texts was clearly affected by fluctuating politico-religious pressures, as I will explore in detail below.

All this being said, to focus exclusively on printed material is to ignore another species of popularity and another venue in which texts circulated: manuscript. Print and manuscript traditions were heavily interdependent when it came to the circulation of older texts. Editions of poets such as Chaucer draw on antiquarian discoveries and methodologies, while antiquarians themselves drew on manuscript sources and re-presented them to readers.[24] Some printed books even flag up their debt to manuscript. For instance, one of Tottel's editions of the laws of Edward III claims that it is published 'non sine accurata multorum manuscriptorum exemplariu{m} collatione' ('not without a careful comparison of many manuscript copies'), and a 1586 edition of the works of St John Chrysostom draws its reader's attention to the use of manuscripts preserved at St John's College, Oxford.[25]

As Richard W. Clement, Peter J. Lucas, and Siân Echard have explored in detail, the publication of texts in Old English often entailed the production of costly sets of special types, based on Anglo-Saxon manuscript models.[26] The first 'Anglo-Saxon' book printed, a text and translation of Ælfric's *Sermo de sacrificio in die pascae*, titled *A Testimonie of Antiquitie* (?1566), appeared in a type made

---

[23]   See *Incipit annus primus Ricardi tertii. De termino Michaelis anno primo Richardi tertii* (London: [?1559]); Robert Brooke, *Anni, regum, Edwardi Quinti, Richardi Tertii, Henrici Septimi, et Henrici Octaui omnes, qui antea impressi fuerunt, iam recens post priores editiones emendati & repurgati* (London: 1597).

[24]   For recent approaches see Trigg, *Congenial Souls*; Jennifer Summit, *Memory's Library: Medieval Books in Early Modern England* (Chicago: 2008).

[25]   *Regis Edvvardi tertii a primo ad decimum (inclusiue) anni omnes* (London: Richard Tottel, 1562); *D. Ioannis Chrysostomi Archiepiscopi Constantinopolitani, homiliae sex ex manuscriptis codicibus Noui Collegij*, ed. John Harmar (Oxford: 1586). Further examples are discussed below.

[26]   See Richard W. Clement, 'The Beginnings of Printing in Anglo-Saxon, 1565–1630', *Papers of the Bibliographical Society of America* 91 (1997): *192–244*; Peter J. Lucas, 'From Politics to Practicalities: Printing Anglo-Saxon in the Context of Seventeenth-Century Scholarship', *The Library*, 7th Ser. 4.1 (March 2003): 28–48; Echard, *Printing the Middle Ages*, pp. 21–59.

under Archbishop Matthew Parker's direction. The font may have been intended to subliminally 'authenticate the antiquity and authority of a text', as Clement argues, but Echard notes that what she terms the 'impulse to facsimile' was qualified by the juxtaposition of 'authentic' language and letter form with an overall design scheme conventional to sixteenth-century books.[27] The somewhat ersatz effect is captured well by Lucas, who writes that 'Parker apparently regarded Anglo-Saxon types somewhat as we regard reproduction furniture, as providing a new substitute for old authenticity'.[28] A claim to antiquity is compromised – or at least modified – by the requirements of the Elizabethan publishing industry.

Period

The publication of older works in the Elizabethan period also raises problems of terminology and periodization. I have been using the terms 'medieval' and 'Tudor', even 'early Tudor', but they have little purchase for the works of continental writers such as Petrarch, Ariosto, Erasmus, or Luther, who are more usually bracketed as 'Renaissance' or 'Reformation'. To examine Elizabethan interactions with the 'medieval' is often to concentrate attention on insular texts. Alternatively, to focus attention on the 'middle ages' (a term used by John Foxe in describing the pre-Reformation church) or '*medium aevum*' (used by Petrarch and other Italian humanists to describe the period between the ancient world and their own day) might be to impose fixed boundaries on what was actually a more fluid set of (multiple) relationships between past and present.[29] The publication of the classics complicates things further: editions and, especially, translations of Greek and Latin works are both relics of the classical past and products of a living Elizabethan tradition.

Moreover, it is also awkward to conceptualize the 'Elizabethan' as a single entity. Patterns of publication shifted rapidly between 1558 and 1603, and this affected old texts no less than new. Some texts appear at regular intervals throughout the period, such as *The Kalender of Shepherdes*, *The Treasure of Gladnesse*, Lily's *A Shorte Introduction of Grammar*, or John Rastell's *An Exposition of Certaine Difficult and Obscure Wordes, and Termes of the Lawes of this Realme*, published in both English and French. Others have left a more patchy record. For instance, the works of Skelton do not seem to have been reissued after the publication of John Stow's edition of *Pithy Pleasaunt and Profitable Workes of Maister Skelton, Poete Laureate* in 1568; Tottel's edition of *Songes and Sonnets* received its last

---

[27] Clement, 'Beginnings', p. 206; Echard, *Printing the Middle Ages*, p. 25, p. 28.

[28] Lucas, 'Politics to Practicalities', p. 28.

[29] My thinking here is influenced by Deanne Williams's 'Shakespearean Medievalism and the Limits of Periodization in *Cymbeline*', *Literature Compass* 8.6 (2011): pp. 390–403. On the problems of periodization see also 'After Periodization', ed. Jennifer Summit and David Wallace, *Journal of Medieval and Early Modern Studies* 37 (2007); Alex Davis, *Renaissance Historical Fiction: Sidney, Deloney, Nashe* (Cambridge: 2011), Introduction.

Elizabethan edition in 1587. The English translation of Raoul Lefèvre's *Recueil des histoires de Troye* appeared regularly before 1559 and after 1603, but only one edition appeared during Elizabeth's reign. Of the Middle English romances printed in large numbers in the 1560s, only a handful were reissued in the 1580s, and still fewer in the following decade. This does not, of course, necessarily mean that they were not available to buy on bookstalls, or second hand, but it nonetheless suggests a decline in interest.

Region

'Elizabethan' also implies a focus on texts produced in England, which is to overlook other parts of Elizabeth's realm, such as Wales and Ireland. The Welsh scholar Humphrey Lloyd was responsible for translations of Pope John XXI's *The Treasurie of Health* (1550, 1570, and 1585) and Caradoch of Llancarvan's *The History of Cambria* (1584), while the 'Old English' writer Richard Stanyhurst, born in Dublin and the descendant of Norman settlers, published a translation of Virgil's *Aeneid* in 1582. It is also to ignore the independent and vibrant Anglophone literary culture that existed in Scotland. Like the reign of their cousin, the reigns of Mary and James VI saw the re-presentation to readers of older texts: Aristotle's *Problems*; laws drawn up under James I and his successors; works by Robert Henryson and David Lindsay; Henry the Minstrel's account of *The Actis and Deidis of the Illuster and Vailzeand Campioun, Schir William Wallace*; and works by English educationalists such as William Lily and John Stanbridge.

Moreover, not all English texts were printed in England, or by the mainstream London presses. Works that contravened the statutes and conventions of the Church of England were often published abroad, or by secret presses within England. While the Catholic martyr Thomas More's *Utopia* was reissued in England in 1597, his more controversial works, *A Dialogue of Cumfort Against Tribulation* (1573) and *A Brief Fourme of Confession* (1576), were published at Antwerp, as was Thomas Stapleton's translation of Bede's *Historia ecclesiastica gentis Anglorum* (1565), complete with a dedication to Queen Elizabeth that urged her to reconcile with Rome for the good of her country. Translations of Johannes Justus Lansperger's *Alloquia Jesu Christi ad animam fidelem* and St Vincent of Lérins' *Pro catholicae fidei antiquitate libellus* were printed on Catholic secret presses in England in 1595–1596.[30] The former was translated by Philip Howard, 13th Earl of Arundel, then imprisoned in the Tower of London; its title page advertises that it was 'translated into English by one of no small fame, whose good example of

---

[30] On the secret presses and their output see Philip Caraman, *Henry Garnet, 1555–1606, and the Gunpowder Plot* (London: 1964); Alexandra Walsham, *Church Papists: Catholicism, Conformity and Confessional Polemic in Early Modern England* (1993; Woodbridge: 1999); Cyndia Susan Clegg, *Press Censorship in Elizabethan England* (Cambridge: 1997), pp. 79–102.

sufferance & liuing, hath and wilbe a memorial vnto his countrie and posteritie for euer'.[31]

A similar dynamic underlies the preparation of *O Read Me, for I am of Great Antiquitie* for the press around 1588. A partial reprint of a Reformation spin-off from Langland's *Piers Ploughman*, titled *I Playne Piers which can not Flatter* (1550), *O Read Me* survives in one incomplete copy, consisting only of signatures A–D2 (British Library C.123.c.16). Some of the pages are printed on one side only, and signatures B and C have proofing marks in the margins; it seems likely that the printing process was interrupted and that no finished copies were produced.[32] Reasons for the book's abortive publication become clearer when we note the ways in which the paratexts link the old text with the pseudonymous Martin Marprelate's attack on the episcopy in the late 1580s. The title page and preface – the latter addressed to 'the puissant paltrypolitanes, vaunting Lord Bishops, Popish parsons, Fickars [*sic*], and Currats, with all that Romish table' – cast Piers as the 'Gransier' of Martin, and the only indication of the place of publication is the information that it was '**Printed either of this side, or of that side of some of the Priestes**' (A21), a formulation that mimics the style of the Marprelate pamphlets. *O Read Me* appears to have been printed by another secret press, here operated by anti-establishment Protestants rather than recusant Catholics. As Mike Rodman Jones points out, *I Plain Piers* was already, on its publication in 1550, a 'polemical, antiquarian attemp[t] to shape the figure Piers Ploughman into a prophetic spokesman of radical religious and economic reform'.[33] *O Read Me* is thus a curiously multilayered text, in which Piers looks back to his medieval and early Tudor antecedents and forward to his 'grandson' Martin.

Obstacles

Many publishers simply ignore the gap in time between the text's original publication and its reappearance. For instance, the 1588 edition of Lynne's *A Most Necessarie Treatise* retains the 1548 edition's dedication to Edward VI (A20; sigs. A2r–A3v), while a late-Elizabethan reprint of *The First Examination of the Worthy Seruant of God, Mystresse Anne Askew* continues to refer to her as 'lately martyred in Smith-fielde, by the Romish Antichristian Broode'.[34] Such texts create

---

[31] *An Epistle in the Person of Christ to the Faithfull Soule* ([English Secret Press], 1595).

[32] See Joseph Black, ed., *The Martin Marprelate Tracts: A Modernized and Annotated Edition* (Cambridge: 2008), p. xcvii. Black argues that 'the failure to correct signature D suggests that printing was interrupted'. On the Marprelate secret presses see also Clegg, *Press Censorship*, pp. 53–54; pp. 73–75; pp. 170–97.

[33] *Radical Pastoral, 1381–1594: Appropriations and the Writing of Religious Controversy* (Farnham: 2011), p. 141.

[34] *The First Examination of the Worthy Seruant of God, Mystresse Anne Askew* (London: [?1585]).

a continuous present, in which the politico-religious pressures that created the original texts are still urgently felt.

Nonetheless, many editions aim to historicize the works they present. According to the title page of *A Sermon No Lesse Frutefull then Famous* (1573), the text was '**founde out hyd in a wall**' (A10), while a 1597 collection advertises poems 'Re-*serued long in the Studie of a* Northfolke Gentleman' (A25). 'Iames Glawcus', the supposed author of *A Knowledge for Kings* (1576), claims to have tracked down the text in the 'chiefe Library' of Constantinople (A12; sig. A4r), and Gervase Markham in *The Gentlemans Academie* (1595) tells his reader, '*I haue reuiued and brought again to light the same which was almost altogether forgotten*' (A23; sig. A3v). A longer account is provided in a preface addressed to '*the industrious and dis*-creet Shoolemaister' [*sic*] in Simon Sturtevant's edition of glosses on the fables of Aesop and Phaedrus, published in 1602. Long thought lost, a manuscript of Phaedrus's fables had been discovered in 1596. Sturtevant accordingly provides his reader with a detailed account of the book's supposed loss and scholars' endeavours to trace it:

> this our Phædrus some ages hath bene mist, enuironed in the mist of obscuritie: and whereas great search hath bene made for auncient copies and Authors … his Proctors continually haue pleaded non inuentius est … vntill that Petrus Pœtheus a diligent searcher of Antiquities put in a yeare or two agoe his Eureca, yea his ioyfull Eureca, and so recalled Phædrus to light and life againe[.]
>
> (A29; sig. G5r)[35]

Punning on 'missed' and 'mist', Sturtevant casts the pioneering editor as the means through which the text is joyfully revivified and recovered from the oblivion of time. Despite their generic differences, these texts are framed with similar conceits, expressed in similar language, as publishers and editors strive to render the antique alluring and desirable.

Editors and publishers also periodically stress the alien qualities of older forms of English. 'Plain Piers' on the title page of *O Read Me* claims that his '**speech is fowlle**' (A21). It is unclear whether this is a function of his age or his status as a '**plough man**', but a claim to plainness is common in editions of old texts. In the preface to *The Gentlemans Academie*, Markham writes,

> I humbly craue pardon of the precise and iudicial Reader, if sometimes I vse the words of the ancient Authour, in such plaine and homely English, as that time affoorded, not being so regardful, nor tying myself so strictly to deliuer any thing in the proper and peculiar wordes and termes of arte, which for the loue I beare to antiquitie, and to the honest simplicitie of those former times, I obserue

[35] See *Phaedri Aug. Liberti Fabularum Æsopiarum libri V nunc primum in lucem editi* (Troyes: 1596). For a detailed account of Phaedrus and Sturtevant see Anne Becher, 'Phaedrus, a New Found Yet Ancient Author: The Rise and Fall of Phaedrus as a Standard School Author, 1668–1828', *Paradigm: Journal of the Textbook Colloquium* 23 (July 1997), <http://faculty.ed.uiuc.edu/westbury/paradigm/becher.html> (accessed 12 May 2012).

as wel beseming the subiect, & no whit disgracefull to the worke, our tong being not of such puritie then, as at this day the Poets of our age haue raised it to[.]

(A23; sigs. A3v–A4r)

Despite the fact that he has changed many aspects of the text's original language, Markham finds value in the plainness and homeliness of the features that he has retained, arguing that they have both decorum and historical authenticity.

A different approach is taken in some literary texts, in which aids to interpretation are provided instead of updating or translation. Thomas Speght's editions of Chaucer, issued in 1598 and 1602, include a dedicatory letter by Francis Beaumont (probably the father of the dramatist), in which he comments on Speght's editorial procedures:

> by your interpretation of the most vnusuall words, that hardnesse and difficultie is made most cleare and easie: and in the paines and diligence you haue vsed in collecting his life, mee thinkes you haue bestowed vpon him more fauorable graces then Medea did vpon Pelias: for you haue restored vs Chaucer both aliue again and yong again, and deliuered many of the doubtfull coniectures they conceiued of him.

(A27, sigs. a3v–a4r)

The 1598 edition accordingly comes with a glossary of 'The old and obscure words of Chaucer, explaned' (A27; sigs. 4A1r–4B1v), corrected and updated in the 1602 edition.[36] Both glossaries are advertised prominently on the title pages of their respective editions, suggesting the extent to which publishers were aware that older works needed additional effort, and the rewards that they saw in making that effort. Tudor editions of Langland similarly provide textual apparatus in the shape of summaries of each part of the book. As Beaumont indicates, Speght additionally seeks to connect new readers with his old texts by providing detailed information about the author's life, a tactic also adopted by other publishers. The preface of John Fortescue's *A Learned Commendation of the Politique Lawes of Englande* (1567), for instance, informs its readers that 'The aucthour of the book was one maister Fortescue knight Seriaunt at the law, and for his Skill and vertues preferred by kinge Henry the .vi. to be Chauncellour of this realme' (A7; sig. A2v) and provides an account of the book's genesis.

Nonetheless, editors and publishers frequently update the language of the texts, and emphasize the pains they have taken in renovating them. Despite Markham's stated fondness for the '*the words of the ancient Authour*', the title page of *The Gentlemans Academie* claims that the text is '*now reduced into a better method*' (A23), while a 1601 edition of *The Ancient, Honourable, Famous, and Delightfull Historie of Huon of Bourdeaux* describes itself as 'now the Third time imprinted, and the rude Eng-*lish corrected and amended*' (A28). Some texts claim to be

---

[36] *The Works of our Ancient and Learned English Poet, Geffrey Chaucer, Newly Printed* (London: 1602), sigs. 3T1r–3U6r.

improvements on earlier translations. The dedication to Sir William Pelham in the 1582 translation of Ratramnus of Corbie's *A Booke of Bertram the Priest* tells him, 'you, and all they that shall heedily reade the same, shall finde it muche cleered, not only in respect of a multitude of darke and vnknowen termes, wherewith the former translation was fraughted, but in respect of sense and matter also' (A17; sig. A6v).

A more complex process of revision affects Raoul Lefèvre's *The Auncient Historie, of the Destruction of Troy*. The 1597 edition claims on its title page to be 'Newly corrected, and the English very much Amended' (A26), and in the preface the publishers promise further corrections:

> And whereas before time, the Translator William Caxton, being (as it seemeth) no English man, had left very many words mere French, and sundry sentences so improperly Englished, that it was hard to vnderstand, wee haue caused them to bee made plainer English: and if leisure had serued, we would haue had the same in better refined phrases, and certaine names that bee amisse, conferred with Authours, and made right. But if wee finde your fauourable accepting heereof to be such, as wee may shortly haue a second impression, we will haue all amended.
>
> (A26; sig. (x)4r)

The promise to amend future editions was still present in the 1636 edition: 'if we find your favourable accepting hereof to be such, as we may shortly have a seventh Impression, by Gods help, we will have all corrected and amended'.[37] Finally, in 1663, nearly 70 years after the initial proposal to further amend the text, the publishers claim, 'What faults escaped in the former Impression, are in this Corrected and amended'.[38]

Antiquity

The final part of this essay examines more closely a set of texts in which age is apparently seen as a route to popularity. None of these texts are marketed specifically as 'medieval' texts, or as products of the 'middle age' or 'medium aevum'. They are, nonetheless, presented as the products of a prior age – however fuzzily defined – and for some of them these marketing tactics appear to have been extremely successful. As we have seen, *The Treasure of Gladnesse* went through at least 12 Elizabethan editions; similarly, *A Sermon No Lesse Fruitfull Then Famous* went through at least 11 Elizabethan editions, *Of the Imitation of Christ* at least 10, and Robert Grosseteste's *The Testamentes of the Twelve Patriarches* at least 5.

Some texts had a sustained tradition in print before their Elizabethan editions appeared – for instance, Juliana Berners's *Book of Hawking*, first printed in 1486, the works of Chaucer, which first appeared in print in 1477, and, to a lesser extent,

---

[37]   *The Ancient Historie of the Destruction of Troy* (London: 1636), sig. *2v.

[38]   *The Destruction of Troy in Three Books* (London: 1663), sig. A2v.

Langland's *Piers Plowman*, Ratramnus of Corbie's *A Booke of Bertram the Priest* and *O Read Me/I Plain Piers*. Others first appeared in print in England during the Elizabethan period, being drawn from manuscript or foreign-language sources. In some cases, a claim to antiquity is suddenly added to the title page of a new edition, or is strengthened in successive editions. For instance, *A Sermon No Lesse Frutefull then Famous* first appeared around 1540 with the claim '**Made in the yeare of our LORDE GOD M.CCC.lxxxvii in these oure latter dayes moost necessary to be knowen. Nether addyng to, neyther demynyshynge fro[m]. Saue tholde and rude Englysh ther of mended here and there**'.[39] In 1573 this was amended and the claim to antiquity expanded: '**Made in the yeare of** our Lord God. M. CCC. lxxxviii. **and founde out hyd in a wall. Which sermon is here set forth by the old copy, without adding or diminishing saue the old & rude English here and there amended**' (A10). In 1582, it was further amended: 'Preached at Paules Crosse, on the Sunday of *Quinquagesima*, by R. Wimbeldon, in the raigne of King Henry the fourth, in the yeare of our Lorde. 1388. *A*nd found out hid in a Wall. *Which Sermon, is* heere set foorth by the olde Copy, without adding or diminishing, saue the olde and rude English, heer and there amended'.[40] The antiquity of the work is apparently seen by successive publishers as its primary demand on the attention of readers, and the claims are accordingly intensified over successive editions.

Elsewhere, inaccurate or spurious claims are made. Thomas Newton's *A View of Valyaunce* declares itself to be '*Describing the famous* feates, and Martiall exploites of two most mightie nations, the Romains and the Carthaginians, for the conquest and possession of Spayne. Translated out of an aun-**cient Recorde of Antiquitie, written by** Rutilius Rufus, **a Romaine Gentleman, and a Capitaine of charge vnder** Scipio, **in the same Warres**' (A16); however, it is actually an abridgement of Appian of Alexandria's *Roman History*, composed more than three centuries later. The original of *A Knowledge for Kings*, which claims to be a translation of an original work by '*Iames Glaucus* a Germaine' (A12) has not been traced and probably never existed; if so, this intensely political text has a fictional pedigree, meaning that it makes a parodic claim to antiquity as part of its bid for the reader's attention.[41]

For many texts, the claim to antiquity is as simple as describing a text or its author as 'old' or 'ancient' on its title page: 'THE Workes of our Antient and lerned English Poet, GEFFREY CHAVCER' (A27); '*Phædrus (a new found yet* auncient

---

[39] *A Sermon no Lesse Fruteful then Famous* ([?London: ?1540]).

[40] *A Sermon no Lesse Fruitfull then Famous* (London: 1582).

[41] The fullest account of this text is in Markku Peltonen, 'Rhetoric and Citizenship in the Monarchical Republic of Queen Elizabeth I', in *The Monarchical Republic of Early Modern England: Essays in Response to Patrick Collinson*, ed. John F. McDiarmid (Aldershot: 2007), pp. 109–27 (pp. 122–27). See also Fred Schurink, '*A Knowledge for Kings*', in *The Origins of English Literature: Recovering Mid-Tudor Writing for a Modern Readership* (Sheffield: Humanities Research Institute, 2007–2008), <http://www.hrionline. ac.uk/origins> (accessed 12 May 2012).

Author*)'* (A29); '**set forth after the Auctours old copy**' (A1); '**newlye imprynted after the authours olde copy**' (A3); 'vetustate antiquissimo' (A8); 'translated in the olde Saxons tyme … newly collected out of Auncient Monumentes of the sayd Saxons' (A9); 'CERTAINE *WORTHYE MANV*-script Poems of great Antiquitie' (A25). Others describe the age of the text more precisely: 'compiled by Iuliana Barnes, in the yere from the incarnation of Christ 1486' (A23); 'Dedicated to K. EDVVARD the 4' (A22); '**Written in latine aboue an hundred yeares past**' (A7); '*made* 170. yeeres since' (A14); '**written in Latin aboue two hundred yeres agoe**' (A11); '*written in the Brytish lan*-guage aboue two hundreth *yeares past*' (A18); 'Drawne out of certaine olde prophecies aboue three hundred yeeres since … with the auncient Pictures therevnto belonging' (A20); 'receaued in the Saxons tyme, aboue 600. yeares agoe' (A5); '**written in Greke aboue. vij. hundred yeres sens, by** Nilus, **an ancient archbyshop of** Thessalonia' (A2); '**written in Latine** … *aboue seuen hundred yeeres agoe*' (A17); '**this Monument was two thousande yeares of Antiquity**' (A12). These simple references place the text in time, insisting on a distance between the original and its new appearance in print.

As we have seen, however, publishers' claims are often more elaborate. 1560s editions of Nicolaus Cabasilas's *A Brief Treatise* and Ælfric's *A Testimonie of Antiquitie* both draw on Biblical authority, including on their title pages a quotation from Jeremiah 6: 'Goe into the streetes, and inquyre for the olde way: and if it be the good and ryght way, then goe therin, that ye maye finde rest for your soules. But they say: we will not walke therein' (A5; see also A2). Others feature complex statements about the origins of their sources. Like *The Treasure of Gladnesse* and *A Sermon No Lesse Frutefull then Famous*, a 1588 translation of St John Chrysostom's *An Excellent Treatise* specifies the material condition of the source text ('*Turned and put into English, out of an* ancient Latine translation*, written in velume*' [A19]), while Robert Grosseteste's *The Testaments of the Twelue Patriarches* (1576) seeks to validate itself by referring to the manuscript on which it is based: '**To the credit whereof an auncient Greeke copye written in parchment, is kept in the Vniuersitie Librarye of Cambridge**' (A13). The authority of the new text is rooted in the material authenticity of its source.

Associations between antiquity and authority are more strenuously applied in controversial texts. St Vincent of Lérins' *The Golden Treatise*, issued by a secret Catholic press around 1596, states that it is published 'For the antiquitie, and vniuersalitie, of the Catholicke Religion: against the prophane nouelties of all Heresies' (A24). In the preface, the translator writes that the work's antiquity was one of the reasons why it appealed to him:

> because it is very auncient, being written aboue an eleue{n} hundred yeres past, for it was composed three yeeres after the general Councell of Ephesus, as appeareth at the conclusion of the booke. And as the Author him selfe is of greate antiquite so is his doctrine more auncient, beeing the selfe same which florished in his time, and came from the Apostles of CHRIST: which thing as it was neuer of any good man doubted of, so is it also most apparant[.]
>
> (A24; sigs. A3r–v)

Similar claims are made by Robert Poyntz in his *Testimonies for the Real Presence of Christes Body and Blood in the Blessed Sacrament of the Aultar* (1566; A6), a text designed to focus attention on the crucial debate around transubstantiation, while Stapleton tells Queen Elizabeth that Bede's *Historia* demonstrates 'a number of diuersities betvvene the pretended religion of Protestants, and the primitiue faith of the english church'.[42]

Protestants similarly sought to demonstrate the antiquity of their interpretation of Christian doctrine through the publication of old texts. Archbishop Parker sponsored editions of Anglo-Saxon texts in the 1560s (see A5, A8, A9), while *The Ruinate Fall of the Pope Vsury*, published around 1580, claims to have been 'reueled by a Saxon of antiquitie' (A15). A dedicatory epistle in *A Booke of Bertram the Priest* is more equivocal about claims to antiquity:

> antiquitie yea, euen then when it is alleadged for the maintenance of Gods trueth, neither doeth nor can much further the same[.] ... [T]here is no reason, why that the bare face of antiquitie, shoulde carry away a falsehood, as though it were veritie, seeing y^t the question betweene vs and our aduersaries, is not so much for the oldnes of any matter, as for the veritie and truth thereof[.]
>
> (A17; sig. A3v–A4r)

However, this statement is made within a book whose title page advertises the fact that it concerns 'the body & blood **of Christe**' and stresses the idea that it was written '*aboue seuen hundred yeeres agoe*'. Even here, the power of the claim to antiquity was evidently felt to override the editor's qualms.

Conclusions

In June 1848 *The Cottager's Monthly Visitor* reprinted an extract from Rev. John East's 1831 book *The Village; Or, Christian Lessons: Drawn from the Circumstances of a Country Parish*. The extract begins,

> ON pulling down the roof of an old house in a village in Somersetshire some time since, a little book was found amongst the thatch, bearing the significant title of 'The Treasure of Gladness.' It was printed in the reign of Queen Elizabeth, as appears from the insertion of her name in the Litany, which forms a part of the book.[43]

The story of the discovery of this copy of *The Treasure of Gladnesse* is followed by some extracts from the book, of which East comments, '[w]e give one or two of the prayers contained in it, merely altering the spelling, which, being in the style

---

[42]   *The History of the Church of Englande. Compiled by Venerable Bede, Englishman* (Antwerp: 1565), sig. *3r.

[43]   'The Treasure of Gladness', *The Cottager's Monthly Visitor* 28 (June 1848), pp. 189–93; p. 189. The litany was added to the 1568 edition and some later editions.

of those days, might hardly be intelligible to some of our readers. It thus opens, like some casket of precious jewels bearing the marks of age, but having lost nothing of their intrinsic worth'. Like the Elizabethan publishers of *The Treasure of Gladnesse*, East stresses the miraculous nature of the book's survival (here, found in a roof rather than 'hid in a wall'), the value of its contents, the lengths to which he has gone to mediate between it and its new readers, and the archaism of the physical text. 'The type', he informs us, 'is the old English black letter commonly used in the infancy of the art of printing'.

Although East does not mention the book's title page, he appears to have absorbed its rhetoric; however, the antiquity of the text is here Elizabethan – the temporal differences to which the original readers would have been attuned are here ironed out, and the book's prayers are described as 'one of the numerous and well-timed efforts made by the Protestants to diffuse through the country a knowledge of Divine truth, which had been so long obscured beneath the errors and tyranny of the Church of Rome'. As these comments suggest, the appeal of *The Treasure of Gladnesse* is not merely nostalgic; like the book's Elizabethan publishers, East is keen to put it to use. His account thus functions not merely as a story of survival, but a polemical statement of the antiquity and value of prayer within the Anglican tradition: 'it was the object of our reformers to substitute spiritual and scriptural prayer as the great means of the soul's communion with God, rendering it "meet for the inheritance of the saints in light." Let us ever keep this in view. ... A PRAYERLESS SOUL IS A HOPELESS SOUL' (192–93).

As East's account of *The Treasure of Gladnesse* suggests, old books can have a powerful and seemingly trans-historical appeal. It is important nonetheless, in concluding this chapter, to acknowledge the historically particular aspects of Elizabethan antiquity publishing, and the variations within it. As we have seen, the Elizabethan industry in older texts had its roots in practices stretching back to the 1470s, with Caxton's editions of Chaucer and the *Recueil des histoires de Troye*, and it often merely amplified the claims made by early Tudor publishers. Particular texts also went in and out of fashion; despite its obvious appeal to the Victorian clergyman, *The Treasure of Gladnesse* does not appear to have been printed after 1601, while many of the Anglo-Saxon texts published in the 1560s did not reappear until the 1650s. The nature and implications of a text's antiquity also shifted over the years, and Chaucer was clearly felt to need more assistance in connecting with readers in 1598 than he had needed in John Stow's 1561 edition.

In its survey of the publication of older texts, and the ways in which they were marketed to readers, this essay suggests not only that older texts, taken as a group, were a prominent and widespread part of the Elizabethan publishing industry, but that there were a number of ways in which they might be popular. Many of the texts examined here are 'popular' in the sense that they are expressions of a (sub-)literary culture often overlooked in traditional accounts of English 'literature', while others were clearly aimed at more self-consciously elite audiences. Individual texts such as *The Treasure of Gladnesse*, *A Sermon No Lesse Frutefull then Famous*, or *Of the Imitation of Christ* were clearly bought in huge numbers, while other texts – such as medieval romances, Anglo-Saxon treatises and histories, or medieval and

Tudor laws – were part of widely circulating groups. To plead 'O read me for I am of great antiquity' was to stake the past's claim to the present's attention, but it was also to acknowledge the role of the present in constructing that past.

Appendix: Works Marketed on Their Antiquity

1. John Lydgate, *The serpent of diuision. Whych hathe euer bene yet the chefest vndoer of any Region or Citie, set forth after the Auctours old copy, by I.S.* (London: Owen Rogers, 1559; STC 17028)

Further Elizabethan editions: *1590*

(Edited by John Stow; earlier version published 1535)

2. Nicolaus Cabasilas, *A Briefe Treatise, Conteynynge a playne and fruitfull declaration of the Popes vsurped Primacye, written in Greke aboue. vij. hundred yeres sens, by Nilus, an ancient archbyshop of Thessalonia and newly tra{n}slated into englyshe by Thomas Gressop Student in Oxforde* (London: Henry Sutton for Rafe Newbery, 1560; STC 4325)
    (Translation of *Peri tes arches tou papa*; issued in Greek 1625)

3. William Langland, *The vision of Pierce Plowman, newlye imprynted after the authours olde copy, with a brefe summary of the principall matters set before euery part called Passus. Wherevnto is also annexed the Crede of Pierce Plowman, neuer imprinted with the booke before* (London: Owen Rogers, 1561; STC 19908)
    (Earlier edition 1550)

4. *Thys booke is called the Treasure of Gladnesse and semeth by the Copy (beeing a verye litle Manuel, and vvritten in velam) to be made aboue CC. yeres past at the least. Wherby appeareth howe God in olde time, and not of late only hath ben truely confessed and honored. The coppy hereof is for the antiquity of it, preserued and to be seene in the Printers Hall. Set forth and alowed, accordyng to the Queenes Iniunctions. And now first imprinted Anno. 1563* (London: [Henry Denham for] John Charlewood, 1563; STC 24190.7)

Further Elizabethan editions: *1564; 1566; 1568; 1572; 1574; 1575; 1577; 1579; 1581; 1590; 1601*

5. Ælfric, *A Testimonie of Antiquitie, shewing the auncient fayth in the Church of England touching the sacrament of the body and bloude of the Lord here publikely preached, and also receaued in the Saxons tyme, aboue 600. yeares agoe.* (London: John Day, ?1566; STC 159.5)
    (Translation of *Sermo de sacrificio in die Pascae*; later editions 1623, 1638, 1675; 1687)

6.   Robert Poyntz, *Testimonies for the Real Presence of Christes body and blood in the blessed Sacrame{n}t of the aultar set foorth at large, & faithfully translated, out of six auncient fathers which lyued far within the first six hundred yeres, together with certain notes, declaring the force of those testimonies, and detecting sometimes the Sacramentaries false dealing, as more plainly appeareth in the other syde of this leaf. By Robert Pointz student in Diuinitie.* (Louvain: John Fowler, 1566; STC 20082)

7.   John Fortescue, *A learned commendation of the politique lawes of Englande: vvherin by moste pitthy reasons & euident demonstrations they are plainelye proued farre to excell aswell the Ciuile lawes of the Empiere, as also all other lawes of the world, with a large discourse of the difference betwene the. ii. gouernements of kingdomes: whereof the one is onely regall, and the other consisteth of regall and polityque administration conioyned. Written in latine aboue an hundred yeares past, by the learned and right honorable maister Fortescue knight, lorde Chauncellour of England in ye time of Kinge Henrye the .vi. And newly translated into Englishe by Robert Mulcaster* (London: Richard Tottel, 1567; STC 11194)

Further Elizabethan editions: 1573, 1599

8.   *Archaionomia, siue de priscis anglorum legibus libri, sermone Anglico, vetustate antiquissimo, aliquot abhinc seculis conscripti, atq{ue} nunc demum, magno iurisperitorum, & amantium antiquitatis omnium commodo, è tenebris in lucem vocati. Gulielmo Lambardo interprete. Regum qui has Leges scripserunt nomenclationem, & quid præterea accesserit, altera monstrabit pagina* (London: John Day, 1568; STC 15142)
    (Reprinted 1654)

9.   *The Gospels of the fower Euangelistes translated in the olde Saxons tyme out of Latin into the vulgare toung of the Saxons, newly collected out of Auncient Monumentes of the sayd Saxons, and now published for testimonie of the same* (London: John Day, 1571; STC 2961)

10.   Thomas Wimbledon, *A Sermon no lesse frutefull then famous. Made in the yeare of our Lord God. M. CCC. lxxxviii. and founde out hyd in a wall. Which sermon is here set forth by the old copy, without adding or diminishing saue the old & rude English here and there amended* (London: John Awdely, 1573; STC 25826)

Further Elizabethan editions: ?1561; 1575; 1578; 1579; 1582; 1584; 1588; 1593; 1599; 1603

(Earlier editions ?1540, c. 1550; later editions 1617, 1629; 1634; 1635)

11. Heinrich Seuse, *Certayne sweete Prayers of the glorious name of Iesus, commonly called Iesus Mattens, with the howers therto belonging: written in Latin aboue two hundred yeres agoe, by H. Susonne* ([London: W. Carter, 1575–1578]; STC 23443.5)

12. *A knowledge for Kings, and a warning for subiects: Conteyning The moste excellent and worthy history of the Raellyans peruerted state, and gouernment of their common wealth: no lesse rare, then strange and wonderfull: and most meete to be published for a speciall example, in these perylous and daungerous dayes. First written in Latine, by Iames Glaucus a Germaine: and now translated into english by VVilliam Cleuer Scholemaster. By speciall recorde, this Monument was two thousande yeares of Antiquity: and so dusked and forworne with age, that being in a plaine writte{n} letter, could scarce be read: And for that it was great pitie, that so precious a Iewell should quite fade out of remembrance I with my painefull indeuour haue now renewed it into fresh memorye* (London: [John Charlewood for] Richard Jones, 1576; STC 11920).

13. Robert Grosseteste, *The Testaments of the twelue Patriarches the Sonnes of Iacob: translated out of the Greeke into Latine by Robert Grosthed, sometime Byshop of Lyncolne, and out of his copye into French and Dutch by others: Now Englished by A. G. To the credit whereof an auncient Greeke copye written in parchment, is kept in the Vniversitie Librarye of Cambridge* (London: John Day [and J. Kingston], 1576; STC 19467)

Further Elizabethan editions: 1574, 1575 (without reference to the manuscript); 1577, 1581, 1595, 1601

(Later editions 1606, 1610, 1633, 1634, 1647, 1658, 1660, 1663, 1666, 1667, 1670, 1671, 1674, 1677, 1681, 1684, 1686, 1693, 1695, 1699)

14. *Of the Imitation of Christ, Three, both for wisedome, and godlines, most excellent bookes; made 170. yeeres since by one Thomas of Kempis, and for the worthines thereof oft since translated out of Latine into sundrie languages by diuers godlie and learned men: now newlie corrected, translated, and with most ample textes, and sentences of holie Scripture illustrated by Thomas Rogers* (London: Henry Denham [1580]; STC 23973)

Further Elizabethan editions: 1582; 1584; 1585; 1587; 1589; 1592; 1596; 1600; 1602

(Later editions 1611, 1614, 1617, 1629, 1640; other versions available)

15. *The ruinate fall of the Pope Vsury, deriued from the Pope Idolatrie /reueled by a Saxon of antiquitie* (London: John Allde for John Hunter [?1580]; STC 24557.5)

16. Thomas Newton, *A View of Valyaunce. Describing the famous feates, and Martiall exploites of two most mightie nations, the Romains and the Carthaginians, for the conquest and possession of Spayne. Translated out of an auncient Recorde of Antiquitie, written by Rutilius Rufus, a Romaine Gentleman, and a Capitaine of charge vnder Scipio, in the same Warres. Very Delightfull to reade, and neuer before this time publyshed* (London: Thomas East, 1580; STC 21469)

(Abridgement of Appian's *Roman History*).

17. Ratramnus of Corbie, *A Booke of Bertram the Priest, concerning the body & blood of Christe, written in Latine to Charles the great being Emperour, aboue seuen hundred yeeres agoe; And translated, & imprinted in the English tongue. Anno Domini. 1549. Since which time it hath been reviewed, and in many places corrected, and nowe newly published, for the profite of the Reader. 1581* (London: [Thomas Dawson] for Thomas Woodcocke, 1582; STC 20751)

(Translation of *De corpore et sanguine Domini*; earlier editions 1548, 1549; later editions 1623; 1624; 1686; 1687)

18. Caradog of Llancarfan, *The historie of Cambria, now called Wales: A part of the most famous Yland of Brytaine, written in the Brytish language aboue two hundreth yeares past: translated into English by H. Lhoyd Gentleman: Corrected, augmented, and continued out of Records and best approoued Authors, by Dauid Powel Doctor in diuinitie* (London, Rafe Newberry and Henry Denham, 1584; STC 4606)

(Later edition 1697)

19. St John Chrysostom, *An Excellent Treatise touching the restoring againe of him that is fallen: Written by the woorthy man Saint Iohn Chrysostome ... Turned and put into English, out of an ancient Latine translation, written in velume: by R.W.* (London: Arnold Hatfield for John Winnington, 1588; STC 14630.5)

(Later edition 1609)

20. Walter Lynne, *A most necessarie Treatise, declaring the beginning and ending of all Poperie, or the popish Kingdome. Drawne out of certaine olde prophecies aboue three hundred yeeres since, and nowe newly set forth with the auncient Pictures therevnto belonging* (London: John Charlewoode, 1588; STC 17116)

(Earlier edition 1548)

21. *O Read me, for I am of great Antiquitie. I plaine Piers which can not flatter A plough man men me call My speech is fowlle, yet marke the matter How things may hap to fall, but now another Ile haue for mee, I thinke it is as fit say, if any my name doo craue, I am the Gransier of Martin mareprelitte. Compiled afore yeaster day, for the behoofe and ouerthrow of all Parsons, Vikars, and Curats, who haue learned their Cathechismes and can not yet vnderstand them, although they be past their grace. Newly corrected, you will say it was by a gréene head, but Ile tell thée true, My head is neither gréene nor blew, You are deceiued bum fay, My head*

is either white or gray. ('Printed either of this side, or of that side of some of the Priestes' [?1588]; STC 19903a.5)

(Partial edition of *I playne Piers which can not flatter* ([London: [? N. Hill, 1550]; STC 19903a)

22.   George Ripley, *The Compovnd of Alchymy. Or The ancient hidden Art of Archemie: Conteining the right & perfectest meanes to make the Philosophers Stone, Aurum potabile, with other Excellent experiments. Diuided into twelue Gates. First written by the learned and rare Philosopher of our Nation George Ripley, sometime Chanon of Bridlington in Yorkeshyre: & Dedicated to K. Edvvard the 4. Whereunto is adioyned his Epistle to the King, his Vision, his Wheele, & other his Workes, neuer before published: with certaine briefe Additions of other notable Writers concerning the same. Set foorth by Raph Rabbards Gentleman, studious and expert in Archemicall Artes. Pulchrum pro Patria pati* (London: Thomas Orwin, 1591; STC 21057)

23.   Juliana Berners,[44] *The Gentlemans Academie. Or, The Booke of S. Albans: Containing three most exact and excellent Bookes: the first of Hawking, the second of all the proper termes of Hunting, and the last of Armorie: all compiled by Iuliana Barnes, in the yere from the incarnation of Christ 1486. And now reduced into a better method, by G.M.* (London: [Valentine Simmes] for Humfrey Lownes, 1595; STC 3314)

(Revised version of text first published in *Here in thys boke afore ar contenyt the bokys of haukyng and huntyng with other plesuris dyuerse as in the boke apperis* ([St Albans: n.p., 1486]; STC 3308) and reissued regularly up to 1556; other versions available in 1580s–1590s)

24.   St Vincent of Lérins, *The Golden Treatise of the Auncient and Learned Father Vincentivs Lirinensis. For the antiquitie, and vniuersalitie, of the Catholicke Religion: against the prophane nouelties of all Heresies: newly translated into English by A.P. Verie profitable for all such as desire in these dangerous times, to imbrace the true Gospell of Iesus Christ, and to remaine free from all infectio{n} of false doctrine as in the Preface more at large is declared* (?London: Henry Garnet's second press, ?1596; STC 24748)

(Translation of *Pro catholicae fidei antiquitate libellus;* later editions 1631, 1651; other translations 1554, 1556; 1563 (in Scots); 1611*)*

25.   *Certaine Worthye Manvscript Poems of great Antiquitie Reserued long in the Studie of a Northfolke Gentleman. And now first published by J.S. 1 The statly tragedy of Guistard and Sismond. 2 The Northren Mothers Blessing. 3 The way to Thrifte* (London: [Robert Robinson] for R[obert] D[exter], 1597; STC 21499)

(Edited by John Stow)

---

44   On the authorship see Julia Boffey, 'Berners, Juliana (fl. 1460)', *Oxford Dictionary of National Biography*, <http://0-www.oxforddnb.com.catalogue.ulrls.lon.ac.uk/view/article/2255> (accessed 11 May 2012).

26. Raoul Lefèvre, *The Avncient Historie, of the destruction of Troy. Conteining the founders and foundation of the said Citie, with the causes and maner of the first and second spoiles and sackings thereof, by Hercules and his followers: and the third and last vtter desolation and ruine, effected by Menelaus and all the notable worthies of Greece. … Translated out of French into English, by W. Caxton. Newly corrected, and the English much amended. By William Fiston* (London: Thomas Creede [and Valentine Simmes], 1597; STC 15379)

   (Translation of *Recueil des histoires de Troye*; earlier editions 1473, 1502, 1553; later editions 1607, 1617, 1636, 1663, 1670, 1676, 1680, 1684)

27. Geoffrey Chaucer, *The Workes of our Antient and lerned English Poet, Geffrey Chavcer, newly Printed. In this Impression you shall find these Additions: 1 His Portraiture and Progenie shewed. 2 His Life collected. 3 Arguments to euery Booke gathered. 4 Old and obscure Words explaned. 5 Authors by him cited, declared. 6 Difficulties opened. 7 Two Bookes of his, neuer before printed* (London: Adam Islip for Thomas Wight, 1598; STC 5077-9)

Elizabethan editions: 1602

(Numerous editions from 1477; other versions of *Works* 1532, 1542, 1550, 1561)

28. John Bourchier, Lord Berners, *The Ancient, Honorable, Famous, and delightfull Historie of Huon of Bourdeaux, one of the Peeres of Fraunce, and Duke of Guyenne. Enterlaced with the loue of many Ladies, as also the fortunes and aduentures of Knights errant, their amorous Seruants. Being now the Third time imprinted, and the rude English corrected and amended* (London: Thomas Purfoot, to be sold by Edward White, 1601; STC 13999)

29. Simon Sturtevant, *The Etymologist of Æsops Fables, Containing the construing of his Latine fables into English: Also The Etymologist of Phædrus fables, containing the construing of Phædrus (a new found yet auncient Author) into English, verbatim. Both very necessarie helps for young schollers* (London: Richard Field for Robert Dexter, 1602; STC 23410)

Chapter 3

'Rare poemes ask rare friends': Popularity and Collecting in Elizabethan England

Helen Smith

In 1581, the schoolmaster Richard Mulcaster declared that a promising gentleman need no longer leave home and suffer the indignities of foreign travel in order to complete his education:

> We haue in that kind thankes be to God for the pen & print, as much at this day as any countrie needes to haue: nay euen as full if we will follow it well, as any antiquitie it selfe euer had. And yong gentlemen with that wealth, or their parentes in that wealth, might procure, and maintaine so excellent maisters and ioine vnto them so choise companions, and furnish them out with such libraries, being able to beare the charge, as they might learne all the best farre better at home in their standing studies, then they euer shall in their stirring residence, yea though the desire of learning were the cause of their trauell.[1]

Mulcaster's gratitude for 'the pen & print' may refer to the endeavours of authors and stationers, writing and setting forth vernacular learning, or to the overlapping realms of scribal and print publication. One thing, however, is clear: it is the unprecedented availability of texts which allows young men of sufficient means (or sufficiently generous parents) to gather a library and undertake their studies 'standing' rather than 'stirring'.

Admiration, and even despair, at the number of books available in Elizabethan England was a commonplace.[2] In his *First part of the Catalogue of English printed Bookes* (1595), the bookseller Andrew Maunsell wondered at 'the great increase in all kind of Learning in this flourishing Realme of England', noting that 'the mysticall Science of Printing, hath been and is, an excellent hand-maide and great furtherer to the same'.[3] Faced with this plenitude, Maunsell suggested, it is 'as necessarie for the Book-seller … to haue a Catalogue of our English Bookes: As the Apothecarie his *Dispensatorium*, or the Schoole-master his *Dictionarie*'. Maunsell invoked his predecessors – Konrad Gesner, Josias Simmler, and John

---

[1]   *Positions … necessarie for the training vp of children …* (London, 1581), sig. Dd2r.
[2]   See Ann M. Blair, *Too Much to Know: Managing Scholarly Information before the Modern Age* (New Haven: 2010).
[3]   Andrew Maunsell, *First part of the Catalogue of English printed books* (London, 1595), sig. ¶3r.

Bale – whose ambitious book-lists, especially Gesner's *Bibliotecha universalis* (1545), were fundamental to the organization of many libraries,[4] but also marked his difference from them:

> They make their Alphabet by the Christen name, I by the Sir name: They mingle Diuinitie, Law Phisicke, &c. together, I set Diuinitie by it selfe: They set downe Printed and not Printed, I onely Printed, and none but such as I haue seene, hauing besides … left blancke roome here and there throughout my booke, that what I haue left out may easily bee inserted, or what new Booke commeth may be placed in due order.

Maunsell's obsessive attention to the details of ordering reflects the problems of classification that marked any attempt to enumerate the products of the press, as well as the impossibility of creating a physical record that could encompass the mobile market in printed texts. Any list – whether a library catalogue, inventory, or booksellers' stock-sheet – tells only part of the story; as Jason Scott-Warren notes, 'it is in the nature of such documents to efface much of the "hard work" and "commerce" that lie behind them … only by the accidental survival of the collection itself or of ancillary documentation is it possible to glimpse the myriad material transactions that collecting entailed'.[5]

The 200-year period between 1431 (the date at which Humfrey, Duke of Gloucester, won the fortune that allowed him to begin a major collection, part of which remains as Duke Humfrey's Library at the heart of the Bodleian today) and 1631 (the date of Robert Cotton's death) witnessed a significant shift: 'At the beginning of this time span, England's most important libraries belonged to its religious institutions; by its end, they had shifted into private hands, to be re-collected by scholars'.[6] Collectors, including Dee, Cotton, and Francis Bacon, urged the Crown to establish a national collection, and – in the first two cases at least – used their own libraries to fulfil something of this function.[7] Emphasizing

---

[4]   Simmler published a new edition of Gesner's *Epitome* of his *Bibliotecha universalis*, and a new edition of the *Bibliotecha*, whilst Bale built on the work of John Leyland to create his *Scriptorum illustrium maioris Brytanniae catalogus*, published in Basel between 1557 and 1559.

[5]   Jason Scott-Warren, 'News, Sociability, and Bookbuying in Early Modern England: The Letters of Sir Thomas Cornwallis', *The Library*, 7th ser., 1 (2000): 384.

[6]   Jennifer Summit, *Memory's Library: Medieval Books in Early Modern England* (Chicago and London: 2008), p. 2.

[7]   For Dee's *Supplication* (1556), see Julian Roberts and A.G. Watson (eds), *John Dee's Library Catalogue* (London: 1990). Cotton's petition to Elizabeth 'for the erecting of her library and an academy' is reproduced in Nicolas Barker (ed.), *Treasures of the British Library* (London: 1996), p. 43. See also Christopher J. Wright (ed.), *Sir Robert Cotton as Collector: Essays on an Early Stuart Courtier and his Legacy* (London and Toronto: 1997); Richard Ovenden, 'The Libraries of the Antiquaries (c. 1580–1640) and the Idea of a National Collection', in Elisabeth Leedham Green and Teresa Webber (eds), *The Cambridge History of Libraries in Britain and Ireland* (Cambridge: 2006), pp. 527–61.

the need to 'read' libraries as spaces that tell us much about how concepts of knowledge, national identity, and the past are brought into being, Summit argues that Renaissance collectors 'constructed libraries in the same way that authors construct books, through a purposeful selection of materials, directed towards specific interests'.[8] Renaissance habits of buying, preserving, or storing books have shaped not only the textual evidence we have inherited, but our ways of accessing and interpreting that information, influencing both our picture of the textual landscape and our habits of organizing and addressing knowledge.

Before 1600, only a handful of English private libraries – including those of Henry Fitzalan, 19th Earl of Arundel, William Cecil, 1st Baron Burghley, and John Dee – amounted to more than 1,000 books, though Francis Russell, 2nd Earl of Bedford, owned over 600 books and manuscripts, and Sir Thomas Smith, Richard Stonley, and William Gent each amassed at least 400 volumes.[9] Even humble collections might be surprisingly extensive: John Maulden, a weaver, barber, and Morris dancer, died in 1576 leaving four chests containing 67 books, valued at 13s 4d.[10] Women, too, possessed small collections: Catherine Bertie, Duchess of Suffolk, had a 'chest full' of books in 1580; and Mildred Cecil, Burghley's wife, possessed her own books as well as making donations to colleges.[11] Jane, Lady Lumley, daughter of the Earl of Arundel, left inscriptions in books from her father's library, suggesting that women might use or have rights in male relatives' collections.[12]

The broad view of book ownership reconstructed by library historians has been supplemented, in recent years, with micro-histories of particular collections, which attend to the evidence of use.[13] Yet records of book ownership, selling, and purchasing are difficult to interpret, and both the plenitude and the gaps which haunted Maunsell still dog the study of buying and collecting in this period. Rather than offering a quantitative overview, this chapter aims to supplement the

---

[8]   Summit, *Memory's Library*, p. 5.

[9]   Pamela Selwyn and David Selwyn, '"The Profession of a Gentleman": Books for the Gentry and the Nobility (c. 1560 to 1640)', in Leedham-Green and Webber (eds), *The Cambridge History*, p. 502. The Selwyns do not include Dee, who had three to four thousand books in his 'Externa bibliotecha', with an undetermined number in other rooms (William H. Sherman, *John Dee: the Politics of Reading and Writing in the English Renaissance* [Amherst: 1995], p. 31; p. 33).

[10]   Margaret Spufford, 'Libraries of the "Common Sort"', in Leedham-Green and Webber (eds), *The Cambridge History*, p. 523.

[11]   Selwyn and Selwyn, '"Profession of a Gentleman"', p. 503; Caroline Bowden, 'The Library of Mildred Cooke Cecil, Lady Burghley', *The Library*, 7th ser., 6 (2005): 3–29.

[12]   Heidi Brayman Hackel, 'The Countess of Bridgewater's London Library', in Jennifer Andersen and Elizabeth Sauer (eds), *Books and Readers in Early Modern England* (Philadelphia: 2002), p. 138.

[13]   For the Elizabethan period, see Sherman, *John Dee*; Colin G.C. Tite, *The Manuscript Library of Sir Robert Cotton (Panizzi lectures)*, 1993 (London: 1994). See also Andrew Watson, *Medieval Manuscripts in Post-Medieval England* (Aldershot: 2004).

resources of the study with those of the schoolyard, adopting a flexible sense of what it means to be 'popular'. By combining the techniques of the textual critic with those of the tween, we may be able, at least in part, to judge popularity on the basis of two apparently reductive but, in reality, complexly coded and fiercely policed criteria: how many friends books had, and what they looked like. This chapter also raises the possibility that, as with the 'in-crowd' in any school, to be 'popular' may be as much to be envied, admired, and inaccessible as to be well liked, open to all, or frequently handled.

As Ben Jonson pointed out to Lucy Russell, Countess of Bedford (daughter-in-law of the bibliophilic second Earl), in a poem which accompanied a gift of Donne's satires: 'Rare poemes aske rare friends'.[14] Jonson's desire to see Donne's poems properly socialized draws on the idea of the patron as 'A defender, a great friend that supporteth one'.[15] The poem implicitly evokes Momus and Zoilus, the archetypal aggressive readers (Momus was the Greek god of satire and censure, whilst Zoilus was a contemporary of Plato who complained of Homer's bad poetry and earned the title 'scourge of Homer'); a good 'friend' might counter readers' carping criticism. Thus in 1579, H.C. begged the reader to 'let my good meaning serue to excuse my rashness … and vouchsafe me thy friendly assistaunce against the slandrous reports of enuious *Zoylus*'.[16] Celebrating a patronal friendship, William Burton linked Lord Wentworth's patronage to his open library, reminiscing: 'when I was as a dry roote remoued, and vnlikely to finde a place to grow in, your Lordship did receiue me … At my departure, your Lordship also furnished me with bookes out of your Librarie, & with other helpes, more then euer I looked for, or deserued'.[17] Burton's position in the Wentworth household and his access to a noble library (as well as his at least temporary acquisition of selected volumes) returns us to Mulcaster's emphasis on the need for a great household to hold a range of texts and the social uses of that library by clients and tutors, as well as a new breed of humanist secretary.[18]

In this context, 'great', like 'rare', is as much a description of political power as it is of personal ties, yet the resurrection of Ciceronian ideals of male amity also allow us to conceive of a more intimate social circle.[19] Thus it seems legitimate to extend the concept of friendship to include the human and bibliographic circles in which books moved as they forged new alliances, their altered identities reinforced

---

[14]   Ben Jonson, 'XCIIII. To Lvcy, Covntesse of Bedford, with Mr. Donne's Satyres', in *The workes of Benjamin Jonson* (London: 1616), sig. Xxx2v.

[15]   John Bullokar, *An English expositor* (London: 1616), sig. L8r-v.

[16]   H.C., *The forrest of fancy* (London, 1579), B1r; Heidi Brayman Hackel charts this trope in *Reading Material in Early Modern England: Gender, Print, and Literacy* (Cambridge: 2005), pp. 122–24.

[17]   William Burton, *Dauids euidenece* [sic] (London: 1592), sig. A2v.

[18]   See Lisa Jardine and Anthony Grafton, '"Studied for Action": How Gabriel Harvey Read his Livy', *Past and Present* 129 (1990), pp. 30–78.

[19]   On friendship see esp. Alan Bray, *The Friend* (Chicago and London: 2003).

through changes in appearance.[20] At Elizabeth's accession many scholarly libraries were still built using lecterns, with books chained to rods along the backs of the desks. By the late sixteenth century, the need for additional space had prompted the adoption of stalls, with reading desks protruding from the walls and books standing upright on adjacent shelves, their fore-edges facing the reader.[21] The title had to be reinscribed on the front of the book block, while old chains had to be moved to anchor the books amongst their new acquaintances. In 1621, Corpus Christi College, Oxford, paid 21 shillings 'for 21 daies work in chayning and unchayning of books'.[22]

While the university libraries received many books ready-bound, both they and private collectors sometimes needed to bind or re-bind texts, either because they had been sold unbound; because they needed to be re-worked to match the other books in a collection, as in the case of Robert Dudley, Earl of Leicester, whose books were stamped with his crest of the bear and ragged staff; or because their very popularity – the rigours of use – had worn out their original bindings.[23] Some books forged new associations through these changes of dress. Both Archbishop Matthew Parker and, in the seventeenth century, Sir Robert Cotton rearranged vast collections of medieval and foreign manuscripts to suit their own categories and organizational conceits.[24] While playtexts, classical commentaries, or political news might enter new alliances when bound together, friendless texts might also find a new home when used to 're-clothe' more desirable texts, concealed within bindings or recycled to repair the edges of decaying pages.[25]

Early modern users often inscribed their names on the flyleaves of books, or interspersed ownership claims and signatures throughout the leaves. As Scott-Warren notes, signing your name on a book might 'at the very least mean inviting

---

[20]   For the conceit that objects have social lives, see Arjun Appadurai, 'Introduction' to Appadurai (ed.), *The Social Life of Things: Commodities in Cultural Perspective* (Cambridge: 1986), p. 5. See also William H. Sherman, 'The social life of books', in Joad Raymond (ed.), *The Oxford History of Popular Print Culture*, vol. 1 (Oxford: 2011), pp. 164–71.

[21]   Esther Potter, 'Bookbinding for Libraries', in Robin Myers, Michael Harris, and Giles Mandelbrote (eds), *Libraries and the Book Trade* (New Castle, DE: 2000), p. 174.

[22]   J.R. Liddell, 'The Library of Corpus Christi College Oxford in the Sixteenth Century', *The Library*, 4th ser., 18 (1938): 385–416 (396).

[23]   On repairs in the All Souls Library, Oxford, see the summary in Potter ('Bookbinding for Libraries'), p. 172. On Leicester see Mirjam Foot, *The Henry Davis Gift: A Collection of Bookbindings* (London: 1978), vol. 1, pp. 27–34.

[24]   Timothy Graham, 'Matthew Parker's Manuscripts: an Elizabethan Library and its Use', in Leedham-Green and Webber (eds), *The Cambridge History of Libraries*, pp. 328–29.

[25]   On the collecting together of texts, see Jeffrey Todd Knight, 'Making Shakespeare's Books: Assembly and Intertextuality in the Archives', *Shakespeare Quarterly* 60 (2009): 304–40; and Jeffrey Todd Knight, 'Fast Bind, Fast Find: The History of the Book and the Modern Collection', *Criticism* 51 (2009): 79–104.

one's "friends" into the copy of a book, making the owning of it a communal ritual
... requiring the presence of witnesses'.[26] Archbishop Parker's extant books contain
evidence of intensive use by Parker and his circle,[27] whilst the Derbyshire minister
William Hull kept a record of book loans on the flyleaves of his sermon notebooks,
'revealing the existence of a network of local clergy and gentry who were able
to borrow new works of theology and religious controversy almost as soon as
they were published'.[28] Some owners made the shared nature of book possession
explicit: Gabriel Harvey is perhaps the best-known English book-owner to have
signed his books '*et amicorum*', indicating shared use, if not ownership, but other
readers, too, signed their books in the name of a social group, including Barnard
Hampton, clerk of the council to Edward VI, Mary Tudor, and Elizabeth I, in his
copy of Robert Recorde's *Ground of Arts* (1543).[29] David Pearson notes that many
sixteenth-century owners adopted a sociable tag, and variations including 'Lyber
Frynde et amicorum eius' and 'Johannes Gowghe mihi et meis' can be discovered
in a range of sources.[30] The recusant Sir Thomas Tresham signed several books
in the names of his friends, and when his son-in-law Thomas Brudenell inherited
the collection he, too, added his signature. To Tresham's inscription, 'Tresami et
amicorum', in Livy's *Le Decho ... delle Historie Romanie*, Brudenell appended
the formula 'Tho: Brudenelli & amicorum suorum & Tresamarum', widening the
book's circle of friends and recording its expanding social life within a Catholic
community.[31]

Across Europe, young men, particularly from German- and Dutch-speaking
regions, invited their friends into the pages of their *alba amicorum*, books which
brought together prints, pictures, and the signatures, mottos, and coats of arms of
'friends' and influential acquaintances into a one-volume library.[32] The antiquary
and herald William Camden signed his name in Abraham Ortelius's friendship
album, inserting himself into the humanist and scientific community of early

---

[26]   Jason Scott-Warren, 'Reading Graffiti in the Early Modern Book', *Huntington
Library Quarterly* 73 (2010): 374.

[27]   Graham, 'Matthew Parker's Manuscripts', p. 332.

[28]   Arnold Hunt, 'Clerical and Parish Libraries', in Leedham-Green and Webber (eds),
The Cambridge History of Libraries, p. 409; citing Dublin Trinity College, MS 709, vols
I–III.

[29]   Scott-Warren, 'Reading Graffiti', p. 374.

[30]   David Pearson, *Provenance Research in Book History: A Handbook* (London:
1994), p. 25. See also G.D. Hobson, 'Et Amicorum', *The Library*, 5th ser., 4 (1949): 87–99.

[31]   I am grateful to Emilie Murphy for this example. The Livy is in the Brudenell
family library at Deene Park, and is listed in Nicolas Barker and David Quentin, *The
Library of Thomas Tresham & Thomas Brudenell, with an introduction by John Martin
Robinson* (London: 2006).

[32]   Margaret F. Rosenthal, 'Fashions of Friendship in an Early Modern Illustrated
Album Amicorum: British Library, MS Egerton 1191', *Journal of Medieval and Early
Modern Studies* 39 (2009): 619–41; 620. See also June Schlueter, *The Album Amicorum
and the London of Shakespeare's Time* (London: 2012).

modern Europe, whilst Dee signed Gesner's *liber amicorum* on 23rd April 1563.[33] Many albums were based on printed books, interleaved with blank pages to allow the addition of autographs and inscriptions, and all testify to 'the intricate networks and the international character of the early modern intellectual world'.[34] Books were not, as the attempt to construct comprehensive catalogues might suggest, immobile, solitary objects, but 'were passed around, and as they circulated, aspects of communal life – the negotiation of relationships, the debating of reputations – rubbed off on them'.[35]

Evidence for book collections comes primarily from catalogues and book-lists, probate inventories compiled shortly after an owner's death, and wills, and thus often fails to capture the reality of lively collections.[36] In an account of the book purchases of Sir Richard Stonley, one of Elizabeth's Tellers of the Exchequer, Scott-Warren compares the inventory of Stonley's possessions taken when he was arrested for embezzlement with his scrupulously kept household account book, noting the purchase of around 50 titles, of which only nine are represented in the inventory, though another was probably cut apart for its engravings 'of the fashions of strange Countries' and hung on the walls of Stonley's gallery in his house on Aldersgate Street.[37] Characteristically, inventories either exclude small books or lump them together as objects of little worth; Alexandra Halasz notes that 145 of the 200 inventories of Cambridge estates published by Elisabeth Leedham-Green 'include one or more entries of "additional bookes unnamed," and such entries often specify that the unnamed books are small-format publications. In some inventories the number of quarto, octavo or duodecimo books unnamed equals or exceeds the named titles'.[38] In a catalogue drawn up in 1583, John Dee was unusual in detailing his ephemeral English texts as extensively as his weighty tomes in learned languages.[39] A little later in the period, Robert Burton's library catalogue also marks an exception, containing pamphlets from writers including

---

[33] Deborah Harkness, *The Jewel House: Elizabethan London and the Scientific Revolution* (New Haven: 2007), p. 39; Sherman, *John Dee*, p. 48.

[34] Schlueter, *The Album Amicorum*, p. 156.

[35] Scott-Warren, 'Reading Graffiti', p. 379.

[36] Useful sources are available in Elisabeth Leedham-Green, *Books in Cambridge Inventories: Book-lists from Vice-Chancellor's Court Probate Inventories in the Tudor and Stuart Periods*, 2 vols (Cambridge: 1986); R.J. Fehrenbach and Elisabeth Leedham-Green (eds), *Private Libraries in Renaissance England: a Collection and Catalogue of Tudor and Early Stuart Book-lists*, 6 vols. to date (Binghamton, NY: 1995 –). On the challenges of probate inventories see Lena Cowen Orlin, 'Fictions of the early modern English probate inventory', in Henry S. Turner (ed.), *The Culture of Capital* (New York: 2002), pp. 51–83.

[37] Jason Scott-Warren, 'Books in the Bedchamber: Religion, Accounting and the Library of Richard Stonley', in John N. King (ed.), *Tudor Books and Readers: Materiality and the Construction of Meaning* (Cambridge: 2010), p. 239.

[38] Alexandra Halasz, *The Marketplace of Print: Pamphlets and the Public Sphere in Early Modern England* (Cambridge: 1997), p. 9.

[39] See Roberts and Watson (eds), *John Dee's Library Catalogue*.

Thomas Nashe, Thomas Deloney, Thomas Dekker, Samuel Rowlands, and John Taylor.[40]

Books listed in wills are often not specified by title, and the deathbed practice of giving away smaller, personal items before dictating a will in front of family members may mean that treasured books were passed on to friends and kin before the listing of remaining property began. Kristian Jensen argues that as more and more books entered circulation, fewer and fewer were listed in assessments of wealth: 'In 1586 the authorities in Oxford by and large stopped listing people's books for probate purposes ... books had become so numerous and so cheap that they were assessed only in the most general way for probate'.[41] As Jensen notes of the Oxford inventory-takers in the plague year of 1577: 'One feels a great deal of sympathy for them when they give up at entry number 228 in the list of books left by James Reynolds, and write "a hundredth parchment old bokes" ... a collection beyond the dreams of any but the most senior academic at the beginning of the century'.[42] While account books and the evidence of extant copies may supplement our understanding of habits of buying and collecting, they, too, are partial: Stonley on several occasions recorded the purchase of 'bookes' without specifying titles or quantities.[43]

It was in the fifteenth century that 'library' came to mean not only a collection of books, but a particular place (drawing, in part, on rediscovered descriptions of the great libraries of the classical past).[44] Writing of the university libraries, Claire Sargent describes the end of the Elizabethan age as witnessing a second 'paradigm shift: the creation of a corporately owned collection aspiring, increasingly, to cover, if not yet the sum of human knowledge, then at least books in the traditional subjects beyond those essential to the syllabus, within a room which promoted study through its architectural form and its furniture'.[45] The provision of specific furniture – presses and shelves – reinforced the division of knowledge into classes: Sir Thomas Knyvett's library catalogue reflects the material practice of grouping his books under such broad subject headings as 'libri theologici', 'medici', 'libri mathematici', 'libri philosophici et aliarum artium humaniorum', 'libri poetici et misici', and 'libri utriusque iuris'. These headings overlapped and were seldom exclusive, with books on a variety of subjects held within each classification, further subdivided by language: Latin, French, English, Italian, Spanish, and

---

[40]   See Nicolas K. Kiessling, *The Library of Robert Burton* (Oxford: 1988).

[41]   Kristian Jensen, 'Universities and Colleges', in Leedham-Green and Webber (eds), *The Cambridge History of Libraries*, p. 352.

[42]   Ibid.; citing Fehrenbach and Leedham-Green (eds), *Private Libraries in Renaissance England*, 127 (IV.4–37).

[43]   Scott-Warren, 'Books in the Bedchamber', p. 239.

[44]   Summit, *Memory's Library*, p. 11.

[45]   Claire Sargent, 'The Early Modern Library', in Leedham-Green and Webber (eds), *The Cambridge History of Libraries*, p. 53.

a small handful of Greek books.[46] The proportion of Latin books in Knyvett's catalogue (75 percent) reflects the ubiquity of Latin texts in learned collections, offering a contrast to notions of popular reading as rooted in vernacular literacy. Not only the books as objects but the texts they held could form part of the visual order of the library: sayings and sentences from books could be inscribed onto walls or (as in the case of Montaigne) onto the beams of the library, so that scholars could read the space as well as its contents.[47]

Throughout this period, however, the conception of the library remained flexible; in his Latin-English dictionary of 1578, Thomas Cooper defined a 'Bibliotecha' as 'a librarie: a study: a great number of books', encompassing both place and quantity as exchangeable criteria for a library.[48] The idea of the library as an accumulation of information could be appropriated for any store of knowledge, even one contained in a single book: Thomas Bentley offered his (admittedly hefty) *Monument of matrones* (1582) as a complete 'domesticall librarie plentifullie stored and replenished',[49] while in a dedication of *Certain tragicall discourses* (1567) to Mary (Sidney) Herbert, Geoffrey Fenton reflected on the utility of 'Histories a librarie or store house of knovvledg'.[50]

Between the extremes of the Bodleian library, founded in 1598 (in part thanks to the prosperity of Bodley's wife, who inherited her first husband's pilchard-trade fortune), and the single, large book lay numerous small collections. Some occupied school shelves, though, as William Barker points out, 'For most schools, the library, if it can be called that, was a small collection of books, usually dictionaries and other works, that were kept on a shelf, often chained, or in a case, to be used by the master or ushers or the senior boys'.[51] Christopher Marlowe, John Lyly, and Stephen Gosson's Canterbury schoolmaster, John Gresshop, however, had a collection of more than 350 volumes. As in many libraries from the period, the classics were strongly represented, as were Reformist writings, the medical works of Galen and Fabritius, history texts, works of vernacular poetry, as well as numerous textbooks and what might now be called pedagogic manuals; how many of these books were available to boys and masters is unclear, though William Urry notes the presence of several texts which resonate throughout Marlowe's

---

[46]   David McKitterick, *The Library of Sir Thomas Knyvett of Ashwellthorpe, c. 1539–1618* (Cambridge: 1978), p. 26. See also David McKitterick, 'Libraries and the Organization of Knowledge', in Leedham-Green and Webber (eds), *The Cambridge History of Libraries*, pp. 592–615.

[47]   Juliet Fleming, 'Graffiti, Grammatology, and the Age of Shakespeare', in Patricia Fumerton and Simon Hunt (eds), *Renaissance Culture and the Everyday* (Philadelphia: 1999), p. 328.

[48]   Thomas Cooper, *Thesaurus linguae Romanae & Britannicae* (London: 1578).

[49]   Thomas Bentley, *The monument of matrones* (London: 1582), sig. A2v.

[50]   Matteo Bandello, *Certaine tragicall discourses*, trans. Geoffrey Fenton (London: 1567), sig. *2v.

[51]   William Barker, 'School Libraries (c. 1540 to 1640)', in Leedham-Green and Webber (eds), *The Cambridge History of Libraries*, p. 436.

later plays and poems.[52] The popularity – or at least intensive use – of some schoolbooks is indicated by their tattered state: a 1599 catalogue of books at the Merchant Taylors' School in London includes 'Cowpers Dictionary folio all rent', 'Epitheta Tectoris [*sic* for Textoris]. 4to all rent', 'Lycosthenis apothegmata. 8° all rent', and 'Textoris officina in 4to all rent'.[53] These were books whose distressed appearance indicates that they were frequently used, even if they made few firm 'friends' among their schoolboy readers.

Some parish churches also built up libraries for the use of local clergy and godly readers. In Bury St Edmunds, Sir Robert Jermyn, a local magistrate, presented a 15-volume set of Calvin's *Works* to the parish, and his example was followed by others 'in what was effectively "a sponsor-a-book" scheme whereby individuals could donate a sum of money to have their name attached to a particular volume'.[54] Though there was no official mandate that all churches must own Foxe's *Book of martyrs*, many godly lay people began to leave either the book or sufficient money to purchase it to their parish churches.[55] The evidence of annotation or repair can tell us whether these books were much used, but the donations suggest that books might be popular because of their prestigious status and materialization of a donor's generosity, rather than because they were eagerly studied. After all, evidence that someone owned a book is not evidence they read it. As Walter Benjamin quipped about his own bibliophilia: 'Suffice it to quote the answer which Anatole France gave to a philistine who admired his library and then finished with the standard question, "And you have read all these books, Monsieur France?" "Not one-tenth of them. I don't suppose you use your Sèvres china every day?"'.[56] We cannot even be sure that each book within a collection definitively reflected the tastes of its owner, since books, like other items, could be received as gifts, lent by well-meaning acquaintances, or purchased wholesale for servants. In 1583, William Parry wrote to Secretary Walsingham, enclosing 'the newest book I could find for a remembrance, wishing it worth 10000 *l.*'.[57] For Parry, the book's worth lay in its novelty, and perhaps in the contrast of its 'newness' with his own 'no news'; we have no record of whether Walsingham read the book, absorbed it into his collection, or abandoned it. The hunger for novelty was a commonplace in complaints about indiscriminate readers in this period: in his *Ortho-epia Gallica* (1593), John Eliot offered a useful phrase for the French tourist wishing to walk in

---

[52]   William Urry, *Christopher Marlowe and Canterbury* (London: 1988), pp. 47–48.

[53]   R.T.D. Sayle, 'Annals of the Merchant Taylors' School Library', *The Library*, 4th ser., 15 (1935): 457–80.

[54]   Hunt, 'Clerical and Parish Libraries', p. 416.

[55]   Ibid., p. 414.

[56]   Walter Benjamin, 'Unpacking My Library', in *Illuminations*, trans. Hannah Arendt (New York: 1968), pp. 49–68; p. 62.

[57]   The National Archives: SP 15/28/1 f. 98.

London: 'Au Cemitiere saint Pol pour achepter [*sic*] vn liure nouueau' or 'To Pauls churchyard to buy a new booke'.[58]

Perhaps inevitably, most evidence for the ownership of books leads us to wealthier, more confidently literate readers, and surviving lists tend to reflect the professional tastes of doctors, ministers, scholars, and lawyers whilst also privileging the university towns of Oxford and Cambridge. The books which were popular (in the simple sense of being widely owned) in these libraries can tell us a great deal about educational fashions (Erasmus, Tully), broadly consensual views of medical practice (Galen, Gesner, Fallopius[59]), influential histories (vernacular chronicles, Caesar's *Commentaries*, Eusebius's ecclesiastical history[60]), religious disputes (Calvin, Luther, Jewel), as well as the most popular sermons and homilies of the Elizabethan age,[61] but may resonate only partially with the tastes and habits of that broader cross-section of the population at the elusive centre of the Venn diagram that charts the overlapping of two vexed terms: 'popular' and 'culture'.

The custodians of significant collections, from time to time, explicitly opposed their endeavours to the texts and formats of 'popular' reading, and participated vigorously in what Alexandra Halasz describes as the 'phobic conception of widely circulated discourses at the emergence of a public sphere'.[62] Notoriously, Thomas Bodley's endeavours to restore the Oxford University library 'to the publique use of students' did not extend to letting them read pamphlets.[63] When his enterprising librarian, Thomas James, reached an agreement by which the Stationers' Company was to supply a copy of every book entered at Stationers' Hall (a move which paved the way for the current British system of Legal Deposit), Bodley grumbled at the prospect that 'idle books, and riffe raffes' – in other words, precisely those categories, including the pamphlet, the almanac, and the jestbook, which contemporary criticism aligns with 'popular culture' – would make their way into the library. Bodley wrote to James, deploring 'the harm that the scandal will bring unto the Librarie, when it shalbe given out, that we stuffe it full of baggage books'.[64]

---

[58] *Ortho-epia Gallica Eliots fruits for the French* (London, 1593), C5r, I2r. John Florio offered an earlier Italian version: 'Anderemo prima a san Paulo. Let vs go first to Paules. / E che faremo la? And what shal we do there? / Compreremo qualche bello libro dinuouo, dicono che é stato stampato vn libro di nouo. We wil buye some fine booke, and new, they say that there is printed a new booke' (*Florio his firste fruites* [London: 1578], sig. E3v).

[59] See Christine Cerdeira, 'Early Modern English Medical Wills, Book Ownership, and Book Culture', *Canadian Bulletin of Medical History* 12 (1995): 427–39.

[60] See D.R. Woolf, *Reading History in Early Modern England* (Cambridge: 2000), pp. 145–49.

[61] See Lori Humphrey Newcomb on Henry Smith, in this volume.

[62] Halasz, *The Marketplace of Print*, p. 2.

[63] Thomas Bodley, *The life of Sir Thomas Bodley* (Oxford: 1647), sig. C4r.

[64] Thomas Bodley, *Letters of Sir Thomas Bodley*, ed. G.W. Wheeler (Oxford: 1926), p. 219; p. 222.

Size mattered: Andrew Perne insisted in his will that books in octavo or decimosexto 'are not so meete for a library', but this distinction applied only to his donation to the library he founded at Corpus Christi College, Cambridge, not to his personal collection. Perne willed that the books he kept at the Bishopric of Ely should go to 'one of the best learned of my name & kyn, willinge notwithstandinge that he which shall haue the said bookes shall lend any of them to any of my name or kyn beinge meete for them taking pawnes for the same'.[65] This bequest at once preserved Perne's books within a collection and insisted that they must be available for sociable use (albeit with a financial guarantee for their return). Still, Perne's belief that a scholarly library needed to be stocked with substantial books, epitomized in his gift to Corpus Christi of 'one of the best and largest sort of all my books of divinitie Lawe, Physicke or of any other Sciences that I haue at Cambridge in folio & in quarto of every sort of Authors', suggests one kind of popularity recognizable in the psychology of the playground: those books which were best-dressed were perhaps recognized as being most desirable, even if their tattered companions possessed more 'real' friends.[66]

The version of popularity painted by available library records is one that sits uneasily with concepts of accessible, portable print. 'It was almost a requirement', notes Leedham-Green, 'that every Cambridge [Doctor of Divinity] had the works of Augustine (in the twenty years 1560 to 1580 every D. D. whose books were inventoried in Cambridge possessed the "Opera", and all but one of the [Bachelors of Divinity])'.[67] This is not to say that the works of Augustine were not popular amongst a much wider audience, but few beyond the universities were likely to have possessed his monumental *Works*. Instead, Augustine's texts circulated extensively in smaller editions and in the pseudonymous *St Austins prayers* (a popular author might collect to himself numerous texts without other authorial 'friends'). The extant 1585 book-list of Roger Ward, a Shrewsbury bookseller frequently imprisoned for infringing patents and pirating popular texts, includes 'i pomand*er* with Austins prayers' and 'i Austens prayers with gou*er*naunce of ve*r*tue', as well as 'i Austines meditac*i*ons'.[68] A manuscript fragment, discovered within the binding of a printed book, details books sent to Cambridge by the bookseller Thomas Chard in 1583–1584, and includes an octavo copy of the *Confessio Augustana*, priced at six pence, and a duodecimo 'Austens Meditations', priced at five pence. Chard sent only one or two copies of most texts to his

---

[65]   Elisabeth Leedham-Green, 'Perne's Wills', in David McKitterick (ed.), *Andrew Perne: Quatercentenary Studies* (Cambridge: 1991), p. 105.

[66]   Ibid., p. 105.

[67]   Elisabeth Leedham-Green, 'Booksellers and Libraries in Sixteenth-Century Cambridge', in Myers, Harris, and Mandelbrote (eds), *Libraries and the Book Trade*, p. 8.

[68]   Alexander Rodger, 'Roger Ward's Shrewsbury Stock: an Inventory of 1585', *The Library*, 5th ser., 13 (1958): 247–68. On the reception of Augustine see K. Pollman and W. Otten (eds), *The Oxford Guide to the Historical Reception of Augustine* (Oxford: forthcoming, 2013).

Cambridge connections, yet his list of authors includes the same doctors of divinity and popular sermon-writers whose texts appeared in grander form in the most extensive libraries, including Gifford and Dering, Bèze, Melancthon, and Calvin.[69] The inventories of bookshops record 'far larger stocks of small-format, relatively elementary texts, than ... of expensive, multi-volume folio sets', in opposition to the evidence of library catalogues.[70] What the two faces of early modern Augustine reveal is not only that the traditions of the learned could find points of contact with more evidently popular print, nor simply a firm divide between the majestic importability of chained folio sets and the decorative, health-giving motility of a 'pomander' of prayers, but also the often-stated but still under-explored ubiquity of religious texts as the most popular of all books.[71] The first part of Maunsell's *Catalogue of English printed Bookes*, which listed texts treating of religion, stood at 123 pages, far outweighing the *The Seconde parte*, concerning 'the Sciences *Mathematicall*, as *Arithmetick, Geometrie, Astronomie, Astrologie, Musick*, the *Arte of Warre*, and *Nauigation:* And also, of *Phisick* and *Surgerie*', at only 27 pages, despite its diligent listing of books concerning topics as diverse as the astrolabe, the benefits of baths, dreams, earthquakes, land-measuring, and urines.

In a survey of Kentish readers, Peter Clark notes 'the ubiquity of the Bible: even amongst those people (often poorer folk) who owned only one work, the volume they chose was the Bible, often a fairly expensive item', a priority that may reflect not only the Bible's centrality to daily devotion but also its status as a family book and heirloom.[72] The only book listed in the inventory of John and Katherine Marlowe, the playwright's parents, is a Bible, whereas the expansive collection of the Canterbury schoolmaster, Gresshop, included not only a Geneva Bible but three Latin Bibles and two Greek Testaments, suggesting the book's continuing primacy in larger libraries.[73] In most libraries, the Bible was not simply the most 'popular' book, but also, quite literally, the 'top' choice, since theology

---

[69]   Robert Jahn, 'Letters and Booklists of Thomas Chard (or Chare) of London, 1583–4', *The Library*, 4th ser., 4 (1923): 219–37.

[70]   Leedham-Green, 'Booksellers and Libraries', p. 6.

[71]   See Brian Cummings, in this collection, on the *Book of Common Prayer*. See also Tessa Watt, *Cheap Print and Popular Piety*, 1550–1640 (Cambridge: 1991); Ian Green, *The Christian's ABC: Catechisms and Catechizing in England, c. 1530–1740* (Oxford: 1996); Peter Lake, 'Religion and Cheap Print', in Raymond (ed.), *Oxford History of Popular Print Culture*, pp. 217–41; and Mary Morrissey, 'Sermons, Primers, and Prayer Books', in Raymond (ed.), *Oxford History of Popular Print Culture*, pp. 491–509.

[72]   Peter Clark, 'The Ownership of Books in England, 1560–1640: the Example of Some Kentish Townsfolk', in Lawrence Stone (ed.), *Schooling and Society* (Baltimore: 1976), p. 103. Woolf notes that 'the overwhelming majority of books in early Tudor wills are religious, except in concentrated scholarly communities such as Oxford and Cambridge' (*Reading History*, p. 135). On Bible reading and ownership see William H. Sherman, *Used Books: Marking Readers in Renaissance England* (Philadelphia: 2007), Chapter 4.

[73]   Urry, *Christopher Marlowe*, p. 40, p. 47.

was 'at the beginning of most classification schemes, with bibles generally first of all'.[74] It is followed in Kentish wills by the New Testament, Service Book, Psalter, and Foxe's *Acts & Monuments*, another expensive and prestigious book.

A moderately wealthy Canterbury widow, Alice Cornelius, died in 1579, leaving behind 'a Bible, Erasmus's *Paraphrase*, the New Testament, a service book, and a volume of Augustine's *Meditations*'.[75] The book-lists of Chard and Ward suggest that Cornelius's collection was representative of small, personal collections, and that it may offer us a glimpse not of a popular 'library' but of a popular bookshelf or bundle. After '5 Dosen of Almanackes', the next most popular items on Chard's list are '24 Moores Catechisme' and 35 copies of the Psalms, 19 in tiny thirty-two-mo (four bound in paper, four 'playn', and twelve in vellum), and 16 in sixteen-mo (four in paper, six in sheep's leather, six in vellum). On the other side of the confessional divide, a Catholic collection might contain similar items, alongside illicit texts. Bundles or packets of 'Popish' books were frequently invoked by searchers as evidence of illegal religious practice. In 1574, for example, Christopher Wandesford arrested one Thomas Wray. A search of 'all Wray's houses and privy places' revealed only 'a small Psalm book, lying upon his study table', but Wray's acquaintance, Robin Smelt, was found to be in possession of a mass book, 'Resolutions of Marcus Antonius Constantius to the objections against the real and carnal presence of Christ in the Sacrament', and 'Boner [Bishop Bonner] upon the sacrament'.[76] The texts appear to have predated the Reformation – Wandesford noted that they were inscribed with the name of John Moore, the late schoolmaster of Richmond – but their persistence and presence as a distinct collection rendered them suspicious.

Ward's inventory also features a cluster of teaching texts, both basic (25 ABCs), and more advanced, including 29 'Terences', 27 'Horaces', and 15 copies of 'Ouides epistles'.[77] It also embraces texts which have more usually been claimed as 'popular' literature, such as Lyly's fashionable *Euphues* (parts 1 and 2), and offers evidence for a previously unrecorded first edition of Robert Greene's popular *Pandosto* (19 copies), as well as some 'how-to' texts, like '2 Bookes of cookery' and 'i Glasse of health', and guides to reading ('i method redinge hystories').[78] Even Ward's detailed list bundles a few books, however, including '69 Bookes at pence', whose titles remain unknown.[79] Ward also sold a number of 'Papire Bookes' and 'copie bookes' (3 'smalest', 3 'largest'), reminding us that booksellers sold writing implements, blank books, and tablets alongside printed and manuscript texts. Do blank books, or the re-usable wax tablets purchased by

[74]　McKitterick, 'Libraries and the Organization of Knowledge', p. 594.
[75]　Clark, 'The Ownership of Books', p. 102.
[76]　The National Archives: SP 15/23 f.122.
[77]　Rodger, 'Roger Ward's Shrewsbury Stock', items 424, 154, 161, 156, 163.
[78]　Ibid., items 121, 132, 133, 315, 329, 345.
[79]　Ibid., item 425.

Richard Stonley, deserve to count as 'popular' books?[80] Was Stonley's account book, to which he so diligently returned, part of a more 'popular' or saleable genre than the copy of *Venus and Adonis* whose purchase has secured his place in literary history?

In Chard's list, Latin texts form more than half the stock, and both the Latin and English texts are predominantly devotional or controversial. However, Chard's habit of alphabetizing reveals some unexpected conjunctions between differently popular texts, blurring the boundaries between genres and sparking conversations between books in ways that raise questions about reading practice and reception: Theodore de Bèze and John Bradford's evangelical writing 'on ye Comandements' flank three copies of *Bevis of Hampton*, whilst Leonard Digges's *Prognostications* are followed by the 'Destruction of Troy' in metre, five copies of *Discouery of ye West Indies*, and six of the *Diall of Destinye*. Chard also stocked 'Penall statutes' and '12 Queens Iniunctions', returning us to Brian Cummings's question in this volume, 'Do we want to call acts of parliament a form of popular literature?'[81]

Perhaps the most significant divide between formal libraries and the evidence of less systematic purchasers' and booksellers' lists lies in the divide between the trade in Latin and other learned languages and the burgeoning cultures of vernacular print. Many collectors looked beyond England for their purchases. John Dee had extensive dealings with the major importers, the Birckmans of Cologne, whilst his time in the Netherlands in 1562–1564 offered him the opportunity to build up one of the largest collections of Hebrew texts in England. Dee was skilled in deploying his own book purchases to impress patrons: in 1563 he wrote to Burghley from Antwerp, boasting that he had 'purchased one boke, for wch a thousand Crownes have ben by others offred, and wch could not be obteyned. A boke, for which many a lerned man hath long sought, and dayly ytt doth seeke … A boke for your honor, or a Prince, so meet, so nedefull and commodious, as in Germayne knowledge, none can be meeter or more behofefull'.[82] Offering the book to Cecil, Dee asked his patron's help in securing him employment upon his return to England.

Many books were sold at the Frankfurt Book Fairs, the most important book-trade events in Europe. Dee and the York Archbishop Tobie Matthew were among the Elizabethan library-builders who owned and annotated Fair catalogues, using them to decide on prospective purchases. Purchasers could also build up relationships with particular stationers; Richard Stonley, for example, bought many of his books from the shop of Edward White.[83] In *Greenes farewell to folly*

---

[80]   Scott-Warren, 'Books in the Bedchamber', p. 239. On tablets see Peter Stallybrass, Roger Chartier, J. Franklin Mowery, and Heather Wolfe, 'Hamlet's Tables and the Technologies of Writing in Renaissance England', *Shakespeare Quarterly* 55 (2004): 379–419.

[81]   See also Mark Jenner, 'London', in Raymond (ed.), *Oxford History of Popular Print Culture*, pp. 294–307.

[82]   The National Archives: SP 12/27 f. 264.

[83]   Scott-Warren, 'Books in the Bedchamber', p. 239.

(1591), Robert Greene's Italian count, Seignor Bernardino, speaks scornfully of the would-be 'scholler', seduced by court fashions and demanding a 'tailer as well to picture out his lineaments, as a Stationer to furnish out his librarie'.[84] The criticism is double-edged: the ostensible target is an obsession with apparel, but the parallel hints at the library itself as a fashionable commodity.

Thomas Bodley not only scoured the Frankfurt Fair catalogues but dispatched the London stationers John Norton and John Bill to find desirable texts: Norton to the Frankfurt book fair, and Bill across Europe, including Paris, Rome, Venice, and Seville.[85] In 1561, Burghley wrote to his son's tutor in northern France, urging his son's continued industry and asking for registers of books 'that I may thereof make choise to garnish my library for I am almost past study', an intriguing hint at a move from business to leisure reading, or even to books as decorative trifles.[86] Thomas Knyvett used as his agent his brother Henry, who secured him books from the Spanish Netherlands and Calais, as well as London,[87] whilst Thomas Goold wrote to Philip Fagan asking him to tell 'brother Galway that I searcht all the booke bynders in Lisbon for his booke, but as god judge me I could fynd neyther newe nor olde, but by chaunce one day in a Church called the misericordia I spied a librarie of olde books, among wch I found this Booke called Estexan de Garribay wherewith I pray you let him content him selfe until I furnish him wth a better'.[88]

Library texts could, as Goold's example suggests, be literal rather than figurative booty: in 1596, Paul Thompson, a chaplain of Lord Burghley, wrote to his employer, identifying two recusants who refused to conform and asking to receive the 'benefit of statute provided for such toward the increase of my librarie'.[89] In 1596 the Earl of Essex plundered the Bishop of Faro's library, and the books soon found their way to the Bodleian.[90] Henry Knyvett, involved in military action at Calais, sent his brother two books, including 'a verye good historie tutchinge the state of Rome'. He noted that 'yow may see by the number figured on the backe of the booke, that it had place, in a very faire Librarie. I woulde it had byn my happe to have seene that Librarie before it was spoyled'.[91] Not all books were removed from their original homes in order to be collected, however, and secretaries and

---

[84]   Robert Greene, *Greenes farewell to folly* (London: 1591), sig. C2v.

[85]   Julian Roberts, 'Extending the Frontiers: Scholar Collectors', in Leedham-Green and Webber (eds), *The Cambridge History of Libraries*, p. 306. See also Julian Roberts, 'Importing Books for Oxford, 1500–1640', in James P. Carley and Colin G.C. Tite, *Books and Collectors, 1200–1700: Essays Presented to Andrew Watson* (London: 1997), pp. 317–33.

[86]   The National Archives: SP 12/20 f. 1.

[87]   McKitterick, *The Library of Sir Thomas Knyvett*, p. 10; p. 12; p. 16.

[88]   The National Archives: SP 63/212, f. 73r-v.

[89]   BL Lansdowne Vol. 83, f. 126.

[90]   Roberts, 'Extending the Frontiers', p. 307.

[91]   Norfolk Record Office KNY 743, cited in McKitterick, *The Library of Sir Thomas Knyvett*, p. 16.

scribes copied rare texts for patrons and bibliophiles. In 1603, Henry Savile wrote to Dudley Carleton introducing James Dalrymple, whom he proposed to 'send into Germany and Italy to write out certain books, wch I desire'. Savile noted that 'He hath also in commission certain bookish matters for my Lord of Northumberland', suggesting that Dalrymple collected commissions to copy texts for noble libraries, and that the most 'popular' texts of European religious houses might be those that received the most visitors, and to whom scholars travelled furthest.[92]

Within England, Matthew Parker collected his manuscripts through networks of clients and friends. John Jewel, Bishop of Salisbury, for example, sent Parker the Sherborne copy of King Alfred's translation of the *Pastoral Care* of Pope Gregory the Great, explaining that he had 'ransacked' his cathedral library and this was the only manuscript 'woorthye the findinge'; Stephan Batman claimed to have collected some 6,700 books for the Archbishop.[93] In 1574, Andrew Perne in turn persuaded Parker to donate 100 volumes to Peterhouse College, Cambridge; Sir Nicholas Bacon, Keeper of the Great Seal, gave 94; Robert Horne, Bishop of Winchester, 50; and James Pilkington, Bishop of Durham, 20, whilst other clerical and lay sponsors presented smaller gifts.[94] Thomas Bodley observed that his great collection was made possible only by his first gathering together a 'great store of honourable friends' to further his bibliophilic ambitions, and the prestige of library donations is evidenced by Dudley Carleton's note to John Chamberlain that the building of Bodley's library was 'approued generallie here in the sheere [shire] and euerie man doth bethinck himself how by some good booke or other he may be written in the skrole of the benefactors'.[95] A book might be popular (in the sense of sought after) not as a reading object but as a prestigious gift to secure its donor's reputation as a patron of learning.

Booksellers sold texts second-hand as well as new, and a lively trade in used books developed around Duck Lane and Little Britain. Roger Ward's list of the stock in his Shrewsbury shop includes a number of 'olde' books, including 'i olde booke of Sermons in latin', 'i Olde booke of phisike', 'i Olde psalter in Englishe', and 'i Olde arte of graffinge', raising the question of the relationship between popularity and endurance. Books from before the Elizabethan period persisted in numerous libraries. In 1549, Edward Seymour, Lord Protector of England, required a new library and took away the entire collection of manuscripts previously gathered at the Guildhall. Though many monastic manuscripts were dispersed at the Reformation and sold to booksellers who used them as waste

---

[92] The National Aarchives: SP 12/287, f. 57.

[93] Graham, 'Matthew Parker's Manuscripts', 325. Rivkah Zim, 'Batman, Stephan (c. 1542–1584)', *Oxford Dictionary of National Biography*, Oxford University Press, 2004; online edn, May 2011 [http://www.oxforddnbe.com/view/article/1704, accessed 5 Jan 2012].

[94] Leedham-Green, 'Booksellers and Libraries', p. 6.

[95] Bodley, *The life of Sir Thomas Bodley*, 19; The National Archives: SP 12/266 f. 120.

paper or wrapping material, the flourishing of antiquarianism in the late sixteenth and early seventeenth centuries saw manuscripts become 'increasingly rare and collectible'.[96] In 1574, John Dee bought a manuscript second-hand 'from a stall in London', whilst in 1589 Lord William Howard purchased the text now known as the *Arundel Psalter* from John Proctor's shop on Holborn Bridge.[97]

Some monastic libraries survived as collections: in the early 1580s, Robert Barker, vicar of Driffield, left a library of approximately 150 medieval books which appear to have been inherited with the vicarage and derived from the Cistercian Abbey at Byland, dissolved in 1538.[98] Smaller libraries could also contain books from pre-Reformation collections. Edmund Skelton gifted a Latin Bible and two other books, probably inherited from his time as a monk at Grosmont Abbey, to the parish church of Egton in 1565, while Robert Pursglove donated eight medieval texts, including works by Augustine, Chrysostom, and Aquinas, to the schoolmaster of the Gisburn grammar school in 1572.[99] These inheritances reveal the vexed politics of book collection after the Reformation: whilst the church fathers could be claimed by both Protestants and Catholics, monastic books continued to signal their Romish heritage as well as their venerability. The keen collector and impeccable Protestant William Cecil possessed a number of Roman breviaries, missals, manuals, and Marian offices.[100] Complex rules governed who could or could not own particular books; Protestant scholars and statesmen, for example, might need to know their enemy in order to contest heretical publications.[101]

For those who could not afford to buy the books they wanted, bookshops might themselves possess a library function. In an address to the reader of his printed miscellany, *A helpe to discourse* (1619), William Basse lambasted the 'curious tasters ... that would not though they reade, vouchsafe to buy it', suggesting the tantalizing possibility that some books were widely read even if their popularity did not translate into roaring sales.[102] On the other hand, booming sales did not always equate to reading: in March 1602, John Blount wrote to William Cecil from Hamburg, giving details of a slanderous book criticizing the Queen and informing Cecil that he had bought all but the three copies already sold in

---

[96]　　Clare Sargent, 'The Early Modern Library (to c. 1640)', in Leedham-Green and Webber (eds), *The Cambridge History of Libraries*, p. 63. See also James P. Carley, 'The Dispersal of the Monastic Libraries and the Salvaging of the Spoils', in Leedham-Green and Webber (eds), *The Cambridge History of Libraries*, pp. 265–91.

[97]　　Ovenden, 'The Libraries of the Antiquaries', pp. 538–39.

[98]　　See Claire Cross, 'A Medieval Yorkshire Library', *Northern History* XXV (1989), pp. 281–90.

[99]　　Hunt, 'Clerical and Parish Libraries', pp. 405–6.

[100]　　Selwyn and Selwyn, '"Profession of a Gentleman"', p. 513.

[101]　　See Cyndia Susan Clegg, *Press Censorship in Elizabethan England* (Cambridge: 1997).

[102]　　*A helpe to discourse* (London: 1619), A4r. I thank Lizzie Swann for drawing this verse to my attention.

order to prevent their circulation.[103] Leedham-Green suggests that students were allowed to borrow and return books from bookshops, noting that the Cambridge bookseller Garrett Godfrey supplied books on approval, and suggesting that, for undergraduates at least, a friendly stationer could be a more useful (and – since undergraduates were not allowed in the University Library – more accessible) source for books which passed from student to student, but have left little in the way of evidence, again suggesting that the most 'popular' scholarly books may be those which have disappeared thanks to heavy use, rather than those which remain on library shelves.[104] Even seasoned scholars found booksellers a useful source of texts. In a copyright dispute over William Fulke's *The confutation of the Rhemish testament*, John Bill recalled: 'Doctor Fulke being not sufficiently stored with bookes to performe it cam[e] to London … where he and two of his men with their horses were mayntained by [George] Bishop for 3. quarters of a yeares space and of Bishop he had such bookes for ye making of the treatise as he wanted', a claim which suggests that Bishop's book-trade contacts and personal library offered a greater variety of reading matter than was possessed by the religious controversialist.[105]

Some desperate souls might go even further to get hold of books; the evidence of theft offers a novel means to measure which books were popular and why. In 1569, Thomas Blague told the cautionary tale of a boy who 'stole his Fellowes Booke out of the Schoole', progressed to worse crimes, and was finally hanged.[106] Leedham-Green, suggesting that 'the disappearance of books from libraries arises more probably from interest than from the need for something to kindle the fire or improve the stability of the librarian's desk', notes that the texts stolen from Cambridge University Library included 'Aristotelian commentaries by Alexander Aphrodisiensis, and Ludovicus Buccaferrea, Cardan on dreams, the works of Gilbert Coignet, Eustathius on the Odyssey, Plotinus, Scaliger (on Aristotle's plants) and, probably, the *Exotericae exercitationes* on Cardan, Ptolemy's *Magna constructio*, Henry Stephanus's *Glossarius duo*, and Glareanus's *Dodecachordon*.[107] In 1568, the Earl Marshal Thomas Howard, Duke of Norfolk, drew up a new code of practice for the College of Arms, which housed a library to serve the heralds. Contesting the need to deposit his books in the collection, Robert Glover complained: 'there hath been much cutting out of leaves of sondrey recordes …

---

[103]   The National Archives: SP 12/283a f. 130

[104]   Leedham-Green, 'Booksellers and Libraries', p. 12. Undergraduates in Edinburgh could use the University Library there.

[105]   The National Archives: SP 14/109, 106–7, cited in Edward Arber, *A Transcript of the Registers of the Company of Stationers of London, 1554-1640 A.D.* 4 vols. (London, 1875-94; rpt. New York: Peter Smith, 1950). vol. 3, pp. 39–40.

[106]   *A schole of wise conceytes* (London: 1569), sig. S1r.

[107]   Leedham-Green, 'Booksellers and Libraries', pp. 11–12.

such stealinge away of the bookes and recordes'.[108] When Sir Christopher Heydon was arrested for his part in the Essex rebellion in 1601, the Privy Council noted, 'there is a great library in one of his houses and that the bookes are purloyned', and instructed the High Sherriff of Nottingham 'to have care that none of them be taken away, but kept together and locked up in the study where they are', perhaps as evidence of Heydon's treason, perhaps so that the 'purloining' might be more formally undertaken by agents of the Crown.[109]

Not all illicit acquisitions necessarily indicated the intention to read. In an unusual case in 1615, one bookbinder, Henry Pyke, was accused of stealing books from another, John Drawwater, including 26 grammars worth 24s, 10 'Virgells' worth 10s, 'Castillian's Dialogues' worth 4d, three copies of 'The Practise of Piety' worth 5s, three of 'Sutten on the Sacraments' worth 2s, and two books called 'To learne to live' worth 2s.[110] On 30th May 1593, James Lee, a yeoman, 'burglariously entered' the dwelling house of Lancelot Loveles and stole 'a Lawe Booke' worth 13s, 4d. Presumably Lee did not need the stolen law book to remind him of the option of benefit of clergy (the provision by which men could escape hanging if they could read the 51st Psalm), as he 'read like a clerk' and was duly delivered.[111] In 1561, John Doone stole a horsecloth worth 2 shillings and a Bible worth 13 shillings from the church at Hackney,[112] whilst in 1573 William Burfield stole a woollen cloak worth 10 shillings and 'an English book called a Bible', also worth 10 shillings. Once again, it was by reading a Bible (though presumably not the one he had recently appropriated) that Burfield escaped hanging.[113] As, on the one hand, a hugely profitable and expensive item (worth the same as or more than a woollen cloak), and, on the other, a means to escape the scaffold, the Bible was popular indeed amongst the criminal fraternity of early modern England.

The British booksellers Waterstone's used to offer a carrier-bag featuring Groucho Marx's observation: 'Outside of a dog, a book is a man's best friend.

---

[108] London, Coll. Of Arms, Heralds MS VIII, fol. 194v, cited in Pamela Selwyn, 'Herald's Libraries', in Leedham-Green and Webber (eds), *The Cambridge History of Libraries*, p. 472.

[109] The National Archives, PC 2/26 f. 105.

[110] 'Sessions, 1615: 28 and 29 March', County of Middlesex. Calendar to the sessions records: new series, volume 2: 1614–1615 (1936), pp. 220–256. http://www.british-history.ac.uk/report.aspx?compid=82341&strquery=book. Date accessed: 17 January 2012. The prosecution was undertaken by Dorothy, Drawwater's wife.

[111] 'Middlesex Sessions Rolls: 1593', Middlesex county records: Volume 1: 1550–1603 (1886), pp. 211–19. http://www.british-history.ac.uk/report.aspx?compid=65962&strquery=middlesex sessions rolls book Date accessed: 17 January 2012.

[112] MSR: 1561', Middlesex county records: Volume 1: 1550-1603 (1886), pp. 37-44. http://www.british-history.ac.uk/report.aspx?compid=65930&strquery=middlesex sessions rolls bible Date accessed: 17 January 2012.

[113] MSR: 1573', Middlesex county records: Volume 1: 1550–1603 (1886), pp. 78–85. http://www.british-history.ac.uk/report.aspx?compid=65942&strquery=middlesex sessions rolls bible. Date accessed: 17 January 2012.

Inside of a dog, it is too dark to read'. The conceit that books might both have and be friends is not a new one: Montaigne, for example, included books, and the spaces of his library, as perhaps the most fulfilling companions in his description 'Of three commerces or societies'.[114] In 1595, Anthony Copley commended the wit of 'The Marques of *Santiliana* [who] was a great student, and being on a time merrily reprehended therfore by his illiterate friends, he said: I conuerse better with my books then with you'.[115] Copley also repeated the story, first told by Antonio Guevara, of King Alonso, who claimed to love 'olde wood for fewel; an olde horse for easie riding; wine of a yeare olde; olde friendes, and olde books', a motto that one early modern reader has underlined in the Huntington Library copy.[116] In *Greenes Vision* (1592), the ghost of Gower advises Robert Greene that 'bookes are companions, and friends, and counsailors', materializing the understanding of books as able to converse with, and direct, their readers.[117] If to be popular is to be possessed of friends, then the books of early modern libraries, collected through extended networks, given as gifts, shelved with new acquaintances, and quizzed in the evenings over a glass of 'old wine', were popular indeed.

---

[114] Michel de Montaigne, *The Essayes Or Morall, Politike and Millitarie Discourses*, trans. John Florio (London: Valentine Sims for Edward Blount, 1603), sigs Tt2v-Tt6r.

[115] Anthony Copley, *Wits fittes and fancies* (London: 1595), sig. C3v.

[116] Ibid., B1v; Antonio Guevara, *The familiar epistles* (London: 1575), sig. H8v.

[117] Anon., *Greenes vision* (London: 1592), sig. G4v.

Chapter 4
Shakespeare's Popularity and the Origins of the Canon

Neil Rhodes

On the Make

The Elizabethan writer who was to become the best-selling English author of all time, and a national literary icon, first announced himself in print not in his mother tongue but in Latin:

> Vilia miretur vulgus: mihi flavus Apollo
> Pocula Castalia plena ministret aqua.[1]

> [Let the masses wonder at cheap things: for me, let golden Apollo
> serve full cups straight from the Castalian spring.]

This is the epigraph to *Venus and Adonis*, Shakespeare's first published work, printed in 1593 by fellow Stratfordian Richard Field, who also printed an edition of Ovid the following year. After a few years of acting and playwriting, partly on a collaborative basis, Shakespeare suddenly makes a very different pitch. The theatres are closed by plague, he identifies a glamorous young nobleman as his patron, and he selects an epigraph from Ovid that commits him unequivocally to an elite rather than a popular route to literary fame. A great deal has been written about Shakespeare and Ovid, but not a great deal about the poem from which this epigraph comes and its resonance for Shakespeare.[2] It's the last poem in the first book of the *Amores* and is in complete contrast to what has gone before, much of which offers fairly cynical observations on relationships, seduction techniques, and other erotic matters. Here, Ovid addresses Envy, claiming that literature will outlast the futile achievements of those who pursue conventional worldly success:

---

[1]   William Shakespeare, *Venus and Adonis* (London, 1593), t.p. [My translation]. We cannot be sure that the epigraph was Shakespeare's choice rather than Field's, but if the latter he certainly seems to have been responsive to Shakespeare's aspirations.

[2]   An important exception is *Shakespeare's Poems*, ed. Katherine Duncan-Jones and H.R. Woudhuysen (London: 2007), pp. 10–12.

Mortale est, quod quaeris opus: mihi fama perennis
Quaeritur, in toto semper ut orbe canar[3]

[Your work is mortal: my quest is for undying fame,
to sing throughout the whole world, forever]

He then lists the great writers, both poets and playwrights, whose work lives on, beginning each couplet with a defiant 'vivet'. In the final couplet this morphs into 'vivam', buttressed by colons in Field's edition:

Ergo etiam, cum me supremus adusserit ignis:
Vivam: parsque mei multa superstes erit[4]

[So I too, when the final fires have consumed me, shall live on
and the greater part of me survive my death]

The couplet selected to preface *Venus and Adonis* is not about the end, however (too hubristic), but the means. Shakespeare signals that he will achieve literary immortality not with crowd-pleasing pap, but by drinking from the fountain of the god himself. In his first publication, in fact, Shakespeare presents himself as Jonson was to do: as an exclusive, high-end writer, defying Envy and hugely ambitious.

Those ambitions were fulfilled in terms that more than matched Ovid's own hopes, but not quite in the way Shakespeare intended, at least in 1593. As a result, in authorial terms Shakespeare and Jonson have always been constructed in opposition to each other. In the first place, though it may have been designed to present Shakespeare's credentials as a writer of class, *Venus and Adonis* was wildly popular, going through more editions than any of his plays.[5] Entire print runs seem to have been read to destruction by eager consumers, and in view of the subject matter of the poem, the epigraph's boasting of pure Castalian waters starts to look rather disingenuous. In an era 'before pornography', as Ian Moulton puts it, the erotic narrative poem filled a prominent gap in the market, and comments by Shakespeare scholars on the books being thumbed to destruction add an appropriately physical touch.[6] Nor was this a nine days' wonder: as late as 1606, the jealous husband, Harebrain, in Middleton's play *A Mad World, My Masters* still

---

[3]   P. Ouidii Nasonis [Ovid], *Heroidum epistolae. Amorum, libri III* … (Book 1, Elegy 15) (London: 1594), pp. 96–97.

[4]   Ibid., p. 97.

[5]   There are known to have been at least 16 editions of *Venus and Adonis* before 1640; see William Shakespeare, *The Complete Sonnets and Poems*, ed. Colin Burrow (Oxford: 2002), p. 7.

[6]   Ian Frederick Moulton, *Before Pornography: Erotic Writing in Early Modern England* (Oxford: 2000); on thumbing see Samuel Schoenbaum, *William Shakespeare: A Documentary Life* (Oxford: 1975), p. 131.

thinks of *Venus and Adonis* and *Hero and Leander* as aphrodisiacs: 'two luscious mary-bone pies for a young married wife!' (1.2.48–9), he says indignantly.[7]

Leaving aside the vexed question of how we define pornography, what *Venus and Adonis* immediately establishes is that the concept of the popular, and therefore of 'popularity', can be understood in at least two different ways, then as now: on the one hand it refers to status, both social and literary, and on the other to success in the market for printed books. As far as the first is concerned, the range of association for Ovid's noun 'vulgus' is represented in English by the 'vulgar', the 'common', and the word that he also uses – 'vile' – which is to be understood principally in social terms in the sixteenth century. And though we can readily take the term 'popular' today to denote a literary kind or category, and the level of its appeal as well as the extent of its appeal, we are more likely to forget that in the 1590s (in Katherine Duncan-Jones's words) 'immediate connections were made between social rank and literary achievement'.[8] Quite simply, a gentleman would have been expected to produce a better class of poetry, a point that Shakespeare seems to have been keenly aware of in the earlier part of his writing life. The correlation between literary and social status was eventually worked into the eighteenth-century concept of taste, and while this wasn't available as an aesthetic touchstone in the 1590s, it nonetheless helps to explain something of the paradox of *Venus and Adonis*. The poem has elite pretensions, but its language is unrefined, often gauchely physical. Its erotic effects, which helped to make it so popular in terms of market success, are achieved at the expense of taste, and in that respect it verges on vulgarity – not just in the strict social sense, or in the modern colloquial sense of 'obscene', but in the more specialized aesthetic sense, which is also socially nuanced. There is a similar quality in Keats, now probably the most popular English-language poet between Shakespeare and Seamus Heaney, who also offered a statement of intent, though more plaintive and less self-confident: 'I want to write fine things that cannot be laughed at in any way', but who was still mocked for the self-exposing tactility of his verse. Aristocratic Byron put it most brutally in his remark on 'Johnny Keats's piss-a-bed poetry'.[9]

What these observations really converge on is the discrepancy between a writer's self-definition and his actual literary achievement, which is another way of looking at the dual sense of popularity. They depend, of course, on there being a functional concept of authorship in the early modern period in the first place, a concept that used to be rejected by historicist criticism in favour of a workshop model of literary production in the case of playtexts. Such a model would imply a third and more fundamental sense of the term 'popular' as

---

[7]   Thomas Middleton, *The Collected Works*, ed. Gary Taylor and John Lavagnino (Oxford: 2007), p. 421.

[8]   Katherine Duncan-Jones, *Shakespeare: Upstart Crow to Sweet Swan, 1592–1623* (London: 2011), p. 97.

[9]   *Letters of John Keats, 1814–21*, ed. Hyder Rollins (Cambridge: 1958), II, 174; *Byron's Letters and Journals*, ed. Leslie A. Marchand (London: 1977), VII, p. 200.

something produced *by* the people *for* the people. It would also tend to move the notion of 'popularity' into the well-traversed field of popular culture, which is not particularly helpful for the present discussion.[10] We need instead to consider the different kinds of role, conceived in terms of literary and social status, that a writer might adopt in the late sixteenth century, and then relate these to market success. The revisionist contention that a concept of authorship did indeed exist in this period has gained considerable ground in recent years and has given us a number of authorial Shakespeares: they include Patrick Cheney's 'national poet-playwright', Lukas Erne's 'literary dramatist', and Jeffrey Knapp's 'Shakespeare only' – the last presenting a Shakespeare who paradoxically achieves 'rareness' and 'glory' as a professional dramatist only by embracing commonness.[11] What these studies help to clarify, in different but mostly complementary ways, is the variety of authorial roles available to Shakespeare as he started to define himself as a writer, as well as the varying degrees of status associated with them. Katherine Duncan-Jones's account of the developing perception of Shakespeare among his contemporaries, from Greene/Chettle's 'upstart crow' to Jonson's 'sweet swan of Avon', stands usefully alongside them. The picture that emerges from this work is of Shakespeare's engagement with three interrelated professional roles in the early 1590s – actor, playwright, and poet – and what is significant about these is not just that they follow an upward trajectory in terms of status, but that none of them is ever really abandoned. The aspirations signalled by Shakespeare's first outing as a published author in *Venus and Adonis* end up being fulfilled later in the decade by his taking a more complex, market-facing route to the eternal fame offered so tantalizingly by Ovid's poem.

'Actor', of course, is not an authorial role, and yet it is one that must be central to any discussion of Shakespeare's popularity. The low status of the acting profession in Elizabethan England is well established: although appearing at court as a member of the premier theatre company, Shakespeare did so as a practitioner of the vile arts of the common player, and the taint of the stage is what he seems to be regretting in Sonnet 110 when he writes that he has 'made myself a motley to the view, / Gored mine own thoughts, sold cheap what is most dear'. Exposing yourself to the public gaze in this way, courting publicity, making yourself cheap, all lead to loss of status. This is the cost of popularity. Shakespeare's professional status as an actor permeates his self-definition as an author, a point that surfaces not just in the Sonnets, but also in his plays, especially those of the late 1590s, in figures such as Hal and Hamlet, as we shall see later. There are dramatic precedents

---

[10] The distinction is between 'popularity' in a socio-economic sense and the socio-anthropological category of 'popular culture'; on the latter see the bibliography to *Shakespeare and Elizabethan Popular Culture*, ed. Stuart Gillespie and Neil Rhodes (London: 2006).

[11] See Patrick Cheney, *Shakespeare, National Poet-Playwright* (Cambridge: 2004); Lukas Erne, *Shakespeare as Literary Dramatist* (Cambridge: 2003); Jeffrey Knapp, *Shakespeare Only* (Chicago: 2009), especially pp. xiii; 39.

for the combined roles of author and actor, notably in Kyd's Hieronimo, who is 'Author and actor in this tragedy' (4.4.147).[12] And the roles were viewed as adjacent in other contexts: one of the best-selling Latin works of the sixteenth century (and beyond), the poetic commonplace-book *Polyanthea*, deals with 'actor' and 'author' together, making a distinction between them under the heading 'definitions and etymologies'.[13] The two words are etymologically different, but the Latin spelling 'auctor' for 'author' continued to be used in English into the early seventeenth century.[14] Although we can't really use 'auctor' as a convenient conflation of the two roles, it is important that we add 'actor-author' to 'poet-playwright' and 'literary dramatist' as job descriptors for Shakespeare,[15] especially in the context of his own rather complex attitude towards popularity in every sense of the term.

For the actor, publicity and popularity are achieved via the stage, for the poet and playwright via print, but print only offers publicity to the playwright if his (or, exceptionally, her) name is assigned to the text of the play. We know that Shakespeare's name was first attached to a poem (in 1593), and it was not until 1598 that he was identified as the author of published playtexts, when his name appeared on the title pages of the first surviving quarto of *Love's Labour's Lost*, the second quarto of *Richard III*, and the second and third quartos of *Richard II*.[16] Quite suddenly, two separate publishers – Cuthbert Burby in the case of *Love's Labour's Lost* and Andrew Wise in the case of the histories – decided that Shakespeare's name was a selling point, and from then on his name is advertised in most printed versions of his plays.[17] Between 1598 and the first collected Shakespeare, Thomas Pavier's abortive project of 1619, there were 36 separate editions of plays by Shakespeare, only eight of which failed to identify him as the author; after 1602 only two editions (*Romeo and Juliet* Q3 in 1609 and *Titus Andronicus* Q3 in 1611) appeared anonymously. Shakespeare is first exposed in person as a performer of plays and then, by name, in print. Initially, his print name is that of poet, but five years on he is also named as the author of what the anti-theatrical William Prynne

---

[12] See Thomas Kyd, *The Spanish Tragedy*, ed. Philip Edwards (Manchester, 1977).

[13] Dominicus (Nanus Mirabellius), *Polyanthea nova*, rev. Joseph Lang (Leiden: 1604), p. 113.

[14] Etymologically, however, *auctor* is Latin for 'progenitor' (*augeo* = 'increase'), offering a concept of authorship that is thematically fundamental to the Young Man sonnets, and the sequence as a whole plays with the *auctor*/author and actor/author meanings.

[15] David Schalkwyck describes Shakespeare as an 'actor-poet' in 'What May Words Do? The Performative of Praise in Shakespeare's Sonnets', *Shakespeare Quarterly* 49 (1998): 251–68; see also Cheney, pp. 207–38.

[16] For the bibliographical data on Shakespeare's publications I follow Andrew Murphy's indispensable *Shakespeare in Print: A History and Chronology of Shakespeare Publishing* (Cambridge: 2003).

[17] See David Scott Kastan, *Shakespeare and the Book* (Cambridge: 2001), p. 33.

called 'Quarto-Play-bookes'.[18] The second of the theatre sonnets (111) offers an interesting gloss on this development. Here Shakespeare regrets that fortune has obliged him to earn his keep by 'public means that public manners breeds', adding 'Thence comes it that my name receives a brand'.[19] The brand is a stigma, the stain of the low-status acting profession, but for us, of course, the term has other associations. What Shakespeare sees as a black mark, we read differently as the making of a name, the beginnings of a global brand, and the fulfilment of the Ovidian dream of universal fame.

So far we have considered the issue of 'popularity' in terms of literary and social status. We could translate this into economic terms by presenting it as evidence of where Shakespeare positions himself in the market, bearing in mind that concerns about social status come with a reluctance to be part of any sort of market. But since the present volume is specifically concerned with the business of the printed book, we need also to ask how popular playbooks were in terms of sales and how successful the Shakespeare brand was in particular. Debate on this issue effectively began in 1997 with Peter Blayney's essay 'The Publication of Playbooks', which contended that playbooks were nowhere near being the bestsellers that earlier bibliographers had claimed. This position was challenged by Alan Farmer and Zachary Lesser in 2005, while the subject of Shakespeare's own success in the print market was discussed in 2009 by Lukas Erne, who demonstrated that Shakespeare was very much more popular than other contemporary dramatists in terms of playbooks sold.[20] Although there have been sharp differences of opinion on the popularity of playbooks in general, all parties base their conclusions on bibliometrical evidence and all agree that the key statistic is reprint numbers. Interpreting the numbers, however, has proved more contentious. For example, it is certainly true that from the early days of playbook publication in the 1580s through to the closure of the theatres in 1642, over three times as many sermons were published as plays. Since most of these didn't make it into a second edition, Farmer and Lesser note, reasonably enough, that 'sermons were reprinted much less frequently than were professional plays'. Not so, responds Blayney, since in terms of volume it is 'irrefutably obvious' that they were not less frequently reprinted.[21] But it is equally obvious that any particular sermon was much less likely than a play to be reprinted, which is presumably

---

[18]   William Prynne, *Histrio-Mastix. The Player's Scourge* (London: 1633), EEBO image 13.

[19]   References to Shakespeare are to *The Norton Shakespeare based on the Oxford Edition*, ed. Stephen Greenblatt et al. (New York: 1997).

[20]   See Peter Blayney, 'The Publication of Playbooks', in *A New History of Early English Drama*, ed. John D. Cox and David Scott Kastan (New York: 1997), pp. 383–422; Alan B. Farmer and Zachary Lesser, 'The Popularity of Playbooks Revisited', *Shakespeare Quarterly* 56: 1 (2005): 1–32; Lukas Erne, 'The Popularity of Shakespeare in Print', *Shakespeare Survey* 62 (2009): 12–29.

[21]   Farmer and Lesser, 'The Popularity of Playbooks Revisited', 21; Peter Blayney, 'The Alleged Popularity of Playbooks', *Shakespeare Quarterly* 56 (2005): 33–50; 44.

what Farmer and Lesser meant, and their more general proposal – that we should consider what they call the 'structures of popularity', based on the four criteria of total number of editions, market share, frequency of reprinting, and profitability – is a helpful way of refining our interpretation of bibliometrical evidence.[22]

Farmer and Lesser divide their discussion of the playbook market into six chronological periods, the second of which (1598–1613) represents the boom years. But even then, and on the most generous reading of the evidence, playbook publication never accounts for much more than 4 percent of the total market, and for the period as a whole it is significantly less.[23] It is possible, they suggest, that supply may not have met demand, and it is noticeable that Blayney never really tackles the question of why any publisher would have ventured into the playbook market in the first place if plays were as unpopular as he contends, but it remains the case that in terms of market share the numbers for reprint rates are not that remarkable.[24] What is more remarkable is Shakespeare's own share of the market and the coincidence in the spike of playbook popularity with the second half of his career. Farmer and Lesser note that 'Shakespeare's plays led the development of this market' (from 1598 to 1613), and Erne discusses the statistics for the number of playbooks with named authors, but we might want to connect these two points in relation to the emergence of the Shakespeare brand.[25] It may not be a coincidence that the popularity of playbooks takes off at the point when Shakespeare has emerged as the leading London dramatist and publishers realize that they will sell more copies of a playtext if they advertise it as being 'by William Shakespeare', and declines again when Shakespeare leaves the stage. This does not mean that all the playbook sales of the fat years were driven by authorship, but that the marketing of the Shakespeare brand created the conditions in which a writer of plays might hope to make a name for himself as a published dramatist. That was exactly the intention of Ben Jonson, whose career was effectively launched in 1598 when the Lord Chamberlain's Men staged *Every Man in His Humour*, with Shakespeare taking one of the parts.

For this reason, if we are to examine the concept of popularity in this period in any depth, bibliometrical work on the playbook market needs to be brought into engagement with the parallel critical discussion of the status of the author and what I have called 'self-definition'. The scholar who has done most to engage these two areas of debate has been Lukas Erne, and as Erne admits towards the end of his discussion of Shakespeare's popularity in print, 'there are other ways of judging the popularity of playwrights than the scope of their bibliographical presence'.[26] It is indeed the purpose of the present essay to explore some of those other ways, and in order to do this, one point we should be clear about is the

---

[22] Farmer and Lesser, 'The Popularity of Playbooks Revisited', p. 5 and pp. 206–13.

[23] Ibid., p. 15.

[24] On supply and demand see ibid., p. 12.

[25] Ibid., p. 11; Erne, 'The Popularity of Shakespeare in Print', pp. 26–28.

[26] Erne, 'The Popularity of Shakespeare in Print', p. 25.

peculiar status of the playbook in the first place. It is surely rather odd to judge the success of a play or the popularity of a playwright by the number of copies sold when the play appears in print. Print survives and speech does not, but it is important to remember that Elizabethan England remained a strongly oral culture and that a significant proportion of a theatre audience would have been illiterate. Shakespeare's popularity as actor-author was initially established by the power of the spoken word.

The discrepancy between what we know was printed and what we can only conjecture was performed has fuelled a vast amount of scholarship, especially with regard to Shakespeare, so it is worth bearing in mind, in the context of the Elizabethan bestseller, that almost nobody buys a playtext nowadays (or a film script, for that matter) except for the purposes of academic study. Since an academic market for English drama did not exist in the 1590s, an alternative market had to be created. This is why we see, at first, very few playtexts being published; then books being advertised as representing the text of a play 'as it was performed' by a particular theatre company; and then, as publishers realized that the print medium demanded something different from the oral medium, an increasing emphasis on what *hadn't* been performed on stage.[27] Ben Jonson, carving a name for himself as a published dramatist, offers the best-known examples of this, and Jonson also illustrates another aspect of the difference between the theatre and the print popularity of plays. *Every Man in His Humour* was published in a single quarto edition, yet we know that it was highly successful on stage. In the modern era it was the perfect choice to open the new Swan Theatre at Stratford in 1986 – and I can vouch at first hand that it was extremely funny – but much of the life of the play dies on the page. Its antitheatrical opposite, *Every Man out of His Humour*, on the other hand, went through three editions in a single year (1600), so in terms of speed of reprints it was a tearaway bestseller. But the text we have could hardly be less suited to theatrical performance, and even The Swan thought that it would have more luck reviving the notoriously unpopular *Sejanus* than *Every Man Out*.

Assessing 'popularity' in the early modern period, then, also requires us to link the role of the author to the media through which that role is performed, and this is another reason why popularity in sense 2 (market success) needs to be seen in conjunction with popularity in sense 1 (literary and social status). The roles of actor, playwright, and poet carry varying degrees of status, but that status is also associated with different media. In the case of poetry those media should include manuscript circulation. Though *Venus and Adonis* gave Shakespeare a print popularity unmatched by any of his plays, the Sonnets circulated 'among his private friends' according to Francis Meres (unpopular in sense 1) before being published in a single edition in 1609 (unpopular in sense 2). In print terms, Shakespeare's career as a poet rather tails off, even as it continues in manuscript. Nonetheless, the Sonnets also give us a clue as to how Shakespeare managed to be

---

[27]   See for example Jonson's preface to *Sejanus* (1605); see Ben Jonson, *Sejanus His Fall*, ed. Philip J. Ayres (Manchester: 1990), p. 52.

successful in the market in ways that Jonson did not. In the lines where he laments the branding of his name in Sonnet 111, he continues:

> And almost thence my nature is subdued
> To what it works in, like the dyer's hand.

What that last, famous phrase points to is Shakespeare's willingness to adapt to and (in the metaphor he chooses) immerse himself in the medium. The Shakespeare brand – what made him popular – was adaptability, versatility.[28] To extend the metaphor and return to Keats, he is the 'chameleon poet', taking on the colour of the different media he works in. What I want to do in the remainder of this chapter is to explore the relationship between Shakespeare's popularity in his own time and the emergence of his canonical status. I want to look first at the concept of popularity in some social contexts and extend the measure of literary success beyond book sales; then ask which of his plays were most popular, and why; and finally examine the literary status of the first folio.

Ranking and Sorting

Whether or not we use the evidence of book sales to demonstrate an author's popularity, the concept of popularity itself is inescapably a social one. This is why we should not try to disengage the statistics of market performance from questions of status: the perceived status of the author and the aspirations implied in the author's choice of literary kind. In modern terminology, we would be talking here about niche markets, though niche markets correlated quite closely with social class. But 'status' is a modern term, of course, eliding social class with market value, and even 'class' itself is a little anachronistic before the 1590s, since it depends upon the perception of there being a large, 'middling sort' of people with an identifiable set of manners and tastes, which was only just emerging in Shakespeare's lifetime.[29] The term that does work for both the sixteenth and twenty-first centuries is rank. In the earlier period it reflects the fixed social order, known in the middle ages as 'estate' or 'degree' and reconfigured in the sixteenth century in the ranked divisions of nobility and commonalty.[30] In our own day, rank (or ranking) is not fixed but volatile, determined by the competitive processes of late capitalism in which everything is constructed as product. We need to find a

---

[28] On Shakespeare as 'Do-all' see Knapp, pp. 90–95.

[29] See Jonathan Barry and Christopher Brooks, eds, *The Middling Sort of People: Culture, Society and Politics in England, 1550–1800* (Basingstoke: 1994), pp. 1–27.

[30] See Keith Wrightson, 'Estates, Degrees, and Sorts: Changing Perceptions of Society in Tudor and Stuart England', in *Language, History and Class*, ed. P.J. Corfield (Oxford: 1991), p. 48. 'Rank' was the subject of a remarkable exhibition at the Northern Gallery for Contemporary Art, Sunderland, in 2009; see the catalogue, *Rank: Picturing the Social Order, 1516–2009* (Sunderland Art Editions North: 2009).

way of positioning the related questions of Shakespeare's popularity and canon formation somewhere between these two versions of 'rank'.

To begin, we might ask where exactly we would rank Shakespeare the individual in social terms. The two guides to the social make-up of Elizabethan England most commonly referred to are William Harrison's *Description of England* (1577) and Sir Thomas Smith's *De Republica Anglorum* (1583). (The dates of publication are slightly misleading: Smith's book was written in 1562–1565 and he seems to have plagiarized an early manuscript of Harrison's.)[31] Both Harrison and Smith identify a two-tier rank of nobility, with the second tier dropping down to 'esquires' and 'mere gentlemen'; next come citizens and burgesses, then yeomen (in the country), and finally, to use Smith's terms, a rank comprising 'day labourers, poore husbandmen, yea marchantes or retailers which have no free lande, copiholders, all artificers, as Taylers, Shoomakers, Carpenters, Brickemakers, Bricklayers, Masons &c.'.[32] Although this list of the lowest ranks goes in reverse social order, there would seem to be no doubt that Shakespeare belongs to it as the son of an artificer (glover and leather-dresser), as do Marlowe (son of a shoemaker) and Jonson (stepson of a bricklayer). However, Smith has earlier contrasted England, where 'we ... divide our men commonly into foure sortes', with ancient Greece and Rome and contemporary France, which have simple, binary divisions between patrician and plebeian, nobility and populace. In England, Smith says, there are 'gentlemen, citizens or burgesses, yeomen artificers, and laborers'.[33] Since John Shakespeare was a man of substance and a voice in the community, he would presumably have qualified as a 'yeoman artificer' and enjoyed a rather higher social rank than the one implied by Smith's later division.

Both the dates of composition for Harrison and Smith's work, and Smith's apparent contradictoriness, are significant. These surveys were written before or at the time of Shakespeare's birth, and during his lifetime he would have witnessed, and participated in, profound social and economic change. This is evident from two sources from the end of Elizabeth's reign, Thomas Wilson's account of the state of England in 1600 (unpublished at the time) and the various editions of John Stow's *Survey of London*. Wilson provides a good deal of social and economic data and focusses particularly on economic change and its social effects. One of the most interesting passages is his description of how, earlier in the century, yeomen had profited from the need of the nobility to turn their lands into cash and obtained long leaseholds from them, which, in the present day, are being squandered by their offspring in a reverse process of economic transfer:

> my yonge masters the sonnes of such, not contented with their
> states of their fathers to be counted yeoman and called John or

---

[31]   Thomas Smith, *De Republica Anglorum*, ed. Mary Dewar (Cambridge: 1982), pp. 157–62.

[32]   Ibid., p. 76.

[33]   Ibid., p. 65.

Robert (such an one), but must skipp into his velvett breches and
silken dublett and, getting to be admitted into some Inn of Court
or Chancery, must ever after thinke skorne to be called any other
then gentleman.[34]

What we see in Shakespeare is a similar project of self-improvement based on
migration from the country to the city, but at a lower point on the social scale and
without the money for fine clothes or a period of residence in the law schools.
And what we can see more generally is an instability at either end of the scale,
at the boundaries between the richer yeoman and the gentleman and between the
'yeoman artificer' and the labouring artificer. This was intensified by the influx
to London, which acted as an ever-expanding social melting pot. Describing this
new metropolis two years earlier, John Stow noted that, considered as a whole, its
inhabitants were

> a mixture of all countries of the [commons of this Realme], by bloud
> Gentlemen, Yeomen, and of the basest sort, without distinction:
> and by profession busie Bees, and travellers for their living in the
> Hive of this common welth, but specially considered, they consist
> of these three partes, – Marchantes, Handicrafts men, and Labourers.[35]

It comes as a surprise here, in a London context, to see that the rank of citizen has
disappeared. What Stow seems to have recognized is the beginnings of a three-
class system with a large middle, concluding 'that they bee a greate multitude, and
that yet the greatest part of them bee neyther too rich no[r] too poore, but doe live
in the mediocritie'.[36] Shakespeare aspired to the rank of gentleman from the low-
ish family background of a provincial artificer; but what he ultimately achieved
was middle-classness.[37]

As the social make-up of England was reconfigured by economic change, so
a more nuanced language of class developed to take account of its new divisions
and distinctions. As Keith Wrightson has argued, this is captured in the term
'sorts', first used extensively by William Harrison and increasingly common in
social commentary in the late sixteenth and early seventeenth centuries. Wrightson
suggests that the expression 'the better sort', for example, developed in order to
express an identity of interest between gentlemen and the higher ranks of the
commonalty.[38] Shakespeare himself uses the term quite frequently, often in a way
that is synonymous with the modern term 'status', as in *Much Ado*:

---

[34]   Thomas Wilson, 'The State of England, Anno Dom. 1600', ed. F.J. Fisher, in
Camden Miscellany 16 (London, 1936), p. 19.

[35]   John Stow, *A Survey of London* (London: 1598), p. 479.

[36]   Stow, p. 480; cited by Wrightson (from 1603), p. 49.

[37]   See especially Theodore B. Leinwand, 'Shakespeare and the Middling Sort',
Shakespeare Quarterly 44 (1993): 284–303.

[38]   Wrightson, 48. See also Wrightson in Barry and Brooks (1994), pp. 28–51.

LEONATO: How many gentlemen have you lost in this action?

MESSENGER: But few of any sort, and none of name.   (I, i, 5–6)

Here, 'sort' means untitled, high status, as distinct from those of titled rank. Elsewhere, Shakespeare uses it more neutrally, as in 'Talk like the vulgar sort of market men' (*1 Henry VI* III, ii, 4), which echoes Ovid's '*vulgus*', or 'Men of all sorts take a pride to gird at me' (*2 Henry IV* I, ii, 7). But what is particularly significant about the language of 'sorts' is that it has the flexibility to cross over from social rank to other kinds of classification. Shakespeare uses it in this way too: 'It is common for the younger sort / To lack discretion', Polonius observes in *Hamlet* (II, i, 116). And Gabriel Harvey may have been unconsciously echoing Polonius when he wrote in the margin of his copy of Chaucer:

> The younger sort takes much delight in Shakespeares Venus, &
> Adonis: but his Lucrece, & his tragedie of Hamlet, Prince of
> Denmarke, have it in them, to please the wiser sort. Or such poets:
> or better: or none.
>   Vilia miretur vulgus: mihi flavus Apollo
>   Pocula Castaliae plena ministret aquae:
> quoth Sir Edward Dier, betwene iest, & earnest.[39]

Harvey may also have been unconscious of the fact that he was echoing the epigraph that Shakespeare used to signal his own ambitions at the start of *Venus and Adonis*, though Shakespeare himself would presumably have been happy enough to be associated with Sir Edward Dyer, as well as to be praised by a Cambridge academic for a stage play. That there was a perceived correlation between social and literary status in the Elizabethan era is not difficult to establish. What we have with the language of 'sorts' is something slightly different – something that hints at modern socio-economic categories of consumer and identifies these with certain kinds of literary taste.

Harvey's use of the language of 'sorts' to make a literary judgement is an early indication of how rank would evolve into ranking. Another example, which combines ranking and sorting, though without using the terms, is Webster's vignette of contemporary dramatists in *The White Divel* (1612):

> For mine owne part I have ever truly cherist my good opinion of other
> mens worthy Labours, especially of that full and heightned stile of
> Maister Chapman. The labor'd and understanding workes of Maister
> Iohnson: The no lesse worthy composures of the both worthily
> excellent Maister Beamont, & Maister Fletcher: And lastly (without
> wrong last to be named) the right happy and copious industry of M.
> Shake-speare, M. Decker, & M. Heywood.[40]

---

[39]   *Gabriel Harvey's Marginalia*, ed. G.C. Moore Smith (Stratford-upon-Avon: 1913), p. 232.

[40]   John Webster, *The White Divel* (London: 1612), sig. A2v.

This was published as Shakespeare was preparing to bow out from professional life, and it is surprising to see his lowly ranking even at this late stage. Harvey's earlier observation, though, since it was written in his copy of Chaucer, is also concerned with the status of vernacular literature, and in this respect it was not just Shakespeare who needed to prove his worth in the 1590s, but English itself. The first three books of *The Faerie Queene* had only been published in 1590, there were few playbooks on the market, and university-educated writers such as Nashe could mock down-market 'English Seneca', with its cheesy commonplaces such as 'Blood is a begger'.[41] Although the debate over the 'adequacy' of English as a literary language had been settled, there was still only hesitant acknowledgement of an emerging national literary canon.

Towards the end of the decade this suddenly changed: a spate of books appeared that staked out the claims of English to literary value by anthologizing extracts from a range of contemporary authors, including (quite prominently) Shakespeare.[42] The first was Nicholas Ling's *Politeuphuia, Wit's Commonwealth* (1597), which was followed by Francis Meres's *Palladis Tamia, or Wit's Treasury* (1598) and two further offerings in the 'Wits' series, Robert Allott's *Wits Theater of the Little World* (1599) and William Wrednot's *Palladis Palatium: Wisdom's Palace. Or the fourth part of wits commonwealth* (1604). Meres's book is much the most famous of these and is frequently cited for its ranking of English poets alongside their classical counterparts, but three other publications were at least as significant in their attempts to establish something like a canon of English literature for the first time. These are John Bodenham's *Belvedere*, Allott's *England's Parnassus*, and Ling's *England's Helicon*, all published in 1600.[43] The last is a poetical miscellany, but the other two are essentially commonplace books, though constructed in different ways. Allott's is a collection of passages taken mainly from non-dramatic poetry, arranged under thematic headings and with attribution to the authors; Bodenham, on the other hand, offers one- or two-line extracts unassigned to author or topic, and runs them together in an enormous literary collage. He also shows considerably more interest in contemporary drama than Allott. The two books are more modestly sized, vernacular versions of the

---

[41] *The Works of Thomas Nashe*, ed. R.B. McKerrow, rev. F.P. Wilson (Oxford: 1958), vol. 3, p. 315.

[42] For commonplacing and the collections made by Ling, Bodenham, and Allott, I draw upon my chapter 'Commonplace Shakespeare' in *Shakespeare and the Origins of English* (Oxford: 2004), pp. 149–88. See also Lukas Erne, *Shakespeare as Literary Dramatist* (Cambridge: 2003), pp. 71–75, whose work appeared too late for me to take account of at the time, and Zachary Lesser and Peter Stallybrass, 'The First Literary *Hamlet* and the Commonplacing of Professional Plays', *Shakespeare Quarterly* 59 (2008): 371-420.

[43] I give the 'authors' of these works as they appear in ESTC. However, the material for Ling (1597), Meres (1598), Allott (1599), and *Englands Helicon* seems to have been collected by Bodenham and then edited by the professional writers. *Belvedere*, on the other hand, is attributed to Bodenham, though edited by Anthony Munday; see Charles Crawford, '*Belvedere*, or *The Garden of the Muses*', *Englische Studien* 43 (1911): 198–228.

voluminous Latin commonplace books, *Polyanthea* and *Poetarum flores*, which had been ransacked for schoolboy compositions for decades, and they were pitched at a rather different audience from the one for those much-used Latin tomes.[44] Their project of valorizing English literature has an eye on the middle-class market, as we can now start to call it. It coincides with other books with a similar target, such as Anthony Munday's popular rhetorical collection, *The Orator* (1596), and with the founding of Gresham College (1597), which provided educational facilities for the rapidly expanding 'mediocrity'. It also coincides with the rise of Shakespeare to the status of premier English playwright.

So what can these books tell us about Shakespeare's popularity and about his presence in the newly emerging literary canon? *England's Parnassus* contains 97 extracts attributed to Shakespeare (including an unpublished sonnet), eight of which are actually from other writers: four from Spenser, two from *The Mirror for Magistrates*, and one each from William Warner and Gervase Markham. The majority of the Shakespeare passages are from poetry, but they also include 30 extracts from five plays (23 plays are represented in the volume as a whole). If we rank the authors in *England's Parnassus* by the number of passages selected from each of them, then Shakespeare comes sixth out of 60–70 named authors, after Spenser, Drayton, Daniel, Warner, and Lodge.[45] As a writer who is primarily a playwright, he comes first. It is more difficult to produce numbers for *Belvedere*, because Bodenham does not assign authors to extracts, but most of them were identified 100 years ago by Charles Crawford, who presented an interleaved copy of his edition of the work, listing all the attributions he could make, to R.B. McKerrow.[46] Crawford's statistics for *Belvedere* show that Shakespeare ranks first overall with 236 extracts (213 excluding *Edward III*) – though Drayton has a large number of single lines – followed by Daniel (208) and Spenser (186).[47] As a poet, Shakespeare is represented by *Lucrece* (91) and *Venus and Adonis* (34). As a playwright, however, he ranks first with 111 entries (88 excluding *Edward III*) represented as follows: *Richard II* (47), *Edward III* (23), *Richard III* (13), *Romeo and Juliet* (12), *3 Henry VI* (10), *Love's Labour's Lost* (5), *1 Henry IV* (1). Perhaps the key point to make about statistics drawn from these anthologies is that they link popularity to status, since presence in a commonplace book implies literary value. In addition to demonstrating Shakespeare's high overall status as a literary

---

[44] See Ottaviano Mirandula, *Illustrium poearum flores* (Strasbourg: Wendelin Rihel, 1538, and many subsequent editions); for the *Polyanthea* see note 12.

[45] See *England's Parnassus: or the choysest Flowers of our Modern Poets* (London, 1600); also *England's Parnassus*, ed. Charles Crawford (Oxford: 1913). (There are problems in identifying the exact number of named authors, and Harington's Ariosto is also strongly represented.)

[46] [Anthony Munday], *Bodenham's Belvedere, or The Garden of the Muses* (Manchester: 1875). BL shelfmark c.116.e.14.

[47] See Charles Crawford, 'Appendix D' in *The Shakespeare Allusion-Book*, ed. C.M. Ingleby, L. Toulmin Smith, and F.J. Furnivall, rev. J. Munro (London: 1932), vol. 2, pp. 498–518.

author, they show that as a poet and a 'name' he is comparable even with Spenser, since in *England's Parnassus* he has passages from *The Faerie Queene* attributed to him, and above all they show Shakespeare's uniquely high status as a poet-playwright, as Patrick Cheney has designated him. In that respect his role in these early constructions of a canon of English literature is absolutely central.

When we focus specifically on *Belvedere*, however, interesting things also emerge about rank, ranking, and sorting. Although the extracts in Bodenham's collection are unattributed, he does in fact begin with a list of authors whom he ranks in terms of social position. Elizabeth comes first, followed by James (still of Scotland only), and then by an earl (Surrey), a marquess (Winchester), and a countess (Pembroke), who are in turn followed by knights (Raleigh, Dyer, Harington). In the bottom tier, where the professional writers reside, small social distinctions are preserved, so Constable appears as 'Henry Constable Esquier'.[48] But the body of the text then dispenses with hierarchy as the quotations are stripped of their names and sorted into their 'common' places ('Here are great store of them digested into their meete places')[49]. What we get here is an extreme process of literary democratization in which all traces of distinction, individuality, and provenance are removed. Even the quotations themselves are malleable: entries from Ling's *Politeuphuia* resurface in altered form; bits of Shakespeare appear in ways not found in any other surviving editions. Traditionally, the commonplace book might be thought of in elite terms, given its function of preserving choice nuggets of text for ornamenting discourse; but the procedure of *Belvedere* exposes the paradox inherent in every commonplace book, which is that its material is by definition *common*, in every sense of the term.[50] What Bodenham produced, in fact, was not so much a rhetorical fashion-accessory for gentlemen as a *Readers' Digest* for the middle classes. And we might also see the levelling processes at work in this rather common commonplace book as a counterpart in the print era to those of the common stage, which is one reason, perhaps, why it was so receptive to material from contemporary vernacular drama.

The English anthologies of the late 1590s (not all of them commonplace books) are revealing because they link the business of canon formation to both rank and ranking. They offer a way of understanding 'popularity', not just in terms of book sales but in relation to social and literary status. At the same time, these texts are themselves part of a process of popularization (vernacularization, making common) that reflects a radical shift in the way English society was being configured at the turn of the seventeenth century. That shift is most pronounced

---

[48]   John Bodenham, *Bel-vedére or the garden of the muses* (London: 1600), sigs. A4r–A5r; see also Mary T. Crane, *Framing Authority: Sayings, Self, and Society in Sixteenth-Century England* (Princeton: 1993), pp. 183–85.

[49]   Bodenham, *Bel-vedere*, sig. A4v.

[50]   We should perhaps note a further ambivalence in the 'elite' role of the commonplace book, since it was used both by gentlemen and by those who saw it as a vehicle for achieving gentlemanly status.

in the city where Shakespeare made his living, as Stow records in his account of the expansion of the 'mediocrity', and the emergence of a national literary canon which included playtexts from the London theatres and miscellaneous gatherings from contemporary English authors is certainly a response to that emerging market. Shakespeare's own popularity is linked to that emerging market, not because he identifies a stable middle ground of taste, but on account of his fluidity – his extraordinary adaptability in terms of professional role and social rank. Alternating between the roles of actor, playwright, and poet, he also manages to occupy at various times and in various ways all of the four social ranks identified by Harrison and Smith.[51] That fluidity and adaptability is perfectly encapsulated in the forum of the theatre itself, and to see how these qualities translate into 'popularity' we need to return to that medium and to certain key plays from the end of the 1590s.

Trading Up and Dumbing Down

The English anthologies of the late 1590s give Shakespeare extensive representation as a poet, but their publication also coincides with his emergence as the named author of playtexts and with the take-off in the popularity of plays as a section of the book market as a whole. From 1598 the Shakespeare brand is increasingly associated with stage plays, not just with narrative poems, though the latter continue to outperform the plays in terms of book sales. And while Shakespeare clearly has competitors as a poet in terms of status, as a print dramatist he now starts to leave the rest of the field behind. By the time the theatres close in 1642, editions of playtexts by Shakespeare outnumber those of his nearest rival by nearly three to one.[52] But since we are particularly concerned here with the relationship between popularity and canonization, we need to focus on the shorter period up to the publication of the first folio.

So which were Shakespeare's most popular plays in print before 1623? First are *1 Henry IV* and *Richard III* (six editions), followed by *Richard II* (five editions) and then *Romeo and Juliet* (four editions). But while it is easy enough to establish the popularity of playtexts on the basis of reprint statistics, it is much more difficult to explain why particular plays were more popular than others. The obvious point about the group just identified is that three of the four are histories, and it is worth noting that the popularity of history is not specific to the theatre. The most successful of Drayton's books of verse, for example, was *England's Heroical Epistles*, which went through six editions from 1597 to 1602, while Daniel's *The First Four Books of the Civil Wars* managed to achieve three editions from 1594 to 1609. And if we put the reprint rankings for Shakespeare's plays alongside their ranking for entries in *Belvedere*, we find not only a correlation between the

---

[51] On the possibility that Shakespeare may have aspired to a knighthood see Duncan-Jones, *Upstart Crow*, pp. 120–28.

[52] Erne, 'The Popularity of Shakespeare in Print', p. 20.

two kinds of list, with *Richard II* coming first, then *Edward III*, *Richard III*, and *Romeo and Juliet*, but also between poetry and history: history is popular in itself, but especially when constructed from rhetorical sound bites and passages of lyric eloquence which can be extracted for commonplacing and anthologization. There is one notable exception. *Edward III* is only partially by Shakespeare, and *Romeo and Juliet* is not a history, of course, but the most interesting discrepancy between the two lists is in the position of *1 Henry IV*, top of one and bottom of the other.

On the basis of its success in both the theatre and the book market, *1 Henry IV* was Shakespeare's most popular play. Nine editions appeared to 1640, when it was still pulling in theatre audiences, as Leonard Digges records in his *Poems* published that year: 'let but *Falstaffe* come, / Hall, Peines [Hal, Poins], the rest you scarce shall have a roome / All is so pester'd'.[53] So why was *1 Henry IV* so popular? Here we can only speculate, but it is clear that what Shakespeare produced in this play was neither the heroic history of the *Henry VI* plays (see Nashe on Talbot); nor the poeticized tragic history of *Richard II*; nor the melodrama and skulduggery of *Richard III*; nor the historical romance (history plus love interest) of *Edward III* and Drayton's *Heroical Epistles*; but history blended with contemporary social realism, and history elided not with tragedy but with comedy. What we get in *1 Henry IV* is popularized history, history made common through a set of remarkable 'characters', as Digges suggests, in which distinctions of rank are collapsed not just in social but also in generic terms. It is as though Shakespeare had looked at Sidney's injunction not to mingle kings and clowns and then tossed it straight in the bin. The play offers the appeal of history as shared national memory combined with the familiarity of the here and now in a formula that was perfectly designed to entertain that greatly expanded 'middling sort' among the London populace. It works because it manages to balance the edginess of its sense of social volatility with the reassuring distance of historical perspective in a way that would have been likely to have greater appeal to the broad 'middling' spectrum of taste than would the more narrowly targeted humours plays of Chapman and Jonson.

Over the centuries, fantasies of social transformation have had an enduring appeal for consumers of fiction across various media. This is typically the lush terrain of romance, but it is also something that is written into the playing conditions of the early modern English theatre. We are so sensitized to the implications of cross-dressing for our reading of gender in this theatre that we may sometimes forget that dress codes also operated with regard to social rank. During Elizabeth's reign there were various attempts to reinforce the 1554 Act of Apparel, which stipulated what certain ranks could or could not wear, but the social flux outlined by Wilson and Stow meant that these became increasingly unworkable in practice. Elizabeth herself was concerned that the flouting of the sumptuary laws was responsible for 'a pestilent canker of the commonwealth, the confusion of all degrees', but the Proclamation of 1597, published while *1*

---

[53]   Leonard Digges, 'Upon Master William Shakespeare', in *Poems: written by Wil. Shakespeare. Gent.* (London: 1640), p. 4.

Henry IV was on the stage, conceded that despite the best efforts of the authorities, 'no reformation at all hath followed', and the laws were eventually repealed in 1604.[54] The most vivid travesty of these regulations was provided, of course, by the theatre, where common players daily put on the silks and velvet breeches of the nobility or pretended to be kings. The fact that the players were often wearing clothes sold on to them by young gallants, who might themselves have traded up from yeoman status, as Wilson describes, simply underlines the ways in which the theatre provided an intense microcosm of late sixteenth-century social mobility and rank-shifting. The aspirational appeal of the stage, and its power to stimulate that through the process of re-clothing, is something that Marlowe immediately recognizes, as Tamburlaine signals his upward social mobility by discarding his lowly 'shepherd's weeds' at the start of the play. But in *1 Henry IV* Shakespeare's characters move in the opposite direction. There we see a prince and a knight slumming in taverns with a motley crew of indeterminate rank. What we have, in fact, is the class version of the gender conundrum: not boys pretending to be girls pretending to be boys, but base pretending to be noble pretending to be base.

The significance of all this takes us to the meaning of the term 'popularity' itself in Elizabethan England and in Shakespeare in particular. 'Popular' appears six times in his plays (four times in *Coriolanus*, once in *Henry V*, and once in *The Tempest*), while 'popularity' appears twice in *1 Henry IV* and once in *Henry V*. In *Coriolanus* the 'popular man' (II, iii, 92) refers to someone who curries favour with the common people and is meant contemptuously; in *As You Like It*, on the other hand, the fact that Orlando is loved by the common people is a sign of virtue (I, ii, 142–44), while in *Hamlet* both Laertes and Hamlet himself are said to be popular in this sense (IV, iii, 4–5; IV, v, 98–104). But the more approving instances of popularity avoid using the term itself, which almost always carried negative associations, either (in adjectival form) of low rank, as in Pistol's challenge to the disguised Henry in *Henry V* ('Or art thou base, common and popular'), or (in noun form) as a potentially subversive wooing of the lower classes in which crowd-pleasing shades into rabble-rousing. James Shapiro has written extremely well on the development of this political sense of 'popularity' in the 1590s.[55] In *1 Henry IV*, though, it can also refer to inappropriately self-demeaning behaviour on the part of the monarch himself. This is how Bolingbroke uses the term when he warns Hal of the dangers of courting public opinion by citing the example of his predecessor, Richard II, who

---

[54] See N.B. Harte, 'State Control of Dress and Social Change', in *Trade, Government and Economy in Pre-Industrial England*, ed. D.C. Coleman and A.H. John (London: 1976), pp. 145–48. On clothing in the theatre see Ann Rosalind Jones and Peter Stallybrass, *Renaissance Clothing and the Materials of Memory* (Cambridge: 2000), especially pp. 175–206.

[55] See James Shapiro, *1599: A Year in the Life of William Shakespeare* (London: 2005), pp. 144–45; also the excellent analysis of Bolingbroke's speech by Jeffrey S. Doty in 'Shakespeare's Richard II, "Popularity", and the Early Modern Public Sphere', *Shakespeare Quarterly* 61 (2010): 183–205.

Grew a companion to the common streets,
Enfeoffed himself to popularity,
That, being daily swallowed by men's eyes,
They surfeited with honey and began
To loathe the taste of sweetness.   (III, ii,.68–72)

Written into Shakespeare's most popular play in print is a critique of popularity itself, a sense of popularity as stigma: 'making an exhibition of yourself' is the modern expression. It is central in the first of the sonnets that expose his feelings about the vulgarity of the acting profession and the branding of his name ('Alas, 'tis true, I have gone here and there / And made myself a motley to the view'), as we saw earlier. Part of the brilliance of *1 Henry IV* lies in Shakespeare's ability to have it both ways. He creates a world that glamorizes the demotic, feeding the social aspirations of the 'mediocrity' with the sense that the nobility is 'just like us', but keeps in reserve a disdainful rejection of the very popularity that helped to make it a print bestseller in the first place.

What Shakespeare seems to be doing in the plays of the late 1590s is projecting a conflict of feelings about his growing popularity onto his characters, where the anxiety is both enacted and palliated by appearing in princely form. The most striking example of this is *Hamlet*. In one sense *Hamlet* is unpopular, aiming to 'please the wiser sort', as Harvey noted, and it was claimed by its publisher, Nicholas Ling, to have been acted 'in the two Universities of Cambridge and Oxford', which, if true, would have been unprecedented for a play from the common stage. But it was not unpopular in terms of its success as a playbook, going through five editions (in different forms) to 1637. While *Hamlet* does not refer specifically to the 'popular' and to 'popularity', it is certainly much preoccupied with commonness and, indeed, with the status of commonplaces. We know from Nashe that one of the features of the original *Hamlet* was its fondness for dumbed-down Senecanism in the form of trite commonplaces, and it is clear that in his own *Hamlet* Shakespeare wanted to be creative in his commonplacing, distinguishing between the common commonplaces of Gertude and Polonius and what we might call the rare observations of Hamlet himself. In her first words to Hamlet, Gertrude delivers the stalest of all commonplaces, that death is common – 'all that lives must die' – which triggers Hamlet's assault on commonness and the commonplace. More empty parental advice is served up in the following scene as Laertes is treated to a slurry of clichés from his busy, shallow father, and *this* son copies his parent when he addresses Ophelia in similar fashion. In both of the early printed versions of the play the speeches of these last two characters are identified as 'sentences' by quote marks, which Zachary Lesser and Peter Stallybrass see as evidence that printed playtexts were starting to be seen as 'literature'; but they also argue that the commonplacing strategy in *Hamlet* is not authorial.[56] It is certainly important to remember that the typographical features of a printed text may not be authorial, but we don't need these markers to recognize creative uses

---

[56]   Lesser and Stallybrass, 'The First Literary *Hamlet*', especially p. 414.

of commonplacing. Besides, it seems rather odd to assert the literary status of professional drama at the same time as denying the author agency in the features that are claimed to define it as literary. It is surely wrong to do so in the case of *Hamlet*, where Shakespeare's perception of the commonplace has shifted towards the modern sense of the term. Hamlet's own extended, searching reflections, though not free of commonplaces in the older sense, are meant to be distinguished both from the stilted sentences of the *Ur-Hamlet* and the banalities of Gertrude, Polonius, and Laertes. What gives them their elite literary status is that they are *not* commonplaces, which is why they are not marked as such in the printed texts.[57]

1 Henry IV and *Hamlet* are both plays that explore the risks of popularity and commonness while achieving popularity themselves in the book market – in the case of *Hamlet*, a 'popularity' somewhat more limited, perhaps, to 'the wiser sort' who could appreciate Hamlet's discriminating attitude towards the commonplace. For modern audiences and readers, they are also both indisputably canonical plays. But their success lies in qualities other than the stock of quotable assets that ensured the more conventional histories and the narrative poems prominence in the English anthologies. In one respect these plays are opposites: the first has the demotic appeal of a sense of community forged through shared national memory in a popularized version of history; the second does the opposite, appealing to the individual's sense that he or she is different, set apart, drinking only from Ovid's Castalian spring. Yet both plays have actors as their central characters and stage unstable relationships between elite and common, nobility and clownishness. In *1 Henry IV* Shakespeare writes about what he really is and what he chooses to be; in *Hamlet* he writes about what he would like to be and what he is forced to do. Between them, the two plays represent the summit of Shakespeare's popularity and the moment of his canonization, but worked into the paradox of Shakespeare's own predicament: that while his career represents a determined attempt at social advancement, the route by which he has chosen to achieve that necessarily impedes its progress.

Canonizing the Popular

Shakespeare's writing life is underscored by a narrative about popularity and its attendant anxieties. The narrative is complex because it traces an interplay between the material and the social and between different and sometimes conflicting interpretations of rank and status, which involve literary genre, the media, and choice of professional role. This narrative is further complicated by its being coupled to a process of canon formation. Even if we did decide that 'popularity' was simply a matter of how an author fared in the league table of book sales, the notion of canonicity would necessarily bring other kinds of status into the equation. The complexity of the narrative is an indication of just how transformational the period of Shakespeare's writing life was, both for the literary

---

[57]   Another creative use of commonplacing is *Othello* I, iii, 198–219; this time it is the parent (Brabantio) who rejects 'sentences'.

profession and for the fabric of English society more generally, and one thing that was certainly transformed over this period was the status of the playtext itself. For Shakespeare, the end product of this sea change was the first folio.

The book that made him popular was a small book of poetry. The book that made him canonical was a large book of plays. There are no Shakespeare poems in the first folio. And if we contrast the publishing history of *Venus and Adonis* with that of the plays, an interesting paradox emerges that vividly captures the change in status of the once despised playtexts. As Andrew Murphy has pointed out, the poems and plays switch places in this respect.[58] Both *Venus and Adonis* and *The Rape of Lucrece* are downsized from quarto to octavo at an early stage in their reprinting, with the former shrinking even further to sextodecimo in 1636. The plays, on the other hand, move from quarto to folio, and after 1623 are much less frequently reprinted as individual, small-format playbooks. What this means is that while the poems head down-market and get cheaper, the plays become a much more expensive, exclusive, high- status commodity. The result is a radical shift in the relationship between the popular and the canonical. In his own lifetime the issues at stake in this relationship pushed Shakespeare into a complex balancing of his professional roles, as he negotiated between his literary and social ambitions and his desire for market success. While the first English anthologies reflect what is still a poetry-based idea of canonicity, the possibility of a different kind of canon is opened up by Shakespeare's plays of the late 1590s, which debate rank, status, and popularity itself. Nine years after his death, however, the picture is enormously simplified. The poetry becomes more marginal, and the first folio defines Shakespeare as a high-status playwright. In a word, the popular becomes canonical.

The precedent for this is usually given as the publication of Jonson's *Workes* in 1616, but there is a different and in some ways more interesting precedent which might point us towards a conclusion. Three years before he brought out the first folio, Isaac Jaggard had already published the first complete *Decameron* in English, also in folio, a venture that proved to be at least as commercially successful as the Shakespeare project.[59] For such an expensive book it seems to have sold remarkably well, since it was reprinted within five years (the first volume only) and again in 1634 (both volumes), but this time in duodecimo, which would presumably have made it cheaper. The Shakespeare folio took nine years to achieve a reprinting and reached a third edition in 1663/1664. The connection between the books is

---

[58] See Andrew Murphy, 'Configuring the Book', *EMLS*, forthcoming.

[59] Italianists have noticed that the *Decameron* and Shakespeare first folios come from the same stable: see Herbert G. Wright, *The First English Translation of 'Decameron'* (Upsala: 1953) and Guyda Armstrong, *The English Boccaccio: A History in Books* (University of Toronto Press, forthcoming), which contains a comprehensive account of the *Decameron*'s publishing history. But this has received surprisingly little attention from English scholars. David Kastan, for example, neatly observes that the co-publisher of the Shakespeare first folio, Edward Blount, who had previously published Florio's Montaigne and Shelton's *Don Quixote*, invented England's 'first Great Books course' (Kastan, *Shakespeare and the Book*, p. 63), but doesn't mention the Jaggard Boccaccio.

reinforced by the fact that they share the same dedicatees, William Herbert, 3rd Earl of Pembroke, and his brother Philip Herbert, 1st Earl of Montgomery. But can the shared provenance of the Boccaccio and Shakespeare volumes tell us anything about the process of canonization in the case of Shakespeare himself?

The translator of the English *Decameron* remains anonymous, but it seems likely to have been John Florio. We also know that a *Decameron* translation was entered to John Wolfe in the Stationers' Register for 1587, and it is possible that the Jaggard edition was based on a manuscript completed at that time.[60] But the relationship between the Boccaccian novella and English drama goes back even earlier than that. The vogue for Italian short prose fiction began in 1566 with William Painter's *Palace of Pleasure*, which began with tales from Livy and other classical writers, but then switched to Boccaccio and Boccaccio-inspired writers such as Bandello and Marguerite de Navarre. The success of Painter's work prompted a spate of similar collections in the decade before The Theater opened in 1576, and they became a rich source of stage-play plots. It was these that Ascham excoriated in *The Schoolmaster* as a threat to English morals.[61] So the appearance of the folio *Decameron* three years before the Shakespeare first folio marks a significant advance in the status of this base matter. But there is an important distinction between Boccaccio and Shakespeare, apart from the fact that the one is known principally for prose *novelle* and the other for plays, and this is that while Boccaccio's material was low and fraught with moral danger, his status as a writer was indisputably high-rank, standing alongside Dante and Petrarch as one of the three masters of vernacular Italian. Painter acknowledged this when he claimed that 'the workes of Boccaccio for his stile, order of writing, gravitie, and sententious discourse, is worthy of intire provulgation', though that final term simultaneously implies Boccaccio's adaptability to Ovid's '*vulgus*'.[62] Boccaccio represents the canonization of the popular in what was then the premier European vernacular.

In that respect Jaggard's publishing agenda in the early 1620s looks extraordinarily prescient. The folio *Decameron* presented Boccaccio to English readers in a form that gave him something of the status that he had long held in Italy. Despite the fact that the tales had become playhouse fodder, here was a publisher who was ready to see them as the work of a major European author. As a European literary translation, the Jaggard *Decameron* is comparable with Blount's Montaigne and *Don Quixote*, but the popularization of the Boccaccian novella by Painter and others, and its role as a source for English playhouse plots, makes it much closer in spirit to Shakespeare's first folio. The Italian's unique combination of elite status and low matter was the perfect prelude to Jaggard's next major project (this time in association with Blount), validating the book that would eventually enable its native English author to outrank and outsell all others.

---

[60]   See Armstrong, *English Boccaccio*, Chapter 3. I am also grateful to Warren Boutcher for advice on this point.

[61]   Roger Ascham, *The Schoolmaster (1570)*, ed. Lawrence V. Ryan (Charlottesville: 1967), pp. 67–70.

[62]   William Painter, *The Palace of Pleasure* (London: 1566), sig. ¶¶ 3.

PART 2
The Elizabethan Top Ten

Chapter 5
Almanacs and Ideas of Popularity

Adam Smyth

The Form

In 1596, Thomas Nashe wrote that selling almanacs was 'readier money than ale and cakes'.[1] Almanacs in England flourished from the 1550s until about 1700, although they also had quieter lives before and after these dates.[2] The market was crowded, frantic and profitable: almanacs constituted a lucrative and vigorously defended monopoly for the Stationers' Company. These texts sold in numbers so large they scarcely seem credible: 'in the sixteenth century, hundreds of thousands were printed; in the seventeenth century several millions.'[3] Many almanacs were updated and reprinted for many years: the almanac initially printed by John Dade in 1589 continued to be revised annually until the eighteenth century. Indeed, almanacs at times acquired a kind of cultural invisibility in the seventeenth century due to their sheer ever-presentness; the ways readers responded to these texts were often similarly naturalized.

Printed almanacs were sold in the last months of each year and provided information about the year to come. These texts were small, generally octavo or duodecimo – their mobility an essential attribute – but they made claims to a kind of totality of coverage. The dominant inclusion was a detailed calendar: a double page for each month, listing the number of days; the moon's positions;

---

[1]   Thomas Nashe, *Have With You To Saffron Walden* (1596), quoted in Bernard Capp, *English Almanacs 1500–1800: Astrology and the Popular Press* (Ithaca and New York, 1979), p. 44.

[2]   The most helpful overviews are Capp, *English Almanacs*; Eustace F. Bosanquet, *English Printed Almanacks and Prognostications: A Bibliographical History to the Year 1600* (London, 1917); R.C. Simmons, 'ABCs, almanacs, ballads, chapbooks, popular piety and textbooks', in John Barnard and D.F. McKenzie (eds, with the assistance of Maureen Bell), *The Cambridge History of the Book in Britain*, vol. IV, 1557–1695 (Cambridge, 2002), pp. 504–13, esp. pp. 506–8; Neil Rhodes, 'Articulate Networks: the Self, the Book and the World', in Jonathan Sawday and Neil Rhodes (eds), *The Renaissance Computer: Knowledge Technology in the First Age of Print* (London, 2000), pp. 181–94; Louis Curth, *Almanacs, Astrology & Popular Medicine, 1550–1700* (Manchester, 2007).

[3]   R.C. Simmons, 'ABCs, almanacs', p. 508. For seventeenth-century figures, see Cyprian Bladen, 'The Distribution of Almanacks in the Second Half of the Seventeenth Century', *Studies in Bibliography: Papers of the Bibliographical Society of the University of Virginia* 11 (1958): 107–16, Table I.

the ascendant sign; the latitude of the moon; the weather; and what almanacs call 'Remarkable days' – church festivals (Whitsunday on May 15th), Saints' days (Ambrose on April 4th) and political anniversaries (the accession of Elizabeth I on November 17th). The other contents of these books – '[t]he necessary furniture of an almanack', as one compiler puts it[4] – included descriptions of local fairs and routes between towns; chronologies of history which mix cosmological, Biblical, social, meteorological and political events ('The Creation of the World ... Noahs Flood ... Coaches first used in England ... The great blazing Star ... The Birth of Charles our Lord and King');[5] tables for calculating financial interest; husbandry advice ('In *March* you may graft; but in planting and grafting chuse a warme time');[6] tables listing the distance, to quote one text, 'of some of the most famous Cities in the world, *from this Honourable City of London*';[7] astrological, medical and agricultural advice; a 'zodiacal body', anatomizing the effect of the planets on parts of the body; and 'predictions of weather, and strange events' ('January ... frosty, serene, and clear'; 'April. Cold blasts and sharp aire').[8] Almanacs were cheap – Sir Edward Dering spent four pence on '2 Allmanackes' in 1619[9] – and utilitarian: farmers might plant crops according to the astrological advice; readers could turn to tables of regnal years when composing legal documents; and wooers might even seek their advice on when to marry. As diminutive volumes that strove for great inclusivity, almanacs represent that Renaissance interest in epitomizing vastness into as small a form as possible – that interest, to use Barabas's words, in conveying 'Infinite riches in a little roome.'[10]

Ten Implications for the Concept of Popularity

The following 10 implications apply in the first instance to almanacs, but also collectively constitute one paradigm for the life-cycle of the Elizabethan print bestseller. They focus, in particular, on the paradoxes of popularity, and the ways in which popularity leads to ephemerality. Popularity is ultimately destructive: it leads, at first, to transformation (the genre is remade, tugged in a variety of directions, by readers, compilers, publishers); then to diffusion (almanac inclusions dissipate into other forms of writing); and eventually to a virtual killing off of the form.

---

[4]   William Salmon, *The London Almanack For the year of our Lord, 1697*, title page (London, 1697).

[5]   Thomas Gallen, *A new almanack for the said year 1668* (London, 1668).

[6]   Jonathan Dove, *Speculum Anni* (1641), sig. C5.

[7]   Thomas Bretnor, *A newe almanacke and prognostication* (London, 1615), no page numbers.

[8]   William Andrewes, *The Celestial Observatory* (1655), sig. C.

[9]   Sir Edward Dering, 'A Booke of Expences for the Yeare 1619' (Maidstone).

[10]   Christopher Marlowe, *The Jew of Malta*, in Roma Gill (ed.), *The Complete Works of Christopher Marlowe*, vol. IV (Oxford, 1995), I, 136–37.

1. Almanacs were printed in huge numbers and, as a result, not many survive.

Perhaps because of the sheer quantity of almanacs, and their explicit ephemerality – title pages fix almanacs to their particular year – almanac survival rates are extremely low. (One paradox of attempts to gauge popularity is that both low and high survival rates are taken to indicate early modern popularity.) Low survival rates are not surprising: almanacs were designed for a single year, and so require a different conception of 'popularity', as a critical category, from other, non-annual publications. There were some exceptions to this pattern of ephemeral use: some readers collected sequences of almanacs running across several years, or bound many almanacs for each year, assembling a kind of permanent archive or database;[11] others added handwritten notes which they turned back to, often decades later (see below). But most almanacs were read and discarded in a single year.

As a result of this rather low life expectancy, almanacs became synonymous with transience. Early modern texts (including almanacs themselves) describe four or five paradigmatic modes of dying – although whether these reflect reality is more doubtful: scholars have perhaps been too quick to take these rhetorical flourishes as reliable evidence. Almanacs were used for lining pie dishes, after their year had passed; for lighting tobacco; as toilet paper; for the 'stopping of mustard pots';[12] for the binding of later books;[13] or, most commonly of all, they were simply discarded. As Eustace Bosanquet notes, 'The entire productions of many of the [almanac] authors of this period have disappeared ... [and] we [only] know of such authors as George Williams, Doctor Harycok ... Barnabe Gaynsforth ... [and] Thomas Stephens, Gent ... by their names appearing among the licenses.'[14] The confluence of these vast production and low survival rates means that almanacs, while intensely, perhaps even prosaically familiar to early modern individuals, remain far less familiar to scholars of the period.

---

[11]   See the run of 1613 almanacs at Bodleian Ash. 66.

[12]   Thomas Dekker, *The Wonderfull Yeare. 1603* (London, 1603), quoted in Capp, *English Almanacs*, p. 66. Many almanacs 'ride post to chaundlers and Tobacco shops in folio', according to Thomas Overbury, *Sir Thomas Ouerbury his Wife. With Additions of New Characters* (London, 1622), sig. I4v. For more on recycling unwanted pages, see Margaret Spufford, *Small Books and Pleasant Histories: Popular Fiction and Its Readership in Seventeenth-Century England* (Cambridge, 1981), pp. 48–50.

[13]   F.H. Stubbings, in 'A Cambridge Pocket-Diary, 1587–92', *Transactions of the Cambridge Bibliographical Society*, V (1971): 191–202, notes that fragments of Gabriel Frende's *Almanacke and Prognostication* (1591) survive 'in the binding of a book at Shrewsbury School' (p. 192).

[14]   Bosanquet, p. 42. Survival rates are hard to gauge with any precision, but parallels may be drawn with the remarkably low figures for popular cheap printed books discussed in John Barnard, 'The Survival and Loss Rates of Psalms, ABCs, Psalters and Primers from the Stationers' Stock, 1660–1700', *The Library*, 6th series, 21: 2 (June 1999): 148–50.

2. Almanacs were read and used by a broad section of society, and so trouble ideas of 'popular culture'.

Almanacs were bought, read and used by men and women across the social spectrum, in town and country – everyone from John Dee and Simon Forman to farmers counting their herd. They thus encourage us to pause and think about 'popular culture' as a category, since in this case it seems not linked, in a straightforward way, to social class. In this sense, almanacs were amphibious texts, floating across class lines.[15] Can we combine a reading of almanacs with a sense of social hierarchy?

Roger Chartier presents one way to respond. He proposes that it is not necessarily a difference in book ownership that reflects (and induces) social hierarchy, but rather the different ways the same books might be read. 'A retrospective sociology,' Chartier writes, 'that has long made the unequal distribution of objects the primary criterion of the cultural hierarchy must be replaced by a different approach that focuses attention on differentiated and contrasting uses of the same goods, the same texts, the same ideas.'[16] What makes reading popular, in other words, is not the book, but the ways in which the book is read.[17]

3. While most almanacs are lost, almanacs live on vividly in early modern discourse.

References to almanacs are common in other forms of writing, particularly in plays and jest-books: 'A calendar, a calendar!', shouts Bottom in *A Midsummer Night's Dream* (1596), 'Look in the almanac. Find out moonshine, find out moonshine!'; 'thou lyest worse than hee that made the last Almanacke,' declares one 'scolding' woman in a jest-book.[18]

What do such references tell us? They are an index of popularity qua *the instantly recognizable*. These references suggest that this recognizability was dependent on almanacs in discourse being symbolically stable: a character calling for an almanac represented, broadly, the same thing across the Elizabethan period, and that thing was some combination of gullibility, doomed social ambition, provincialism and ignorance. Literary representations of almanacs, in other words,

---

[15]   Peter Burke uses the idea of 'amphibiousness' to describe individuals who engaged with both popular and elite culture. See, for instance, Peter Burke, *Popular Culture in Early Modern Europe*, 3rd edition (Farnham, 2009), p. 56.

[16]   Roger Chartier, 'Texts, Printing, Readings', in L. Hunt (ed.), *The New Cultural History* (Berkeley, 1989), pp. 154–75, p. 171.

[17]   See also Roger Chartier, 'Reading Matter and "Popular" Reading: From the Renaissance to the Seventeenth Century', in Guglielmo Cavallo and Roger Chartier, *A History of Reading in the West* (Cambridge, 1999), pp. 269–83.

[18]   *A Midsummer Night's Dream*, III, i; Robert Chamberlain, *A New Booke of Mistakes. Or, Bulls with Tales, and Buls Without Tales But No Lyes by any Meanes* (London, 1637), pp. 26–27.

become early modern shorthand for representing a particular kind of the popular, defined against the elite, the urbane or the informed. In fact, this stereotype is not an accurate depiction of actual readers: almanacs were read by a wide social spectrum. But this more inclusive reality was quashed beneath the symbolic weight of debased almanacs and their debased readers.

It may be worth noting that when almanacs are cited, they are almost always invoked by the compiler's name: Leonard Digges's almanacs from the 1550s and 1560s were Digges; Gadbury's were Gadbury. 'What says Bretnor?', asks Chough when deciding when to marry, in *A Fair Quarrel* (1617).[19] This is perhaps surprising, given scholarship's sense of the rather low presence of authorship as a category of literary definition: almanac compilers had a vivid cultural presence, enjoying, even, a form of textual celebrity. As a consequence, William Lilly included a brief autobiography at the start of his *Anglicus, peace or no peace* (1645), since, he claimed, 'Many desire to know what I am'.[20] And compilers often used almanacs as a space in which to advertise their other services: in his *A newe almanacke and prognostication* (1615), Thomas Bretnor advertised that 'Arithmeticke', 'Geometry', 'Nauigation', 'Astronomy' and 'Astrology' 'are taught by the author in *English, Latine, French* or *Spanish*'.[21]

4. The popularity of almanacs led to increasingly specialized titles.

There is a pattern of increasing particularity over time. What might be called 'general' almanacs were followed by more specialized titles: almanacs addressing particular professions – William Woodhouse's *An almanacke and prognostication* (1602) was pitched at 'lawyers, marchants, mariners, husbandmen, trauellers' – and also almanacs linked to particular locations. Alexander Mounslowe's *An almanacke, and prognostication* (1579) 'Referred to the meridian of the citie of Chester'; Thomas Buckminster 'gathered and made' his *New almanacke* (1589) to serve 'specially for the meridian of this honorable citie of London'; and Walter Gray's *An almanacke and prognostication* (1591) was 'Rectified for the elevation and meridian of Dorchester seruing most aptly for the west partes.'

5. As a popular form, almanacs became a medium through which other debates were staged.

We see this most clearly in post-Elizabethan almanacs: during the Civil War, almanacs grew highly politicized, as evidenced in the acrimony between Royalist George Wharton and Republican John Booker. John Gadbury – former Leveller and follower of Abiezer Coppe – published strongly Royalist almanacs, and also

---

[19]   Thomas Middleton and William Rowley, *A Fair Quarrel*, in Gary Taylor and John Lavagnino (eds), *Thomas Middleton: The Complete Works* (Oxford, 2007), V, i, 131.

[20]   William Lilly, *Anglicus, peace or no peace* (London, 1645), sigs. A3v–A4v.

[21]   Bretnor, *A newe almanacke*.

the astrological biography *The Nativity of the Late King Charles* (1659). As a result of their popularity, almanacs became an available language or set of forms through which other subjects could be addressed.

6. Almanacs were used by readers in ways that compilers did not anticipate; they were turned into different forms of text; they had unpredicted social lives.

The popularity of almanacs exposed them to multiple uses (and I think 'use' – following Bradin Cormack and Carla Mazzio's terminology – is preferable to 'reading', given the range of things readers did to books).[22] These uses were not generally foreseen by compilers and publishers. The best example is the practice of readers adding marginal annotations to their almanacs: readers frequently inscribed almanacs with handwritten notes, either on the printed page or on inserted blanks, relating to (most commonly) family births and deaths; health and the body; the weather; travel ('Mr Dye my Cosen & I went to Cromer'); financial accounting; legal or employment contracts; and husbandry ('they begun Harvest').[23] This practice was widespread, across a diverse social spectrum: well-known autobiographers such as John Evelyn and Anthony Wood began their life-writings with series of notes in almanacs, which they later turned back to and revised into fuller narratives.[24]

Early printed almanacs seem not to have envisaged this practice, but Elizabethan almanacs began to signal an awareness of this mode of consumption. Thomas Purfoote's *A blanke and perpetuall Almanacke* (1566) was 'a memoriall ... for any ... that will make & keepe notes of any actes, deedes, or thinges that passeth from time to time (Worthy of memory, to be registered)', and, in 1571, Thomas Hill's *An almanack* was offered 'in forme of a booke of memorie necessary for all such, as haue occasion daylie to note sundry affayres, eyther for receytes, payments, or such lyke'.[25] Purfoote's and Hill's texts, which included blanks and encouraged readers to 'make & keepe notes', were responding to, reinforcing, but not initiating this practice. In 1582, Evans Lloyd's *An almanacke and prognostication* included pages for accounts, blank except for printed column headings for pounds, shillings and pence. These practices and innovations were enabled by the profound popularity of the Elizabethan almanac: popularity catalyzed transformation.

Such invitations to add notes suggests a model for a reader-text-publisher dynamic in the instance of popular texts: the printed almanac, rather than simply prescribing reading modes through its material form (although it did do this), reorganized its material form in response to new modes of reading. Other popular

---

[22]	Bradin Cormack and Carla Mazzio (eds.), *Book Use, Book Theory: 1500–1700* (Chicago, 2005).

[23]	Arthur Hopton, *New Almanacke* (1613), Bodleian Ash. 66, 'August.'

[24]	Adam Smyth, *Autobiography in Early Modern England* (Cambridge, 2010), pp. 35–38.

[25]	Thomas Purfoote, *A blanke and perpetuall Almanacke* (London, 1566), title page; Thomas Hill, *An almanack* (London, 1571), title page.

sixteenth-century forms follow a similar paradigm: *alba amicorum*, for example, or (largely European) friendship albums, in which compilers gathered signatures and aphorisms of friends and admired acquaintances, often began as printed books (Andrea Alciato's *Emblemata* was a common choice) interleaved by readers with blank pages. Publishers responded to this demand, printing books specifically designed to serve as skeletons for albums: Jean de Tournes' *Thesaurus Amicorum* (Lyon, 1558) includes witty sentences, portrait medallions and blank pages surrounded by woodcut borders, awaiting the addition of signatures.[26]

Michel de Certeau, in his critique of the notion of consumption as inertia, described ways in which the consumer might be not a passive figure, but a dexterous improviser, subtly resisting and remaking a culture's prescriptions and rituals. The model of reading operating in almanacs, and other printed bestsellers, shows an even more dynamic version of this idea: not only do readers improvise with an apparently imposed culture, but that imposed culture, in the form of the printed almanac, is materially reworked as a result of consumers' creative responses to the book.[27]

7. These surprising uses extended as far as physical remaking.

Surviving almanacs have often been materially remade, through the pinning in of scraps of paper or the creation of pockets to hold loose notes (book lists; letters; business cards; dried flowers.) More strikingly, other almanacs have been physically cut up. Most of the examples come from post-Elizabethan texts, since such patterns of use are typically associated with texts some time after their initial popularity. Thus a copy of Edward Pond's *An almanack for the Year of our Lord God 1696* (Cambridge, 1696) includes not only copious manuscript notes, but also stubs indicating cut-out pages: usually whole pages have been cut out, but sometimes only the top third of a page.[28] Royalist Sir John Gibson produced a commonplace while imprisoned in Durham Castle in the 1650s, hoping that the text would serve and aid his son as a 'companion some times to looke upon, in this Vale of teares'.[29] The volume features several pages cut from printed volumes, including almanacs, and glued into the pages of the manuscript, to which Gibson has added his own handwritten notes. Sometimes almanacs prescribe this remaking. John White's *Briefe and easie almanack for this yeare* (1650) instructs

---

[26]   June Schlueter, *The Album Amicorum and the London of Shakespeare's Time* (London, 2011), pp. 12–13.

[27]   Michel de Certeau, *The Practice of Everyday Life*, trans. Steven Rendall (Berkeley, 1984).

[28]   Folger V.a. 515. For more stubs and cut pages, see Cardanus Rider, *British Merlin* (London, 1680); Folger A2254.5; George Wharton, *Calendarium Carolinum* (London, 1664); Folger A2655.

[29]   British Library Additional Manuscript 37719, f. 5v; Adam Smyth, '"Rend and teare in peeces": Textual Fragmentation in Seventeenth-Century England', *The Seventeenth Century* 19.1 (Autumn 2004): 36–52.

readers to snip out 'the whole kalender' for 1650 for use elsewhere: 'which being cut out, is fit to be placed into any book of accompts, table book, or other.'[30] Such prescriptions produced composite texts of a complex materiality, often the products of combining different forms, both manuscript and print – a complexity obscured by scholars preoccupied with a modern conception of the book.

One consequence of popularity, then, was the exposure of almanacs to these kinds of inventive and vigorous models of consumption. The texts, by being popular, were cut apart.

8. The popularity of almanacs sparked satirical writing which, initially registering (and feeding off) popularity, eventually contributed to the almanac's demise.

This satirical strain is most evident in the form of mock almanacs and prognostications: printed texts that parodied the almanac form, such as *A Wonderfull, Strange and Miraculous, Astrologicall Prognostication* (1591), by Adam Fouleweather, 'student in asse-tronomy', and Simon Smel-knave's *The Fearfull and Lamentable Effects of Two Dangerous Comets* (1590), 'wherein both man and woman shall find theyr naturall inclination, and accidentall or necessarie mischiefes.' Thomas Dekker's *The Ravens Almanacke* (1609) and Thomas Middleton's *The Owles Almanacke* (1618) also used the almanac form as a vehicle for satire. Parodies grew more intense over time: a compiler styling himself 'Poor Richard, Knight of the Burnt Island' began publishing the parodic *Poor Robin's Almanack*. 'This month', the 1664 text confidently predicted, 'we may expect to hear of the Death of some Man, Woman, or Child, either in Kent or Christendom.'[31]

Two points are worth making here. First, that the mock almanacs are very close to the originals: there is a curious alignment of parody and original; a sense, even, of satire lagging behind its object. We see this as mock almanacs took aim at readers' annotations. *Poor Robin* includes mock reader notes printed in the margins: 'Lost my best Shirt off the hedge'; 'Nell laught at the story of the Fryer & Boy till she pist'; 'Rainy weather, and yet the Almanack said it would be fair'.[32] If

---

[30] John White, *Briefe and easie almanack for this yeare* (London, 1650), title page.

[31] See also Thomas Dekker's *The ravens almanacke* (London, 1609) and *The Owles almanacke* (London, 1618), the latter 'found in an Iuy-bush written in old characters and now published in English by the painefull labours of Mr. Iocundary Merry-braines.'

[32] *Poor Robin 1673 an almanack after a new fashion* (1673), sig. B2v. Noted by Capp, *English Almanacs*, p. 62. For further mockery of almanac readers, see Thomas Middleton, *No Wit, No Help Like a Woman* (1611), and Middleton and Rowley, *A Fair Quarrel*. It was not only readers of almanacs who were mocked: almanacs themselves were also subject to sustained ridicule. For a sample of typical abuse, see Matthew Stevenson, *Norfolk Drollery* (London, 1673), pp. 30–33: 'Observations upon Lillie's Almanack' ('An *Almanack's* a store-house, where old wives / May furnisht be with Fables all their Lives'); and *Sportive Wit*, pp. 35–36: 'The Mercury' ('He that writ this, ne'er writ before').

these mock notes possess a comic specificity and bathos, then genuine handwritten annotations – 'June 1ˢᵗ the black cow tooke the Bull'[33] – frequently match them.

Second: Parody and satire functioned for a time as a register of popularity; but this body of satirical writing soon contributed to the demise of the form – rather as Cervantes' *Don Quixote* (1605) and Samuel Rowlands's *Melancholie Knight* (1615) reflected the popularity of romance, but eventually drove it from high cultural visibility.[34]

9. Almanac inclusions migrated into other forms of writing: almanacs, because of their popularity, were diffused across culture.

As a result of their popularity, almanacs migrated into other forms of writing: diaries; newspapers; ballads; novels; developing theories of medicine and science. The notebooks of one Henry Sturmey in Gloucester contain his own almanac-style astrological charts that attempt to fathom whether, when and where to marry, whether to have children and what names to choose: he's appropriated those aspects of almanacs that were most useful to him, and so dispensed with the original form.[35] We see this today in traces of almanacs that survive in the desk diary (listing the moon's positions and religious holidays) and newspaper columns of astrological predictions. This diffusion is a kind of destruction: the contents of the early almanac scattered across other, later forms of publication.

10. An awareness of the cultural ever-presentness of almanacs allows us to recontextualize and reread familiar literary texts.

Edmund Spenser's *Shepherd's Calendar* (1579) appeared just as almanac annotating was becoming widespread; Spenser's text, constructed as a calendar, features a sea of annotations by EK. One way to use the popularity of almanacs would be to reread Spenser's text through the prism of almanac annotations. Shakespeare's sonnets also respond to almanac popularity. Sonnet 77, for instance – 'Thy glass will show thee how thy beauties wear' – describes a narrator bequeathing three gifts that track passing time: a mirror, a sundial and 'a book of vacant leaves'. New interpretative possibilities open up if we consider that those vacant leaves could be an interleaved almanac. What other new readings of familiar literary texts come into view when we approach them armed with a knowledge of the near omnipresence of Elizabethan almanacs?

---

[33] Cardanus Rider, *Merlinus, Cambro-Britannus* (London, 1654), Folger A2243.5.

[34] Helen Cooper, *The English Romance in Time: Transforming Motifs from Geoffrey of Monmouth to the Death of Shakespeare* (Oxford, 2008), p. 39.

[35] Gloucester Record Office, D 2375 / F10.

Chapter 6
Print, Popularity, and the
Book of Common Prayer

Brian Cummings

Whatever a best-selling book was in the early modern period, the *Book of Common Prayer* is it. Ian Green in *Print and Protestantism in Early Modern England* has established a working criterion for a 'steady selling' book of five re-editions over a period of 30 years, starting either from an original appearance in print or a subsequent edition.[1] Depending on how we define an imprint, there were perhaps 525 re-editions of the *Book of Common Prayer* in early modern England, of which 117 were in the reign of Elizabeth.[2] Of the calendar years from 1558 to 1603, only 1593 and 1602 did not see a fresh imprint, judged by surviving copies; some years saw as many as six. In addition, print runs for the *Book of Common Prayer* were permitted to exceed the usual limits. At least 200,000 copies must have been printed in Elizabethan England, and many more remained in circulation from the reign of Edward VI. The only books to rival it were bibles and psalters, along with books of religious instruction such as *The Christians ABC*. This last text Green considers may have been the most reprinted item of all, with perhaps several imprints per year of upwards of 2,500 copies each. It was produced very cheaply, sold equally well, and was used so readily, indeed, that most copies do not survive.[3] Yet this text, too, can be seen as an ancillary of the *Book of Common Prayer*, containing as it did the catechism and many short prayers and biblical citations lifted straight from it. Many other catechistical books were abbreviated from the *Book of Common Prayer*, and other printings were made of liturgical lectionaries of collects and bible readings. Surviving copies of other widely reprinted texts like Geneva Bibles and Sternhold and Hopkins's Metrical Psalter were often bound in with copies of the *Book of Common Prayer*, so that in terms of print run and dissemination it is even difficult to distinguish between them.

---

[1]   *Print and Protestantism in Early Modern England* (Oxford: Oxford University Press, 2000), p.173.

[2]   The figure for the period 1549–1640 is derived from the STC as interpreted by Green. For the Elizabethan period, I have used the list in David N. Griffiths, *The Bibliography of the Book of Common Prayer 1549–1999* (London: British Library; Delaware: Oak Knoll Press, 2002), p. 69–82.

[3]   Green, *Print and Protestantism*, p. 183.

Religious books, as Green has argued, in the past often fell below the radar in accounts of 'popular literature' in early modern England.[4] Compilers of such lists sometimes ignored the religious, perhaps as intrinsically 'unpopular'. Even lists of religious publications sometimes omitted bibles and prayer books either on principle, or else out of quiet despair at the sheer bibliographical scale involved. Yet the hesitation also has some justification. The primary object in printing large numbers of copies of the *Book of Common Prayer* when it was first introduced in 1549 was in supplying every church in the land with a workable liturgy. This also accounts for the volume of copies produced in early printings of the Great Bible in 1539 and 1540, and the Bishops' Bible in 1569. There were over 700 parish churches at the Reformation in Norfolk alone. Edward Whitchurch and Richard Grafton produced between them 15 folio editions of the 1549 version of the *Book of Common Prayer*. A large proportion of these copies were used up simply in fulfilling the conditions of the Act of Uniformity in establishing a vernacular service order, 'the Unyformytie of Service and Admynistracion of the Sacramentes throughout the Realme'.[5] This shows an immediate problem with our use of the word 'popular' in relation to the printing press.[6] Leah Price has recently made a stringent attack, in relation to Victorian books and their readership, on the unwritten assumption that 'acquiring a book implies choosing it' – which she calls 'bookish liberalism'.[7] With early modern printing it is even less the case that readership implies choice. While it is an obvious measure of popularity to count numbers of editions and print runs, the first and most pressing orders to printers came from government: prayer books and primers, of course, but also proclamations and statutes. Do we want to call Acts of Parliament a form of popular literature?

The revised Edwardian *Book of Common Prayer* in 1552 was issued in large numbers in order to supplant the version of 1549, which was no longer legal religious tender. The same thing happened again with the new Act of Uniformity in 1559, with the added urgency that the Marian repeals of 1554 had ordered the wholesale destruction of the 1549 and 1552 orders. In restricting our attention specifically to Elizabethan bestsellers, there are three editions that bear the year date 1559 (although one may be later). Even allowing for 2,000–3,000 copies each, they do not cater for much beyond church use, especially when we reckon in

---

[4]	Ibid., p. 170.

[5]	2 & 3 Edward VI, Chapter 1, *The Statutes of the Realm. Printed by Command of his Majesty King George the Third. In Pursuance of an Address of the House of Commons of Great Britain. From Original Records and Authentic Manuscripts*, ed. A. Luders and others, 12 vols (London: George Eyre and Andrew Strahan, 1810–1828), iv, 37.

[6]	Brian Cummings, 'Acts of Uniformity: Pluralization and the Vernacular in the First Book of Common Prayer', in *Pluralisierungen: Konzepte zur Erfassung der Frühen Neuzeit*, ed. Jan-Dirk Müller, Wulf Oesterreicher, and Friedrich Vollhardt (Berlin: Walter de Gruyter, 2010), p. 149.

[7]	*How to Do Things with Books in Victorian Britain* (Princeton: Princeton University Press, 2012), p. 150.

the needs of parish priests beyond use in church. Is the *Book of Common Prayer* therefore a public book but not a popular one; or a bestseller that does not have a reading public? Immediately, then, the concept of the prayer book raises profound methodological problems. It is printed and sold in numbers which would make a historian of play texts weep with envy, yet its commercial success instantly raises questions about how we measure 'popularity' against it.

Here, the seeming synonyms 'people', 'popular', and 'popularity' play uneasily against each other. Indeed, religious history has much to teach book history in the sophistication with which it examines such terms:

> In talking about elite religion or popular religion, are we contrasting notions of orthodoxy with heterodoxy or superstition, or the religion of the clergy with the religion of the laity, or the religion of the rich with the religion of the poor, or the religion of the polite and educated with the religion of the unwashed and unlettered, or the religion of the thinking individual over against the religion of the undifferentiated multitude?[8]

Eamon Duffy, in asking these questions, proposes to 'subvert' them, and to show that the distinctions they imply are hard to maintain. However, the word 'popular' has a long history in debates about the Reformation. When J.J. Scarisbrick stated in *The Reformation and the English People* (1984) that 'the English Reformation was only in a limited sense popular and "from below"', he was responding to a longstanding tradition in the opposite direction.[9] Part of the assumption here in the past had been that the translation of bible and ritual into the vernacular was by definition 'popular'.[10] Yet the introduction of the new English services in Devon and Cornwall on Whitsun 1549 was the occasion of opposition turning into full-scale rebellion. Third in the list of demands in the manifesto at Exeter was 'Item we will have the mass in latten, as was before'.[11] Scarisbrick suggests resistance to the new liturgy was a popular cause well into the Elizabethan period.[12] In the opposite direction, evidence has been found of a groundswell in favour of Protestant reform in 1549 in the Midlands and East Anglia. Some rebels in Norwich appointed a minister to say the new offices of Morning and Evening Prayer for them.[13] Judith Maltby has attempted to trace a 'popular' religious sentiment based on the *Book*

---

[8]   Eamon Duffy, 'Elite and Popular Religion: the Book of Hours and Lay Piety in the Later Middle Ages', in *Elite and Popular Religion*, ed. Kate Cooper and Jeremy Gregory, *Studies in Church History* 42 (Woodbridge: The Boydell Press, for the Ecclesiastical History Society, 2006), p. 140.

[9]   *The Reformation and the English People* (Oxford: Blackwell, 1984), p. 1.

[10]   A.G. Dickens, *The English Reformation*, rev. ed. (London: Fontana, 1967), p. 303.

[11]   *Tudor Rebellions*, ed. Anthony Fletcher and Diarmaid MacCulloch, 5th ed. (Harlow: Pearson, 2008), p. 151.

[12]   *Reformation and the English People*, p. 140–41.

[13]   Ethan H. Shagan, *Popular Politics and the English Reformation* (Cambridge: Cambridge University Press, 2003), p. 282–3.

of Common Prayer in the Elizabethan reign and after.[14] The idea of 'prayer book piety' nonetheless remains difficult to quantify. Attachment to ritual could be just as much evidence of Catholic survivalism; and godly zeal in favour of the vernacular might be more a sign of a radicalism that wished for a more Genevan style of prayer and worship. Whereas in past generations, particularly in Victorian times, the *Book of Common Prayer* was appealed to as the epitome of consensus religion, now it can equally appear as the squeezed middle, between traditionalist and radical.

The question I wish to ask here is whether a bibliographical approach might help to illuminate this problem, while in return seeing how arguments about 'popularity' in the English Reformation should cause us to rethink the history of the book. In this latter direction, the dissemination of religious texts broadens the conceptual scope of our inquiry into how books work in early modern culture. A 'best-selling book' easily evokes a sense of popularity through an image of individual readers rushing to the printer's shop. At the same time, we know that simply by virtue of advanced literacy and the wherewithal to buy books, individual readers are already a very exclusive clientele. However, in a mixed oral and literate culture, book-owning is only one of the ways in which printed texts reached an audience.[15] We could call this 'socialized' literacy. The *Book of Common Prayer* permeated society like no other text, since millions who were not otherwise literate heard weekly Morning and Evening Prayer, and could be fined if they did not.[16] Even groups who for religious reasons avoided the rites of the official church would attend weddings, baptisms, and funerals, either on their own part (to avoid illegitimacy) or to assist friends or neighbours.[17] Evidence of the influence of the printed text *heard* rather than seen can be found in sophisticated readers as well as the unlettered. Shakespeare has long been known to cite biblical texts from a number of different sources, probably often from memory. At times he appears to be quoting from the Bishops' Bible, used in church services, but at others from a Geneva Bible, which he may even have owned. At other times, an allusion is closer to the version in the *Book of Common Prayer*, which still followed the 1540 text of the Great Bible (including the Psalms).[18]

---

[14] *Prayer Book and People in Elizabethan and Early Stuart England* (Cambridge: Cambridge University Press, 1998), p. 1–19.

[15] Green, *Print and Protestantism*, p. 24.

[16] Communion was a much rarer experience: most parishioners only attended once a year at Easter; see Arnold Hunt, 'The Lord's Supper in Early Modern England', *Past & Present* 161 (1998): 39–83; discussion of communion attendance on p. 41–43.

[17] On non-conformists attending church for baptism, see David Cressy, *Birth, Marriage and Death: Ritual, Religion and the Life-Cycle in Tudor and Stuart England* (Oxford: Oxford University Press, 1997), p. 102–4; and marriage, p. 341–42.

[18] See the discussion in Richmond Noble, *Shakespeare's Biblical Knowledge and Use of the Book of Common Prayer* (London: SPCK, 1930), p. 58–89.

However, the *Book of Common Prayer* widens the concept of socialized literacy in other ways. Parts of it, such as the official short catechism, might be read and heard in groups in church, or in other contexts outside. Devotion could take place in private or in public. Religious books in general were used beyond the study (the social location for learned books and perhaps also for narrative and play texts), in the bedchamber or outside the house; prayer books, like other edifying works, were read aloud by the head of household among family and servants; or in the houses of gentry, by the lady of the house among the women. These create what Green calls 'fluid, overlapping readerships', or 'communities of interpretation' rather than Edmund Burke's more modern concept of the 'reading public'.[19]

These things we can say from our knowledge of books in general, but what can be gleaned by examining surviving material copies of the *Book of Common Prayer*? As with bibles, this is a peculiarly under-researched area, perhaps, paradoxically, because of the richness of the corpus. The printing of the *Book of Common Prayer* was carefully protected by license. Grafton in 1549 was the King's Printer and Whitchurch his business partner. John Oswen was also licensed to print the *Book of Common Prayer* in Worcester for sale in Wales and the Marches, but after 1552 there was no further printing outside London until Cambridge University Press in 1629. In 1559, when the Elizabethan regime restored the Protestant service book along with the monarch's supremacy, Grafton at first attempted to revive his monopoly, but he was quickly supplanted by the Queen's Printers, Richard Jugge and John Cawood. Cawood died in 1572 and Jugge in 1577. Thereafter, Christopher Barker took up the monopoly, one that his family inherited as Royal Printers (with a number of partners and assigns) for more than a century.

A first consideration is one of formats. The first editions of 1549 by Whitchurch and Grafton are in Folio and are designed for church use. However, Oswen, as well as a Folio, also produced a 1549 Quarto edition. Whitchurch produced his first Quarto *Book of Common Prayer* in 1552; Jugge and Cawood supplemented their 1559 Folio with a Quarto.[20] Grafton and Whitchurch both produced an Octavo *Book of Common Prayer* in 1553, the first ever made; new editions in both Quarto and Octavo were produced throughout the Elizabethan reign.[21] The first Sextodecimo was printed by Jugge and Cawood in 1570 and editions in this size were commonly produced from the 1580s onwards.[22] In the smaller formats, Roman type was sometimes introduced (beginning with the 1570 Sextodecimo). Yet Roman never supplanted blackletter founts, which were favoured for the Folio church editions until well after the Restoration edition of 1662. What do these

---

[19]   Green, *Print and Protestantism*, p. 26. The *OED* gives the first reference to 'reading public' as a phrase in 1812 (Walter Scott, *Letter to Byron*, 3 July 1812).

[20]   Whitchurch's 1552 Quarto is STC 16288; the Jugge and Cawood Quarto of 1559 survives in three different states: STC 16293, 16293.3, and 16293.5.

[21]   STC 16290 and 16290.5.

[22]   STC 16300. Griffith lists five Sextodecimos produced in a six-year period (in 1586, 1587, 1590, 1591, and 1592).

different formats imply? The rule goes, the smaller the size the more private the use; yet prayer books as in other respects may make us wary of general bibliographical rules. Smaller editions may have been handy for a minister at his reading desk by the side of the altar or for a richer parishioner in the pew. The smallest editions may have been carried as 'jewel books' rather than read. The fount in the 1570 Sextodecimo is truly minuscule, with tiny illuminated xylographic initials. It only survives in one copy; there is an ownership mark but no other annotation.[23]

A second issue is how copies of the *Book of Common Prayer* were bound in with other books. Maltby comments that the 'practice of binding up the whole Prayer Book with the Bible increases dramatically in the second half of the 1570s'.[24] However, Quarto copies of the *Book of Common Prayer* were bound with related materials from the beginning. It is not always possible to determine at what point a binding has taken place, but both the British Library and the Houghton Library copies of the Oswen Quarto of 1549 are bound with the same items, each from the same printer in the same year: a psalter (STC 2378) and a copy of the official homilies, *Certayne Sermons* (STC 13645).[25] Such a combination was evidently practical, since the psalter was required for daily prayers, and the homilies were used at Communion whenever a new sermon could not be provided by a minister. An early Elizabethan Quarto of 1560 was bound in the same combination, and another of the same year with a psalter alone.[26] The psalter was not at this time officially part of the *Book of Common Prayer* (as it became after 1662), but printers routinely printed one in identical format to an edition of the *Book of Common Prayer* and the two seem to have been sold together. In other cases, as with expensive books in general, customers seem to have bought books in loose leaves and had them bound together in a combination to suit their own pleasure.[27] My own survey of Elizabethan Quartos shows Sternhold and Hopkins's Metrical Psalter, first printed in 1562, frequently used in this way; from 1567 another common companion was the *Godly Prayers*. In the 1580s, when the reprinting of the Geneva Bible became more widespread, this, too, was bound in with the *Book of Common Prayer*, sometimes also with a biblical concordance.[28]

What evidence does this provide of personal ownership or of private use or reading, that is, outside of a church service? How far the laity owned personal copies of the *Book of Common Prayer* has long been a vexed question. Eamon Duffy has compared the *Book of Common Prayer* unfavourably with late medieval

---

[23] Bodleian 8° C 35 Th. Seld. The BL copy is destroyed.

[24] *Prayer Book and People*, p. 26.

[25] BL C.10.a.10(1); and Houghton Library, Harvard University STC 2378.

[26] BL C.25.h.12; and Bodleian C.P. 1560.e.1.

[27] Maltby, *Prayer Book and People*, p. 27.

[28] Durham University Library SB 2186/1 contains a BCP of 1586; a psalter of the same date; a Geneva Bible (Christopher Barker, 1586); *Two right profitable and fruitfull Concordances* (Christopher Barker, n.d.); and a Sternhold and Hopkins (John Day, 1584).

Books of Hours in this respect, in his study of sixteenth-century printed Hours.[29] Patrick Collinson has commented on the infrequency of mentions of the *Book of Common Prayer* in probate inventories in wills. However, Maltby has argued that in many cases, as we have seen, a *Book of Common Prayer* might be bound up with a Bible, so that inventories hide such evidence. The pricing of the *Book of Common Prayer* by the 1590s suggests its affordability for lay readers, and the sheer quantity on the market – half a million by the time of the civil wars – is way beyond what is required for church use or clerical use outside of church. Here the material evidence of surviving copies can help us, although as always such evidence takes a deal of unpacking and adds new complexities.

One clear distinction emerges through looking at formats. Folio, as opposed to Quarto, editions of the 1549 text are hardly ever bound in with other books; one exception, John Cosin's copy of Whitchurch's March edition, which is bound in with a 1552 edition by Grafton, is clearly an exception, a private binding presumably for his own scholarly use in the mid-seventeenth century. 1552 editions also tend not to be bound with other books. It is only in the Elizabethan period that the psalter, even though published by the same printers at the same time since 1549, becomes bound in with the *Book of Common Prayer*. Quarto copies show a different practice from the beginning. Such copies might be for clerical use but they certainly appear to be designed as an aid to private study, not for liturgical practice. The *Godly Prayers* were not part of any of the divine services, but were adapted from them specifically for use in the home. This suggests that Quarto copies were used either for acts of domestic worship or, when combined with bibles and other study aids, for private study.

Some more detailed reflection is possible via ownership marks and other forms of annotation. My own researches in this area are in progress and are subject to the usual caveats. Collectors over the years have favoured clean copies, especially in major research libraries. (An exception is the James R. Page Collection in the Huntington Library, since Page not only loved collecting the *Book of Common Prayer*, he also loved used books.) Any annotation is idiosyncratic and has to be handled with care. With the *Book of Common Prayer* there is the additional difficulty that the book had such an extraordinary shelf life, so copies are passed down from generation to generation, and who is writing what, and when, can only be deciphered with care, and sometimes evades us entirely. However, the second-hand and inherited legacy of the *Book of Common Prayer* also has important consequences for how we view 'popularity' and 'private' use. Assessing Elizabethan popular literature includes the continuous re-use of books printed before 1558. Copies even of the 1549 edition, which was out of date by 1559 and included many versions of services no longer current, passed out of church use and into private libraries, seemingly for a variety of purposes. One copy in the Huntington Library contains annotations in two different hands, both indicating a

---

[29] *Marking the Hours: English People and their Prayers, 1240–1570* (New Haven and London: Yale University Press, 2006), p. 165.

somewhat learned or ecclesiastical intervention in the text, with an interest in the development of the liturgy. The earlier hand, dateable to the late sixteenth century (unfortunately cropped in a later binding), makes notes in Communion, and also underlines sections of text. One of these is of the words of consecration in the Eucharist, the most important single change between the 1552 and 1559 editions.[30] This might suggest a priest, or someone else interested in the development of doctrine and ritual. On the other hand, the British Library copy of the same 1549 edition has a signature on the verso of the colophon, next to the price of the original volume, and in the same sixteenth-century hand and ink, the word 'Quene' has been written in next to the printed word 'Kyng', indicating ownership in the reign of Queen Elizabeth.[31] The signature is of 'Margret Slater'; whoever she was, we can be certain she was not a priest.

It is in fact commonplace for copies of the *Book of Common Prayer* to record revisions of the text handwritten into the earlier printed text. Sometimes this is of changes in sacred ritual; sometimes it is to show deletions, such as the mention in the Litany of 'the tirrany of the bishop of Rome and all his detestable enormities' which appeared in the 1549 and 1552 editions but was cut in 1559 and subsequently; sometimes it is to record changes in the name of the monarch and other members of the royal family in the State Prayers. This shows the continuous use of the book, but it also shows the practical commitment to the text, to what we might call getting it right. Sometimes this may have been to enable the recycling of books for church use to save money; but there is also plenty of evidence of second-hand church copies passing into domestic use. As it happens, Cosin's 1549 copy shows layers of annotation, which suggests several owners before he acquired it in the mid-seventeenth century. Probably the earliest markings are a highly curious set of upward marks between words in the offices, especially of Communion, Baptism, Matrimony, Burial of the Dead, and Purification of Women. In Communion there are also small crosses at points of ritual significance in the words of the priest. The best explanation of the marks is that they help in parsing or chanting the text, while the crosses indicate the manual actions of the priest. Since the 1549 service of Communion was defunct after November 1552, these marks were presumably made before the death of Edward VI. However, a second set of annotations records changes to the *Book of Common Prayer* after 1552: the ritual anointing used in Baptism, banned in 1552, is crossed out; also, the words of consecration, not from 1552 but from 1559, are added.[32] This shows a second, Elizabethan layer of ownership. Another mark of ownership is a record of donation from 'Joannes Siskas' to 'Daniel Wykes'. The former of these names is signed in Greek, so the writer is either a minister or a scholar; it may be, of course, that he is the author of the annotations marking revision after 1559. However, the donation definitively takes us into domestic ownership: three members of the Wykes family add their

---

[30]		Huntington Library 62273, sig. Y4ᵛ.
[31]		British Library C.25.l.14, sig. ¶F7ᵛ.
[32]		Durham University Library SB+ 0851/1, sig. 2A4ᵛ and Y4ᵛ.

names, Daniel, Thomas, and Elizabeth, who records herself as Thomas's daughter. Elizabeth, wonderfully, adds a small ink drawing of a cat with a banderole, like a speech bubble, saying 'sister Tilby'. This multiply owned and inter-generational copy shows the passage of the *Book of Common Prayer* into everyday life. It is a book at one point used in church, at another in the home, by the learned for studying, and by a child for doodling. Children very often made marks in copies of the *Book of Common Prayer*: partly, perhaps, because the book was lying around, although in other cases, where alphabets and suchlike are inscribed, it may be the book was used instructionally for teaching reading and writing in the home.

When we turn to copies printed in the reign of Elizabeth, even Folio copies can show personal marks. Private ownership is therefore not limited to Quarto and smaller formats, as might have been surmised. A copy of Jugge and Cawood bearing the date 1559 (but perhaps printed in 1560 or 1561) records in the Kalendar 'borne dec. 1561'.[33] Use of the *Book of Common Prayer* for family genealogy was not yet common, as it became in early bibles, but it did happen. The Kalendar is often the place where the owner shows his or her intervention, whether on behalf of the family, or to record lucky and unlucky days of more individual significance.[34] Sometimes, if very rarely, the annotation is more anecdotal: a 1564 copy takes the trouble to record that 'yᵉ yonge mane that dyd take suppr of mr [anger?] …' on the reverse of the title page.[35] Marking the inside of a copy of a prayer book with everyday business may have been felt to be somewhat blasphemous, and many copies are completely clean, even when well thumbed. An occasional copy completely breaks this rule and shows the book crossing over fully into private use. A 1566 Folio now in the Page Collection has copious annotations in a sixteenth-century italic hand, beginning with a verse prayer on the reverse of the title page. All of this annotation is ample evidence of a personal copy which, while we do not know the owner's identity, gives an individual's stamp of identity (with monograms and banderoles) and a particular personal piety emphasizing death and consolation, with a lacing of attitudinizing about the passage of time and the rites of life from cradle to grave.[36]

Smaller formats do not necessarily show the increase in annotation that we might expect. The distinction between Folio and Quarto uses increasingly breaks down in the Elizabethan period, although it is hard to be exact since markings can only be dated by handwriting. As already stated, binding in with other books is often a good indication of domestic use. Later Elizabethan imprints in smaller formats sometimes were printed without the full readings of the Epistles and Gospels, which are given only citations. The same edition may be printed simultaneously with a psalter, however, which suggests a demand for devotional

---

[33]   BL 6.d.9.

[34]   Lambeth Palace Library H5145.A4 1559 has a note of ownership and many markings in the Kalendar.

[35]   BL C.12.i.1 (1).

[36]   Huntington Library, Page 783.

use outside of church. Surviving copies are bound with a Geneva Bible, too, so that readings could have been readily found by hand, or alternatives as well. A copy in the Bodleian reminds its user: 'Marke this well', and gives the instruction to cleanse the heart through scripture, 'by the margant and the notes'.[37]

In silent copies, however, bindings, too, can reveal ownership and use or re-use. A 1566 Folio copy proudly bears the new lettering 'WILLIAM ALYN/ LORDE MAIOR/ 1571'.[38] Smaller books might be more elaborately covered. A 1582 Quarto in the Huntington Library is bound in a very pretty needlework binding which is Elizabethan in provenance. The edgings of the paper are also gilded with an indented scrolled patterning. The binding itself preserves considerable evidence of the reverence with which it was owned and used: it is either a show-copy or a devotional object in its own right.

An expensive and lettered binding, or the use of embroidery, shows all the problems of evidence attaching to the idea of 'popularity'. Such an owner was well off and even gentrified. Yet it also attests to the ways that the *Book of Common Prayer* breaks out of the framework of books defined entirely by official or purposeful usage. By the end of the reign of Elizabeth, the *Book of Common Prayer* was a commonplace object. It bore all the signs of familiarity and even ordinariness that everyday objects possess. In that sense, it is much more of a household presence than most books, even ones that we think of as more 'popular' in cultural affect, such as a play text or even a pamphlet copy of a sermon.[39] This everyday quality to some extent acquires a universal aspect. Of course, many Elizabethans were Catholics, and many more were becoming puritans. But just as there were church papists there were also prayer book papists (and puritans). They might have disputed, disliked, or even despised the doctrine and organization of the church, and perhaps transferred these feelings to the book itself (from the Prayer Book rebellion of 1549 to the civil wars this was a politically divisive text), but they still knew what it was and what it did. Most people were conformist to the extent that they attended christenings and weddings, and so heard it in practice. In addition, prayer books, much more than almost any other book, are levelling objects. One individual copy may be more expensive than another, certainly more richly decorated, but it is in essence, and largely in use, the same thing when used by people of different classes and genders. Not only was it – through weekly and often daily divine service – the book through which more people filtered their experience than any other, it was also the book which placed people face to face with the ordinary fears and yearnings of life more completely than any other. 'In the midst of life we are in death', the order for burial maintains: the *Book of Common Prayer* expresses common experience in ritually adapted forms, which almost anyone in Elizabethan England would have recognized.

---

[37]   Bodleian: Bib. Eng. 1598.e.3 (1).

[38]   BL C.108.aaa.3 (1).

[39]   Compare here the chapter by Abigail Shinn in the present volume.

Chapter 7
International News Pamphlets

S. K. Barker

Of all the genres in the early modern book world, news was the area where printers looked forward as much as they looked back. A changing and challenging form of print which demanded that printers kept up to date with the latest techniques, as well as the latest events, news printing evolved as part of a complicated hybridized information culture led by consumer demand. Cheap, deliberately provocative and out to snare the reader's attention, news pamphlets showcased the ingenuity of the printer, and as such give the modern reader great insight into the concerns and tastes of the Elizabethan print consumer. Frequently polemical, more often than not didactic, if not downright preachy, early modern news pamphlets gave the public what it wanted: sensation, danger, information and ultimately the hope of resolution in uncertain times. Elizabeth's reign was part of a wider continental struggle for Europe's soul. This was the era of the French Wars of Religion and the Dutch Revolt, the Council of Trent and the Battle of Lepanto. Heathens were on the edges of Europe and heretics were on both sides of the channel. People needed to know what was happening, to keep their place in the conflict and to work out the significance of each battle, each siege, each declaration. They needed to know how God was working in the world, both in England and abroad. This chapter examines how readers in Elizabethan England kept up to date with the major happenings in the wider world through translations of foreign language news texts.[1] These pamphlets had a multi-faceted societal role: they informed readers about events happening on the continent, which served to confirm their understanding of the ongoing battle between the forces of good and evil, whilst also allowing printers to make money and develop new techniques of establishing a relationship between the book and the reader.

News was a highly sought-after commodity in Elizabethan England. It was traded between friends, colleagues and even strangers. In its simplest form, news was exchanged orally, as it had been for centuries.[2] This was undoubtedly how

---

[1]   This investigation is based on an analysis of the news translations catalogued in the *Renaissance Cultural Crossroads* project, based at the University of Warwick. The accompanying online catalogue can be found at http://www.hrionline.ac.uk/rcc/.

[2]   This form of news exchange is most readily seen in the plays of William Shakespeare. Act 3, Scene 1 of *The Merchant of Venice* opens with a fairly typical demand of this kind: 'What news on the Rialto?' Furthermore, swapping news (and getting the news wrong) is central to the plots of *The Comedy of Errors* and *The Two Gentlemen of Verona*.

most people received their news, particularly local and national news. Not always entirely distinguishable from gossip, oral news moved quickly within and between communities, passing along trade routes. Within these communities, it was also used as a test, both for the information transmitted between news-giver and news-consumer, and for the personal relationship between the two parties. People would judge how much they trusted the information shared by what they knew of the character of the news-bearer, whilst making judgements on the credibility of the same news-bearer resulting from how reliable the news they brought turned out to be. Manuscript newsletters worked within similar trust parameters: the recipient made a judgement about the contents of the newsletter based on what he thought of the sender, and his own relationship with that person, just as the sender would have had to make a similar judgement about his relationship with the recipient and his circle, and decide what to include in the letter accordingly.[3]

Concerns about credibility and trust thus underpinned early modern news culture, and were clearly visible in the move to print, as shall be seen. Regular periodical print would not emerge in England until the Corantos of the 1620s and would not be maintained long-term until much later in the seventeenth century, although people already had been reading about interesting events for decades. From 1513, when an account of the Scots' defeat at Flodden Field was printed by Richard Facques, readers could purchase occasional individual pamphlets designed to give information about events when they happened.[4] By the later decades of the sixteenth century, pamphlets reporting the news and current events of the day had become almost commonplace in Europe, alongside professional manuscript newsletters.[5] England was slower to catch on, but not immune to the attractions of printed information pamphlets: by the early seventeenth century, news culture was so established as to be worthy of satire in Ben Jonson's biting *The Staple of News*, which emphasized both the public's appetite for news and the printing industry's eagerness to give it to them.[6] A range of title page keywords

---

[3]   Harold Love, *The Culture and Commerce of Texts: Scribal Publication in Seventeenth-Century England* (Oxford, 1998), particularly pp. 9–22; David Randall, *Credibility in Elizabethan and Early Stuart Military News* (London, 2008), especially Chapter 1, 'From Oral News to Written News' and Chapter 2, 'Sociable News'.

[4]   STC 11088.5, *Hereafter ensue the trewe encounter or ... batayle lately done between Engla[n]de and Scotlande* (London, 1513?).

[5]   Richard Streckfuss estimated that of the 26,000 plus items in the *Short Title Catalogue of Books Printed in England, Ireland & Scotland* and *English Books Printed Abroad, 1475–1640*, some 1,250 items could be classified as News publications, excluding Ballads and Official Proclamations. Richard Streckfuss, 'News Before Newspapers', *Journalism and Mass Communication Quarterly* 75/1 (1998): 84–97 (84). On handwritten newsletters, see Zsuzsa Barbarics-Hermanik, 'Handwritten Newsletters as Interregional Information Sources in Central and Southeastern Europe', in Brendan Dooley (ed.), *The Dissemination of News and the Emergence of Contemporaneity in Early Modern Europe* (Farnham, 2010), pp. 155-78.

[6]   Ben Jonson, *The Staple of News*, ed. Anthony Parr (Manchester, 1988).

emerged that indicated to readers that the contents of particular pamphlets partook of this phenomenon of gathering up and sharing stories: as well as news, titles enticed their readers by offering them a 'Discours', a 'Report', some 'Tidings' or a 'Journal'. One of the most potent of all such terms, 'Relation' or *'Relazione'*, has recently been the subject of a workshop and related proceedings.[7]

To a modern reader, these pamphlets might not seem worthy of any of these terms. The items are almost unbearably polemical, but early modern news was not designed to be impartial. In the heat of the Reformation century, the sense of right and wrong which lay behind the reporting of the news made it all the more attractive to its readers, and in no small measure helped its passage across linguistic barriers. Commercial imperatives also had a role to play, however: for every reader interested in events, there was a printer interested in financial return. Throughout most of the early modern period, the English authorities prohibited the printing of news tracts covering the domestic situation.[8] No worthy government would allow for open debate of its policies, particularly not when the King's marital affairs, and later his daughter's lack of them, had consequences for the spiritual well-being of the entire nation. As pamphlet culture emerged from the printing houses of London, government took it upon itself to batten down the hatches.[9] Yet this was not the last word in the matter. A public hungry for information and printers with an eye for profit quickly turned abroad for news.[10]

What made a potential purchaser stop, pick up a news pamphlet and decide to buy it? At the core of this process lay the subject matter of the news itself. People bought these pamphlets because they were interested in the contents.[11] Whereas the rationale behind the purchase of a Bible or martyrology might combine devotional

---

[7]   The workshop, 'The Relation: The Relazione' was held in Toronto in 2009, and the proceedings have recently been published as 'Things not easily believed', with a forward by Natalie Zemon Davis and contributions by Thomas V. Cohen & Germaine Warkentin and Filippo de Vivo, amongst others, in a special issue of *Renaissance and Reformation* 34/1–2 (Winter–Spring 2011). My thanks must go to Professor Davis for making me aware of both the workshop and its general themes.

[8]   The extremely complicated history of press censorship and its implementation cannot be addressed fully here. Key points of interest include Henry VIII's proclamation of 1538 and the Elizabethan Injunctions of 1559. These and other sources are in the online archive *Primary Sources on Copyright (1450–1900)* http://copy.law.cam.ac.uk/cam/index. php.

[9]   Cyndia Susan Clegg's work on press censorship gives the best overall view of these problems in the sixteenth and seventeenth centuries: *Press Censorship in Elizabethan England* (Cambridge, 1997), *Press Censorship in Jacobean England* (Cambridge, 2001) and *Press Censorship in Caroline England* (Cambridge, 2008).

[10]   It is intriguing that within the vibrant scholarship surrounding early news production in the British Isles, translation is frequently alluded to, but rarely analyzed.

[11]   Andrew Pettegree has challenged some of the scholarly assumptions behind the purchasing of books by early modern readers in *Reformation and the Culture of Persuasion* (Cambridge, 2005), p. 157.

commitment with content interest, the acquisition of a news pamphlet was not such an evident statement of confessional allegiance. News pamphlets were not bought to show off one's sophistication and erudition. These books, more than any other book except perhaps the Bible, were primarily purchased for their content. Undoubtedly one of the elements that made international news pamphlets so enticing to their readers was their topicality. The intellectual news space was one where printed works had to battle with oral and manuscript sources for consumers, and it was a battle that could only be won over time. The earlier decades of the sixteenth century saw only a handful of news pamphlet translations, even though events were already being reported in print in different languages. The apparent language/translation gap was first discussed by Matthias A. Shaaber, who noted that despite the existence of Latin and French accounts of the Field of the Cloth of Gold, no English printed account of this event appeared to have been made.[12] Just over a dozen news translations were made before Elizabeth's accession, and these were mostly produced in the 1530s and 1540s, charting Charles V's struggles in the Holy Roman Empire. During Elizabeth's reign, production shot up. It was when continental Europe became the physical battlefield for the forces of good and evil, which for Englishmen meant Protestantism vs. Catholicism, that the news industry found both its professional capacity and its audience. Lots of interesting and important things happening meant more foreign source pamphlets and more opportunities for translations. In 1589, for example, news-related publishing made up about 40 percent of all printed translations in England.[13] By the time of Elizabeth's death in 1603, around 250 translations of foreign-language news pamphlets had been printed. Events in northern Europe drew the most attention in print. French was the most prevalent source language, with nearly 140 translations made, followed by Dutch with just under 60 items. This language distribution mirrored the interest Englishmen had in the confessional struggles of the Huguenots and the Dutch Protestants, as well as the strong trade links that printers, like other businessmen, had with northern Europe.[14] After the resolution of these conflicts, former co-religionist allies could go back to being

---

[12]   Matthias A. Shaaber, *Some Forerunners of the Newspaper in England, 1476–1622* (Philadelphia, 1929), pp. 9–11.

[13]   A full survey of this material in the sixteenth and early seventeenth centuries, in particular its chronological spread, can be found in S.K. Barker, 'Newes Lately Come: European News Books in English Translation', in S.K. Barker and Brenda M. Hosington (eds), *Renaissance Cultural Crossroads: Translation, Print and Culture in Britain, 1473–1640* (Leiden, forthcoming).

[14]   The *Renaissance Cultural Crossroads* project has been able to clarify that a number of items previously thought to be translations from German were in fact made from Dutch, using the *Short Title Catalogue Netherlands* (STCN) and the *Short Title Catalogus Vlaanderen* (STCV) databases. The STCN can be accessed at http://www.kb.nl/stcn/index-en.html and the STCV at http://www.vlaamse-erfgoedbibliotheek.be/oude-drukken.

foreign enemies.[15] Only a dozen items were translated from Italian and around 20 from Spanish, a quarter of which were produced during the late 1580s during the heightened circumstances of the Spanish Armada. Even then, readers were given little leeway in their interpretations of their reading matter, with titles like *A packe of Spanish lyes, sent abroad in the vvorld* and on one occasion a reply set alongside the translation entitled *An answer to the vntruthes, published and printed in Spaine, in glorie of their supposed victorie atchieued against our English Nauie*: such explicit titles left readers with no uncertainty as to the editorial concerns of the pamphlet maker, and their own anticipated understanding of the contents.[16]

Getting the reader's attention mattered when putting together a pamphlet. English readers seem to have been very similar to their continental counterparts in their love of a name to give their reading some shape, be it a person's name or a place name. Only a couple of items had no reference to a person or place (outside of any pertinent publication details) on their title pages. Individual names were most commonly found on title pages, with around 120 items in the sample being distinguished in this way. Also common was combining a personal name or names with a location, to give even more detail. Around 90 items fall into this category. Places on their own as identifiers were a bit less common, but not unheard of, with just under 50 title pages making reference to a place, typically a town or towns. Using a person's name on the title page of a news pamphlet did several things for the reader. It made up for the unfortunate lack of attributable authors of news pamphlets, something which was potentially problematic for consumers used to having a name or a face through which to trace their news and decide its value. It is telling that many of these pamphlets still today are catalogued as though authored by the characters whose exploits are recounted within their pages. Making the protagonists of the various events so prominent also allowed printers and readers to establish quasi-personal relationships with these otherwise distant characters. Henri IV's victory at Ivry in 1590 was glorious for him, for his armies and for all his readers: reading *The true discourse of the wonderfull victorie, obtained by Henrie the fourth, the French King, and King of Nauarre, in a battell against those of the League, neere the towne of Yurie*, all shared in the glory together.[17] Even relatively anonymous works could be given a veneer of personality with a judicious title. An account that was attributed to a 'a Frenche gentilwoman to an other gentilwoman straunger' or *A letter lately written from Rome, by an Italian*

---

[15]   Bernard Capp discusses chapbook prognostications against the 'villainous Dutch and French' in the later seventeenth century. Bernard Capp, 'Popular literature', in Barry Reay (ed.), *Popular Culture in Seventeenth-Century England* (London & Sydney, 1985), p. 228.

[16]   STC 23011, *A packe of Spanish lyes, sent abroad in the vvorld* (London, 1588) and STC 17132, *An answer to the vntruthes, published and printed in Spaine, in glorie of their supposed victorie atchieued against our English Nauie* (London, 1589).

[17]   STC 13145, *The true discourse of the wonderfull victorie, obtained by Henrie the fourth, the French King, and King of Nauarre, in a battell against those of the League, neere the towne of Yurie* (London, 1590).

gentleman, to a freende of his in Lyons in Fraunce still carried an expectation of the kind of person the author was, merely through acknowledgement of his or her social standing and nationality.[18] The same formulas were followed for news of a more sensational nature, with the famous werewolf Peter Stumpp not merely being named on the title page of the 1590 pamphlet outlining his deeds, but also acknowledged as 'a most wicked sorcerer' alongside his lycanthropic incarnation.[19] This fascination with people tells us something about the personal nature of early modern European society, and how these concerns interacted with print to allow everyone the opportunity to create his or her own public personality, or at least have a personality created by a printer. Readers were not buying pamphlets about unknown anonymous figures, but about people whom they felt they knew, people they could care about and make judgements about.[20]

Places were just as important as people in this setup. Places were constant, places did not move. Englishmen could visit places, have a personal knowledge of them, in a way that they were unlikely to know the French King or Peter Stumpp the werewolf. Pamphlets could be very broadly geographical, such as *Nevves from Spayne and Holland conteyning. An information of Inglish affayres in Spayne*, *Newes out of France*, or *Credible reportes from France, and Flanders. In the moneth of May. 1590.*[21] These gave a basic location for the story, one which would draw the reader's attention as a kind of general theme, but gave little more hint than that. Most items were more specific, with the geographical location being integral to the reporting of the event in question, as in *A True relation of taking of Alba-Regalis in the German tongue, called Sfullweissenburgh [sic], the chiefe cittie in Nether-Hungarie, which was taken by the Christian armie, the twentith [sic] of September last past, 1601* or *A Most straunge and wounderfull accident happened at Weersburch by Franckford, by a most fearefull earthquake and daknesse [sic], with a mighty tempest of thunder and lightning.*[22] Battles and

---

[18]   STC 24565, *The translation of a letter written by a Frenche gentilwoman to an other gentilwoman straunger, her frind, vpon the death of the most excellent and vertous ladye, Elenor of Roye, Princes of Conde, contaynyng her last wyll and testament* (London, 1564) and STC 21292a, *A letter lately written from Rome, by an Italian gentleman, to a freende of his in Lyons in Fraunce (London, 1585)*.

[19]   STC 23375, *A true discourse. Declaring the damnable life and death of one Stubbe Peeter, a most wicked sorcerer, who in the likenes of a woolfe committed many murders* (London, [1590]).

[20]   Bernard Capp has discussed similar tendencies within ballads in 'Popular Literature', pp. 205–6.

[21]   STC 22994, *Nevves from Spayne and Holland conteyning. An information of Inglish affayres in Spayne* (Antwerp, 1593); STC 11285, *Newes out of France* (London, 1592); STC 11265 *Credible reportes from France, and Flanders. In the moneth of May. 1590* (London, 1590).

[22]   STC 256.5, *A True relation of taking of Alba-Regalis in the German tongue, called Sfullweissenburgh [sic], the chiefe cittie in Nether-Hungarie, which was taken by the Christian armie, the twentith [sic] of September last past, 1601* (London, 1601);

Natural disasters alike needed to be securely and precisely located, in order for their true providential worth to be assessed. If the end of the world was coming, readers needed to know where it was coming from.

News rarely escaped its sensationalist background, no matter what the subject matter of an individual pamphlet might be. Readers were presented with evidence that the end of the world was nigh, and this was proved just as well by an account of a battle in France as it was by the reporting of a monstrous birth in Flanders. According to Lisa Ferrarro Parmelee, the French material translated in the 1580s and 1590s had tacit governmental support. The authorities were happy for printers like John Wolfe to produce translations of French pamphlets as long as they were bringing news of Protestant successes against the Catholic enemy. When the French tide turned, and Henri IV abjured his Protestant faith for the sake of internal peace, the translations dried up.[23] Parmelee's argument needs some nuancing with regard to the reader. Translations of French pamphlets were indeed the mainstay of the industry, but news from the Low Countries was of almost equal interest. Readers might not have had quite so many pamphlets about the Prince of Orange or the challenges faced by Parma in the Netherlands as they did about the edicts of the French king or the military successes of Henri IV, but they did have some. The conflicts were of equal and connected confessional bearing, particularly given the frequency with which the two wars overlapped. And whilst political and military pamphlets were plentiful and varied, English readers wanted to read about other stories too, stories which had similar providential overtones, which also explained the world unfolding around them but were not as lofty as battles between kings and nobles. Accounts of floods and fires, monstrous births and miraculous apparitions appeared steadily throughout the period, as did stories about the Turk and Eastern threats to Christendom. It is unlikely that government support lay behind the translation of a pamphlet about the murder of an innkeeper, his wife and child by a 22-year-old man in Normandy.[24] The translator of this particular pamphlet owned that he made the English version because of the interest shown in a similar murder story already rendered into print, and, one imagines, a good seller. Audience response shaped news translation: printers had translated what they thought the public would want to read and did their best to manage audience anticipation. In the note to the reader that prefaces *Aduertisements from Brittany, And from the Lovv Countries In September and October*, the publisher not only discusses how he got hold of the material from contacts in Brittany, but also declares that 'If I may finde this to be acceptable to the Reader, I shall be willing to acquaint him

---

STC 25219.5, *A Most straunge and wounderfull accident happened at Weersburch by Franckford, by a most fearefull earthquake and daknesse [sic], with a mighty tempest of thunder and lightning.* (London, 1600).

[23] Lisa Ferraro Parmelee, *Good Newes From Fraunce: French Anti-League Propaganda in Late Elizabethan England* (Rochester, NY, 1996).

[24] STC 11377, *A most straunge, rare, and horrible murther committed by a Frenchman of the age of too or three and twentie yeares* (London, [1586]).

with the rest, as it shall come vnto my hands.'[25] The reader was made part of a news network, not just a consumer but a participant complementing the traditional oral network.

The different words used to indicate news content have already been noted. Printers further played on reader sensibilities by including a qualifier such as 'true' or 'veritable' in the title. This spoke to the need to establish credibility and to cut other news sources out of the equation, by making a pamphlet appear more trustworthy than its competitors. Printers were not shy about making the most of what they had, in particular their source materials. Drawing attention to the links in this supply chain drew the reader in, as the end point in an international news network. Much of this was done through techniques used on the title page, the printers' best advertising space. Translated titles frequently employed the word 'copy', emphasizing that the title had already appeared elsewhere.[26] Where possible, details of the source language pamphlet were given, to give the networks some detail. The most basic way of doing this was to note the language that the translation had been made from, as in *The strange and marueilous newes lately come from the great kingdome of Chyna ... . Translated out of the Castlyn tongue, by T.N.*[27] A slightly more sophisticated version would include details of the original place of publication, as in, for example, *The letters pattents of the Kings declaration for the referring of the generall assemblie of the princes, cardinals, dukes and peeres*, which noted that it was 'Faithfullie translated out of the French copie printed at Caen'.[28] The most evolved pamphlets would give the name of the original printer: *A true discourse of an ouerthrow giuen to the armie of the Leaguers in Prouince* informed the casual browser very clearly that it was 'Translated verbatim out of the French copie, printed at Tours by Iamet Mettayer'.[29] If a reader so wished, he could search out a copy of Mettayer's text and compare the two accounts. This quest to make the origins of a work as transparent as possible could take other forms, with the names of witnesses to the

---

[25]   Not in ESTC, *Aduertisements from Brittany, And from the Lovv Countries, In September and October* (London, 1591).

[26]   'Copy' did not always indicate a translation, and indeed was sometimes a direct rendering of the source title, as in STC 333, *A true copy of a letter sent by the Prince of Parma to the generall states of the lowe cuntries, assembled at Antwerpe* (London, [1579]) a translation of a French original through a Dutch intermediary, where the French original, *Copie d'une lettre du prince de Parma, envoyée aux Estats Généraux des Païs Bas, assemblez en Anvers* (Antwerp, 1579), used the term to indicate the move from manuscript to print.

[27]   STC 5141, *The strange and marueilous newes lately come from the great kingdome of Chyna, which adioyneth to the East Indya* (London, 1577).

[28]   STC 13113, *The letters pattents of the Kings declaration for the referring of the generall assemblie of the princes, cardinals, dukes and peeres* (London, 1590).

[29]   STC 11290, *A true discourse of an ouerthrow giuen to the armie of the Leaguers in Prouince: by Messieurs D'Esdiguieres and Lauallette. Translated verbatim out of the French copie, printed at Tours by Iamet Mettayer* (London, [1591]).

events in question, and their location. Although paratextual materials were not particularly common, where present, they also served to illuminate this network setup, and to include the reader in the story's continued dispersal. *An example of Gods iudgement shew[n] vpon two children borne in high Dutch la[nd] in the citie of Lutssolof* includes a paratext which makes plain what a reader was meant to take from these stories: with the Bible as an example they are exhorted to consider such events and repent, like the people of Nineveh, rather than ignoring the signs sent by God, as did the people of Sodom, Gomorrah and Jerusalem.[30]

Where possible, an image might be included as part of the title page to further pique interest. These could be elaborate, such as the tripartite woodcut that introduced *A true coppy of the admonitions sent by the subdued prouinces to the states of Holland*, which combined a time-lapsed narrative with allegorical cartouches, a map representing the Armada and the salacious promise of 'A mayden buried alive at Brussels. 1597.'.[31] Images were frequently used in sensational texts. Pamphlets dealing with the threat from the east would frequently include an image showing men of war. *Newes come latle frõ Pera*, for example, included a small, square woodcut of two armies fighting, men on horseback with swords drawn, discarded weapons and fallen comrades lying scattered on the ground.[32] The savagery of the battle is unmistakable, even if the soldiers in the image are not particularly exotic in their appearance. Seventeenth-century images of the East would be far more vivid: when this particular story was reprinted in 1606, the title-page image was far more menacing, even though it now showed men ready for battle rather than engaged in combat, as the individual fighters were given clear features and they carried a range of weapons, all with one hand ready to draw and fight.[33] Even more disturbing were the images that advertised the tales of monstrous births and natural disasters. *An example of Gods iudgement shew[n] vpon two children borne in high Dutch la[nd] in the citie of Lutssolof* included an image of the first child described in the pamphlet, with his head shaped like a bishop's mitre, one hand shaped as a sword and the other as a rod, and with the skin of a 'Negro or Blackmore'. The text referred the reader to this image, before recounting the sensational events of the child's short life.[34] Other images were indicated on the title page but were in fact embedded in the text, and so could essentially only be investigated further once a purchase had been made. A good example of this is *A most strange and wonderfull herring*, where it is explained that the fish is inscribed with images 'having on the one side the picture of two

[30]   STC 10608.5, *An example of Gods iudgement shew[n] vpon two children borne in high Dutch la[nd] in the citie of Lutssolof, the first day of Iulie* (London, [1582?]).

[31]   STC 18465, *A true coppy of the admonitions sent by the subdued prouinces to the states of Holland* (London, 1598).

[32]   STC 4102.3, *Newes come latle frõ Pera* ([London], [1561]).

[33]   STC 4102.5, *Newes from Rome. Of two mightie armies, aswell footemen as horsmen: the first of the great Sophy* ([London], [1606]).

[34]   *An example of Gods iudgement.*

armed men fighting, and on the other most strange Characters, as in the picture is here expressed'. A reader would have to turn to the end of the pamphlet to see the men and characters discussed on the title page and in the text.[35] But the promise was evident from the title page.

The extent to which foreign imports fascinated the English reader and profited the English printer is seen in how such products were abused. Reports of news and events that might more readily be considered domestic were advertised as having non-English origins. *Newe Newes containing A shorte rehersall of the late enterprise of certaine fugytiue Rebelles* proclaimed that it was translated from a Dutch original, and included a supposed date of translation, but it was a discussion of the Second Desmond Rebellion of July 1579.[36] There could be several explanations as to why the printer felt the need to claim a Dutch origin. Obviously, there was the underlying problem of government prohibitions of the printing of domestic news. Giving a story a foreign source allowed a printer to skirt round this issue, even if the contents as stated on the title page indicated the unlikelihood of these claimed origins. The writer of this pamphlet made a considerable effort to place this as an international pamphlet, mentioning the 'cankered Court of the Spanish Inquisition', the Irish rebels' connections in Rome and Spain, Don John's taking of Namur, as well as various maritime connections which included Civitavecchia (identified as 'a sea towne'), Genoa, Lisbon and even the Barbary coast.[37] Such elaborate detail suggests that translated news had a worth and a cachet which was valued by the consumer and there to be exploited by the producer. We get a sense of how successful this could be from *A true discourse of a cruell fact committed by a gentlewoman ... First printed in French at Roan: and now translated into English*, an item packaged as a typical sensational news story, but in fact a rendering of one of Matteo Bandello's *Novelle* into news pamphlet form.[38] Whether or not the printer knew that this was not a news story but a fictional tale is unclear. What is undeniable is that the reading public wanted good stories on a regular basis, and printers had to find ways to meet this demand. News which came from abroad was evidently taken seriously and trusted, so much so that these credentials could be abused to get other material in under the radar.

Printing was a trade where practitioners and consumers frequently tested the waters to see what they could get away with. Nowhere were the lines quite so

---

[35]   STC 13239, *A most strange and wonderfull herring, taken on the 26. day of Nouember 1597, neere vnto Drenton sometime the old and chiefe cittie of the kingdome of Norway* (London, 1598).

[36]   STC 23406, *Newe Newes containing A shorte rehersall of the late enterprise of certaine fugytiue Rebelles* ([London], [1579]). No Dutch language source pamphlet has so far been traced, and given the content and tone of the pamphlet, foreign origins of the type indicated on the title page seem particularly unlikely.

[37]   Ibid., Aiiir-vv.

[38]   STC 3469, *A true discourse of a cruell fact committed by a gentlewoman towardes her husband, her father, her sister and two of her nephewes* (London, 1599).

fuzzily drawn as in relation to current events publishing. Through the translation of news pamphlets from across Europe, but mainly from the continental Protestant allies, Englishmen could understand that they were part of the wider contest for the soul of Christendom. These pamphlets gave Englishmen's reading lives an international perspective that has been little acknowledged outside the realms of literary translation, but which evidently constituted a vibrant and growing market, where printers worked hard to tailor their wares to the tastes of their audience, where the political was highly personal and the next newsworthy event could not come soon enough.

Chapter 8
Spenser's Popular Intertexts

Abigail Shinn

Written by and for a privileged group of educated readers, Elizabethan poesy was allied to the rhetorical arts and claimed as the inheritor of the Ciceronian plea that rhetoric should teach, delight and move.[1] This endeavour was to be accomplished through the skilful use of figures and tropes, rhetorical flourishes which had the potential to restore eloquence to a post-lapsarian world mired in a linguistic muddle of 'galimaufrey and hodgepodge'.[2] Poesy can therefore be understood as setting itself up in opposition to forms of cultural production which lack a rhetorical, Latinate foundation. As Roger Chartier has noted, however, when we go looking for well-defined boundaries between cultural forms, those 'cultural cleavages' which would allow us to differentiate between social groups, we instead find evidence of 'fluid circulation ... blurred distinctions'.[3]

Natalie Zemon Davis responds to this model of cultural fluidity by focusing upon tracing patterns of meaning across different forms, potentially defining the popular as that which is most mobile.[4] The effect of this interaction between cultural types in poesy can be to draw attention to instances where appropriation forms part of the act of literary construction, the borrowing of different cultural objects helping to shape the role adopted by the poet. In order to explore one example of how cultural borrowings interact with forms of literary self-fashioning, this chapter will trace a series of appropriations in the work of Edmund Spenser, arguing that his impulse towards textual and cultural copiousness stems from a fascination with the medium of print as a discursive force which can influence and change the course of English poesy.[5]

---

[1]   Cicero, *De Inventione, De Optimo Genere Oratorum, Topica*, trans. H.M. Hubbell (Cambridge, MA, 1949), I, 3, p. 356.

[2]   Edmund Spenser, epistle to 'The Shepheardes Calender', in *Edmund Spenser: The Shorter Poems*, ed. Richard A. McCabe (London, 1999), p. 27. All further quotations are from this edition.

[3]   Roger Chartier, *The Cultural Uses of Print in Early Modern France*, trans. Lydia G. Cochrane (Princeton, 1987), p. 3.

[4]   Natalie Zemon Davis, 'Towards Mixtures and Margins', *American Historical Review* 97 (1992): 1414–15; Susan Wiseman, 'Popular Culture: A Category for Analysis?', in Matthew Dimmock and Andrew Hadfield (eds), *Literature and Popular Culture in Early Modern England* (Farnham, 2009), p. 21.

[5]   Roger Chartier, 'Culture as Appropriation: Popular Cultural Uses in Early Modern France', in Steven Kaplan (ed.), *Understanding Popular Culture: Europe from the Middle Ages to the Nineteenth Century* (New York, 1984), p. 233.

For Spenser print culture, in all its forms, was a valuable ally in his quest for 'a kingdome for our owne language',[6] providing a storehouse of images and analogies which would enable him to forge his identity as 'England's new Poete' (epistle, 25). He engaged with a variety of printed formats, from the ribald and frequently scatological adventures recounted in jest books and the instantly recognizable yearly prognostication and calendar of the almanac to the beast epic's anti-clerical Aesopian satire and the collections of erotic novella found in storybook compilations. These popular, widely disseminated, relatively stable and bestselling texts (particularly in the case of the almanac) garnered a wide readership but also stand testament to the role of elite culture in mediating the popular, as all were produced by educated men even if their influences and consumers came from more varied groups.[7] As a result, Spenser's appropriation of these printed formats not only tells us about the construction of his literary identity, but also reflects the many layers of cultural interaction which have to be negotiated when approaching the 'popular' in the early modern period.

Jest Books

Evidence for Spenser's varied reading can be found in a much quoted marginal annotation from Gabriel Harvey's copy of Murner's *Howleglas* (1528), in which Harvey records how Spenser lent him some 'foolish Bookes':

> This Howletglasse, with Skoggin, Skelton, and L[a]zarill, given me at London, of M[r] Spensar XX. Decembris, 1[5]78, on condition [I] shoold bestowe the reading of them over, before the first of January [imme]diately ensuing; otherwise to forfeit unto him my Lucian in fower volumes. Whereupon I was the rather induced to trifle away so many howers, as were idely overpassed in running thorowgh the [foresaid] foolish Bookes.[8]

Howleglas was the name given to the German trickster Till Eulenspiegel, who appears in a number of English jest books which survive from the sixteenth century, the first of which was published in 1519. 'Skoggin' invokes *The iests of Skogyn* (1570) by John Scogan, a jest book which produced offspring in the form of George Dobson's *Dobsons drie bobbes sonne and heire to Skoggin* (1607). The reference to Skelton may indicate that Spenser gave Harvey a copy of *Merie Tales Newly Imprinted & Made by Master Skelton* (1567), a jest book in which Skelton himself

---

[6]   Edmund Spenser, 'Three Proper and wittie, familiar Letters', in Edwin Greenlaw, Charles Grosvenor Osgood, Frederick Morgan Padelford, and Ray Heffner (eds), *The Works of Edmund Spenser: A Variorum Edition, The Prose Works* (Baltimore, 1949), p. 16.

[7]   Garret Sullivan and Linda Woodbridge, 'Popular Culture in Print', in Arthur F. Kinney (ed.), *The Cambridge Companion to English Literature, 1500–1600* (Cambridge, 2000), p. 277.

[8]   Virginia F. Stern, *Gabriel Harvey: His Life, Marginalia and Library* (Oxford, 1979), p. 228.

is a figure of fun, although this could also be the John Stow edition of Skelton's works, *Pithy pleasaunt and profitable workes of maister Skelton*, published by Thomas Marsh in 1568. 'Lazarillo' refers to the Spanish picaresque novella *La Vida de Lazarillo de Tormes, y de sus fortunas y aduersidades* (1554) by Diego Hurtado de Mendoza, translated into English as *The pleasaunt historie of Lazarillo de Tormes* (1586) by David Rowland. These texts may seem a strange trade for Harvey's 'Lucian in fower volumes', but as Spenser and Harvey's relationship was in many respects a literary one, the marginal note not only provides evidence that their book exchanges included popular texts (albeit as a form of blackmail) but also undoes any assumption that they adhered to a strict classical model for their intellectual trading, as Andrew Hadfield notes: 'Harvey's comment appears to suggest that Spenser was eager to test the boundaries and limits of Harvey's Cambridge culture and to show him that humour did not begin and end with the classics'.[9]

While three jest books and a picaresque novella are a relatively flimsy foundation on which to build a picture of Spenser as a popular reader, and in no way undo the evidence of Spenser's classical and Italianate influences, they do remind us of the poet's ability to act as a cultural mediator. Spenser and Harvey's transaction, in which ephemeral, popular texts are swapped for four volumes by a witty and humorous classical writer, may in itself be a jest as Spenser punctures Harvey's inflated view of himself as a serious scholar. This raises the possibility that when Spenser appropriates aspects of the wide-ranging field of Elizabethan print culture in his own work, he is engaging in a similarly playful process of negotiation between the Humanist tradition of classical learning (one which, lest we forget, produced Erasmus and Thomas More's mischievous and frequently scatological offerings) and the popular products of the printing press. In doing so Spenser simultaneously plays a joke on the reader and highlights his work's position within an inclusive national print culture, a culture in which jest books and classical works can share both shelf space and readers.

Almanacs

The patterns left by ephemeral print can be found throughout Spenser's work, nowhere more so than in *The Shepheardes Calender* (1579). In the *Calender* Spenser adopts a style reminiscent of the standard almanac format: the 'twelue Aeglogues proportionable to the twelue monethes' (23) mimic the almanac maker's month-by-month prognostications, and the inclusion of newly commissioned woodcuts which head each eclogue also imitates many almanacs (see Adam Smyth's chapter

---

[9]   Andrew Hadfield, *Edmund Spenser: A Life* (Oxford, 2012), p. 72; see also Andrew Hadfield, 'Spenser and Jokes: The Kathleen Williams Lecture', *Spenser Studies* 25 (2010): 1-19.

in this volume).[10] This produces a collision between an established classical model in the form of the eclogue and a recognizable contemporary publication. Most striking, however, is Spenser's decision to name his publication *The Shepheardes Calender*, as E.K. notes in the epistle 'applying an olde name to a new worke' (168) and directly associating his poem with the frequently reprinted French *Compost et calendrier des bergères*, a large perpetual almanac that included religious teaching alongside astrological and medical advice, first translated into English as the *Kalender of Shepardes* in 1503.[11] The *Kalender* also incorporated detailed woodcuts which may have influenced the layout of Spenser's publication.

In the epistle to *The Shepheardes Calender* the unidentified E.K. praises the poet's use of 'naturall English words, as haue ben long time out of vse and almost cleare disherited' (81) and places him within a literary tradition headed by Chaucer. This positioning of the poem within a national literary framework underscores Spenser's use of the almanac model. During the sixteenth century, English almanacs had begun to diverge from their Continental counterparts and were becoming more geographically specific.[12] One of the ways in which English almanacs asserted their nationality was through their choice of meridian, as is demonstrated by Leonard Digges in the preface to his almanac for 1555: 'Here note (Reder) wher as the eleuate Pole, & Meridian should be considered: in this work it is performed for London: bycause I wisshe this Meridian, Situation, or Clime the exact truthe of thinges'.[13] England was usually on the periphery of Continental almanacs, its astrological forecast based upon a European meridian and Alison Chapman has argued that the growing geographical specificity of English almanacs came at the behest of a readership which 'enjoyed the idea that their local time and place were unique in relation to the heavens'.[14] This anglicized view of the almanac tradition corresponds neatly to E.K.'s insistence in *The Shepheardes Calender* that 'our Mother tongue [is] truly of it self … both ful enough for prose and stately enough for verse' (82–3).

The choice of typeface in the first edition of *The Shepheardes Calender* also mirrors the almanac's geographical specificity. The eclogues are printed in blackletter, the epistle and glosses in roman type. Steven K. Galbraith argues that the

---

[10]   Ruth Samson Luborsky, 'The Illustrations to *The Shepheardes Calender*', *Spenser Studies* 2 (1981): 19–21; Stephen Orgel, 'Textual Icons: Reading Early Modern Illustrations', in Neil Rhodes and Jonathan Sawday (eds.), *The Renaissance Computer: Knowledge Technology in the First Age of Print* (London, 2000), p. 68.

[11]   Bernard Capp, *Astrology and the Popular Press: English Almanacs 1500–1800* (London, 1979), p. 144.

[12]   Abigail Shinn, '"Extraordinary discourses of vnnecessarie matter": Spenser's *Shepheardes Calender* and the Almanac Tradition', in Matthew Dimmock and Andrew Hadfield (eds), *Literature and Popular Culture in Early Modern England* (Farnham, 2009), pp. 135–49; Capp, *Astrology and the Popular Press*, pp. 270–74.

[13]   Leonard Digges, *A Prognostication of Right Good effect* (London, 1555), sig. *3ᵛ.

[14]   Alison Chapman, 'Marking Time: Astrology, Almanacs, and English Protestantism', *Renaissance Quarterly* 60 (2007): 1264.

choice of blackletter over roman type for the eclogues is a moment of 'Englishing' because blackletter was known as 'English' type and closely associated with the vernacular.[15] The almanac was one of the most pervasive forms of vernacular print available, and commonly printed in blackletter. The English almanac tradition thus afforded Spenser a useful template that would consolidate his interrogation of the value attributed to English poetry, not only through an association with a geographically specific form but by allying his work to a culturally resonant aspect of print which conflated the popular with the national.

Beast Epic

Mother Hubberds Tale, published in 1591 as part of the *Complaints*, has become defined by its relationship to the tangled web of Spenser's biography and the tantalizing hints that its publication may have had a detrimental effect upon his efforts to gain favour at court. The *Complaints* was famously 'called in' – copies were removed from circulation – because of *Mother Hubberds Tale*'s satirical look at Elizabethan politics and the shadowing of Lord Burghley in the figure of the crafty fox.[16] This biographical focus, however, has resulted in the poem's literary and generic influences being largely neglected. *Mother Hubberds Tale* is a beast epic, belonging to an old tradition of speaking beasts used to produce morality tales and satire. Spenser's recounting of the adventures of Sir Reynold the fox draws upon a large body of medieval satire, principally anti-clerical in tone, which related the comic exploits of a wily fox called Reynard as he sought to fill his belly and confound his enemies. This tradition was dominated by the widely disseminated French collection of Reynard stories, the *Roman de Renart*.[17] Spenser's poem follows this literary model, which had spread throughout Europe by the late medieval period and was defined by a long history of adaptation and translation. A comparison of *Mother Hubberds Tale* and Caxton's *The booke of Raynarde the foxe* (1550) produces multiple points of connection between

---

[15] Steven K. Galbraith, '"English" Black-Letter Type and Spenser's *Shepheardes Calender*', *Spenser Studies* 23 (2008): 26.

[16] See Edwin Greenlaw, *Studies in Spenser's Historical Allegory* (New York, 1967), p. 112; Richard S. Peterson, 'Laurel Crown and Ape's Tail: New Light on Spenser's Career from Thomas Tresham', *Spenser Studies* 12 (1998): 1–35; Hadfield, *Edmund Spenser*, pp. 265–74; Thomas Herron, 'Reforming the Fox: Spenser's "Mother Hubberds Tale", the Beast Fables of Barnabe Riche, and Adam Loftus, Archbishop of Dublin', *Studies in Philology* 3 (2008): 336–87; A.C. Judson, 'Mother Hubberd's Ape', *Modern Language Notes* 63 (1948): 146; Bruce Danner, *Furious Muse: Edmund Spenser's War on Lord Burghley* (Basingstoke, 2011).

[17] Kenneth Varty, *Reynard, Renart, Reinaert and other Foxes in Medieval England: The Iconographic Evidence* (Amsterdam, 1999), pp. 23–24; Jill Mann, *From Aesop to Raynard: Beast Literature in Medieval Britain* (Oxford, 2009), p. 52.

this popular form and Spenser's satire, links that run far deeper than the initial correlation between Spenser's Sir Reynold and the beast epic's Raynard the fox.[18]

The *Raynard* stories were well known in Europe (although there is no textual evidence for a Reynardian tradition in English prior to Caxton's publication of the *Booke of Raynarde the Foxe* in 1481), and the figure of Raynard was found in manuscript and print, his stories taught in grammar schools, incorporated into sermons and represented in woodcuts and on wall paintings.[19] The beast epic also had an important position within a storytelling tradition, and by co-opting a genre with an oral dimension Spenser reminds his reader of the unfixed nature of satire when passed from storyteller to audience. The narrator of Spenser's poem emphasizes that Mother Hubberd is a common storyteller with no finesse, stating 'bad her tongue that it so bluntly told', simultaneously demanding that the reader interrogate any pleasure that they derive from the tale and identifying the source for the story as part of the oral tradition.[20] Spenser explicitly separates that tradition from classically inspired genres: 'No Muses aide me needes hereto to call; / Base is the style, and matter meane withal' (43–44). It is also important to consider that many fables or ballads recited or performed to an audience were also found in print and if Spenser's poem was ever read out loud, his tale would travel from an imagined storyteller in the form of Mother Hubberd to the reader indulging in an oral performance to entertain their friends and neighbours.[21] This movement has serious implications for how we frame our understanding of popular orality, as it highlights the impossibility of separating literate and oral practices.

Spenser's debt to Caxton's *Raynarde the Foxe*, and the wider tradition to which it belonged, is readily apparent.[22] His poem follows the wily Sir Reynold and his ape companion as they wander the countryside looking for food, adopting a series of disguises in order to trick and dissemble until they end up at court, where the ape usurps the lion-king's crown while the fox acts as chief courtier. The *Booke of Raynarde the Foxe* features a litany of complaints made to the 'lyon kynge

---

[18]   This 1550 edition of Caxton's text was published by Thomas Gaultier and is based on Caxton's 1481 English translation of Gheraert Leeu's *Die Hystorie van Reynaert die Vos* (1479).

[19]   Mann, *From Aesop to Reynard*, p. 220; Adam Fox, 'Popular Verses and their Readership in the Early Seventeenth Century', in James Raven, Helen Small and Naomi Tadmor (eds), *The Practice and Representation of Reading in England* (Cambridge, 1996), p. 135.

[20]   Edmund Spenser, 'Mother Hubberds Tale', in McCabe (ed.), *Edmund Spenser: The Shorter Poems*, p. 271, l. 1388. See Mary Ellen Lamb, *The Popular Culture of Shakespeare, Spenser and Jonson* (London, 2006), pp. 180–86, on the role of old wives' tales and childhood fairytales in *The Faerie Queene*.

[21]   Robert A. Schwegler, 'Oral Tradition and Print: Domestic Performance in Renaissance England', *The Journal of American Folklore* 93 (1980): 435–49.

[22]   Richard Dutton examines the relationship between Ben Jonson's *Volpone* and the Reynardian tradition and also traces a series of connections between the play and *Mother Hubberds Tale*, in *Ben Jonson, Volpone and the Gunpowder Plot* (Cambridge, 2008), p. 74.

of all beastes' about Raynard's immoral behaviour.[23] Charged with slander, rape and murder by the other beasts at court, his crimes are made more savage by his dissembling; he claims to have repented and dwells in a 'heremitage ... and doth greate penaunce for his sinnes' (B1ʳ), but it is while disguised as a penitent that he tricks Chaunteclere the cock and kills his daughter.

The animals that take on the fabulist role of beasts of burden in beast epics allow writers to assert a satirical force at one remove. Given that *Mother Hubberds Tale* includes a series of incidents of false speech and dissembling on the part of the fox and the ape at court, this satirical impulse becomes associated with the dangers of false counsel, calling into question the roles of both the courtier and the counselor poet. This strategy is further emphasized by the poem's association with the popular Reynardian tradition, as the harnessing of a popular form allows the text to reach beyond its printed readership to a larger community governed by storytelling, rumour and gossip. This leaves those who would peddle false counsel and 'play the Poet' (810) open to the ridicule not only of their social equals, but of the wider audience familiar with the bawdy and messy tales of Raynarde. *Mother Hubberds Tale* was potentially at greater risk of censure precisely because it broadcast its satirical intent through a format which was recognizable to a wide and, from the point of view of those policing cultural output, potentially low-born audience. The beast epic's inherent familiarity – particularly in relation to the stock character of the wily fox – meant that *Mother Hubberds Tale* could be easily retold and embellished, resulting in a printed text becoming oral performance, a slippery transfer which would have allowed Spenser's beasts to 'wander' far from the margins of his poem.

Storybook

In *The Faerie Queene* Spenser produces a series of sexually charged images of fallen women and predatory men, from Acrasia in the Bower of Bliss (Book II) to the pursuit of Florimell (Book III). While this is reminiscent of European models such as Ariosto's *Orlando Furioso*, similar accounts were included in popular storybook compilations, disguised, through a series of literary deflections, as educational morality tales. The way in which popular, erotic material, such as that contained in storybooks, established an instructional relationship with its audience produces a blurring of cultural distinctions. The tales' employment of deflective strategies provided a point of correspondence with elite forms of cultural production which wished to appeal to the body as well as the higher faculties.

The phenomenon of pleasurable reading was explored, and indeed revelled in, by the translators and compilers of popular Elizabethan storybooks such as William Painter's *Palace of Pleasure* (1566 and 1567) and George Pettie's *A petite Pallace of Pettie his pleasure* (1576). Painter and Pettie depict scenes of rape and

---

[23] William Caxton, *The booke of raynarde the foxe* (London, 1550), sig. A1ᵛ.

lust while directing their readers to view their stories as instructional, part of a didactic or educational process which, like Spenser's 'Letter to Raleigh' appended to *The Faerie Queene*, insists upon the text's ability to aid moral development. Both Painter's and Pettie's collections went through several reprints, and their tales were widely disseminated. The storybooks included the tales of the rape of Lucrece, Titus Andronicus, Pygmalion, the Duchess of Malfi and Minos and Pasiphae; stories which would be reworked in print and onstage by a variety of writers including Shakespeare and Webster.[24] The fact that these storybooks became source books for playwrights is representative of the common transferral of tales from a printed medium to an oral one, suggesting a movement from an audience defined by a reasonable level of literacy (or at least access to a willing reader) and purchasing power, to one epitomized by the potentially limited literacy of the groundlings in the playhouses. Paradoxically, this process would come full circle with the publication of popular play texts.

Many of the novellas compiled by Painter and Pettie, which include translations from Matteo Bandello and Boccaccio, belong to the Continental and classical traditions of prose romance; consequently, it is unsurprising that both storybook compilations utilize the cultural perception that romance was a feminine genre which could both educate and arouse the (commonly male) reader.[25] In the *Palace of Pleasure* Painter goes to some pains to emphasize the moral purpose behind his compilation. He claims in the preface that all his tales will 'be both profitable and pleasant, and will be liked of the indifferent Reader':

> Profitable I say in y^t they doe reueale ye miseries of rapes and fleshly actions, the ouerthrow of noble men and Princes by disordered gouernement, the tragicall endes of them that vnhappily doe attempt practises vicious and horrible. Wilt thou learne how to behaue thy selfe with modestie after thou hast achieued any victorious conquest, and not to forget thy prosperous fortune in the glorious triumphe of the same ...[26]

Painter claims to be offering instruction to his betters by mining stories of bad governance provoked by lust, but, despite his protestations to the contrary, he could also be provoking licentious behaviour in his readers, as his examples, time and again, prove that those in power are in fact weak and prone to sexual

---

[24]   Robin Kirkpatrick, *English and Italian Literature from Dante to Shakespeare* (London, 1995), pp. 239–53; Ernst de Chickera, 'The Theme of Revenge in Elizabethan Translations of Novelle', *The Review of English Studies* 11 (1960): 1–7; Helen Hackett, *Women and Romance Fiction in the English Renaissance* (Cambridge, 2000), p. 33; G. Harold Metz (ed.), *Sources of Four Plays Ascribed to Shakespeare* (Columbia, 1989), pp. 3–129.

[25]   Hackett, *Women and Romance Fiction*, pp. 10–11. For a study of Spenser's use of native English romance in *The Faerie Queene* see Andrew King, *The Faerie Queene and Middle English Romance: The Matter of Just Memory* (Oxford, 2000).

[26]   William Painter, *The Palace of Pleasure* (London, 1566), sig. ¶¶3^v.

inconstancy. The result is a text which simultaneously promises moral exemplarity and titillation:

> By the first face and view, some of these [histories] may seme to intreat of vnlawfull Loue, and foule practises of the same, yet being thoroughly read and well considered, both olde and yong may learne howe to auoyde the ruine, ouerthrow, inconuenience, and displeasure, that lasciuious desire, and wanton will, doth bring to the suters and pursuers of the same. (*3ᵛ)

Pettie's preface to his storybook also makes a claim for moral didacticism, but, unlike Painter, he directs his work specifically 'To the gentle Gentlewoman Readers'.[27] Whilst the preface is signed with the initials R.B., frequent allusions to the gentlewoman reader throughout the text indicate that Pettie himself had a hand in its composition. R.B. claims that his motivation for seeing Pettie's tales printed was altruistic: 'I thought I could not any way do better pleasure or better service to your noble sexe, then to publish them in print, to your common profit and pleasure' (A2ʳ). Pettie's attempts to mould a female readership by claiming a 'flirtatious intimacy'[28] with his target audience appears to deflect any unwanted criticism as to the implied subjectivity of a male reader, but as the vast majority of the literate book-buying public, and doubtless Pettie's own readership, was male, it rings slightly hollow.[29] The result is a text which Juliet Fleming argues is 'structured as a dirty joke, exchanged between men across the evoked but absent figure of a woman'.[30]

Painter's and Pettie's efforts to shape a readership for their storybooks reach for the moral high ground, while simultaneously alluding to the voyeuristic pleasures of both reading about fallen women and imagining women reading.[31] This paradox is echoed in the tone of Spenser's 'Letter to Raleigh', in which he famously claims that 'The generall end … of all the booke is to fashion a gentleman or noble person in virtuous and gentle discipline', a process which will be achieved through 'historicall fiction, the which the most part of men delight to read, rather for variety of matter, then for the profite of the ensemple'.[32] Pleasure will lead to moral profit,

---

[27]   George Pettie, *A petite Pallace of Pettie his pleasure* (London, 1576), sig. A2ʳ.

[28]   Katherine Wilson, 'Revenge and Romance: George Pettie's *Palace of Pleasure* and Robert Greene's *Pandosto*', in Mike Pincombe and Cathy Shrank (eds), *The Oxford Handbook of Tudor Literature 1485–1603* (Oxford, 2009), p. 691.

[29]   Margaret Spufford, *Small Books and Pleasant Histories: Popular Fiction and its Readership in Seventeenth-Century England* (London, 1981), pp. 34–36.

[30]   Juliet Fleming, 'The Ladies' Man and the Age of Elizabeth' in James Grantham Turner (ed.), *Sexuality and Gender in Early Modern Europe* (Cambridge, 1993), p. 166.

[31]   Hackett, *Women and Romance Fiction*, p. 12; Wendy Wall, 'Disclosures in Print: The "Violent Enlargement" of the Renaissance Voyeuristic Text', *Studies in English Literature* 29 (1989): 38; Caroline Lucas, *Writing for Women: The Example of Woman as Reader in Elizabethan Romance* (Milton Keynes, 1989), pp. 52–73.

[32]   Edmund Spenser, *The Faerie Queene*, ed. A.C. Hamilton (London, 1977), p. 737.

but in a similar manner to Painter's and Pettie's storybooks, Spenser's work will also risk a far from virtuous return, a danger most keenly felt in the erotic potency of the Bower of Bliss episode in Book II, canto xii.[33] The abiding popularity of Painter's and Pettie's storybooks and their theatrical counterparts was based, at least in part, upon the often salacious nature of their narratives, but it is the nature of the pleasure derived from these texts and their ability to prompt a variety of different reader responses, not least a bodily one, under the guise of a form of informational reading, which illuminates Spenser's interest in this popular format.

More specifically, Spenser appears to allude directly to Painter's *Palace of Pleasure* and, potentially, Pettie's later *A petite Pallace of Pettie his pleasure* in Book II of *The Faerie Queene*. In an episode laden with echoes of the myth of Diana and Actaeon, Belphoebe stumbles upon a bewildered Braggadoccio cowering in a bush while she pursues a 'bleeding Hind' (II. iii. 32, 7). She throws scorn upon Braggadoccio's assertion that she would be better suited to life at court than in 'this wilde forrest, where no pleasure is' (39, 2), successfully repulses his advances when he is overcome with 'filthy lust' (42, 5) and proffers the following moral:

> But easie is the way, and passage plaine
> To pleasures pallace; it may soon be spide,
> And day and night her dores to all stand open wide. (41, 7–9)

It is unlikely that Spenser was unaware of the previous publications that had joined the alliterative 'p' of pleasure and palace, and this allusion potentially references the popularity of these texts, which are available 'to all' while also highlighting the voyeuristic nature of their contents through the dilatory image of female openings. This is the only point in Spenser's epic when 'palace' and 'pleasure' are coupled in this manner, although there are references to the House of Pride as 'a stately Pallace' (I. iv. 4, 1) and the destruction of the Bower of Bliss is described in the following terms: 'But all those pleasant bowres and Pallace braue, / *Guyon* broke downe, with rigour pittilesse' (II. ix. 83, 1–2). Belphoebe's dismissal of 'pleasures pallace' therefore reinforces the contrast between her chastity and the licentious sinfulness of Duessa, Acrasia and Lucifera, who all draw hapless knights into vice-riddled palaces of pleasure. As a result this brief excerpt reveals Belphoebe as a model for the virtuous (female) reader, who, like Pettie's 'gentle Gentlewoman Readers', is subject to the voyeuristic tendencies of the (male) gaze. This allusion to a popular text playfully asks whether the reader will be astute enough to recognize the reference, and it may even afford the knowing reader a moment of comedy, insinuating that the readership for Painter's and Pettie's storybooks and for Spenser's poem could be the same.

---

[33]   Stephen Greenblatt, *Renaissance Self-Fashioning: From More to Shakespeare*, London, 1980), pp. 171–78.

Conclusion

Spenser was happy to engage with, and incorporate into his work, culturally diverse objects as part of a strategic dialogue with debates about the value and form of English poesy. Importantly, this dialogue is partly framed around the discursive output of the printing press, placing bestselling and widely disseminated texts at the heart of Spenser's construction of his identity as an English poet. The self-conscious adoption of familiar bibliographical techniques, particularly in *The Shepheardes Calender*, alongside references to texts with a wide readership and broad cultural register places Spenser's work within a cultural marketplace in which transactions are varied and fluid. Sometimes this process of exchange affords a knowing glance at his elite audience's and his own reading habits or situates his work within a cultural framework defined by the English vernacular, but the wider implications of this blending of influences is a closing of any perceived gap between a canonical poet and the more easily accessible, or popular aspects of their cultural environment.

Chapter 9
Household Manuals

Catherine Richardson

This article argues that we must attend to the way books were used if we want to understand popularity in contemporary terms, as appreciated by early modern readers. It argues for an understanding of 'local popularity', defined by individuals' knowledge of a book's status within an early modern community – who owned it and how they used it – and therefore in many ways separable from measures of 'national popularity' calculated by, for instance, print runs. The argument for judging what is popular at a local level is made in relation to household manuals – substantial didactic texts that purport to offer their readers domestic bliss by outlining the mutual responsibilities of those who lived under the same roof, because, as William Perkins put it, 'Among al the Societies & States, wherof the whole world of mankind from the first calling of *Adam* in Paradise, vnto this day, hath consisted, the first and most ancient is the Familie'.[1]

The household was an especially complex subject for a book in the period after the Reformation, when for the first time family life became the principal ideal, as chastity was abruptly replaced as the ultimate expression of humanity. In the abstract, theoretical sense, it was given unprecedented political relevance by an over-determined set of ideologies and discourses around family life and civil order, circulating both orally and textually: authority over the household was crucial because it was analogous to government of the state; the husband was 'reckoned worthie to rule a common wealth, that with such wisdome, discretion, and iudgement, doth rule and gouerne his owne house'.[2] Men proved their worth as state rulers by governing their households effectively: 'he may easilie conserue and keepe his Citizens in peace and concord, that hath so wel established the fame in his owne house and familie.'[3] But the management skills of those men who were not civic leaders were also important, as order in the local sphere of the house literally made harmony in the larger one of the nation: 'the common wealth ... standeth of seuerall families'[4] – it was a patchwork made up of many small pieces of domestic harmony.

---

[1]   William Perkins, *Christian oeconomie: or, A short survey of the right manner of erecting and ordering a familie according to the scriptures*, trans. Tho. Pickering Bachelar of Diuinitie (London, 1609), Epistle dedicatory.

[2]   Robert Cleaver, *A godlie forme of hovseholde government* (London, 1598), p.13.

[3]   Ibid.

[4]   Ibid.

In the particular, everyday sense, the household was an equally complex conglomeration of things, spaces, practices and emotions with implications for the formation of gendered identity, social and moral status. The Elizabethan period saw it expand physically, as medieval halls which had been open to the roof were ceiled over to provide extra rooms above – new chambers in which a wide range of newly acquired goods could be stored – and central open fires gave way to chimneys which heated lower and upper rooms more efficiently. As larger proportions of the population had access to more than the basic household possessions, so new behaviours were expected of them – not only being able to use something like a fine linen napkin with dexterity, but also showing one's understanding of the kind of morality which went hand in hand with elevated status. A range of texts offered advice or something stronger about what was expected, in terms which might strike us as rather disproportionate. Women, for instance, were admonished that the disobedient wife rose up 'not so much against her husband, as against GOD',[5] and men that 'The honour and authority of God and of his son Christ Jesus is maintained in and by the honour and authority of a husband'.[6] So great was the political importance of the household that drawing direct connections between domestic behaviour and respect due to God was both appropriate and essential.

Household manuals made no secret of their understanding that the moral, religious, political and economic significance of their subject made domestic life an extremely complicated business. They dealt explicitly with recalcitrance. Talking of wives' subjection to their husbands, for instance, William Whately stated that 'This duty had so much more need to be pressed because though it be so plain as it cannot be denied, yet it is withal so hard that it can hardly be yielded unto.'[7] Indeed, it was the complexities of domestic life that made household manuals necessary – its difficulties were central to the way they marketed themselves as resources for knowledge which would lead directly to domestic harmony. Robert Cleaver's *A godlie forme of hovseholde government* pointed out on the first page that familial management 'is not a thing that men can stumble on by chance, but wisdome must leade vs to it.'[8] Manuals therefore laid out the duties of each individual family member with great care, including tables of contents and diagrams of the prominent domestic relationships, their connections and distinctions.

Despite this intricacy, the underlying framework on which the books were based was both straightforward and strikingly uniform, founded on one essential division: 'The household order hath 2. parts' says Dudley Fenner, and he brackets them together in his text, one under the other: 'The first, of those which concerne the governours of the familie. The second, of those which are gouerned in the

---

[5]   Cleaver, *A godlie forme*, p. 228.

[6]   William Gouge, *Of Domesticall Duties Eight Treatises* (London, 1622), p. 468.

[7]   Willam Whately, *A Bride-Bush or, A Direction for Married Persons. Plainely Describing the Duties common to both, and peculiar to each of them* (London, 1619), p. 260.

[8]   Cleaver, *A godlie forme*, p. 13, following the dedication.

same.'[9] The remainder of these often lengthy texts (Gouge's runs to nearly 700 pages, for example) was given over to the nature of authority or subjection for each category of household member, laying this out in a series of statements which display their basis in holy scripture prominently, either in the text or the margin. At all stages, then, the manuals attempted to tie biblical ideals to everyday practice, and therefore the eternal and spiritual to the mundane and quotidian, to give an urgency to daily life by connecting it to apocalyptic timescales: 'These Scriptures shew, that God hath put the rod of correction in the hands of the Gouernours of the familie, by punishment to saue them from destruction; which if the bridle were let loose vnto them, they would runne vnto'.[10]

The status of the household in this period raises particular issues for texts written about it, and indicates a rather different set of questions about popularity to those raised by some of the other genres in this section. First, what exactly might you have been buying when you bought a household manual? The significance of domestic life, its development and its complexity, generated a whole range of texts. Volumes on household work and husbandry such as cookbooks, receipt books, dietaries, husbandry manuals and books detailing the management of beasts addressed the practicalities of domestic labour. A range of Godly texts addressed the household as a space for devotion by offering prayers for each moment of the day spent at home and encouraging meditation upon quotidian tasks. Further volumes gave advice on conduct within the home – on appropriate behaviour for those who considered themselves above the common sort. Still others considered one aspect of household relationships – usually the relationship between the husband and wife, but occasionally between parent and child – and the former were often versions of didactic sermons given at a particular marriage, expanded to make them more widely pertinent.[11]

Closely connected to elements of each of these, household manuals sit at the centre of the overlapping circles of textual interest in domestic life, containing information on or allusions to each of these areas. Buying one of these books must, as a result, have involved making an intervention into a much broader discursive field than that represented by one's individual text. As the books themselves captured more extensive print and oral discourses within their own texts like flies in amber, so the reader must have heard verbal echoes which made references

---

[9]   Dudley Fenner, 'The Order of Houshold: Described Methodically out of the Word of God with the Contrary Abuses Found in the World', in *Certain godly and learned treatises written by that worthie minister of Christe, M. Dudley Fenner; for the behoofe and edification of al those, that desire to grovv and increase in true godlines. The titles whereof, are set downe in the page following* (Edinburgh, 1592), p. 2.

[10]   Cleaver, *A godlie forme*, p. 59.

[11]   The divisions between such texts were not always clearcut, and they altered across the period. Lynette Hunter sees this as a symptom of wider changes in the market for popular print as their appeal broadened; see 'Books for daily life: household, husbandry, behaviour', in John Barnard and D.F. McKenzie (eds), *The Cambridge History of the Book in Britain*, Volume IV, 1557–1695 (Cambridge, 2002), p. 521.

to other works as they read. Obviously, explicit biblical references go to make up the intertextual wisdom on which the manuals' authority depends, but there are also consonances with both the language and the advice given in the other genres outlined above which suggest a community of interests amongst prose texts across which ideas move.[12] And the material covered by different manuals was very similar: based on a narrow range of biblical examples and in several cases borrowing significant passages of text from one another, they may well have been seen as fairly interchangeable – authors appear to have written hoping to give a more lively or expressive voice to a familiar ideal rather than to supersede the advice given by their peers. You would, therefore, only need to own one of these books. So we might ask, how does the popularity of individual texts relate to the significance of such 'super topics' as the household, where discourses are so interwoven? Does owning one such volume allow one to make connections to a range of other texts? How might such a 'super topic' relate to Farmer and Lesser's 'supra-categories'?

Thinking about a family only needing one domestic manual raises a further issue: domestic books presuppose a very different kind of audience to other types of text. As their tables of contents suggest, they are addressed to the household as a whole, and the ideal readership they imagine is a grouping of parents, children and servants, all equally enthralled by their message. Their focus is on the mutuality of responsibility: the duties of householders towards their servants, for instance, are 'that not onely according to justice they pay them their due wages, but also otherwise helpe them, comfort them, liberally reward them, as far as christianitie, liberalitie in equalitie shall binde them', whereas 'household fellows' are to be helpful to their masters both 'in outward behaviour' and inwardly, 'in subjection and obedience'.[13] Although the concentration on the interaction between authority and subjection indicates that their advice was usually intended to be filtered through the male head, it was nevertheless aimed at all those for whom he was responsible, and focused on their identity *as a group*, in relation to one another. So those definitions of popular literature which concentrate on a broad appeal to diverse audiences and a consideration of social relations are nuanced by a focus on domestic manuals – the diversity of audience is in microcosm here, bounded by residence within the same four walls.

But the family focus also invites a more individualized sense of popularity, because it forces us to address the links between book purchase and the lifecycle. If we take the case of one individual who, we know, bought a copy of Gouge's *Of Domestical Duties*, we can see that there was a particular spur: Nehemiah

---

[12]   Elizabeth Fowler and Roland Greene argue that 'the boundaries of particular works often matter less in prose than they would in other media, as contemporaneous audiences look intuitively to prose texts of different orientations to complement, augment, and contextualize one another', in *The Project of Prose in Early Modern England and the New World* (Cambridge, 1997), p. 7.

[13]   Fenner, 'The Order of Houshold', p. 51; p. 54.

Wallington, the seventeenth-century Puritan and London artisan, purchased his copy shortly after his marriage 'so everyone of us may learn and know our duties and honor God every one in his place where God has set them', and he subsequently drew up a list of '31 articles for my family for the reforming of our lives', to which his household set their hands.[14] Several texts make this focus on the early modern rite of passage from single man to married householder explicit: 'he that doth marry must cast off all childishness', says Vives, 'this age requireth another manner of life, and other manners'. Whately reveals the nature of a good householder by offering the nightmare vision of his opposite: 'lightness – Foolish, childish, unstayed tricks, that have no stamp nor impression of gravity or discretion seen upon them but savor strongly of a kind of puerility and boyishness'.[15] We might want to think about the purchase of such a text as being a part of the transition from subjection to authority for a domestic ruler, and as an element in the establishment of the household in which it is read. In other words, these were books which built households.

That connection between subject matter and location, and between theory and practice, is another aspect of the texts' popularity. Household manuals' treatment of their own locations for consumption must have produced a striking mirror effect, and it is one which they self-consciously exploit, using their setting both literally – as the material context which they aim to subordinate to the spiritual well-being of its inhabitants – and metaphorically. In the latter case, the idea of a house offers an image with which other types of building might be thought through: wisdom must lead to good household management, '*Though wisedome (saith Salomon) is an house builded, and with understanding it is established and by knowledge shall the Chambers therof bee filled with all precious pleasant riches*'; or the house as biblical metaphor is brought into comparison with its earthly equivalent to show the householder how he must inspire his subordinates: '*I reioyced when they said unto me, wee will goe into the house of the Lord*'.[16] The effect of these different narrative images of the house is to use the context in which the book is being read actively – to draw attention to it as the imperfect, earthly element in a thought-provoking pair.

Although manuals might cover very similar issues to a marriage sermon, it is their self-consciousness about location which makes these texts work differently. One might listen to a preacher's sermon in an abstract space of spiritual ideals and try to think about how such principles might translate into forms of behaviour. In one's home, reading out a manual oneself to one's household, one is forced to deal much more directly with its practical application. We cannot be sure, because there is little evidence for how they were used, but it seems likely that some sections, at

---

[14]   Paul Seaver, *Wallington's World: A Puritan Artisan in Seventeenth-Century London* (London, 1985), p. 79.

[15]   Vives, Juan Luis, *The Office and Duty of an Husband*, trans. William Whately (London, 1553), p. 250.

[16]   Cleaver, *A godlie forme*, p. 13; p. 36.

least, of domestic manuals formed a part of the 'group activities' of the household. They themselves draw attention to the duty of the householder to ensure the spiritual well-being of his subordinates, Perkins lists as the head's first duty the need to act as 'principal agent, directer and furtherer of the worship of God within his familie ... by praying for and with his household ... instructing them in the holy Scriptures'.[17] Central to the role of domestic leader is the organization of those events which take place on a household scale – the responsibility for those things that concern everyone who is part of the domestic unit, 'which only ought to be done jointlie of the whol familie, and then the superious must bee there, the chiefe directors of them'.[18] These events focused on domestic devotion as a microcosm of a worshipping community. Such a setting would presumably have been inappropriate for discussion of the duties of wives, and perhaps of husbands also (as opposed to masters or fathers). Other parts of the detailed lists of responsibilities of subservience which these texts give (most especially the ones relating to children and servants), not to mention the behaviours through which subservience was to be performed, would, however, lend themselves very well to presentation at the coming together of the group whose mutual responsibilities bound them to pray together.

We can begin to reconstruct the context within which these books might have been read if we expand on the description of the shape of the early modern house given at the start. For all but the grandest of houses, the two main reception rooms were the hall and the parlour, the latter a relatively new development in the Elizabethan period. The hall was the main public room, and the parlour was increasingly used for the family to retire to alone or with small groups of social equals, in order to dine away from servants and casual visitors.[19] Such evidence as there is for domestic piety suggests that prayers and Bible reading probably took place in the parlour, all those who were a part of the household in its widest sense invited in, their status in most cases raised by the invitation, in order to participate in a religious observance that bound them together as a group. It seems probable that domestic manuals, or at least sections of them, were read here too, with the intention that, whilst only the head *read* the text, those subordinate to him might *live out* an appropriate subjection in the hours which followed. There is some evidence that debate was diffused into other areas of the house as the group returned to their labours after household devotion, passages of Scripture attracting further discussion in the kitchen as meals were prepared, for instance, and the

---

[17] Perkins, *Christian oeconomie*, p. 164. He suggests morning, evening and mealtimes as appropriate for prayer, p. 6.

[18] Fenner, 'The Order of Houshold', pp. 9–10.

[19] For more information on these changes see C. Platt, *The Great Rebuildings of Tudor and Stuart England* (London, 1994; Catherine Richardson, *Domestic Life and Domestic Tragedy in Early Modern England: The Material Life of the Household* (Manchester, 2006), Chapter 2.

same relationship between authoritative reading to a group and later digestion during labours may have been the intended aim with household manuals.[20]

The early modern household was a highly decorated space, from printed broadside ballads pasted onto walls, through textual and pictorial wall paintings and painted cloths, to tapestries. Households at all social levels displayed narratives which commented explicitly or implicitly on domestic behaviour. Imagining the reading of a manual which played out its biblical exemplars into an array of different configurations gives us a sense of how the volume itself might fit into the household materially – might set off thought-provoking, meaningful echoes between theory and practice. For example, reading the stress upon peaceable living which the texts offer as the key to both domestic and national stability in a space bearing the text 'Better is a dinner with greene hearbes where love is, then a fat oxe and hatred therewith'[21] makes for a particular sense of intellectual and moral coherence. Similarly, the numerous overmantles carved with the moment at which Abraham's sacrifice of Isaac is brought to a halt take on a rather different meaning when seen in the context of the statement that 'The very name of a wife, is like the Angell which staied *Abrahams* hand, when the stroke was coming'.[22] In this context it is not so much the typological significance of this Old Testament sacrifice which is brought to the fore, but the patterning it sets up between the rushed confusion of earthly relationships, with their physical momentum which outruns reason, and the calm omniscience of the intervening deity. The image is perhaps an apposite one for the manuals themselves – offering models of behaviour which are measured, thought through and prepared in advance in an effort to head off the instinctive responses which escalate dissention.

These are brief examples of the remarkable consonances between the subject matter and concerns of domestic manuals, their textual form, and the nature and decoration of the spaces in which they were read. If we return to our imaginary household head, seated in his parlour reading aloud to his household on the subject of their duties, then we might want to push our reconstruction of his sense of the popularity of his manual one stage further: how did he see himself in relation to his peers? There is no evidence that large numbers of individuals in early modern communities owned such manuals. Compared to the Bible or the *Book of Common Prayer* the numbers must have been rather small, and the evidence suggests that those who owned a household manual would have owned these other texts

---

[20] William Hinde, *A faithfull remonstrance of the holy life and happy death of John Bruen of Bruen-Stapleford, in the county of Chester, Esquire* (London, 1641).

[21] The text, from Proverbs 15.17, adorns the walls of No1 Church Lane, Ledbury, as well as Cowside Farmstead, Langstrothdale, Upper Wharfedale, North Yorkshire.

[22] Cleaver, *A godlie forme*, p. 214. For detailed analysis of examples of the image see Tara Hamling, *Decorating the 'Godly' Household: Religious Art in Post-Reformation Britain* (New Haven, 2010), passim.

too.[23] In other words, ownership of a copy was an excess, an extra, and therefore offered a more exclusive popularity – if prayer books are 'levelling objects', then manuals are elevating texts.[24] This superiority was presumably a significant part of a book's attractiveness for its owner. Whilst his neighbours may have taken up the oft-repeated injunctions to pray with and educate their households, he may well have known that he was one of a select few who was able to instigate an explicit discussion of household structure, behaviour and obligations in relation to an apposite text. Our putative owner did not see himself as a percentage of a purchasing public on a national scale, but rather at the local level of his parish, village or town. His understanding of his book's status depended on his and his peers' awareness of the organization and horizons of the dissemination of ideas. Reading as a way of marking oneself apart from the majority of one's neighbours on a *local* level may have been one of the sources of these manuals' comparative popularity on a *national* level, where they stood amongst the middling ranks of the relatively frequently printed genres.

Such an analysis suggests that one source of these texts' popularity was their ability to give detailed substance to forms of behaviour which a particular social group felt appropriate to their sense of their status, their morality and the quality of their spirituality. The people who consumed these manuals are often said to have been of the 'middling sort', but focusing on the nature of the texts' popularity helps us to see their agency here – buying one of these books offered aspirant readers a clear sense of the behaviour required of such a group, and they may thereby have given form to their owners' ambitions. There are certainly indications of a particular ethic as one reads between them; there is a focus on active management of the household and an emphasis on hard work: an 'idle and vnthrifty husband, and a prodigall and slothfull wife, are two ready waies to destruction'. The repeated denigration of luxury suggests a point of tension for those whose wealth was growing – a spiritual spur to control the appetites of consumption – 'a sweete tooth & a veluet mouth, that is, daintinesse, or choicenesse in diet, is an enemie to frugalitie'.[25] It is this social group who were most likely to have decorated their houses with the Biblical narratives and injunctions which appear as models for early modern domestic behaviour within the manuals' pages.

One aspect of the popularity of these texts, then, is their implication in the creation of middling identity through their influence on appropriate behaviour (from the way to chastise servants to whether to call one's husband by a pet name and what kind of clothing might be seemly). Using them in the way just imagined would then form a part of that behaviour. They have, it seems, a kind of 'middling

---

[23]   Peter Clark, 'The ownership of books in England 1560–1640: the Example of Some Kentish Townsfolk', in Lawrence Stone (ed.), *Schooling and Society* (Baltimore, 1976), pp. 95–111.

[24]   See Brian Cummings, 'Print, popularity, and the *Book of Common Prayer*', in the current volume.

[25]   Cleaver, *A godlie forme*, pp. 187, 78.

popularity' which is situated interestingly in relation to the binary terms – elite and popular – between which the debate about appreciation is usually conducted. They force us to ask how the application of those terms to readers or reading practices might be made to relate to early modern social groups.

The essential quality of behaviour and viewpoint to which these texts give shape, however, is a confessional one: these men and women were most explicitly interested in learning to be good Protestants. The books were popular because they gave confessional identity a clear and unequivocal shape; they were valuable because they were insistently moral, and their readers' interest in learning their lessons in itself demonstrated their election. Earthly harmony and eternal bliss were popular concepts worth paying money to learn more of.

That gives household manuals a curious popularity nowadays, one which concerns serious matter and the morality of reading. To read and to teach they are hard texts, involving very different pleasures to the ones we expect to find in literature today. Historicizing pleasure is obviously a complicated business, but it must be attempted if we are fully to understand popularity. How can we conceive the intense satisfaction they offered to Nehemiah Wallington and others like him? Although household manuals are eagerly consumed in snippet view today, presented as representative examples of a patriarchal relationship between the sexes in which the duties of wives are often divorced from the obligations of husbands, let alone of children and servants, they are very rarely, I think, read in full. That is a great shame, as in their entirety they offer a patterning of language and ideas that develops in a way which offers the comfort of repetition with alteration. That patterning, seen in the division into chapters and in tables of matching virtues and obligations and played out in detail in the rhetoric of the chapters themselves, permits, indeed invites, a meditation on what it means to live together in a patriarchal society.[26] It does not invite debate or dissention, but it does encourage self-analysis, meditation and mutuality. The fact that it sends the quest for domestic perfection both inwards and outwards by requiring its early modern readers to examine their own subtly distinct behaviours of subservience in relation to their fellows' tells us a good deal about how the manuals' readers viewed themselves as members of a community. The polar opposite of texts like the almanacs discussed in this section, domestic manuals offer a textual form of

---

[26] For instance, the chapters pack many examples together, but they are controlled and structured by the duties through which they progress in orderly fashion: the husband's 'first dutie is called Harting, that is, hartie affection', says Henry Smith, 'His next duetie … to let all things be common betweene them', 'Lastlie, he must tender her as much as all her friends, because he hath taken her from her friends, and couenaunted to tender her for them all', a list which organizes four pages of explication, *A Preparative to Mariage* (London, 1591), pp. 49–53. In Cleaver's famous example of rhetorical pattern, p. 170: 'The dutie of the husband is, to get goods: and that of the wife to gather them together, and saue them. The dutie of the husband is, to trauell aborad to seeke liuing: and the wiues dutie is to keep the house. The dutie of the husband is, to get monie and prouision: and of the wiues, not vainly to spend it …'.

ideas to be thought through over a period of years, perhaps over a lifetime, not only as and when they are read but as the situations they discuss are experienced, maybe first as servant and then as master; first as child and then as mother. Lengthy moral texts show very clearly how difficult the bridges between modern and early modern notions of popularity can be to cross.

Chapter 10
Damask Papers

Juliet Fleming

Ephemera are things that last – continue or hold out -– for a day or less. If we are thinking rigorously there is nothing ephemeral in nature: flowers are the reproductive organs of certain plants whose life cycles continue beyond their appearance, while the famously short-lived mayfly, whose winged state can last as little as 30 minutes, first spends a year in its larval stage. More than this, the ephemeroptera, the order of insects to which the mayfly belongs, dates back 300 million years. Before we call an organism ephemeral we must decide where and when it begins or ends, and to do this we will have to follow the paths of evolutionary biology into a field from which there is no easy exit.

But are literary historians any better off? In library catalogues the term ephemera indicates a taxonomical hiccup: in them ephemera – things whose survival beyond their occasion is a matter of some surprise – are precisely not ephemeral, except in the sense that all things are. Judged transient, base, peripheral to learning, ephemera survive in the place where thousands of other more worthy items might have been preserved: indeed an archivist may class as ephemera those things she feels *ought not* to have outlived their occasion. Still, resentment can't be the whole story. We all love survivors, and want to extend to them the protection that elsewhere came too late. Besides, the term ephemeral suggests the consequence of the quotidian. An ephemeris is a record of daily occurrences, such as a court book or journal, and in his posthumous publication *Christian Morals* (1716) Thomas Browne advised his readers to 'Register not, only strange, but merciful occurrences, let ephemerides, not olympiades, give thee account of His Mercies'.[1] Even as we marvel at the inclusion of matchboxes, napkins and grocery bills among the special collections of our libraries, we have to admit, with Iago, that there is a 'daily beauty' in such things. Ephemera engage and hurt us because they are the traces of life, because they are beautiful in their vulnerability, and because they tell us that we ourselves, like even the most celebrated of our achievements, must pass.

The product whose consequence I have chosen to defend for this volume is damask paper – decorative paper that could be used for wallpapers, lining papers, bookbindings, pattern sheets and other decorative purposes. But I am not going to attempt to adjudicate whether these were either ephemeral or popular. Although they are representative of the kinds of objects that librarians classify

---

[1]   Thomas Browne, *Christian Morals* [1761] (London, 1863), p. 31.

as 'ephemera', damask papers are no more or less ephemeral than any other product of the early English press. Patterns are collocations of visual, affective and cognitive resources, so even if we could separate the contents of 'lasting' poems or wallpaper designs from the sheets of paper that gave them material support we would still be unable to discriminate between them in terms of their influence or endurance. Both the single motifs and the larger compositions of damask sheets were reproduced at various locations and in various media (painted onto walls, carved into wood, embroidered into fabric, adapted for the manufacture of luxury goods such as lace, ceramics and metal work), and, like any 'enduring' poem, they remain available today for our use and enjoyment. As for popularity, I am only going to argue that damask paper came off the early modern press in extremely large quantities (thousands, perhaps tens of thousands of sheets at a time, which means that a single damask sheet could have a much wider circulation than even the most popular book), that it was fashionable, profitable and alluring, and that its purchase was neither restricted to nor unusual within elite households.

In 1563 Delft printer Herman Schinkel answered charges that he had printed prohibited ballads by claiming that they 'were printed in his absence by his servant, and on his return he refused to deliver them and threw them in a corner intending to print roses and stripes on the other side, to paper attics with'.[2] The court discounted his defense and Schinkel was executed for printing heretical material, but the practice he described of printing decorative designs on the reverse of waste papers was certainly followed in early modern Europe, and has left its traces in court records and other archives in England. But the history of damasking has never been fully investigated, and is complicated by the fact that the process serves more than one function: in one blow it cancels texts, produces new products, and recycles waste paper.[3] While the term 'damasking' was used in the second half of the seventeenth century to describe a specific mandate to cancel offensive printed work, the practice of cancelling and reusing pages by over-printing them with decorative patterns is as old as type printing itself.

Schinkel's stated intention in preserving the sheets whose reverse he intended to print 'with stripes and roses' was self-correction: realizing that his workman had printed something likely to be prohibited by the licensing authorities, he meant to cancel the print job and to re-coup the financial loss thus incurred. By the second half of the seventeenth century the term damasking began to be used in England to

---

2   James Knowles, 'Papering Rooms', *Notes and Queries*, 2nd series 27: 2 (1856): 7–8.

3   In 1935, correcting some previous contributors to a discussion in *Notes and Queries* as to what 'damasking' meant, W.W. Greg provided one of the few unexceptionable descriptions of the practice: 'The old suggestion quoted from *Notes and Queries* to the effect that 'to damask' paper was to demasquer, unmask [actually, deface] or change its appearance can hardly be entertained. I imagine that damask paper is patterned or diaper paper: *domino* paper is the French term. It was printed over with some design in black and white and used for lining boxes and the like … . If so, to damask paper was to impress such a pattern upon it, and confiscated sheets were over-printed in that manner to deface them and then used as waste', *Review of English Studies* 11: 44 (October 1935): 479. See *Notes and Queries*, 2nd series, 8 (November 26 and December 18, 1859): 430, 541.

describe this method of dealing with works whose cancellation had been ordered by the authorities of the State: in 1673 the Bishop of London issued an order to 'seize, and damask' ['or obliterate'] a second edition of Hobbes's *Leviathan*.[4] Such orders speak to a heightened interest in the State control of the press, and a concern to see that proscribed print work did indeed get cancelled.[5] The earliest, from the Council of State in 1651, required that the printer Edward Crouch be bound for £100 to 'damask the scandalous papers formerly taken from him, now to be restored, and put them to no other use'.[6] Later orders were made in accordance

---

[4]   11 December 1673 'These are to Require you to Damask or obliterate whatsoever sheets you have seised of a Book, intitled, Leviatan: and for your so doing this shall be your Warrant', in Robin Myers (ed.), *Records of the Worshipful Company of Stationers, 1554–1920* (Teaneck, NJ): Chadwyck-Healey, c. 1985, microform reel 97, envelope 3. See also November 2, 1674, order from the Stationers' Company Court that 'the Damask Sheets of a Booke called Hobbes Leviathan' be given to the Beadle for delivery to John Williams and Thomas Sawbridge, SCDf. 240 v; D.F. Mackenzie and Maureen Bell, *A Chronology and Calendar of Documents Relating to the London Book Trade 1641–1700*, 3 vols (Oxford, 2005), II, p. 77. For a full description of this complicated event, which unrolled over several years, see Noel Malcolm, *Aspects of Hobbes* (Oxford, 2002), pp. 336–79.

[5]   The orders for which there is evidence in the records of the Stationers' Company Court before 1695 concern 27 named or identifiable texts, while others refer simply to 'Popish', Quaker, and other books, which may be those otherwise named. Lists of orders and other records concerning damasking in the Stationers' Company records and elsewhere can be found in Charles Rivington, *The Records of the Worshipful Company of Stationers* (London: 1883), pp. 33–34; Edward Arber, *A Transcript of the Registers of the Company of Stationers of London, 1554–1640 A.D.* (London, 1875–1894), II, pp. 784, 808; W.W. Greg, *A Companion to Arber: being a calendar of documents in Edward Arber's transcript of the Registers of the Company of Stationers in London, 1554–1640* (Oxford, 1967), p. 386; Robin Myers (ed.), *The Stationers' Company Archive: An Account of the records 1554–1984* (Winchester, 1990), pp. 85–86; McKenzie and Bell, *A Chronology and Calendar*, III, p. 438; and Alison Shell and Alison Emblow, *Index to the Court Books of the Stationers' Company 1679–1717* (London, 2007), pp. 25–26, 197. John Barnard records a further reference to damasking in 'The Stationers' Stock 1663/4 to 1705/6: Psalms, Psalters, Primers and ABCs', *The Library*, 6th series, 21 (1999): 369–67. I have noted these references in my notes. Some additional undocumented records can be found in Robin Myers (ed.), *Records of the Worshipful Company of Stationers, 1554–1920* (Teaneck, NJ: Chadwyck-Healey, c. 1985), microform reel 97, envelope 3; I make reference to these by reel and envelope number only. Further orders may well have been lost (several entries in the Court records that instruct the Stationers to search for previous damasking orders suggest how easily they could go astray) or left unrecorded in Court books and State papers; and some will have eluded my own searches.

[6]   *Calendars of the State Papers, Domestic Series* (London, 1649–1650), pp. 522–23; MacKenzie and Bell, *A Chronology and Calendar*, I, p. 301. The order probably refers to the *The Man in the Moon*, a Royalist newsbook printed by Edward Crouch between 1647 and 1649. For an account of his career see Jason McElligott, 'Edward Crouch (c. 1622–1676), A Poor Printer in 17thc London', *Journal of the Printing Historical Society* (n.s.) 1 (2000): 49–73.

with the notorious Act of Parliament of 1662 'for preventing the frequent abuses in printing seditious, treasonable and unlicensed books'.[7] The Act expired in 1679, but was renewed in 1685 and continued until 1695, when the Commons refused to renew it. It is worth noting that extant damasking orders usually invoke the Act, and were issued to the Stationers' Court only during years that it was in force, 1673–1679 and 1685–1695. But even then the number of State damasking orders is small: those for which there is evidence in the records of the Stationers' Company Court before 1695 concern 27 named or identifiable texts, and over half of these orders were issued by one man, Henry Compton, Bishop of London from 1676 to 1714.[8]

The political functions of these late seventeenth-century orders cannot be mapped onto the largely commercial damasking practice of the sixteenth century. But their details are revealing. Although comparatively few titles were ordered damasked the number of sheets of paper involved was large. Porters with packhorses and carters with wagons had to be employed to transport them: 250 reams, or 120,000 folio sheets, taken for damasking from Pindar's coffee house; loose sheets for 'about 1900' copies of 'a book Entituled Confession of Faith and the larger and shorter Catechisme' seized in 1677; 'three cartloads' of books from printer Andrew Sowle.[9] What did it take to damask all these sheets? The earliest order in the Company records, sent from the King's Commissioners in 1673, contains unusually careful instructions. The Stationers were told 'to cause all those books called King's Psalters then in their custody and taken from one Thomas Rookes to be damasked or the Characters in such manner obliterated as might hinder the reading thereof'. And the Stationers recorded their intention to comply: 'It is this day therefore in obedience to his Majesties and Commissioners ordered that every particular sheet shall be damasked on both sides to the end that the Contents thereof may [not be read].'[10] As interpreted by the Stationers' Court, patterns were to be over-printed on both sides of the sheets, of sufficient density to 'obliterate' the characters. 'Hindrance' and 'obliteration' are, however, relative

---

[7]   *Anno Regni Caroli II* (London, 1662), p. 438. For an excellent description of this act, its provisions and consequences, see Michael Treadwell, 'The Stationers and the printing acts at the end of the seventeenth century,' in John Barnard and D.F. McKenzie (eds), *The Cambridge History of the Book in Britain*, Vol. IV, 1557–1695 (Cambridge, 2002), pp. 755–76.

[8]   For a full account of Compton's divided allegiances during these years (for he was 'equally committed to international Protestantism and Tory principles'), see Edward Carpenter, *The Protestant Bishop: Being the Life of Henry Compton, 1632–1713* (London, 1956), pp. 59–77.

[9]   For Pindar see Myers, *Records of the Worshipful Company of Stationers*, reel 97, envelope 5; for *The Assembly's Catechism* see SCDff. 290–290v, in Mackenzie and Bell, II, p. 267; for Sowle see SCDff. 285–285v, in Mackenzie and Bell, II, p. 155.

[10]   SCDf. 224v, MacKenzie and Bell, II, p. 65: their transcription reads 'to the end that the Contents thereof may be 'totally obliterated', but damage to the paper means that both our readings are speculative.

terms: very few instances of over-printed sheets survive, none from the sixteenth century, and none that can be identified as resulting from these seventeenth-century orders. But of the few seventeenth- and eighteenth-century papers extant, not one so obscures the characters that nothing of the underlying text can be read. Indeed, each case allows some show-through, while in some instances the patterns are so sparse, or so lightly imposed, that they can almost be ignored by the reading eye. And this need not surprise us. If texts were ordered damasked in order that they could circulate the news and evidence of their own proscription, there would be no need to ensure that every word was illegible. On the contrary, while the reading of such texts must be 'hindered', it should not be altogether precluded, for the full efficacy of the gesture can be achieved only when a text is still recognizable. Juridically damasked texts, we might think, *should* remain partially legible, since anyone attempting to read them would then be traumatized, or alternatively edified, by understanding that they had been damaged, and parts of them lost. Schinkel's defence is interesting in this context: he claims to have thought that, having printed prohibited texts on one side of his paper, he might remedy matters by printing patterns on the other – as if the offence would be removed once each ballad was thus marked, on its reverse, as cancelled.[11] The obvious weakness of this proposal may explain why Schinkel specified that the decorated sheets would be used for papering attics, for the ballads could do no harm stuck face down to the walls and ceiling of a scarcely used room. But other records confirm his sense that sheets could sometimes be cancelled by over-printing one side only. In 1690 William Wilde received £4 19s from the Warden of the Stationers' Company for damasking 198 reams 'of Crowne and Fooles Cap wast[e]', and almost the same amount, on the same day, for damasking 99 reams of an unspecified size. Either the sheets in the second set were twice as large as those in the first or they were damasked on both sides, where the first set was over-printed on one side only.[12]

But however high the number of sheets that could be involved in a single case, damasking for State-ordered censorship purposes appears to have been a relatively minor, and perhaps personal, epiphenomenon within the wider context of the censorship of the English press during the second half of the seventeenth century.[13] Before 1670, English damask paper was produced and understood primarily as a commercial product, and after this date it continued to be produced primarily as such. In 1668 Francis Kirkham dedicated his continuation of *The English Rogue*

---

[11]   In his last letter to his wife, Schinkel described how he had explained that the ballads had been printed by the servant in his absence: 'Want ick quam t'huys, eer dat sy gelevert waren, ende doe en woude ick niet gedoogen, dat mense leveren sonde, maarick schichtese in een Noeck, om roosenen stricken op d'andere zijde te drucken, daer men Solders mede bekleet.' [When he came home, and found they were not delivered, he refused to deliver them and threw them into a corner, intending to print roses and stripes *on the other side*, to paper attics with – italics mine]. Knowles, 'Papering Rooms', p. 7.

[12]   Myers, *Records of the Worshipful Company of Stationers*, reel 97, envelope 3.

[13]   For a good discussion of the difficulties of assessing the incidence and consequence of censorship in the period see Jason McElligott, *Royalism, Print and Censorship in Revolutionary England* (Woodbridge, 2007), pp. 210–24.

to the book-sellers of London on the grounds that an author who does not seek the favor of that powerful group may see his work end as 'loose sheets at Cooks and Tobacco-shops ... or at best (after more cost than was intended by the Author in damasking and figuring it) used in Truncks and Hat-cases'.[14] Throughout both periods, when the Stationers' Company Court ordered work damasked it was probably acting to adjust trade interests: the first recorded case concerns Thomas Rooke's edition of *The King's Psalter*, which was ordered damasked on both sides not because its contents were inimicable (on the contrary, it was a child's primer containing psalms, other Scripture passages and an illustrated ABC), but because under a patent granted them by James I the Stationers claimed the exclusive right to print all psalters and primers, and Rookes was not a member of their Company.[15]

Over the years the Stationers had developed their own ways of dealing with 'disorderly' printing, that is, when a printer printed something without first entering his or her claim in the Court Register. Sometimes the offender had simply been trying to save the registration fee, in other cases he or she would have printed a work registered to another printer,, or one that formed part of the English Stock (the collection of lucrative titles whose copy was the possession of a cartel of powerful printers).[16] Such cases were common, and adjudicating them according to the severity of the infraction was one of the regular tasks of the Stationers' Company Court. Under the Decrees of 1586, any printer who worked contrary to the ordinances of the Company was liable to the destruction of his press and the fount of type used to print the offending items, as well as a fine, a prohibition against practicing as a printer again and six months' imprisonment. In practice the Court tempered these penalties considerably, especially during years when Company policy was to aim for a wider distribution of books among its members.[17] If the case touched on the rights of another printer the disorderly work was sometimes simply confiscated and given to the injured party, who could then sell it as an imprint of his own.[18] In cases where the wrongdoing was more aggravated or directed against the English Stock or other interests of the Company, additional fines were imposed, while in the most serious cases the Court ordered the surrender, for destruction, of the spindle or press bar, as well as of the fount of type used in the printing of the work.

---

[14]   Francis Kirkham, *The English Rogue Continued* (London, 1668), A2r–A2v.

[15]   SCDf. 224v, Mackenzie and Bell, II, p. 65.

[16]   See W.W. Greg and E. Boswell (eds), *Records of the Court of the Stationers' Company, 1576–1602: from Register B* (London, 1930), pp. lx–lxxvii.

[17]   For an account of these developments within the Stationers' Company see Cyprian Blagden, 'The English Stock of the Stationers' Company in the Time of the Stuarts,' *The Library*, 5th series, XII, 3 (1957): 167–86 and *The Stationers' Company: a History, 1403–1959* (Stanford, 1960), pp. 63–77; also D.F. McKenzie, 'Stationers' Company "Liber A": An Apologia', in Robin Myers and Michael Harris (eds), *The Stationers' Company and the Book Trade, 1550–1990* (Winchester: St. Paul's Bibliographies, 1997), pp. 46–50.

[18]   See, for example, the case adjudicated between John Kingston and Christopher Barker in 1583 in Greg and Boswell, *Records of the Court of the Stationers' Company*, pp. 13–14.

Disorderly printing was most often discovered in the middle, or at the end, of a print run, which meant that there were numbers of printed sheets to be disposed of. In the sixteenth century, work containing 'matters unfit to be published' was usually burned, but books and sheets that were merely unlicensed, or that had infringed copy but could not be given over to the printers who held the right to them, were typically ordered to be 'disposed to the use of the poor of the Company'.[19] The protocols of this disposal are not detailed in the records, but completed books were probably sold as such, with or without new imprints, while loose sheets that could not be so used might be sold as waste paper. In both cases any profit went into the Company funds to relieve the poor after the expenses of search and confiscation were deducted. But sheets that came from interrupted print runs, particularly those printed on one side only, would not have been most economically disposed of in being sold for waste, and it is these sheets in particular that would have been earmarked for the manufacture of damask papers, and distributed for printing among those poorer members of the Company who, owning little copy themselves, were always hungry for work.

Damask papers were also produced outside the pressroom. While sixteenth-century woodblocks were deliberately made to the same standard depth as type, so that the two could be fitted together on the press-bed, a printing press is not necessary for the production of a woodcut, for impressions can also be taken by pressing an inverted woodblock down onto a sheet of paper, or by laying a sheet of paper over a woodblock and rubbing the back of it.[20] Anyone who owned a woodblock and knew how to make ink of the right consistency could make damask paper. A testamentary inventory made in 1578 of the belongings of Cambridge bookbinder and stationer John Denys lists among 'all such tools as be in the workhouse ... 2 prints for the cover of books'. These 'prints' are valued at 3s 4d each, which led editors Gray and Palmer to speculate that they might be 'blocks for sides of bound books,', but they are more likely to have been woodblocks used to make damask papers designed for the specific purpose of covering books.[21] For the stock of books at Denys's death included a significant number 'in paste boards uncovered' (that is, in cardboard bindings), and beyond his 'prints for the

---

[19]   For example, in 1593 the Court heard that Edward White had printed 'the spanish tragedie belonging to Abell Jeffes,' while Jeffes had printed 'the tragedie of arden of kent belonginge to Edw White,' and ruled 'that all the bookes of eche ympression shalbe as confiscated and forfayted according to thordonnance. diposed to thuse of the poor of the companie for that eche of them hath sev'ally transgressed th'ordonnances in the seid impressions'. SCR, May 1593, Greg and Boswell, *Records of the Court of the Stationers' Company*, pp. 42, 44; for a discussion of this case see W.W. Greg, '"The Spanish Tragedy": A Leading Case?', *The Library*, 4th series, 7 (1926): 47–53. For an account of the funding and operation of the Stationers' Company pension fund see W.C. Ferguson, 'The Stationers' Company poor book, 1608–1700,' *The Library,* 5th series, 31 (1976): 37–51.

[20]   See John Jackson, *A Treatise on Wood Engraving* (London, 1839), p. 131.

[21]   G. Gray and W.M. Palmer, *Abstracts from the Wills and Testamentary Documents of Printers, Binders and Stationers of Cambridge from 1504 to 1699* (London, 1915), p. 56.

cover of books' he also owned 'a pot to make ink' and 'a large pot to make black in'. We can imagine him selecting the size and colour of paper he required, and printing off covers that could be stitched to a pamphlet as a wrapper, or glued to the pasteboard cover of a book. Technically known as binder's wrappers, such covers would have protected and decorated Denys's stock and also marked each book as coming from his shop.[22]

Damask papers could also be produced from metal plates. Unless they are done in relief, metal engravings cannot be printed simultaneously with type but must be printed on a rolling press, which forces the paper into the incisions on the plate where the ink is retained. The use of the term 'roll' in the Decrees of 1586, which required the registration of 'any printing press, roll, or other instrument, for imprinting,', is intended to specify that the decrees covered not only the work of the letter press, but the production of printed material all told, including engravings made with rolling presses and 'other printing instruments'.[23] The records of the Stationers' Company for 26 March 1619 note that the Court ordered that John Pemberton, who was not a member of the Company, 'shall have his Rolling press when he has entered into bond not to imprint any unlawful thing'.[24] Similarly, on 7 February 1618 license was granted to Reynold Smith 'to imprint his table and Computation that he has made and to sell them without interruption of the Company'.[25] Such entries, like the Decrees of 1586, underline the fact that printers were printing things other than books and, conversely, that certain print jobs – particularly single sheets or broadsides – were undertaken by craftsmen who were not members of the Stationers' Company.[26]

Nevertheless, the Company was quick to claim the manufacture of damask papers as a concern of its own. In 1575 its members had successfully petitioned Lord Burghley against the granting of a proposed privilege for the sole printing of 'ballads, damask paper, and books of one quire,' while in 1583 the Commission on Privileges answered the complaints of four printers who had protested against the monopoly of privileges and patents held by other Company members by reminding them that members of the Stationers' Company 'have liberty of damask paper.

---

[22]   In 1928 E.P. Goldschmidt was able to identify almost 20 early Italian and German paper covers and to distinguish 'binder's decorations', which are 'applied to any book of the appropriate size', from publisher's wrappers, which occur on several copies of the same book. Goldschmidt, *Gothic and Renaissance Bookbindings* (London, 1928), I, pp. 163–64.

[23]   23 June 1586, 'The New Decrees of the Star Chamber for Orders in Printing' (*Dom. Eliz.* Vol 190, Art. 48); Arber, *Transcript*, II, p. 808.

[24]   William A. Jackson (ed.), *Records of the Court of the Stationers' Company 1602 to 1640* (London, 1957), p. 109.

[25]   Ibid., p. 107.

[26]   By the charter of its incorporation, members of the Stationers' Company had the sole right to print throughout England, always excepting the holders of the royal grant of letters patent. On the other hand, a member of any one of the London Companies had traditionally been allowed to practice the trade of another. See C.B. Judge, *Elizabethan Book Pirates* (Cambridge, MA, 1934), p. 16.

Which costs nothing in copy or composition'.[27] The rulings indicate that damask papers were not considered privileged copy, and that the right to produce them was unrestricted among printers and others. But in 1618 this freedom was threatened when Marin Boislore, a French courtier, requested a patent for things printed on one side only on parchment and paper. The Stationers protested, with kettle logic, that under their Charter nothing could be printed without their sanction; that the objects of the proposed patent were anyway 'mean, and not worthy of your Majesty's privilege'; and that the printing of them was 'settled already', since according to their custom it was assigned to their poorer members. But the Solicitor General noted that the right to print playbills, indentures, licenses and other items included in the patent application had, for years, been monopolized by a few powerful members of the Stationers' Company, and advised the King that the patent could be granted, cautioning only that it should be made out to Boislore's English assignees.

On 30 October 1619, letters patent were accordingly granted to Roger Wood and Thomas Symcock, giving them 'sole power and privilege to Imprint, Impress, Role, Stamp, work, publish, utter, sell, distribute and disburse' all things printed on one side only, except for 'proclamations and such belonging to the King's Printer,', ballads, prognostications, almanacs and other things granted elsewhere by letters patent. In 1623, a new abstract of the patent added damask papers to the list of products included there, while in 1628 a third abstract once again omitted them.[28] This uncertainty as to whether damask papers could be subject to a patent reflects their unique status as a printed product whose freedom from copy restrictions was both traditional and assured.[29] Unlike other items subject to the

---

[27]   5 February, 1575/6, Suit from the Stationers to Lord Treasurer Burghley against the granting of a proposed privilege for the sole printing of ballads, damask paper, and books up to 24 sheets [leaves?] *MS. Lansdowne* 48, *art.* 76 (*fol.* 176) in Arber, I, p. 468; Greg, *A Companion to Arber* I, p. 17; Greg and Boswell, *Records of the Court of the Stationers' Company,* lxv. And 18 July, 1583, 'The Final Report of the Augmented Commission from the Privy Council on the Controversy in the Stationers' Company' (*Dom. Eliz.,* vol 161, art. 1 (III); Arber, *Transcript,* II, pp. 783–84; and Greg, *A Companion to Arber*, pp. 126–27.

[28]   Printed broadsides (STC 8615 and STC 8903) each contain 'an abstract of His Majesties Letters Patent granted, unto Roger Wood and Thomas Symcocke', see Greg, *A Companion to Arber*, pp. 59, 75.

[29]   In 1598 Simon Stafford, who was a printer by training but a member of the Draper's Company, was given permission by the Archbishop of Canterbury to set up a press. Displeased, the Stationers obtained an injunction against him, on the grounds that as a non-member of their Company he had no right to print. In this tight spot Stafford printed a ballad that had been licensed to him by the Bishop of London and 'certen damaske paper', and he further testified that once he had been called to answer for his behavior to the Star Chamber Court he had printed nothing 'other then only a lyttle damaske paper wch he prynted for & at the request & charge of one Iohn Harrison the younger a Stacyoner ... being formerly bound to the sd harrisson so to doe'. Damask paper appears in Stafford's deposition as the product whose printing is least likely to cause legal or other offence (Star Chamber Elizabeth S8 3/39), in Judge, *Elizabethan Book Pirates*, pp. 112–31, 179–81.

patent, damask papers were, it seems, customarily assigned to the poorer members of the company, and Symcock and Wood may have been advised to leave them alone, either for ethical reasons or because the attempted annexation of a practice at once customary, petty and widespread, both among and beyond the members of the Stationers' Company, would have proved more trouble than it was worth.

The production of early English damask papers is attested by their survival on walls, in deed-boxes, and bound into book covers. Damask paper can usefully be thought of as a single product with various uses, but in the early twentieth century Hilary Jenkinson, one of the group of curators and local historians who first began to notice, identify and conserve sheets and fragments of English damask paper, devised a useful taxonomy of their types: 'true wall papers,', where the design is incomplete without the juxtaposition of a number of sheets; book-covers, which have 'large margins of blank paper left by the printer for turn-in at the edge'; box linings, where the design is complete on a single sheet, and usually of small scale; and 'pattern or diaper papers', which might be suitable for any purpose. All the papers identified were produced in England between 1500 and 1700, and were of approximately standard size – a little over 14 by 11 inches, which means their designs fitted onto the average-sized sheet of folio paper. And with the exception of the book covers, which are on a 'practical grey paper,', all had been printed on white paper in black, or, occasionally, red printers' ink. [30]

The circumstances and the quantities in which these papers were made have still to be fully explored. They are usually considered to be the first European wall papers, and such evidence as has been gathered tends to be cast in that light. There is only one mention of 'painted paper hangings' in the monastic inventories of the sixteenth century, but since they were attached to the surfaces on which they appeared and had little independent value they would not have been registered in inventories and wills, and it is certainly possible that, as C.C. Oman once speculated, many rooms for which no hangings are mentioned were really decorated with damask papers.[31] However, while damask papers were doubtless used on walls in much larger numbers than surviving evidence can indicate, it

---

[30] Hilary Jenkinson, *English Wall-Papers of the Sixteenth and Seventeenth Centuries* (London, 1925), pp. 237–53. Other early discussions of these papers are in P. Ackermann, *Wallpaper: Its History, Design and Use* (London, 1923); N. McClelland, *Historic Wall-Papers* (Philadelphia, 1924); C.C. Oman and J.C. Hamilton, *Wallpapers: A History and Illustrated Catalogue of the Collection of the Victoria and Albert Museum* (London, 1982); A.V. Sugden and J.L. Edmondson, *A History of English Wallpaper 1509–1914* (London, 1926); Preston Remington, 'Elizabethan Wallpapers', *Bulletin of the Metropolitan Museum of Art* 22: 6 (June 1927): 168–70. For a description of some early printed paper book covers and wrappers see Paul Kristeller, 'Woodcuts as Bindings', *Bibliographica* 1 (1895): 249–51; E.P. Goldschmidt, *Gothic and Renaissance Book Bindings*, I, pp. 163–64; M. Ivins, 'A Tudor paper Book Jacket,' *Bulletin of the Metropolitan Museum of Art* 22 (1927): 224–26; and William A. Jackson, 'Printed Wrappers of the Fifteenth to the Eighteenth Centuries', *Harvard Library Bulletin* VI (1952): 313–21.

[31] Oman and Hamilton, *Wallpapers,* p. 11.

does not follow that they were intended primarily for such use. Besides their use as lining or wrapping papers they were also valuable for the visual information they contained and disseminated. Sheets with the same or with slightly modified patterns have been found in disparate parts of the country: circulating as pattern sheets for workers in cloth and other media, they worked to spread decorative designs throughout England. Trade purposes aside, we can imagine sixteenth-century men and women buying damask papers from stationers' shops and stalls, sometimes with a specific use in mind, otherwise drawn by a design they had not seen before. These papers would be admired, hoarded, shown to neighbors or given to children; they could be meditated on and dreamed over; painted, cut to fit boxes and drawers or used to create decals for decoupage and other purposes; and their motifs could be copied and adapted for further use.

The earliest surviving English damask paper was clearly used as a wallpaper. It was discovered in Christ's College, Cambridge, in 1911, attached to the lath and plaster of rooms that had been built in 1506 for Margaret Beaufort, founder of the College. Fragments were recovered from 29 sheets, each measuring 16 by 11 inches: their repeatable design has a central pomegranate motif flanked on either side by the letter 'H' and a goose, the rebus of Yorkshire printer Hugo Goes. They had been printed on the reverse of various 'waste' papers, including an Indulgence of Pope Julius II and a poem on the death of Henry VII, both printed by Wynken de Worde, and a proclamation from the first year of the reign of Henry VIII by an unknown printer, perhaps Goes himself.[32]

The recycling of waste papers in this manner might have been something of a specialty among certain of the earliest printers in England. In this case Goes owned the woodblock and used it, not only on his own waste papers but also on those from the shop of Wynken de Worde and possibly others. The practice could have formed a useful sideline for a small printer, or even the bulk of his business since, labor aside, it would have cost him nothing beyond the woodblock, ink, and waste paper.[33] But waste paper was a real factor in the balance sheet of every print shop. According to Cyprian Blagden, in 1663/4 £1211 were expended on purchasing paper for printing of the English Stock, while £8 were returned from the sale of waste; in 1664/5 the outlay was £400, with £60 in income from waste; in 1665/6

---

[32] It is likely that all these sheets date from the middle or the end of 1509. The find is described by Charles Sayle, who painstakingly restored the sheets, in *Cambridge Fragments* (Cambridge, 1913); earlier versions of this work appeared in *The Library* (October 1911) and in the *Christ's College Magazine* XXVI (1911–12). My description closely follows Sayle's account; Ann Keith of the Christ's College Library kindly drew it to my attention, and allowed me to examine the wallpaper fragments.

[33] In *A History of English Wallpaper,* p. 25, Sugden and Edmondson suggest that 'The early letterpress printers, not only in this country, but on the Continent, contributed a good deal to the evolution of wallpaper, possibly as a secondary product as time, occasional demand, or caprice suggested.'

the outlay was £961, with £30 in income from waste.[34] Earlier in the century, in 1602, the Stationers' Company Court received £3 10s for 'fourty reames of wast pap at xxjd the reame,' which is approximately one penny for a quire of 25 sheets; while in 1621 the Court paid the stationer Richard Gubbins 22d a ream 'for so many Reams of Accidences as the company had of him, being waste pap.'[35] These prices are surprisingly high, and since the Company itself was paying them, may have been for waste paper printed on one side only, not yet folded or stitched, which could thus be used for the best-quality damask paper.

Among entries recorded in the fragmented papers of a mid-sixteenth-century bookseller listing items supplied to one George Grosser in Southwark are two quires of 'paper damasked,' priced 6d; four quires of white paper at 8d; two more quires 'damasked' at 6d, and another quire of white paper at 2d; another customer was supplied with one quire of 'ruled paper,' 6d. Leslie Oliver, who discovered the record and identified it as a stationers' account book, notes that the entries do not indicate the size or quality of the paper, which would have had an effect on prices. But we can still perhaps reconstruct a tentative scale of values and prices whereby in the middle of the sixteenth century plain paper cost 2d per quire, damask paper 3d, and ruled paper 6d (Oliver speculates that these are retail rather than wholesale prices, which raises the question of what Grosser intended to do with his 100 sheets of damask paper: perhaps this is an instance of wall-papering).[36] The entries would then confirm what we might expect: that damask paper is worth something more than plain paper but not as much as paper that has been customized for another purpose. The value of waste paper, initially considerably less than that of unprinted paper, was palpably enhanced – and therefore the wasting largely redeemed – through the process of damasking.[37]

As late as 1710 the statute of Queen Anne that first granted copyright to authors and their assignees included a clause stating that, in the case of piratical printing,

---

[34]   Cyprian Blagden, 'The English Stock of the Stationers' Company', p. 179, Tables IV and V. It has sometimes been argued that overrun or extra copies and waste sheets were regarded as the property of the printers' workmen, who could sell them as their perquisite, but this was not a practice enforced by the Stationers' Court; indeed, a note for March 3, 1627 specifies that printers for the English Stock, at least, must return to the Stock-keeper the 'overplus books' and 'the waste … which they are always to do upon the finishing of every Impression', William Jackson, *Records of the Court of the Stationers' Company*, p. 200.

[35]   Greg and Boswell, *Records of the Court of the Stationers' Company*, p. 86; William Jackson, *Records of the Court of the Stationers' Company*, p. 134.

[36]   Leslie Mahin Oliver, 'A Bookseller's Account Book, 1545', *Harvard Library Bulletin* 16: 2 (1968): 144–54.

[37]   In 1620 the Stationers' Company Court valued a ream (20 quires) of waste paper for damasking at around 12d, that is, at a little over a halfpenny a quire: prices and values for the different kinds of paper may have changed over the intervening 50 years, but damask paper would still have cost more than plain paper, and represented a significant recuperation of the value otherwise lost when paper was wasted.

'the offenders shall forfeit such book or books, and all and every part or parts of such book or books, to the proprietor … of the copy thereof, who shall forthwith damask and make waste paper of them'. Sixty-four years later, when the House of Lords was debating the question of literary property, Mr. Baron Perrott claimed to be baffled by this provision: 'By damasking he understood turn to waste paper and line trunks, which linings were figured like damask. What remedy was this? None in the world'.[38] Puzzling to later centuries, the clause speaks to and from a moment in which writing mattered, but paper mattered too, and spoiled sheets retained too much value to be wasted on a fire or allowed as a journeyman's perk. Instead, throughout the sixteenth and seventeenth centuries the Stationers' Company Court used damasking as a way of re-cycling and redistributing waste paper through regulated channels. In doing so it created a source of revenue that could be used to pay costs of search and seizure, compensate copy-holders whose privileges had been infringed and printers whose work had been wasted, and look after the poorer members of the Company by providing work for idle presses. This process, in its turn, supported the manufacture and promulgation of pattern sheets, whose presence and influence must have been of considerable consequence within the visual environment of early modern England.

---

[38] William Cobbett, *Cobbett's Parliamentary History of England* (London, 1812), Vol. XVII, p. 984.

Chapter 11
Sermons

Lori Anne Ferrell

'When I should have preached under the Crosse', declared the London lecturer Henry Smith from the outdoor pulpit at St Paul's in 1587 or 1588, 'I mused what text to take in hand to please all, & to keep myself out of danger'. Smith chose Ecclesiastes 11.9, 'Rejoice O young man in thy youth … But remember for all these things thou must come to Judgement', an apt enough text for a rowdy urban congregation.[1] In choosing and declaring his text, however, Smith took altogether the wrong tone. Within the year, John Aylmer, Bishop of London, hammer of Puritans and the overseer of the Paul's Cross pulpit, had banned Smith from any pulpit, citing persistent rumors of his non-conformity and, more to the point, the fact that Smith was not licensed to preach, at least not in London.

Smith was luckier in his patron, William Cecil, Lord Burghley, royal minister and hammer of Aylmer. Cecil promptly stepped in and Smith was soon restored to the grateful and godly congregants of the London parish, who had secured him as an unbeneficed lecturer. First published in 1591, Smith's sermon was reissued at an extraordinary rate in the 1590s; as part of two collections, it continued to be reprinted at least seven times between 1592 and 1624. Henry Smith was Elizabethan England's best-selling preacher. We have barely heard of the man since.

Of course the exception proves the rule, and this exception came in a brief spate of English sermon analyses mostly undertaken in the middle of the last century. 'Henry Smith's great popularity demands notice', wrote A.F. Herr in one such, his 1940 survey of the Elizabethan sermon, 'but it also presents a problem'.[2] For Herr, the problem was that the Preacher was, for his purposes, unclassifiable: neither Anglican nor Puritan, neither plain nor ornate, Smith seemed to be a scholar *and* a gentleman, whose sermons against sin carried a worldly note that altogether suited his city pulpit but not, perhaps, his Calvinist bona fides.

In the reinvigorated and busy world of current early modern sermon studies – now populated by rigorous scholars like Peter McCullough, Mary Morrissey, Arnold Hunt, David Colclough, and Jeanne Shami – eccentric and opinionated works like Herr's, W. Fraser Mitchell's (1932), John Lievsay's (1947), J.W.

---

[1]   Henry Smith, *The Trumpet of the Soule, Sounding to Judgement* (London, 1592), A3r.

[2]   A.F. Herr, *The Elizabethan Sermon: A Survey and a Bibliography* (Philadelphia, 1940), p. 99.

Blench's (1964), and Horton Davies' (a 1986 outlier, and all the quainter for it) – have been consigned to time out of academic mind.[3] In their day, though, they all found Henry Smith remarkable in *his*. Mitchell called Smith 'multiform' and 'multivarious'; Blench praised his capacity to 'bridge' the divide between metaphysical and Puritan *elocutio*; after admitting his inclusion of Smith in a book about English metaphysical preaching was 'unusual', Davies went on to describe Smith's seemingly incongruous combination of 'Puritan training', Calvinist divinity, and witty wordplay. Almost to a man, the critics of the early and mid-twentieth century professed amazement that such elegance could be found in plain style; such cosmopolitanism in a Calvinist; such winsomeness in a Puritan.

These days we have little problem locating Smith in his time and place. To slightly refit a phrase of Peter Lake's, Smith was an *avant garde* Puritan: uncompromisingly Calvinist, yet not concerned overmuch with matters indifferent and, in fact, thoroughly enamored of the beauties of linguistic holiness. He was, in other words, just one more fascinating specimen of late Elizabethan churchmanship, variegated enough to please a councilor like Burghley (who was also related to Smith by marriage) and annoy a bishop like Aylmer. Given the role he played in the ongoing drama of the Elizabethan Settlement, Smith would have made a perfect subject for recent studies of the multiform and multivarious early modern Church of England, but little note has been taken of him since those charming, earlier studies of English pulpit oratory.[4] Henry Smith's current obscurity not only demands redress, then, but also forces us to acknowledge that popularity is a time-bound value, which depends as much on the attention spans and value systems of modern scholars as it did on those of early modern congregations.

To bring this exceptionally popular Elizabethan preacher back to our attention, my essay will consider the circumstances surrounding one of Smith's best-known sermons, *The Trumpet of the Soule Sounding to Judgement*, the only sermon Smith preached at Paul's Cross, in pursuit of a larger methodological issue. It will do so, therefore, partly at the expense of content analysis. For an edited collection with the title *Elizabethan Bestsellers*, many other sermons by Smith would qualify

---

[3] Jeanne Shami, *John Donne and Conformity in Crisis in the Jacobean Pulpit* (Cambridge, 2003); Peter McCullough, *Lancelot Andrewes: Select Sermons and Lectures* (Oxford, 2005); Arnold Hunt, *The Art of Hearing: English Preachers and their Audiences, 1590–1640* (Cambridge, 2010); for Morrissey, see below; still others are represented in P. McCullough, H. Adlington, and E. Rhatigan (eds), *The Oxford Handbook of the Early Modern Sermon* (Oxford, 2011), and/or constitute the editorial team assembled by McCullough for the forthcoming multi-volume *Oxford Edition of the Sermons of John Donne*, to be published by Oxford University Press. The first volume in that series, edited by David Colclough, is in press.

[4] Here the exception is provided by Paul Seaver, whose *The Puritan Lectureships* (Stanford, 1970) outlines the specifics of the kind of post held by Smith, wherein, without benefice or license from the bishop of London, one could be employed, in essence, privately, by a rector and a congregation, to preach. These 'lectureships' established a strong, proto-Puritan preaching campaign to reform London.

– all his sermons were bestsellers. *Trumpet*, however, widens the evaluative setting in which we might consider the life and work of a popular preacher. Given its controversial political and religious valences, its remarkable print and reception history, and its specific place of preaching, *Trumpet* is an interestingly representative sermon. Most important here, however, is that it makes a case for a text's popular success that need not depend exclusively on style and content, nor largely on the print record. This essay, then, privileges context over content.

We could simply take the past at its word, for example. Smith's contemporaries and near-contemporaries stated, without qualification, that Henry Smith was the most acclaimed preacher of that eloquent decade, the 1580s. Anthony Wood called him the 'wonder of his age, for his prodigious memory, and his fluent, eloquent, and practical way of preaching'. Thomas Nashe, in an unguarded, un-ironic turn, mourned his passing in *Piers Penniless*. Thomas Fuller listed him among the Worthies, reminding his readers that Smith was 'commonly called "the silver-tongued"' – a historical detail that has proved so useful that one invariably distinguishes this particular Henry Smith with that particular modifying phrase.[5]

More recent assessments followed up by following suit, albeit playing the subjunctive hand. 'One might well imagine Smith's popularity', mused Davies after parsing a particularly analogy-laden section in Smith's sermon *The Young Man's Taske*. 'His posthumous popularity', wrote Mitchell, 'and therefore the influence of his works, must have been extraordinary.' 'The works of this silver-tongued preacher can indeed still provide literary pleasure', enthused Blench. ('Some reason must be found for this popularity', insisted Herr, perhaps channelling the Elizabethan Bishop of London.)[6]

Sixteenth- and seventeenth-century reports convey little, however, beyond the fact that Smith was well known: observers praised his preaching by commenting upon the size and enthusiasm of his auditory. So the sermon scholars of the mid-twentieth century attached intricate formal analyses to the early modern report, accounting – or not – for late sixteenth-century tastes by comparing them to their own rhetorical preferences. They cited Smith's use of apt and vivid similes, Blench pointing out that a homiletic passage like Smith's 'every man hath a part, some longer, and some shorter: and while the Actors are at it, suddenly Death steps upon the Stage, like a Hawk which separates one of the Doves from his flight' showed not only the preacher's brave way with metaphor, but also his astute gauge of an audience familiar with similar contentions in *As You Like It*. Mitchell pointed out that such stage-savvy lines showed that Smith 'was accustomed to appeal to citizens of the type depicted in the plays of Jonson and Dekker', noting his astute calculation of decorum in a city congregation. With less admiration Herr (whose ardor was reserved for the likes of Richard Hooker, and whose distaste for Puritans indicted every conformable Calvinist of Elizabeth's reign) cited Smith's relentless approach to sermon structure: 'he announces his text and then enlarges

[5]   Wood, *Athenae Oxonienses*, 1.603.

[6]   Herr, *Elizabethan Sermon*, p. 99.

on it, beats down all opposition to his view, and ends by applying the moral.' The silver-tongued Enigma, we would conclude, then, combined the commonsense and user-friendliness of plain style architectonics with the unforgettable flights that characterized metaphysical preaching. This hybrid approach, which made every line of Smith's sermons memorable both practically and aesthetically, was one source of Smith's singular homiletic power.[7]

These formal analyses of individual sermon passages have mostly stood the test of time, but the method has not. Rhetorical style cannot in itself argue for rhetorical success. The enthusiasms of post-war Anglican partisans tell us little about the homiletic tastes forged in the first great age of English preaching (if quite a lot about what sort of scholar read Elizabethan sermons for a living in the 1940s, 50s, and 60s). These days we assess the effect of an early modern sermon a bit less genteelly and far less piously, drawing on theories of reading and reception; studies of manuscript, print, and political culture; and views on the importance of occasion and location.[8]

Religious content remains, of course, the touchstone of sermon analysis. But historical and cultural contextualization allows us to comprehend the appeal of a theology like Calvinism beyond the elegance (or, for that matter, inelegance) of its articulation. What confused an earlier generation of analysts – how Smith could be eloquent, witty, *and* Puritan – no longer confounds us. So while we cannot gauge their worth with reference solely to our own enjoyment in or approval of their sentiments, the age proclaimed Smith's success, and that alone should earn the man and his work another look.

The word 'popularity' itself undertook its first major definitional shift in this period, when the old meaning of the term – wherein it referred to democratic styles of government – made an unhappy intersection with an up-and-coming usage: one that indicated, with implicit disapproval, the condition of being liked, admired, and supported; or, by extension and with explicit disapproval, described the ambitious seeking of such admiration.[9] Early modern popularity thus carried a dangerous edge: of mongering and pandering, of rebellion and treason. The arousal of the people's devotion could lead to agrarian uprising, religious petitioning, and parliamentary clamor against royal policy. But men like Robert Devereux, the second earl of Essex (or, later, George Villiers, first Marquis and Duke of Buckingham), thought there were political benefits in seeking not simply the monarch's but also 'the people's love', whether the 'people' were commoners

---

[7]   J.W. Blench, *Preaching In England* (New York, 1964), pp. 186–87; W. Fraser Mitchell, *English Pulpit Oratory* (London, 1932); Herr, *Elizabethan Sermon*, p. 99.

[8]   These last two are best covered, generally speaking, in Peter McCullough, *Sermons at Court* (Cambridge, 1998), and, more recently, Mary Morrissey, *Politics and the Paul's Cross Sermons, 1558–1642* (Oxford, 2011).

[9]   See, in this volume, Andy Kesson and Emma Smith, 'Introduction', and Neil Rhodes, 'Shakespeare's Popularity and the Origins of the Canon', for further information on these points.

or in Commons. To court popularity in either high or low places, therefore, was to court political disaster. In the early modern political realm, 'popularity' was a modifier best applied to monarchs and their policies, neither to be sought nor shared with others.[10]

One cohort to whom Archbishop John Whitgift's pointed 1574 query about the dangers of such ambitions – 'in whome hath not popularity wrought these effects?' – did not necessarily apply was the clergy.[11] Unlike politics in an age of unrepresentative government, preaching aimed at popularity as Protestant necessity. Elizabethan preachers, especially in the second half of the sixteenth century, would have felt the need and even been encouraged to cultivate their popular reach – within limits. To be popular in the religious realm was both to court official disapproval – the writings of such disparates as John Foxe and William Allen alike present eloquent and hair-raising testimony to this fact – and to be doing the job well, even unto the glory of God.

Calvinism thus presents an interesting text case, with observers then and scholars now assailing its doctrines – predestined election, limited atonement, and perseverance in particular – as either off-puttingly unpopular or destabilizingly populist. Elizabethan preachers worked within the bureaucratic, quality-controlling, and doctrinally incongruous structure of a Protestant state church, wherein all the queen's subjects were required to assemble, but in which all would not, in the end, be saved. In Elizabeth's Church of England, moreover, what of saving faith was to be had was reckoned to come in at the ear. After the shaky restoration of Calvinist Protestantism after six years of Marian Catholicism, the captive audiences of the kingdom's parishes were now to be captivated anew, trading enforced (if not always unenthusiastic) participation in the Mass for enforced (if not always enthusiastic) Bible reading and sermon-listening. Only a sustained attention to the Word, reformed doctrine taught, could acquaint the elect to salvation with the knowledge of the saving grace of God. And so the pulpit, not the altar, became the divine instrument of religious transformation in Elizabethan England.

What of popularity we can comfortably ascertain in the late sixteenth century, then, is most reliably to be found in the environs surrounding that pulpit. And after being elected by the rector and congregation to a lectureship there in 1587, Henry Smith occupied one of the highest-profile pulpits in London: that of the church of St Clement Danes, a large parish of Westminster, located along the Strand and bounded by Lincoln's Fields and the Inns of Court. The parish provided catchment for a diverse range of inhabitants that included both illiterate artisans and the educated inhabitants of the Inns. From this enviable location, Smith could build

---

[10]   For example, see the essays contributed by the editors in Thomas Cogswell, Richard Cust, and Peter Lake (eds), *Politics, Religion, and Popularity: Early Stuart Essays in Honour of Conrad Russell* (Cambridge, 2002), pp. 211–89.

[11]   John Whitgift, *A Goodly Sermon* (London, 1574), sig. Bvii, also cited in the OED entry for 'popularity'.

an enviable reputation: Thomas Fuller wrote that on Sundays the Church of St Clement Danes had standing room only, with people jostling in the aisles for the chance to hear the silver-tongued Smith expound on his text. We should, perhaps, not be quite surprised at this. They had voted for him, after all. Henry Smith's popularity in the St Clement Danes pulpit came without license or benefice. The holder of one of the new 'lectureships' that now allowed the laity of the Church of England to secure the kind of preaching (inevitably Puritan) they preferred, Smith held a truly popular mandate to proclaim the word of God to the city of London.[12]

Trumpet of the Soule, however, was preached in another venue, one with a much higher profile – arguably the highest profile (and with the longest reach) in the kingdom: the outdoor pulpit situated next to the London Cathedral of St Paul's. St Paul's Cross was both a location and a series of events, by no means all of these involving the delivery of sermons. The most prominent of the traditional 'pulpit crosses' (open-air preaching spaces located next to churches in order to allow for increased attendance at notable occasions) in which pre-Reformation England abounded, Paul's took on new and even greater significance, both sacred and secular, after Elizabeth I's accession in 1558. The historical sources are full of references to the proclamations, sermons, and preachers to be heard; the book-burnings, plague notices, libel postings, and acts of penance to be experienced in this prime location. When the Earl of Essex decided to entice a crowd to accompany him in unlawful incursion into Elizabeth I's court in 1601, he chose Paul's Cross as his muster-yard. When Elizabeth's government explained its choice to execute Essex for treason shortly thereafter, it chose the Cross from whence to broadcast its rationales to a populace still unsure of their allegiances in a highly charged situation. [13]

It is easy to see why. Paul's Cross reliably attracted a significant number of the city's inhabitants and visitors: privy councilors (often), church and court officials and their hangers-on (frequently), members of Parliament when it was in session (occasionally), the Lord Mayor and his aldermen (regularly), and any other citizens or visitors who could squeeze into either the outdoor bleachers or a variety of flimsily covered buildings. Foreigners interested in practicing their English language skills were encouraged to attend sermons at the Cross. All in all, attendance was reckoned up by thousands, although a large congregation could not ensure a large auditory – in fact, of course, it worked against it. This still meant, however, that a sermon preached at Paul's was a sermon thereafter associated with

---

[12]   Seaver, *The Puritan Lectureships*, pp. 135–36.

[13]   This paragraph and the three that follow are so heavily indebted to the recent exemplary work of Mary Morrissey – whose 2011 *Politics and the Paul's Cross Sermons* has finally provided a useful corrective to Millar MacLure's *The Paul's Cross Sermons* (Toronto, 1958) and also reintroduced sermon scholars to essential work done by Peter Blayney (*The Bookshops in Paul's Cross Churchyard* [London, 1990]) – that I should just write passim here and leave it at that; however, see especially pp. 1–34, 86–93, and, of course, passim.

the largest event venue in early modern England; the London theatres had nothing on the Cross.[14]

Here, we might recall that Henry Smith shared the large, noisy theatre commonly known as urban London with such celebrities as the Earl and his men (and Elizabeth I, and the stage clown William Kempe, and any number of baited bears and performing dogs); those who commented on Smith's own magnetism in the pulpit and capacity to draw crowds, after all, would have logged Smith, at least in part, in this register of entertainment. The popularity of Smith's sermon was largely the consequence, then, of his performative popularity; all his best-selling sermons can be considered postscripts to performance. Given its once-in-a-lifetime venue, however, none were more so than *Trumpet*.[15]

Paul's was, after all, a thriving marketplace of people and ideas. In its immediate vicinity you could hire a servant, read a libel, take in a play, or listen in on the latest gossip. And you could purchase a book that re-affixed and inscribed onto pages the words – and by extension, the faith – that had once simply come in by the ear. The churchyard of Paul's Cross was lined with bookstalls, providing the requisite conditions for what Morrissey has called the 'symbiosis' between preaching at Paul's Cross, the book trade of the Cross yard, and the startlingly precipitate rise of interest in the printed sermon that dates from 1583.

In short, Smith could not have found a better venue, ecclesiastical or mercantile, from whence to establish himself as the preacher of a best-selling sermon. He was already popular as a London lecturer who possessed an enviable way with words and an enviable set of highly placed patrons, so Smith's sermon at the Cross should have proceeded as politicly as he declared himself prepared to proceed in its opening remarks. That it did not simply reminds us once again that words out of context are denied meaning.

Silver-tongued Smith may have been, but that metal carried a well-honed edge. One characteristic of his style (at which the mid-twentieth-century critics, with their remarks about the precision and aptness of his city similes, perhaps hinted) is *knowingness*: a kind of irony that, in *Trumpet*, employed self-reference at the outset to drive his sermon's theme. *Trumpet of the Soule* is a sermon about heedless inattention to the consequences of self-indulgence.[16] This story turns, then, on the exact cast of those opening words – which, given Smith was already known for a kind of brash popularity, now seem in reconsideration not at all humble but too

---

[14] MacLure quotes, with some small scepticism, John Jewel's claim to Peter Martyr in 1560 that 6,000 were in a recent auditory: 7–9; fn I.6. Theatre crowds were also reckoned up by thousands – but overall, sermons at the Cross were more reliably had than plays (and, of course, free).

[15] Thanks are due here to my editors, who pointed out the consequences of my own argument and helped me to make it more pointedly by suggesting the phrase 'performative popularity'. Compare this challenge to the focus on print as a popular medium with Peter Kirwan's chapter, 'Mucedorus'.

[16] *Trumpet*, sig B3r.

clever by half: his claim to try 'to please all, & to keep myself out of danger', in fact, seems so provocative as to ensure he would do neither.

Not, at least, where his immediate superior was concerned. The Cross was closely managed by Aylmer, who took as his general brief the suppression of Puritanism, and as his specific brief the suppression of Puritanism from the Paul's Cross pulpit – in which he took not simply the requisite professional responsibility but also a great personal interest. We have no records telling us what specific administrative decisions brought Smith to the Cross pulpit, but given the bishop's oversight of the venue; the rumors of Smith's unwillingness to conform; the galling fact he was an unbeneficed, unlicensed lecturer hired by a congregation that had taken it upon themselves to pay his salary and thus bypass the bureaucratic oversight of the Church of England; in short, given Smith was a popular Puritan preacher with a conformable nature and more than a modicum of self-awareness, we might think that, at Paul's Cross, he would have done well to curb that silver tongue of his.

But confident in the relative power of the bishop and his own patron – Aylmer was not much favored by Elizabeth and seems, in fact, to have spent most of his professional life pleading his virtues to her and her chief minister in a fashion described even by his *ODNB* biographer as 'groveling' – Smith opened his sermon at the Cross with a bold and backhanded swipe at the episcopal power that brought him to such unprecedented public notice. Preaching before the largest, the most diverse, and the most powerful congregation he would ever face, he gambled on his capacity to talk a potential political disaster into a career changer by immediately drawing his auditory's attention to that very fact. It surely drew the attention of his patron: all in all, it is difficult to construe Smith's intentions as innocent.

His inevitable reckoning took another, all-too-mortal form. The Providence that governed Smith's works and days was not to crown his ultimate success with worldly laurels. After rousing Cecil to action and returning in triumph to St Clement Danes, Smith was favored to receive the benefice upon the death of the incumbent, who had been his supporter throughout. That the sinecure went to another, a nonentity named Richard Webster, cannot be attributed to political backlash but almost certainly to the fact that by 1589, after only a few short years in the pulpit 'without the Temple Bar', Henry Smith was a dying man. Never having married, he retired to his family home and lived one more year, expiring, aged 31, on 4 July 1591.[17]

But it is here, at the end of Smith's life, that we see the promise of his opening remarks at the Cross come, post-ironically, to life. Sometime before that command performance Smith preached two sermons on the art of hearing, wherein he recommended to his congregation the practice of note-taking using both their hands and their minds. 'Record every note in thy mind, as the preacher goeth', he stated, 'and after, before thou dost eat, or drink, or talk, or do anything else,

---

[17]   ODNB.

repeat all to thyself.'[18] When illness forced Smith to retire, he took with him not only his, but also their sermon notes. He spent the final year of his life editing and correcting his sermons for publication, seeking a kind of assurance in the memory of his words (in both the past and future senses of that phrase) as, good Calvinist that he was, he surely sought as earnestly in the matter of the eternal disposition of his predestined soul.[19]

No doubt this was, in part, simply to correct the record. Smith's sermons were already beginning to circulate, probably in manuscript, as was so often the case, but also in pirated editions first taken down by the new and inaccurate art of 'charactery' and published, without Smith's permission, during his lifetime. The year of his death, 1591, was a big year for Smith's printed sermons, and interest in them did not soon wane: for a decade it waxed, reissuing with assurances that the words therein were the preacher's own. By 1593, a collection, *The Sermons of Master Henry Smith*, stated in subtitle that its contents were *printed according to his corrected copies in his life time*; in 1593, readers of *The Sinful Man's Search* were assured they held in their hands a *true corrected copy*. In 1595, *Jacob's Ladder, or the High Way to Heaven* went on to declare that this series was '... the last sermons that Master Henry Smith made. And now published not (as so many forged things have beene in his name) to deceive the Christian reader, but to instruct and prepare him'.[20]

For all we know, then, Smith added *Trumpet*'s insolent opening disclaimer as he lay dying. His final earthly labor to secure his reputation in print might lead us to yet one more argument for this sermon's – or any sermon's – popularity as indelibly and most essentially linked to the undeniably growing popularity of print in this period. And this would not be incorrect, not exactly, but it would miss an important point about what made the book worth buying in the first place. What made Smith's work an Elizabethan bestseller was his risky, charismatic, mocking performance at the Cross, and his final determination to remind Elizabethans that he – and they – had once been there.

---

[18] John C. Miller (ed.), *The Works of Henry Smith*, vol 1 (London, 1846), p. 335. Also quoted in John T. Lievsay, '"Silver-tongued Smith", paragon of Elizabethan preachers', *Huntington Library Quarterly* 11.1 (November 1947): 13–36 (35).

[19] *Trumpet of the Soule* was entered in the Stationer's Register in 1591 by the printer Edward Allde and the bookseller John Perrin (who vended the sermon from his shop at the sign of the Angel in Paul's churchyard, capitalizing on Smith's recent passing by recognizing the prescient power in Smith's text on that occasion, Ecclesiastes 12.1: 'remember thy maker in the days of thy youth').

[20] For Smith's sermons and the cunning art of charactery, see Mitchell, *English Pulpit Oratory*, p. 36; on the problem in general see Lori Anne Ferrell, 'Method as Knowledge: Scribal Theology, Protestantism, and the Reinvention of Shorthand in Sixteenth Century England', in Pamela H. Smith and Benjamin Schmidt (eds), *Making Knowledge in Early Modern England: Practices, Objects, and Texts, 1400–1800* (Chicago, 2007), pp. 163–77.

Chapter 12
The Psalm Book

Beth Quitslund

A volume called 'The Elizabethan Top Ten' perhaps inevitably invites a popularity contest between the various kinds of print artefacts that it treats, and a corresponding variety in what 'popularity' means. By nearly any measure, the anthology of psalm paraphrases, hymns, and prose prayers known to Elizabethan and Jacobean English people as 'the psalm book' and to its late seventeenth-century opponents as 'Sternhold and Hopkins' is a strong contender for the palm, if not necessarily the poet's laurel. *The whole book of Psalmes, collected into English metre, by T. Sternhold, J. Hopkins and others* (*WBP*) was among a handful of the most frequently printed titles, making its patent owners a fortune and regularly testing the Stationers' capacity to control piracy. By the middle of Elizabeth's reign it was used by virtually every English Protestant in public worship, and by many in household devotions. Although ubiquitous, the *WBP* was never specifically mandated for use by any national authority, which meant that it depended largely on custom for its continuance. Finally, for most of the Elizabethan period it seems to have been generally enjoyed and appreciated by an audience that included literati as well as artisans, and in the seventeenth century, when the critical reputation of its psalm paraphrases began to decline, it inspired an enormous number of alternative metrical psalters.

Though I will generally refer to this work as the *WBP*, the essay takes its title from Elizabethan usage in order to direct our attention away from the metrical psalm texts themselves and toward the ways that the physical book entered into and changed in response to its purchasers' devotional practices. When literary scholars talk about 'metrical psalms', they generally mean a lyric genre to which a substantial number of Elizabethan writers contributed, including Anne Lock, George Gascoigne, Philip Sidney, the Countess of Pembroke, Samuel Daniel, Abraham Fraunce, John Harington, Richard Verstegan, Richard Stanyhurst, and, probably, Edmund Spenser. Despite the important literary experiments and achievements of these works, however, I am going to ignore them, because from the perspective of book history they were niche publications – when printed at all. Only one collection of metrical psalm paraphrases other than the *WBP* went through multiple editions in the Elizabethan period, William Hunnis's *Seuen sobs of a sorrowful soule for sinne* (printed eight times from 1583 to 1602 and a further seven times in the seventeenth century).[1] This is impressive, but literally a different

---

[1] A set of very long songs meditating on the Penitential Psalms, Hunnis's work was not treated as 'psalms in metre' for the purposes of copyright.

order of magnitude from the *WBP*. The ESTC records 149 English imprints of the complete psalm book from the first edition in 1562 through 1602, a total which does not include incomplete Elizabethan editions of its psalm paraphrases (twelve), editions printed abroad (three), or the harmonizations of the tunes which did not print the whole psalm texts (four versions, with a total of five imprints). It is also certain that the surviving examples understate the total number of printings: though not as fragile or inexpensive as basic pedagogical texts like the *A.B.C.*, it was nevertheless heavily used and easily replaced, and small-format editions on cheap paper are far less likely to have been preserved than more expensive larger editions or those bound with other valuable books like the Bible and the Book of Common Prayer.[2] Nor was this popularity limited to the years of Elizabeth's reign: the *WBP* descended from an Edwardian smash bestseller, *Al such psalmes of Dauid as Thomas Sternehold late grome of [the] kinges Maiesties Robes, didde in his life time draw into English Metre* (11 editions from December 1549 through 1553), and was produced in vaster quantities yet over most of the seventeenth century, with more than 600 imprints (again as catalogued by the ESTC) between 1603 and 1700.[3]

The heart of the *WBP* was, of course, the Book of Psalms. From 1577 on, most editions contained a total of 156 psalm paraphrases in the metrical psalter portion of the book: all 150 psalms paraphrased in full at least once, with six of them in two versions each. The majority are in the alternating eight- and six-syllable iambic quatrains now known as Common Meter but often referred to in the mid-sixteenth century as 'Sternhold's meter'.[4] The rest are in poulter's meter or one of a number of stanzaic forms borrowed from the French metrical psalter. A prose summary or argument preceded each psalm, and somewhere between 40 and 60 of the psalms, depending on the edition, were printed with a tune overlaying the first song verse. The remainder name a tune printed elsewhere that fits the words (e.g., 'Sing this as the iii. Psalme'). The metrical psalter, however, was

---

[2]   For example, lists of wholesale books sent to Cambridge booksellers in 1583 and 1584 show a very high proportion of 32mos (at least 21 out of 52 total copies). The first three editions in that format listed by the ESTC, however, are from 1569, 1577, and 1590. Even given the unusual characteristics of the Cambridge book market, the lists strongly suggest that there must have been multiple 32mo editions lost to us from the period between 1577 and 1590. Robert Jahn, 'Letters and Booklists of Thomas Chard (or Chare) of London, 1583–4', *The Library* 4th ser., IV.3 (1923): 219–37.

[3]   Counting editions in the seventeenth century is hopelessly imprecise: the *WBP* may at times have been continuously printed, and at the least mixed copies are not uncommon. In addition, the standard print run for each set of forms was also increased early in the seventeenth century, so that the number of copies in circulation was probably greater than the number of identifiable imprints would suggest. See Ian Green, *Print and Protestantism in Early Modern England* (Oxford, 2000), pp. 508–9; D.W. Kummel, *English Music Printing 1553–1700* (London, 1975), pp. 36–42.

[4]   For the term, see Beth Quitslund, *The Reformation in Rhyme: Sternhold, Hopkins and the English Metrical Psalter, 1547–1603* (Aldershot, 2008), pp. 22–23, 70–71.

surrounded by sets of ancillary texts never suggested by the title page but also never absent except in a handful of the very cheapest editions. These include prose prefaces intended to clarify the use of the psalms or the printed music or both; a set of hymns with music immediately before the psalms that included traditional ecclesiastical texts (e.g., Veni Creator) as well as paraphrases of biblical texts (e.g., the Magnificat and Decalogue) and some original hymns; another set of hymns following the psalms, with a mix of biblical and original texts that in some cases duplicated those already paraphrased at the front of the volume; and 'A forme of Prayer to be vsed in priuate houses', usually comprising 12 domestic prayers before 1577 and a variable number after. In addition, more than half the editions after 1569 add a 'Confession of the Christian Faith' either before or after the prose prayers, and all editions end with tables for locating the psalms and hymns. When Elizabethans bought a psalm book, then, they generally got a version of the psalms contextualized by a complex exegetical framework and model of devotion.

The question of who was doing all this buying, and why, goes to the heart of what *kind* of popularity the *WBP* enjoyed. While there is some external evidence for how early modern readers and singers used the psalm book,[5] the surviving copies themselves are the single richest trove of information. The testimony they offer, however, is not always easy to interpret. While it is evident that texts omitted from many editions or dropped altogether in later printings were less frequently used – if only because they weren't available – it is far less obvious that everything that *did* remain in most copies of the book was there because of demand from purchasers. During the sixteenth century, the *WBP*'s publication was controlled by the two individuals holding the patent, the printer John Day and his son Richard. As a result, John Day's religious, political, and aesthetic preferences shaped the original compilation, and one or both of these men either drove or acceded to all subsequent modifications until 1604. At that point, James I granted the rights to print metrical psalms to the Stationers' Company as a central part of the English Stock. While there were a few intentional innovations in the publication of the *WBP* over the seventeenth century, most assigned printers reproduced it fairly mechanically and automatically from previous copies. For several reasons, then, the physical books available in shops could be unresponsive to changes in use. Nor, unfortunately, did many early owners leave marks that give us much more help. Nevertheless, it is difficult to explain the trajectory of Elizabethan printings without concluding that the Days were keen to make the most of the potential market for the psalm book, and harder still to imagine the main body of the Stationers' Company preferring to make a particular religious point over making

---

[5]   Discussions of use can be found in Hannibal Hamlin, *Psalm Culture in Early Modern England* (Cambridge, 2004), pp. 19–50; Christopher Marsh, *Music and Society in Early Modern England* (Cambridge, 2010), pp. 391–453; and Nicholas Temperley, *Music of the English Parish Church* (Cambridge, 1979), pp. 53–75. Other sources are listed below in conjunction with particular practices.

a profit. I am thus, very cautiously, reading the history of the *WBP*'s contents as a partial guide to the practices that it enabled and accompanied.

Public congregational singing most obviously drove demand for the psalm book. Casual references to parish psalm-singing by the 1580s make it clear that around London, at least, the practice was an ordinary and expected part of common prayer.[6] By the early seventeenth century the belief that the *WBP* was an officially required part of the liturgy had become widespread enough that George Wither felt he needed to refute it before embarking on his own metrical psalm paraphrases. (His intervention had no lasting effect: writers through the end of the century continued to freshly discover the psalms' unofficial status.)[7] In fact, some Elizabethan and early Stuart bishops did try to enforce the use of the singing psalms in their Visitation Articles, despite the lack of higher-level injunction.[8] The long-lived title page is probably more to blame for the confusion, however. Early editions noted that the book was 'Faithfully perused and alowed according to thordre appointed in the Quenes maiesties iniunctions', referring to the 1559 Injunction requiring all books to be examined by the Bishop of London before publication. Beginning in 1566, though, the reference of 'allowed' drifted so that it at least seemed to apply to the psalms' public use: 'set foorth and allowed to bee soong of the people together, in churches, before and after morning and euening prayer: as also before and after the sermon'.[9] The initial spread of psalm-singing in church and before or after public sermons in other venues does not seem to have begun with any ecclesiastical authority but out of genuine lay enthusiasm. John Jewel reported some 6,000 Londoners singing psalms at St Paul's Cross in March 1560, and other early evidence for the metrical psalms' use comes from reports of conflicts between singers and local officials who saw them as disruptive.[10] Elizabeth's first generation of bishops generally sided with the singers, but it is

---

[6]   See Jonathan Willis, *Church Music and Protestantism in Post-Reformation England: Discourses, Sites and Identities* (Aldershot, 2010), pp. 121–31; Quitslund, *The Reformation in Rhyme*, pp. 240–46.

[7]   George Wither, *A Preparation to the Psalter* (London, 1619; STC 25914), pp. 10–11. Later examples include Peter Heylin, *Ecclesia restaurata* (London, 1660–1661), p. 50; John Birkenhead, *The assembly-man* (London, 1662 [1663]; Wing B2961), p. 15; *Concavum cappo-cloacorum* (London, 1682; Wing C5692), pp. 29–30; and John Cosin, letter quoted in Richard Watson, *The Right Reverend Doctor John Cosin* (London, 1684; Wing W1094), pp. 13–14.

[8]   For example, Robert Horne in 1562 and 1571, in W.H. Frere and W.P.M. Kennedy (eds), *Visitation Articles and Injunctions of the Period of the Reformation 1536–1575* (London, 1910), III, pp. 138, 322; Matthew Wren, *Articles to be inquired of vvithin the dioces of Norwich in the first visitation* (London, 1636; STC 10298), B3ʳ.

[9]   From STC 2430 (1562) and 2437, respectively. The 1559 Injunction on liturgical music allowed for 'an hymn or such like song' before and after common prayer. Paul L. Hughes and James Francis Larkin (eds), *Tudor Royal Proclamations* (New Haven, 1964), II, p. 130.

[10]   Hastings Robinson (ed.), *The Zurich Letters* (Cambridge, 1842), p. 71; see also Quitslund, *The Reformation in Rhyme*, pp. 240–41, 196–7.

probably fair to say that the *WBP* established itself through collaboration between a minority's evangelical fervor, the majority's pleasure in the activity of singing, and highly sympathetic church authorities.

Public singing directly accounts for two sources of demand for the book, one smaller and one much more substantial. As Green notes, the early editions of the *WBP* tend to have large print suitable for an organist or for holding at arm's length in a choir, and some early Elizabethan church wardens' accounts note the purchase of a small number of psalm books, sometimes specifically recorded as for the choir.[11] These folios and one-column quartos – the only formats of the *WBP* that Day produced from 1562 to 1567, with the exception of one octavo in 1564 – represent a major shift from the octavo format in which every single incomplete English metrical psalter had previously appeared in either London or Geneva. Those were unostentatious books primarily for personal use, but by 1562 Day clearly foresaw a more institutional future for the completed collection. In most cases, choirs or singing boys probably would have led the congregation in unison singing, but especially in the 1560s the metrical psalms sometimes served for anthems as well, using harmonizations like those which Day printed in 1563.[12] From 1569 at the latest, however, regular production of smaller volumes resumed, including the first surviving 32mos and two-column quartos (the latter for binding with a Bible in the same format). The massive number of editions at an increasingly wide set of price points as the century wore on means that ownership of the *WBP* must have seemed desirable or necessary to English people in a variety of economic circumstances, and the best explanation is that they brought them to church. Thinking of the psalm book as an accessory for public devotion might at least account for one of the stranger comments to come out of the conflicts over its patent. In a Star Chamber complaint of 1584, John Wolfe alleged that Day took advantage of the public to make excessive profits from his rights to the psalm book. Among the price-gouging practices he detailed was 'prynting books of the halfe psalms whiche are souled for bookes of the whole Psalmes to suche as are vnlearned and Can not reade'.[13] For Wolfe's assertion to make any sense at all there must have been some use for the books quite aside from the words they contained – for instance, as status symbol carried to prayers in a London parish.[14]

---

[11] Ian Green, pp. 509–10, 512; see also Willis, pp. 122–28.

[12] Ian Green, p. 509, n31.

[13] Quoted in Harry R. Hoppe, 'John Wolfe, Printer and Publisher, 1579–1601', *The Library*, 4th ser., XIV.3 (1933): 256. Wolfe must have been reaching back to his apprenticeship to Day in 1569, when Day printed the last edition of *The first parte of the booke of psalmes* (STC 2439.7).

[14] Ian Green (pp. 510–11) does give a convincing case for a market among school children, who were in some cases to bring their psalm books to school with them. A number of schools, however, seem to have mandated psalm-singing in the 1560s, (probably) before there were large numbers of cheap editions available, suggesting that at the beginning the psalms were transmitted without private copies for the students. The psalm book's use as a required textbook must, to some extent, have evolved in tandem with the expanding supply of inexpensive copies, and in turn stimulated even larger production of small formats.

Finally, some Elizabethans drew on the *WBP* for domestic recreation and devotion. From 1579 to 1599 five different sets of harmonizations designed for domestic part-singing, solo instrumental accompaniment, or small consorts were published.[15] With the exception of Thomas East's version, these did not include the full texts of the psalms and so formed supplements or companions to the *WBP* itself. Though these music books had a select audience compared to the basic psalm book, they were apparently enough in demand to recompense the publishers; East's went through four editions by 1611. Probably an even greater number of households incorporated psalm-singing from the *WBP* into daily prayers. By the end of the sixteenth century, devotional manuals – particularly those aimed at the 'godly' – routinely urged that families sing psalms together as part of domestic prayers. Indeed, the best-selling such manual of the seventeenth century, Lewis Bayly's *Practice of Pietie* (1613), gave detailed directions for singing psalms in the evening, as well as encouraging their use in the morning and after returning home from church on Sunday.[16] Printed sermons beginning in the 1590s make clear that domestic psalmody was becoming negatively associated with 'puritanism', but the practice was not, in fact, limited to sectarians or even the more precise brand of conformists. In addition to the future Bishop Bayly's enthusiastic endorsement, John Donne praised Magdalene Herbert Danvers for regularly leading her own family in evening psalms.[17]

Frequent reprinting of the psalm book meant that Day could adjust it to fit the ways that it was being used, and he did so several times. In the first few years of publication, he made repeated attempts to get the number and placement of psalm versions and hymns right. Unlike his earlier partial metrical psalters, which included alternate versifications of some psalms, the first edition of the *WBP* included only one version of each (with the exception of a second Psalm 51). His choices did not, apparently, reflect the preferences of the singing public. In 1563, immediately following 'the ende of the psalmes of Dauid in meter' are

---

[15] William Daman, *The psalmes of David in English meter* (London, 1579; STC 6219); Daman, *The former booke of the musicke of M. William Damon* and *Cantus. The second booke* (London, 1591; STC 6220 and 6221); Thomas East, *The whole booke of Psalmes: with their wonted tunes* (London, 1592; STC 2482, 2nd edn 1594; STC 2488); *The whole booke of Psalmes ... composed into foure parts. Compiled by sundrie authors* (London, 1598?; STC 2495); Richard Allison, *The Psalmes of Dauid in meter* (London, 1599; STC 2496 and 2497).

[16] Lewis Bayly, *The practise of pietie* (London, 1613; STC 1602), pp. 464–68, 606–8. Others offering similar advice included Robert Openshaw, *Short questions and answeares* (London, 1579; STC 18816), A4r–5r, A8r; Robert Cleaver, *A godly forme of household gouernment* (London, 1598; STC 5383), C3r–v; Richard Rogers, *Seuen Treatises* (London, 1603; STC 21215), pp. 335, 396.

[17] John Donne, *A sermon of commemoration of the Lady Da[n]uers* (London, 1627; STC 7049), p. 133. For domestic psalmody more generally, see Quitslund, 'Singing the Psalms for Fun and Profit', in Alec Ryrie and Jessica Martin (eds), *Private and Household Devotion in Early Modern Britain* (Aldershot, 2012), pp. 237–58.

'Sertayne other Psalmes that be vsually song': the versions of Psalms 50, 100, and 125 that had been eliminated the previous year. In addition, three other psalm paraphrases that had been treated as hymns and included either before or after the metrical psalter returned to their previous spots. The folio of 1565 included 'another of the same' for five psalms within the metrical psalter (51, 50, 100, 125, and now also 23). In every case, the one that Day had ousted preceded the version from 1562. The publisher did not restore all of the alternate paraphrases from his earlier collections; some, apparently, were *not* 'vsually song'. (The last alternate version, of Ps. 136, was added from the Scots psalm book in 1577.) Similarly, in 1569 Day permanently rearranged the order of the hymns, promoting one from the back section to the front and moving another up to become the second in the book. These revisions not only signal the relative popularity of the hymns (at least in London congregations), but demonstrate how devotional practice changed the book's contours.

As the variety of formats diversified through the Elizabethan period, the psalm book's shape changed in physical terms as well. By 1603, the public had been offered folios, quartos, and octavos in one column of blackletter and in two columns of either blackletter or roman type; octavos in one column in blackletter or roman type or in two columns of roman; either blackletter or roman-type 16mos and 32mos; and roman duodecimos and 24mos. Although not all formats were reprinted as frequently as others, by the 1580s it is usual to see at least three different formats each year and sometimes as many as five or six. A number of these formats seemed designed to match and be bound with other religious texts, most commonly the complete Bible, the New Testament (in English or Latin), the Book of Common Prayer, the liturgical prose psalter, or some combination of these texts.[18] Others, especially in smaller formats, seemed to have been sold alone. Seventeenth-century octavos were sometimes bound at the end of a book of blank sheets for sermon notes or prayers.[19]

Nor were the differences in these editions only a matter of number of words on the page and the quality of the paper: beginning in the late 1570s, the Days differentiated the market for the *WBP* by varying its textual contents. By and large, the omissions and additions are tailored less to religious orientation than to purse size. Aside from the frequent absence of a preface on how to use the Psalms translated from Athanasius, the most common kind of variation is in the private prayers at the back of the volume. Printed in full up to 1577, with (two editions excepted) no additions other than the Confession of Faith, these were abbreviated

---

[18]   Ian Green (pp. 511–19) notes the regular coincidence of format for most of these books, though not the prose psalter, which surviving booklists from the bookseller Thomas Chard suggest may have been one of the most common combinations. See Robert Jahn, 'Letters and Booklist of Thomas Chard (or Chare) of London, 1583–4', *The Library*, 4th ser., IV.3 (1923): 219–37.

[19]   The Folger Library has three examples from the 1620s and 1630s: Folger STC 2608, 2626, and 2678.

in a variety of ways from that point on. The prayers for before and after meals were most likely to be omitted, probably because households were less likely to be singing psalms then than in morning or evening devotions. In some editions, their absence made room to include a long anti-Catholic prayer by John Foxe, the pseudo-Augustinian prayer 'Against the Devil', or both. Though the Foxe prayer participates in highly confessionalized polemic and the pseudo-Augustine looks very traditional, not to say medieval, they frequently appear together and so were not apparently intended for different audiences.

The effort to reduce the number of pages, and almost certainly the cost, led some small-format volumes to omit more prayers, and even some songs. Four prayers that seem to have been treated as the core of the collection – those for morning and evening, 'A Godly prayer to be said at all times', and a confession of sin – remain in most editions. Otherwise, the principle of selection in the shorter volumes seems to have been to print just enough prayers to take up extra pages in the last sheet. Other measures for reducing cost by cutting matter also show up in later Elizabethan editions. Most versions printed for binding with octavo Bibles or 16mo New Testaments, as well as the very slenderest 32mos, omit the prose arguments to individual psalms. The number of tunes provided plummets at the lower end of the market, from about 65 in the early editions and most complete later ones to a low of 46 in a 24mo of 1603. Finally, some 32mo editions beginning in the 1590s do not print *any* tunes, and one series also eliminates some alternate psalm versions and winnows the hymns to 15 from the usual 23.[20]

At the same time, the publishers also continued to issue more complete or spaciously printed editions, albeit in lower numbers. The two editions with the largest total apparatus of prefaces and prayers, including several not otherwise included in the *WBP*, are 32mos from 1569 and 1577. Though neither survives in later printings, a similar, relatively luxurious series of 32mos stretched from 1593 into the seventeenth century and would qualify in Ian Green's terms as a steady seller in its own right by appearing exactly five times in 30 years. Its production rate is modest, however, compared to those of many other formats – like the two-column blackletter quartos coming out annually and often in two independently set editions.

Thus the Days, and later the Stationers, adjusted the size of the book with an eye to market and cost. But in the midst of these adjustments they also kept an eye on what they thought, or what they believed their audience thought, was the essential nature of the book's identity. This essential nature had several parts.

First and foremost, it was a book for singing, whether or not the owner could read music. Despite the fact that musical literacy was more limited than verbal literacy, most editions included printed tunes. These did not necessarily guide the singing, however. East's harmonizations, first published in 1592, according to the title page contains 'the Church tunes … carefully corrected, and thereunto added other short tunes vsually song in London, and other places of this Realme'; the next edition, in 1594, identifies four tunes not found in standard editions of

---

[20]   Starting in 1617, most roman 12mos also omit music.

the *WBP* as those to which 'The Psalmes are song … In most churches of this Realme'.[21] Support for East's assertions is found in the 1603 *Certaine Psalmes* by Henry Dod. He chose them, he tells us, because their unusual stanza forms in the *WBP* has rendered them 'heretofore much out of vse, because of their difficult tunes', whereas his own are 'Reduced into English meter better fitting the common tunes.' While the first of them, Psalm 104, specifies the tune proper to Psalm 25, the rest do not have any such notes, and Dod may well be thinking of 'common tunes' outside the *WBP*.[22] Nor is the *WBP* itself always much better at helping the singer. In editions that cut down the number of tunes, it is not difficult to find notes directing the reader to 'Sing this as' another psalm that is also printed without music. Finally, the music seems frequently to have been set by compositors without musical training and to have remained uncorrected thereafter.[23] The difference between printing unpopular music that has descended through a line of un-proofread editions and not printing tunes at all is largely a difference of appearance and perception – of the buyer's expectations for what the book *is,* regardless of how she will actually use it.

It was also a book of devotion. The prose arguments distilling the psalms' context and application disappeared in the most minimalist editions and in those bound with small-format Bibles, but otherwise remain a standard feature of the book. They could not be consulted during congregational singing, and thus point to an idea of the psalm book as a repository of sacred texts for individual edification. Likewise, while it is impossible to know how many owners of psalm books used the household prayers at the back of the volume, their continued presence in some form marks the book as a domestic devotional resource. In fact, while readers' marks on surviving copies of the *WBP* are uncommon, two copies at the Huntington Library update the private prayers by striking out references to the Queen and replacing them with 'King'.[24]

Finally, it was the Book of Psalms. Though in verse, its legitimacy for many English worshipers derived from its status as a complete unit of scripture. Wolf considered Day's 'books of the halfe psalms' scandalous despite the evidence suggesting that a substantial number of the paraphrases included in the *WBP* went largely unsung. Not until the end of the seventeenth century did collections of *selected* psalms for public singing begin to appear as complete hymnals in their own right. Before that could happen, literally dozens of writers over the seventeenth century published singing psalms meant to displace the *WBP*, some in the form of complete metrical psalters, and others in smaller batches, as often leaden trial balloons. Although the Stationers' monopoly and popular inertia colluded in maintaining the *WBP*'s popularity, much of the Restoration audience had come to view its versifications as one of many possible ways of singing the psalms, and not the best way at that. Elbowed by rivals, it could no longer be *the* psalm book.

---

[21]   East, 1594, B1r.

[22]   Henry Dod, *Certaine Psalmes of David* (Edinburgh, 1603; STC 2730), A3r, tp.

[23]   Kummel, *English Music Printing*, p. 73.

[24]   Editions from 1566 (Huntington 438000:597) and 1569 (Huntington 62361).

Chapter 13
Serial Publication and Romance

Louise Wilson

To attempt to define the popularity of early modern romance is to embark on a journey as errant and as fraught with difficulties as any of the genre's protagonists ever undertook. Native medieval romance persisted in the sixteenth century, given new impetus by print, and this was joined by classical Greek and continental romance translations and, increasingly, original romances by English writers. Often romance emerged as a mode at play in other genres including the epic, the novella, and drama.[1] The pervasiveness of romance in much literary writing of the Elizabethan period testified to its widespread appeal both for writers, who continued to find creative inspiration in it, and for consumers who continued to enjoy it. Given its prevalence in early modern literary culture, it was unquestionably a popular genre in both quantifiable and unquantifiable terms: both a bestseller and a crowd-pleaser. While certain romances were aimed towards a more restricted readership – such as Edmund Spenser's *The Faerie Queene* and Sir Philip Sidney's *The Countess of Pembroke's Arcadia* – the genre was not generally elite: it appealed to the widest range of readers, from the highly educated to the least literate, who had the narratives read to them. As Roger Chartier points out, 'in the Renaissance the same texts and the same books often circulated in all social milieus.',[2] and as Helen Cooper observes, 'Romances, like novels, can appeal to readers of every level of intelligence, although (unlike the most intellectually demanding, and

---

[1]   On the difficulty of defining early modern romance and its relation to other genres, see, for example, Nandini Das, *Renaissance Romance: The Transformation of English Prose Fiction, 1570–1620* (Farnham, 2011), p. 14; Alex Davis, *Chivalry and Romance in the English Renaissance* (Cambridge, 2003), p. 2; Barbara Fuchs, *Romance* (London, 2004), pp. 66–78; and Helen Moore, 'Shakespeare and Popular Romance', in Stuart Gillespie and Neil Rhodes (eds), *Shakespeare and Elizabethan Popular Culture* (London, 2006), p. 92. Lori Humphrey Newcomb, 'Romance', in Joad Raymond (ed.), *The Oxford History of Popular Print Culture, Volume 1, Cheap Print in Britain and Ireland to 1660* (Oxford, 2011), pp. 363–76, provides a useful discussion of popular romance and print in early modern England.

[2]   Roger Chartier, 'Reading Matter and "Popular" Reading: From the Renaissance to the Seventeenth Century', in Roger Chartier and Guglielmo Cavallo (eds), A *History of Reading in the West*, (trans.) Lydia G. Cochrane (Oxford, 1999), p. 270.

therefore elitist, novels) they always do their audience the kindness of placing a primacy on telling good stories.'[3]

It is the very accessibility of romance that sustains its pre-eminence in the early modern marketplace of print, where a number of the genre's titles can lay claim to the status of bestseller, particularly John Lyly's *Euphues, the anatomy of wyt* and *Euphues and his England,* and Robert Greene's *Pandosto: the Triumph of Time* (later *Dorastus and Fawnia*).[4] *Euphues, the anatomy of wyt* was printed 16 times between 1578 and 1617, *Euphues and his England* was printed 15 times between 1580 and 1617, and *Pandosto* was printed 8 times between 1588 and 1619.[5] As the example of Lyly's two volumes of *Euphues* shows, demand for a romance often led to a subsequent volume even as the print popularity of the first continued, and a number of romances generated bestselling sequels: for example, Emanuel Forde's *Parismus the renoumed prince of Bohemia* was first printed in 1598, and its sequel, *Parismenos: the second part of* [...] *Parismus the renowned prince of Bohemia,* was printed in 1599. Each went through four editions to 1615 and – after the first editions – the two volumes were usually bound together. Richard Johnson's prose romance, *The most famous history of the seauen champions of Christendome,* published in two parts in 1596 and 1597, was published two further times to 1616, and the two parts were also bound together.[6] Sequels were not only quantitatively successful editions in their own right, but also a qualitative marker of the popularity of the original, trading on narrative continuity or similarity and also indicating their relation to the first title in their various paratexts, particularly the title page. As the numbers show, they also often enjoyed a similar level of print popularity; but while the popularity of one sequel is relatively easy to quantify in bibliographic terms, accounting for the long-term serial publication of some romances presents a greater challenge.

The issue of print popularity has been given particular attention in recent years in the debate on the popularity of playbooks between Peter Blayney on the one hand and Alan B. Farmer and Zachary Lesser on the other.[7] While disagreeing in

---

[3]   Helen Cooper, *The English Romance in Time: Transforming Motifs from Geoffrey of Monmouth to the Death of Shakespeare* (Oxford, 2004), p. 12.

[4]   On the complex publication history of *Pandosto,* see Lori Humphrey Newcomb, *Reading Popular Romance in Early Modern England* (New York, 2002); on Lyly, see Andy Kesson, *John Lyly and Early Modern Authorship* (Manchester, 2013).

[5]   This may seem an arbitrary cut-off point, but it signals the end of the period of intensive printing and initial reprinting of the Iberian chivalric romances on which this chapter focuses.

[6]   See Naomi Conn Liebler, 'Elizabethan Pulp Fiction: The Example of Richard Johnson', *Critical Survey* 12 (2000): 71–87. Liebler points out that the rate of publication of *The Seven Champions* is equal to that of Sir Thomas North's translation of Plutarch, *The Lives of the Noble Grecians and Romanes,* with 'fifteen printings in eighty years, five of them during the period 1596–1639 (cf. North's editions 1579–1631)', p. 71.

[7]   See, in order of publication, Peter W.M. Blayney, 'The Publication of Playbooks', in John D. Cox and David Scott Kastan (eds), *A New History of Early English Drama* (New

method, their shared emphasis on reprint rates of editions as a sign of continuing demand for a title remains the focus for many bibliographic studies of print popularity. This method measures the saleability of a single title over time; I want to propose that we also pay attention to collective popularity in order to understand the enduring popularity of a sequence of texts over time. This chapter, therefore, makes the case for serial publication as a marker of print popularity. To do this, it examines the long-term publication of Anthony Munday's translations of the Iberian chivalric romance cycles, *Amadis de Gaule* and *Palmerin*, and links this to the relationship between their paratextual and narrative features to propose that the distinctive open-endedness of the genre, coupled with its emphasis on genealogical continuation, marries with the public demand for editions to create a cumulative form of popularity unparalleled in Elizabethan literature.

The several volumes of the *Amadis de Gaule* and *Palmerin* cycles were translated into English by Munday from the early 1580s until 1602. These romances had already enjoyed a very high level of popularity throughout Europe from their print origins in Spain and Portugal.[8] In France, the two cycles began to be translated and published discretely after the flow of new Iberian volumes had stopped, and demand was so high for the ongoing exploits of *Amadis de Gaule* in particular that when the Iberian originals were exhausted, the translators and publishers looked to Italian continuations to sustain the public appetite. When Munday took up the challenge of translating the romances into English from the French editions, he conflated the two cycles so that they formed one long project.[9]

York, 1997); Alan B. Farmer and Zachary Lesser, 'The Popularity of Playbooks Revisited', *Shakespeare Quarterly* 56.1 (2005): 1–32; Peter W.M. Blayney, 'The Alleged Popularity of Playbooks', *Shakespeare Quarterly* 56.1 (2005): 33–50; and Alan B. Farmer and Zachary Lesser, 'Structures of Popularity in the Early Modern Book Trade', *Shakespeare Quarterly* 56.2 (2005): 206–13. For a discussion of the implications of this debate, see the introduction to the present volume.

[8]   On the popularity of the Iberian cycles in continental Europe, see, for example, Daniel Eisenberg, *Castilian Romances of Chivalry in the Sixteenth Century* (London, 1979); Helen Moore (ed.), 'Introduction', in *Amadis de Gaule, Translated by Anthony Munday* (Aldershot, 2004); Andrew Pettegree, 'Translation and the Migration of Texts' in *The French Book and the European Book World* (Leiden, 2007), pp. 203–18; Andrew Pettegree and Malcolm Walsby (eds), *French Vernacular Books: Books Published in the French Language Before 1601* (Leiden, 2007); Elizabeth Spiller, *Reading and the History of Race in the Renaissance* (Cambridge, 2011), esp. pp. 12–14; and Henry Thomas, *Spanish and Portuguese Romances of Chivalry* (Cambridge, 1920), pp. 41–118.

[9]   1588 is the date of the earliest extant edition of any of Munday's chivalric romance translations, *Palmerin d'Oliva* (Part One), which was also chronologically the first volume of the Spanish and French *Palmerin* cycles – but there is a possibility that Munday's translation of *The First Part of Palmerin of England* was published earlier in the 1580s and then suppressed or lost, as parts one and two were entered in the Stationers' Register to John Charlewood on 13 February 1581 and Munday also mentions an earlier published translation in his preliminaries to *Palmerin d'Oliva*. For fuller bibliographic details of the publication of the romances see Donna B. Hamilton, *Anthony Munday and the Catholics,*

A precedent for the serial publication of chivalric romance in England had been set a few years earlier with the translation of the Spanish cycle, *Espejo de principes y cavalleros*; the first part, written by Diego Ortúñez de Calahorra, had proved extremely popular in Spain and inspired three continuations. In England, the four volumes – translated directly from the Spanish – were divided into nine. Book one of part one was translated by Margaret Tyler as *The Mirrour of princely deedes and knighthood* and printed in 1578, 1580, and 1599;[10] book two of part one was translated by R.P.[11] and printed as *The second part of the first booke of the myrrour of knighthood* in 1585 and 1599; book three of part one was also translated by R.P. as *The third part of the first booke of the mirrour of knighthood* and printed in 1586 and 1598 or 1599. The second part by Pedro de la Sierra was translated by R.P. and its two books were printed as *The second part of the myrror of knighthood* in 1583 and again in 1598. Book one of part three, by Marcos Martínez, was translated by R.P. as *The sixth booke of the myrrour of knighthood* and printed in 1598; book two of part three was translated by L.A. as *The seventh booke of the myrrour of knighthood* and printed in 1598. Book one of part four, also by Marcos Martínez, was translated by L.A. as *The eighth booke of the myrror of knighthood* and printed in 1599; and book two of part four was translated by R.P. as *The ninth part of the mirrour of knight-hood* and printed in 1601. Although the translation and publication of the several parts of *The Mirror* between 1578 and 1601 suggest an appetite for long chivalric narratives, the low reprint rates of the individual titles indicate that the series did not enjoy the same level of popularity as other romances in the period; nonetheless, they provide a model for the serial publication of several volumes of a chivalric cycle that Munday and his printing agents would follow. Perhaps looking to its huge success in France, his stationers appear to have recognized the potential for the *Amadis*, in particular, to be a bestseller and were keen to secure the right to produce several volumes of the cycle. A year after the initial publication of *Palmerin d'Oliva* (Part One) in 1588, the first two books of *Amadis de Gaule* – which appeared in separate volumes – were entered in the Stationers' Register to Edward Allde on 15 January 1589; books two through five were entered to John Wolfe on 10 April 1592; and books two through twelve were entered to Adam Islip and William Moring on 16 October 1594.

Taking one particular volume of either cycle, the reprint rate would be respectable but not outstandingly high for fiction in the period: for example, *Palmerin d'Oliva* (Part One) was printed four times in around 30 years – in 1588,

---

1560–1633 (Aldershot, 2005), esp. pp. 199–206; Gerald R. Hayes, 'Anthony Munday's Romances of Chivalry', *The Library*, 4th ser., 6 (1926): 57–81 and 'Anthony Munday's Romances: A Postscript', *The Library*, 4th ser., 7 (1926): 31–38.

[10]   Several of the dates of publication in this paragraph are conjectured by STC, as they do not feature in the imprints of the editions. On the publication of Tyler's editions, see Joyce Boro (ed.), *Margaret Tyler, The Mirror of Princely Deeds and Knighthood*, MHRA *Tudor and Stuart Translations* (London, 2013), Introduction.

[11]   The translations have been attributed to either Robert Parke or Robert Parry.

1597, 1615, and 1616 – whereas some romances that were first printed at the same time reappeared much more frequently: as previously noted, Robert Greene's *Pandosto* was first printed in 1588 and went through eight editions to 1619; and Sidney's *The Countess of Pembroke's Arcadia,* also printed for the first time in 1588, went through seven editions to 1621. However, taking Munday's translation project as a whole, the figures are more significant. With this approach, we can see a steady stream of editions from either the *Amadis* or the *Palmerin* cycle published between at least 1588 and 1602, totalling at least 11 or 12[12] editions in around 15 years:

Palmerin d'Oliva [Part One] (John Charlewood for William Wright, 1588)
Palmendos (John Charlewood for Simon Waterson, 1589)
The first booke of Amadis de Gaule (Edward Allde, 1590)
The second booke of Amadis de Gaule (Adam Islip for Cuthbert Burby, 1595)
The first booke of Primaleon of Greece (John Danter for Cuthbert Burby, 1595)
Palmerin of England [Parts One and Two] (Thomas Creede, 1596)
The second booke of Primaleon of Greece (John Danter for Cuthbert Burby, 1596)
Palmerin d'Oliva [Parts One and Two?] (Thomas Creede, 1597)
The fift[h] booke of ... Amadis de Gaule (Adam Islip, sold by Hugh Jackson, 1598)
The third ... part of Palmerin of England (James Roberts for William Leake, 1602)

This completed the early run of first editions and reprints. After a short lapse of time, 12 further editions – many of them printed together as composite editions – appeared over 11 years:

Palmerin of England [Part One] (Thomas Creede, 1609)
Palmerin d'Oliva [Part One] (Thomas Creede, 1615)
Palmerin d'Oliva [Parts One – a reissue of the 1615 edition with a cancel title page – and Two] (Thomas Creede and Bernard Alsop for Richard Higgenbotham, 1616)

---

[12]   The exact figure for this period is difficult to state with certainty owing to the incomplete nature of the evidence. My analysis is necessarily based on extant editions, but there is little doubt that others have been lost; for example, it is widely noted that editions of *Palmerin of England*, Parts One and Two, are likely to have appeared in the early 1580s (see n. 9). Hayes presents compelling evidence that the first edition of the second part of *Palmerin d'Oliva* appeared in 1588 ('Anthony Munday's Romances of Chivalry', p. 60). Furthermore, the edition of the first part of *Palmerin d'Oliva* bound with the first extant edition of the second part of *Palmerin d'Oliva* (1597) has missing preliminaries, so it is impossible to say with certainty whether it is a new edition – as STC conjectures – or a first edition bound with the later volume.

Palmerin of England [Parts One and Two] (Thomas Creede and Bernard
    Alsop, 1616)
Amadis de Gaule [Parts Three and Four] (Nicholas Okes, 1618)
Amadis de Gaule [Parts One and Two] (Nicholas Okes, 1619)
Primaleon of Greece [Parts One, Two, and Three] (Thomas Snodham, 1619)

The comparatively low reprint rate of individual titles is offset by the frequent
printing of related titles in the cycles and, in total, at least 23 editions appeared
between 1588 and 1619. The great length of the texts may also be an inhibiting
factor with regard to reprints: *The First Part of Palmerin of England* stretched to
over 400 pages in quarto compared to, for example, *Pandosto* at 56 quarto pages,
so there was a more significant economic investment in materials and labour to
produce Munday's texts for the press.

The serial publication of chivalric romance cannot, however, simply be ascribed
to market demands: its narrative form – errant, episodic, and often open-ended and
multi-generational[13] – had always been particularly conducive to continuations.
In the *Palmerin* romances, for example, the narrative loosely follows the family
line with sons and grandsons and their friends dominating later editions after the
initial protagonist dies: the first volume of *Palmerin, Palmerin d'Oliva*, concerns
the titular hero, who is the illegitimate grandson of the emperor of Constantinople.
Munday divides the French translation of this into two parts which are published
separately, and then takes the first 20 chapters of the Spanish *Primaleón* and
publishes those as *Palmendos*, the third volume of the English series. Palmendos is
one of Palmerin d'Oliva's sons; the fourth volume, *Primaleon of Greece*, is about
another son of Palmerin d'Oliva as well as another protagonist, Prince Edward of
England. This volume ends with the death of Palmerin d'Oliva, leaving Primaleon
as his successor. Three volumes of *Palmerin of England* follow, concerning the
hero who is the son of Prince Edward, and named after his father's friend's father;
he has a twin, Florian, and so these volumes also have two protagonists.[14] Thus,
along with the provisional or deferred nature of the ending of chivalric romance,
the possibility to extend through the genealogical line in such a manner means
that, if the series continued to prove appealing to book purchasers, the narrative
could be extended into further editions to capitalize on its continuing saleability.

Both print and narrative continuities are programmed in the paratexts of the
romances. As a number of scholars have pointed out, Munday was particularly
adept at advertising forthcoming volumes of the cycles in the front and back

---

[13] Numerous studies examine the open-endedness of romance. See, particularly,
Patricia A. Parker, *Inescapable Romance: Studies in the Poetics of a Mode* (Princeton,
1979); Nandini Das explores the wide significance of generational thinking to romance in
Renaissance Romance.

[14] For fuller plot summaries, see Mary Patchell, *The Palmerin Romances in
Elizabethan Fiction* (New York, 1966), pp. 129–33; for a summary of the narratives of the
various volumes of *Amadis de Gaule*, see Thomas, *Spanish and Portuguese Romances of
Chivalry*, pp. 43–47.

matter of editions, whether he was simply assuring his patrons or readers that his translation of the next edition was well under way and close to completion, or offering a specific advertisement of the forthcoming narrative to the reader.[15] At the end of his original Euphuistic romance, *Zelauto* (1580), Munday promised his patron, Edward de Vere, the Earl of Oxford, that 'Not long it will be before the rest be finished and the renowned Palmerin of England with all speede shall be sent you';[16] and a host of similar claims appear in the paratexts of the romances themselves, including *Palmerin d'Oliva* (Part One), in which Munday writes in another dedicatory epistle to the Earl of Oxford, 'the second part, now on the presse, and well neere finished I will shortly present my worthie Patrone.'[17]

While these paratextual promises of future volumes are usually read as a commercial strategy that responded explicitly to the dual demands of Munday's printing houses and book purchasers, they did not, in fact, originate with the English editions; Munday borrowed this particular practice from the producers of the French *Amadis* editions, who regularly pointed to forthcoming titles in the same cycle. Rather than being simply documents of intense literary labour, the paratexts also hint at modes of readerly engagement. Virginia Krause, discussing the French *Amadis* cycle, suggests that the conscious print serialization of the narrative developed as a means of engendering desire in the reader. In this way, serial publication became enmeshed with the deferral of narrative closure of chivalric romance, and a transformation in book marketing took place in the course of translating and publishing the later volumes of the cycle: 'beginning with the fourth book … narrative modes begin to encourage readers to keep reading from one book to the next, using each new book to program a desire for a sequel',[18] and the sense of an ending was countered with a sense of expectation.

The French translator, Michel de Herberay, Seigneur des Essars, had altered the ending of the fourth *Amadis* volume from the Spanish original so that the characters were suspended, waiting for the fifth book to commence to resume their adventures. This also seems to be a feature that Munday emulated in at least one

---

[15]   On this feature, see Hamilton, *Anthony Munday and the Catholics*, p. 79; Tracey Hill, *Anthony Munday and Civic Culture: Theatre, history and power in early modern London, 1580–1633* (Manchester, 2004), pp. 83–87; Helen Moore, 'Anthony Munday', in Gordon Braden, Robert Cummings, and Stuart Gillespie (eds), *The Oxford History of Literary Translation in English: Volume 2 1550–1660* (Oxford: Oxford University Press, 2010), p. 76; and Joshua Phillips, *English Fictions of Communal Identity, 1485–1603* (Farnham, 2010), esp. pp. 144–45. On the late sixteenth-century reorientation of paratextual material from the patron to the reader-purchaser, see Steve Mentz, *Romance for Sale in Early Modern England: The Rise of Prose Fiction* (Aldershot, 2006), esp. Introduction.

[16]   Anthony Munday, *Zelauto* (London, 1580), sig. ¶iiii^v.

[17]   Anthony Munday (trans.), *Palmerin d'Oliva* (Part One), (London, 1588), sig. *ii^v.

[18]   Virginia Krause, 'Serializing the French *Amadis* in the 1540s', in Marian Rothstein (ed.), *Charting Change in France around 1540* (Selinsgrove, 2006), p. 45. On the apparent insatiability of the romance reader, see A.C. Hamilton, 'Elizabethan Romance: The Example of Prose Fiction', *ELH* 49 (1982): 287–99 (297–98).

of his English translations, but, rather than altering the ending from the French, he added an authorial address to the reader at the end of the volume. *Palmerin d'Oliva* (Part One) ends in medias res, followed by Munday's short address. He begins by recounting the events that have just occurred:

> Thus Gentlemen haue wee left the Prince Trineus transformed into the shape of a Dogge, in the Isle of Maljada, by the Enchantresse: the English Princesse Agriola, in the custody of the Turkish Pirate Olimael: Ptolome and Colmelio carried into Aethiopia, and Palmerin raunging in the Islande with his Hauke for his delight.

Having detailed these various cliff-hangers, any sense of suspense on the part of the reader is quickly dissipated as he goes on to publicize the narrative developments of the next volume:

> Right straunge will bee the meeting of all these friendes againe, after the hazards of many perillous fortunes. For Agriola thus separated from the Prince her husband, is married to the great Emperour of Turkie: howe wonderfully the ring which Palmerin gaue her, preserues her chastitie, will be worth the hearing. How Palmerin gaines his Polinarda, Trineus his chast wife Agriola, Ptolome his Brionella, and all Honors meeting togither in the Emperours Court of Allemaigne, wil be so strange as the like was neuer heard: and all this performes the second part, which shall be published so soone as it can be printed.[19]

The assurances that these events 'will be worth the hearing' and 'so strange as the like was neuer heard' promise future pleasure in reading even as they admit that the narrative is not yet available. This particular strategy of pointing to forthcoming continuations does not, however, provide a full account of either Munday's or the readers' engagement.

Munday did not translate the romances in narrative order, so while he was always promising a forthcoming edition, it was rarely the next instalment in the sequence. While acknowledging the disjunction, the preliminaries emphasized the interdependence of the individual volumes and their value to the larger narratives of the romance cycles: 'When I finished my seconde parte of *Palmerin of England*, I promised this worke of *Palmerin D'Oliua*, because it depended so especially on the other',[20] writes Munday in his epistle 'To the courteous Readers' in the first part of *Palmerin d'Oliva*. Introducing new folio editions of parts one and two of *Amadis de Gaule* with a dedicatory epistle to Sir Philip Herbert in 1619, he describes the third and fourth parts of the cycle, which had appeared together a year earlier, as 'a body without an head, because these former Bookes are the guide and direction to them all'.[21] In his epistle to Frances and Susan Young preceding a new edition of the first part of *Palmerin d'Oliva* in 1615, he writes that 'by the reprinting of

---

[19]   Munday, *Palmerin d'Oliva* (Part One), sig. Z4ʳ.

[20]   Munday, *Palmerin d'Oliva* (Part One), sig. *iiiʳ.

[21]   Anthony Munday (trans.), *Amadis de Gaule* (Part One), (London, 1619), sig. A2ʳ.

them [i.e. the *Palmerin* romances] ouer againe, at length they will come to a iust order, ... will perfect the whole history, and make it complete in euery part.'[22] The earlier editions of the 1580s and 1590s had imagined readers in their paratexts who read the volumes in their initial printing order rather than their narrative order, but later reprinting, new front matter suggested, remedied this unsatisfactory state of affairs. Owners had attempted to impose continuity on the early editions by having copies bound together in sequence, such as the British Library copy of *Palmerin d'Oliva*, parts one and two [STC 19158] from 1588 and 1597, respectively.[23] The later reprints in the 1610s made much of the repositioning of the volumes in their correct sequences to provide a more pleasurable and profitable experience for the reader. Volumes were printed and marketed as composite editions, too, as, for example, the three parts of *Primaleon of Greece* by Thomas Snodham in 1619, which, Munday claims, 'all the seuerall parts compared together, and ordered as they ought to be; they will seeme as a Chronologie of so many famous mens liues',[24] a reorganization of the order of publication seemingly transforming the lowly romance into a more prestigious form.

Romance bestsellers reached their peak in print popularity at the same time as they achieved their greatest notoriety: as Barbara Fuchs notes, 'the marginalization of romance as a lesser form begins at exactly the same point that it achieves its broad popularity via print circulation'.[25] The Iberian romances experienced renewed cultural visibility in the parodic plots of Francis Beaumont's play *The Knight of the Burning Pestle* (perf. 1607) and Thomas Shelton's English translation of the first part of Cervantes' *Don Quixote* (1612), which indicate an audience deeply familiar both with the narratives of the romance cycles and with concerns over the unintelligent devotion they were thought to inspire in the uneducated reader or listener. These literary redirections of romance narratives occur at the same time as the second intensive phase of reprinting of Munday's translations (1609–1619), suggesting that the comic treatment of the narratives and their readers did nothing to dampen demand for the originals and may in fact have fuelled it further. Although the status of chivalric romance was clearly under revision in the early decades of the 1600s, the many volumes of the Iberian cycles continued to be printed throughout the century. The *Amadis* and *Palmerin* romances are unusual examples of early modern popular fiction, both in terms of the length of their individual editions and also the scope and duration of the series' publication, but paying attention to their collective popularity shows that they enjoyed a long-term prime position in the early modern book market.

---

[22] Anthony Munday (trans.), *Palmerin d'Oliva* (Part One), (London, 1615), sig. A3r.

[23] See Hayes, 'Anthony Munday's Romances of Chivalry', p. 66.

[24] Anthony Munday (trans.), *Primaleon of Greece* (Part One), (London, 1619), sig. A4v.

[25] Fuchs, *Romance*, p. 97.

Chapter 14
Mucedorus

Peter Kirwan

The Popular Play

By virtue of the very nature of Elizabethan drama, there are particular challenges for anyone attempting to determine the most 'popular' play of the period. Drama offers two primary modes of consumption, through the communal experience of theatregoing and the relatively private experience of reading, and success in the one format need not necessarily translate to popularity in the other. Further, our methodologies for measuring both are partial and arguably misleading. This chapter takes the case of a specific play, the anonymous *Mucedorus*, to interrogate some of the problems in defining and articulating print popularity in the case of drama, and the effects of popularity on the text's afterlife. *Mucedorus,* which tells the story of the titular prince who, disguised as a shepherd, woos a foreign princess, kills a savage woodland dweller and unites two kingdoms, is particularly helpful for its relative obscurity in the present day, despite apparently being one of the bestsellers of its time.

Little quantitative evidence survives to help us ascertain the popularity of plays before they reached print. With the obvious exception of Henslowe's account book, few financial records of Elizabethan playhouses survive, leaving us in most cases to conjecture how long a given play was in the repertory, how often it was played and whether or not it sustained recurring audiences.[1] We are dependent, rather, on the evidence of printed playbooks, which poses new problems. One longstanding school of thought, for example, suggests that a play would only pass into print once it had exhausted its life on stage;[2] if so, then the theoretical possibility needs to be acknowledged that the most popular plays may have waited years to be printed, or may not have been printed at all, while less popular plays were retired early and printed quickly, or not at all.[3] For book scholars, the popularity of the play begins with its first publication, which becomes an origin point eliding the prior commercial history of the play.

---

[1]   See R.A. Foakes (ed.), *Henslowe's Diary*, 2nd ed. (Cambridge, 2002).

[2]   For a summary of positions, see John Jowett, *Shakespeare and Text* (Oxford, 2007), pp. 9–10.

[3]   Elizabethan plays apparently popular onstage but not published for many years include the anonymous *The Famous Victories of Henry V* (usually dated to the 1580s; first published 1598) and Marlowe's *The Jew of Malta* (c.1590; first published 1633).

The very fact of a play text reaching print may imply failure on stage (as in Jonson's *Sejanus* and *Catiline*) or overwhelming success (as in *Romeo and Juliet*, which 'hath often been [with great applause] played publiquely').[4] Print publications both substitute for and consolidate the reception of the plays as staged, and both success and failure are used to sell printed texts.[5] The additional danger of a presentation that justifies publication through success or failure on stage is that it implies a monodirectional line of transmission from performance to print, when of course evidence suggests that many plays did remain in the company's repertory after publication.[6]

Our methodologies for determining popularity through sales, reprints and rates of publication have been the focus of ongoing debate, particularly in the work of Alan Farmer, Zachary Lesser and Peter Blayney, discussed elsewhere in this volume.[7] Nonetheless, it needs to be noted that however we interpret the evidence provided by the reprinting and republication of playbooks, there is no simple quantitative formula for determining popularity. The 'most spectacularly and scandalously popular play of the English Renaissance' in terms of box-office success was Middleton's *A Game at Chess*, running for an apparently unprecedented nine consecutive performances at the Globe in 1624;[8] yet its popularity in print is confined to an extraordinary flourish – three quartos within 18 months and six extant manuscript versions, testifying to the immediacy of its impact at a significant political moment in Jacobean London rather than to continuous stage life. This was a short-term bestseller, an immediate smash. Conversely, *Mucedorus* does not appear to have been printed until almost a decade after its first performance, but its publication history is then continuous for 70 years; the Elizabethan equivalent of a 'sleeper hit' in print, divorced from its initial moment of creation. Finally, of course, the popularity of a play might be more qualitatively discussed in terms of its cultural saturation; the legacy of a play such as *The Spanish Tragedy*, *Tamburlaine* or *Romeo and Juliet*, reflected in references, adaptations, tributes and other media.

---

[4]   *An excellent conceited tragedie of Romeo and Iuliet As it hath been often (with great applause) plaid publiquely, by the right Honourable the L. of Hunsdon his Seruants* (London, 1597), title page.

[5]   See also the title page of *The nevv inne. Or, The light heart A comoedy. As it was neuer acted, but most negligently play'd, by some, the Kings Seruants. And more squeamishly beheld, and censured by others, the Kings subiects. 1629. Now, at last, set at liberty to the readers, his Maties seruants, and subiects, to be iudg'd* (London, 1631).

[6]   Examples include Shakespeare's *Much Ado about Nothing*, *1 Henry IV* and *The Merry Wives of Windsor*, all performed at court in 1612–1613. See Roslyn Lander Knutson, *The Repertory of Shakespeare's Company 1594–1616* (Fayetteville, 1991), p. 140.

[7]   See Alan B. Farmer and Zachary Lesser, 'The Popularity of Playbooks Revisited', *Shakespeare Quarterly* 56.1 (2005): 1–32; and Peter W.M. Blayney, 'The Alleged Popularity of Playbooks', *Shakespeare Quarterly* 56.1 (2005): 33–50.

[8]   Gary Taylor, 'Thomas Middleton: Lives and Afterlives', in Gary Taylor and John Lavagnino (eds), *Thomas Middleton: Collected Works* (Oxford, 2007), p. 49.

A play's popularity, then, may best be thought of in terms of a conglomeration of measures, acknowledging the approval of the state, physical reprints of books and/or the cultural work done by the play. Yet 'popular' does not solely, of course, imply 'successful'. Michael Hattaway notes that '[t]o the Elizabethans, in fact, "public" and "popular" were virtually synonymous ... "Drama for the people" therefore is one definition of popular drama. Another might be "drama of the people".'[9] 'Popular' exists in implicit opposition to notions of the private, elite, sophisticated and artistic, a set of oppositions that is challenged usefully throughout Hattaway's important monograph. Nonetheless, it remains the fact that our understanding of the correlation between the market for the auditing of drama and that for the reading of printed plays remains necessarily hazy. However, we should note the fundamental problem of measuring the 'popular' – which I will continue to use with awareness of the dual meanings of 'successful/acclaimed' and 'of the people' – through its textual manifestations. In a society of increasing but still limited literacy, there is an element of exclusivity to printed drama in terms of the education and financial background of its consumers, which inevitably reframes the popular within a less 'popular' format.

Despite these caveats, however, one may still assert with Victor Holtcamp that '*Mucedorus* was arguably the most popular Elizabethan play of the 17th century'.[10] This anonymous play can be positioned as popular in all senses of the word, across platforms and measuring criteria. Its publication history is unmatched by any other early modern play: by 1668, no fewer than 18 quartos had been published, including, between 1610 and 1626, an average of one new printing every two years.[11] Although the first quarto of the play appeared in 1598, the text is usually conjecturally dated to the late 1580s or early 1590s, suggesting some form of ongoing company investment, if not continuous performance, for its first decade of life.[12] There are several allusions to the play in the literature of the period: Rafe, in Beaumont's *The Knight of the Burning Pestle* (1607), is announced to have played the title role, in an imagined amateur performance by apprentices 'before the wardens of our company', and the play is mentioned again in Cowley's *The Guardian* (1642).[13] This kind of citation is one of our most important forms of

---

[9]   Michael Hattaway, *Elizabethan Popular Theatre* (London, 1982), p. 1.

[10]   Victor Holtcamp, 'A Fear of "Ould" Plays: How *Mucedorus* Brought down the House and Fought for Charles II in 1652', in Douglas A. Brooks (ed.), *The Shakespeare Apocrypha* (Lampeter, 2007), p. 141.

[11]   For identification of the eighteenth, which only survives in fragments, see Richard Proudfoot, '"Modernizing" the Printed Play-Text in Jacobean London: Some Early Reprints of *Mucedorus*', in Linda Anderson and Janis Lull (eds), *'A Certain Text': Close Readings and Textual Studies on Shakespeare and Others* (Newark, 2002), pp. 18–28.

[12]   Terence P. Logan and Denzell S. Smith (eds), *The Predecessors of Shakespeare: A Survey and Bibliography of Recent Studies in English Renaissance Drama* (Lincoln, 1973), pp. 229–30.

[13]   Francis Beaumont, *The Knight of the Burning Pestle*, ed. Sheldon P. Zitner (Manchester, 2004), Induction, l. 84.

qualitative evidence for a play's popularity in a broader discourse; as, for example, in the reference to *Romeo and Juliet* by the scholars of *1 Return from Parnassus*, on which René Weis remarks, 'they know Shakespeare's dramatic verse and are quoting heard lines from memory.'[14] While evidence of this nature is purely anecdotal, it is indicative not only of the availability of a play, but also of engaged reader/audience response.

If these allusions are to be taken seriously as referring to continuous popular performance, they offer some corroboration of the claims of the quarto title pages that the play was performed 'sundrie' times around London, presented as 'very delectable and full of mirth.'[15] *Mucedorus* was performed at both the Globe and Whitehall by the King's Men, demonstrating the company's usual versatility with space. The relationship between the two is difficult to interpret in terms of the direction of popularity, as Hattaway suggests:

> [t]he play must have enjoyed sufficient repute in the public playhouses for it to be commanded at Court, but it is also important to remember that the play and others of its kind may have derived their popular appeal from the fact that they gave the public playhouse audiences a taste of the dramatic fare offered before the monarch.[16]

That amphitheatre and banqueting hall work together to consolidate a play's position in the popular mind-set seems apparent, the new court performance serving to add new legitimacy in 1610 to a play that had already enjoyed popular success in London.

We also know that the play survived as a performance piece into the Interregnum, at least in the provinces, where it famously caused an accident at an illegal performance in Witney. The preacher, Nicholas Rowe, sternly (but not without some glee) recounts the incident, in which the floor of the venue collapsed mid-performance, prompting Rowe to acknowledge God's judgment against the players.[17] In this instance, the play's popularity with its provincial audience, leading to an overcrowding of the Witney inn, went some way towards consolidating its unpopularity with the authorities, Rowe and, by extension, God, as an exemplar of an out-of-favour form of entertainment.

The Witney incident reminds us that popularity is not a homogeneous phenomenon; what is popular among one group may be unpopular in other eyes, and the question of censorship comes into play in other instances where popular opinion is at odds with an institutional perspective, as the repression of *A Game*

---

[14]   William Shakespeare, *Romeo and Juliet*, ed. Rene Weis (London, 2012), p. 55.

[15]   *A most pleasant comedie of Mucedorus the kings sonne of Valentia and Amadine the Kings daughter of Arragon with the merie conceites of Mouse. Newly set foorth, as it hath bin sundrie times plaide in the honorable cittie of London. Very delectable and full of mirth* (London, 1598), title page.

[16]   Hattaway, *Elizabethan Popular Theatre*, p. 130.

[17]   Holtcamp, 'A Fear of "Ould" Plays', provides a full discussion of this incident.

at Chess demonstrates.[18] More broadly, the popular is subject to vogue, as both a play and its form become more or less fashionable. In the case of *Mucedorus*, its apparent early modern popularity has become the cause of subsequent unpopularity in critical discourse; in 2007, Richard Preiss pointed out that only 17 articles on the play had been published in the previous 50 years, 'or one for every (extant) early modern printing.'[19] There are few good modern editions of the play, and its stage history over the last 200 years is negligible, confined primarily to amateur and festival performance.[20]

The unpopularity of *Mucedorus* can be attributed to two factors. The first is its association, in the early 1630s, with the name of William Shakespeare by the compiler of a volume entitled 'Shakespeare Vol. 1' which made its way into the library of King Charles I.[21] The attribution was picked up by Francis Kirkman, and *Mucedorus* subsequently entered the extended group of anonymous and misattributed plays that came to be known, in C.F. Tucker Brooke's edition of 1908, as 'The Shakespeare Apocrypha'. From the point of its association with Shakespeare, subsequent scholarship on the play focused almost entirely on the question of its authorship. This positioned it as in some way 'other' to Shakespeare, whether entirely dissimilar (often with the value judgment of 'not good enough') or as a simpler, more rudimentary version of Shakespeare that represented his juvenilia. Positioned in inverse relationship to an authorial canon of unusual cultural standing, criticism of *Mucedorus* became focused on what it was *not*.

The second, related factor is the aesthetic and literary depreciation of the play, routinely dismissed as a crude, folksy or rough entertainment. Its popularity is often discussed in the form of embarrassment at the poor taste of our ancestors. Charles Knight summed up the general impression: 'A more rude, inartificial, unpoetical, and altogether effete performance the English drama cannot, we think, exhibit.'[22] Knight's remark remains typical, and even today critical discussion of the play tends to relate it to popular drama where 'popular' equates to 'populist', which is read in turn as non-Shakespearean, non-professional and/or non-literary. Hattaway concludes his essay on the play with the dismissive statement, '[n]o one could claim that *Mucedorus* has much in the way of literary or even dramatic merit. It is a gallimaufry, a pleasant pastime – reassuring in its romantic view

---

[18]   See Gary Taylor: The play 'had the longest consecutive run of any English play before the Restoration, and that run would certainly have continued if the play had not been suppressed' (Taylor and Lavagnino, *Thomas Middleton*, p. 1825).

[19]   Richard Preiss, 'A Play Finally Anonymous', in Brooks, *Shakespeare Apocrypha*, p. 118.

[20]   For a review of the play in relatively recent performance, see Joseph H. Stodder, 'Mucedorus and The Birth of Merlin at the Los Angeles Globe', *Shakespeare Quarterly* 41.3 (1990): 368–72.

[21]   See Peter Kirwan, 'The First Collected "Shakespeare Apocrypha"', *Shakespeare Quarterly* 62.4 (2011): 594–601.

[22]   Charles Knight (ed.), *The Pictorial Edition of the Works of Shakspere: Doubtful Plays &c.* (London, 1841), p. 306.

of the world',[23] and even Preiss, in his reclamation of the play as an important company property, begins with Philostrate's apology that it is 'nothing, nothing in the world'.[24] Gestures towards its lack of literary quality are particularly interesting, as the primary basis for the play's retention of any interest for early modern scholars has been its privileged material existence as a hugely successful book; yet references to its rudeness and artificiality encourage us to think about it as something unworthy of print at all.

The popularity of *Mucedorus* has thus become a problem for the play, with narratives being concocted to account and, indeed, apologize for this anomaly. The processes by which this play became so successful on stage and in print must, it appears, be understood differently to the processes that consolidated the cultural status of Shakespeare and the King's Men. The play's attempts to court popular appeal through the appearance of bears, cannibals and prominent clowns is seen as a weakness that has led to the play being recast as an exemplar of a different kind of popularity that exempts it from association with author, company and more prestige forms of theatrical entertainment. It is these attempts to refigure the popular that form the subject of the remainder of this chapter.

Mucedorus for the Masses

The publication record of *Mucedorus* is primarily Jacobean. The play was first printed in quarto in 1598, again in 1606, and then with revisions and additions in 1610.[25] It is at this point that republication becomes particularly frequent, consolidating this popular Elizabethan play as an even more popular Jacobean book.

Richard Preiss's recent contribution to studies of *Mucedorus* seeks to account for the play's popularity according to relatively modern concepts of intellectual property and brand management. He notes that the run of reprints beginning in 1610 followed the Star Chamber inquest into the touring practices of Lord Cholmeley's Men, who toured the country performing from printed books including *Pericles* and *King Lear*.[26] Preiss argues that the King's Men, hearing of their plays being performed from 'allowed' books in the provinces, 'suddenly became aware that they could not control their own dissemination, neither of their identity as 'the King's Men' nor of the dramatic material that constituted it.'[27] He suggests that the

---

[23]   Hattaway, *Elizabethan Popular Theatre*, p. 140.

[24]   Preiss, 'A Play Finally Anonymous', p. 117.

[25]   *A most pleasant comedie of Mucedorus the Kings sonne of Valentia, and Amadine the Kinges daughter of Aragon With the merry conceites of Mouse. Amplified with new additions, as it was acted before the Kings Maiestie at White-hall on Shroue-sunday night. By his Highnes Seruantes vsually playing at the Globe. Very delectable, and full of conceited mirth* (London, 1610).

[26]   Preiss, 'A Play Finally Anonymous', pp. 124–26.

[27]   Ibid., p. 127.

company, realizing that the King's Men's 'brand' would be disseminated with or without their involvement, made the decision to give away *Mucedorus*, explaining the sudden increase in reprints. In giving away something that was never really its own, the company attached its 'brand' to a play that would boost its profile around the country while dissuading amateur performances of its more valuable, more jealously guarded properties. In effect, 'the King's Men were surrendering a single product to disseminate an entire platform.'[28] Popularity, in this scenario, is exploited for commercial and capital gain, pleasing the masses while developing the company's market reach.

The key evidence for this intention underlying the play is the presence of a doubling chart in the first and all subsequent quartos. In the 1598 quarto, this takes up A1[v] and is headed 'Eight persons may easily play it'. In the 1610 quarto, this is revised to 'Ten persons' to acknowledge the inclusion of new characters in the additions. The assumption of critics is that the doubling chart was designed to promote the play as a working script for performance, actively encouraging amateur companies to perform it without the need for license. While this argument explains an implicit invitation for readers to perform the play, Preiss overreaches by yoking this to a particular strategic moment in the history of the King's Men. The play carried this invitation from its earliest publication; it is not a Jacobean innovation. The difference is not in the fact of the play being offered for performance, but in the readjustment of the doubling chart to 'Ten persons' and the increased rate of publication. To attribute the increased rate to a new strategy of product dissemination would suggest that the King's Men retained some interest in the play that allowed it to dictate the rate of publication; but this does not in itself suggest why the play suddenly began selling so well. London reprint rates of one new printing every two years from 1610 seem overmuch if we are to believe that *Mucedorus*'s primary platform was provincial performance during this period. The adjusted doubling chart is also careless, adding two new actors for two new characters who only appear in brief scenes and could be far more economically integrated.[29] The information contained within the paratexts is updated to be accurate, but it is not suggestive of a strategy newly geared towards amateur playing.

More careful consideration, however, is given to the revisions to the play that fit it towards court presentation. In 1606, as Richard T. Thornberry has pointed out, someone carefully revised the play's Epilogue in order to change the gender of the addressed monarch.[30] Comedy's line 'Yeelde to a woman' changes to 'Yeeld to King *Iames*' and Envy's 'forst me stoope vnto a womans swaie' to

---

[28] Ibid.

[29] The two new characters are the King of Valencia and Anselmo. Two other new named characters, Roderigo (who speaks seven words) and Borachius (silent), are not accounted for.

[30] Richard T. Thornberry, 'A Seventeenth-Century Revival of *Mucedorus* in London before 1610', *Shakespeare Quarterly* 28.3 (1977): 362–64.

forst mee stoope vnto a Worthies Sway'.[31] Thornberry deduces from this that the play received a court revival in or around 1606. The second period of revisions came between 1606 and 1610, when a substantial set of additions were written. The additions serve to reveal from the start that Mucedorus is a prince, where the original text has the prince only reveal his true identity to his onstage and offstage audience at the play's end, and to add some comic business for the clown, Mouse, and the bear who dominates the play's opening action. A new Prologue dedicates the play to James, and an extended Epilogue creates a masque-like finale in which the allegorical character Envy promises defiance but is defeated by the splendour of James. The 1610 quarto boasts of these additions and also of the play's performance at Whitehall, for which it seems reasonable to assume that they were written.[32] The presentation of the play at court is, of course, further evidence of the company's ongoing investment and interest in the play.

That *Mucedorus* may have had a particularly prominent role in court performances has been further asserted by Teresa Grant, who notes that *The Winter's Tale* and the masque *Oberon, the Fairy Prince* were also written for the King's Men around the time of the revisions to *Mucedorus*.[33] She suggests that the three plays were performed together to take advantage of the availability of two polar bear cubs recently brought to the country and resident in the King's menagerie. The use of real bears in performance has been disputed by Helen Cooper and others, who maintain that the dangers of incorporating wild animals would have been too great, particularly given the close proximity of Prince Henry to the animals in *Oberon*.[34] The confluence of bear plays at this particular moment is undeniable, however, and *Mucedorus* is in keeping with the popular fascination at this time with performing animals and the representation of bears onstage; a context which *Mucedorus*'s obscurity has all but removed from discussion of *The Winter's Tale*.[35]

Preiss's argument that *Mucedorus* was farmed out at this time for provincial players is at odds with the scale of investment in text to fit it for court performance. The new scene with the bear adds additional challenges for any company attempting to mount the play, and the Epilogue specifically calls for the presence

---

[31]   *Mucedorus* (1598), F4ᵛ; *Mucedorus* (London, 1606), F4ᵛ.

[32]   *Mucedorus* (1610), title page.

[33]   Teresa Grant, 'White Bears in *Mucedorus*, *The Winter's Tale* and *Oberon, The Fairy Prince*', *Notes and Queries* 48.3 (2001): 311–13. See also George F. Reynolds, who similarly argues for the play's popularity based on its utilization of bears: '*Mucedorus*, Most Popular Elizabethan Play?', in Josephine W. Bennett, Oscar Cargill and Vernon Hall, Jr. (eds), *Studies in the English Renaissance Drama* (London, 1961), pp. 248–68.

[34]   Helen Cooper, 'Pursued by Bearists', *London Review of Books* 27.1 (6 January 2005), accessed online 25 July 2011, http://www.lrb.co.uk/v27/n01/letters#letter1.

[35]   For a near-exhaustive discussion of readings of the bear, see Maurice Hunt, '"Bearing Hence": Shakespeare's "The Winter's Tale"', *Studies in English Literature 1500–1900* 44.2 (2004): 33–46.

of the monarch, rooting the revised text firmly in Whitehall performance.[36] The one-way passage from company to amateurs, city to provinces is, in fact, reversed. The play was long available to the masses, as evidenced by the 'Eight persons' doubling chart and by the familiarity with the play implicit in the Induction to *The Knight of the Burning Pestle*. Performance at court follows this, the popular play revised, complicated and re-presented in a light intended to be particularly flattering to James; and perhaps elevated alongside William Shakespeare's new play and Ben Jonson's new masque. MacDonald P. Jackson has made an isolated but persuasive argument for at least the possibility that the additions – which echo *Twelfth Night* in the King of Valencia's 'Enough of Musicke, it but ads to torment'[37] – may have been written by Shakespeare in his capacity as the company's resident dramatist, an argument that recognizes the importance to the King's Men of the play pleasing the King.[38] Across the first 20 years of the play's life, then, *Mucedorus* appears to have enjoyed an increase in popularity and status, finally being canonized in a major court performance. This may well have been the climax of the play's London performance history, but to speak of the play as an undesirable property farmed out for the provinces is misleading. The only change in *Mucedorus*'s fortunes after this point was a substantial increase in the regularity of publication by London-based printers, in quartos that capitalized on the prestige performance and metropolitan popularity of the play.

The 1610 Additions

The third quarto of *Mucedorus* in 1610 thus stands in unusually complex relation to discourses of popularity. It offers prestige to a play hitherto associated with apprentice performance and amateur playing, simultaneously appearing to lend court authority to the play for the further dissemination of a King's Men's 'product'; and it rewrites the play for a specific prestigious occasion while spearheading a massive increase in the rates of publication that would see it become the most widely available of early modern dramas. Furthermore, as shall now be explored, the revisions act to distinguish the play from current 'popular' concerns, marking it deliberately as out of date at the same point as it was made newly famous.

Mucedorus is a romance narrative, chronicling the adventures of the titular prince as he roams the forests and courts of a foreign land in disguise. As Abigail Scherer points out, in the same year as the revised play was published, James I introduced a special statute for control of vagrants and wild men as they impinged

---

[36]   *Mucedorus* (1610), F3^v.

[37]   *Mucedorus* (1610), D3^r.

[38]   MacDonald P. Jackson, 'Edward Archer's Ascription of *Mucedorus* to Shakespeare', *Journal of the Australasian Universities Language and Literature Association* 22 (1964): 233–48.

on the royal forests.[39] Scherer suggests that the presence of the untamable Bremo, the play's cannibal and self-professed 'king' of the forests, may have stirred up feelings of vulnerability in court performance, speaking to very real Jacobean concerns. The play establishes an opposition between court and forest, tame and untamed spaces, between which the disguised Mucedorus moves freely in his pursuit of Amadine. In both the original and revised texts, Mucedorus is the tamer of wild spaces; he slays the bear that pursues the cowardly Segasto and the princess in Act One, and then later ingratiates himself with Bremo and kills the outcast with his own club. Bremo is disorder personified, the failure of society.[40] For the court audience in 1610, then, the play speaks to topical – a further aspect of 'popular' – concerns, potentially serving to allegorize James's own pursuit of local control.

The significant difference between the two versions of the play, however, is in Mucedorus's perceived social identity at this point. In the 1598 text the character only appears to the audience as a shepherd until the final scene; while a reader has the privileged information of the doubling list and title page, the spoken text includes no reference to Mucedorus's true princely status. The scene plays as a cross-rank romance, with the shepherd transgressing social norms in his usurpation of the courtly Segasto's role as Amadine's suitor. In this reading, Mucedorus enacts the self-regulating practices of excluded spaces, dispensing a form of forest rather than courtly justice in his execution of Bremo via a trick. His triumph is cast as one of individual human virtue over baseness, good over evil; he is a folk hero.

In the revised 1610 text, Mucedorus's true identity is explicit from the start. The Valencia scenes act to assert and remind audiences of his status as prince, and to state his dynastic marriage with Amadine as the object of his quest. Understood as a prince entering the forest, his taming of wild spaces enacts a reassertion of law-abiding society and a display of monarchical power. The prince, as the proxy of the state, colonizes and takes over the space of exclusion, restoring justice and liberating virtue. As Arvin Jupin suggests, his role is to temper the 'uncivilized impulses which can also lead to tragedy if left uncontrolled', thus keeping the social threat firmly within safe, comic conventions in the manner of other disguised ruler plays such as *Measure for Measure*.[41] It is no accident that, in both texts, it is in the forest that Mucedorus's true identity is subsequently revealed to other characters: having conquered an excluded space, he then uses that setting to enact a resumption of his public persona. The reunion of both Mucedorus and Amadine with their parents subsequently occurs in what Tucker Brooke fittingly describes

---

[39] Abigail Scherer, '*Mucedorus's* Wild Man: Disorderly Acts on the Early Modern Stage', in T.H. Howard-Hill and Philip Rollinson (eds), *Renaissance Papers 1999* (Rochester, 1999), p. 57.

[40] Ibid., p. 63.

[41] Arvin Jupin (ed.), *A Contextual Study and Modern-Spelling Edition of Mucedorus* (London, 1987), p. 40.

as 'an open space' outside Aragon's court;[42] a liminal space between court and forest which dissolves the dichotomy between civilized and newly tamed spaces and restores monarchical control over the whole kingdom.

The transformation of Mucedorus's known identity for the bulk of the play affects the experience of watching it, resituating the play explicitly within a Jacobean discourse of disguised ruler plays and the effective, centralized exercise of power. However, the removal of the play's surprise ending marks an interesting divergence from current theatrical trends. Mucedorus's surprise revelation of his identity is almost without precedent in Elizabethan drama.[43] Andrew Gurr, however, points out that these revelations are a regular and deliberate feature of Jacobean tragicomedy, beginning with Beaumont and Fletcher's *Philaster* in 1609. Gurr argues that these plays in fact 'depended on their ability to hold the audience in suspense until the surprise revelation.'[44] Such endings are commonplace in the period: King's Men's plays such as *A King and No King*, *Philaster*, and later *The Renegado* all hinge on the final surprise revelation, as does Jonson's contemporaneous *Epicoene* for the Children of the Queen's Revels.[45] The revelation normally reconciles a previously untenable situation; for example, the incestuous love of *A King and No King* is proven lawful when the lovers are revealed to be unrelated. In this, the 1598 text of *Mucedorus* is surprisingly anticipative of the later structural trend. The incompatibility of shepherd and princess is a recurrent theme throughout the play, and even Amadine refers to Mucedorus almost invariably as 'Shepherd', both directly and indirectly.[46] However, the use of a revelatory ending changes the rules at the last moment and sanctions a conservative dynastic marriage.

By removing this feature, associated with the newer tragicomedies, *Mucedorus* was retrospectively cast as a more dated, conventional pastoral romance. In this,

---

[42] C.F. Tucker Brooke (ed.), *The Shakespeare Apocrypha* (Oxford, 1908), V.ii.0.1.

[43] Hints are given at 3.1: 'More may I boast and say; but I / Was never shepherd in such dignity' (4–5), and again at 4.1: 'Now, Mucedorus, whither wilt thou go? / Home to thy father, to thy native soil, / Or try some long abode within these woods?' (1–3). The former deliberately plays with the audience's lack of knowledge, while the second hints at a real identity while still being attributable to the 'shepherd.' Quotations taken from Brooke, *Shakespeare Apocrypha*.

[44] Andrew Gurr, *The Shakespeare Company 1594–1642* (Cambridge, 2004), p. 46. In this, the genre followed Tasso's *Il Pastor Fido*; see Marco Mincoff, '*The Faithful Shepherdess*: A Fletcherian Experiment', *Renaissance Drama* 9 (1966): 163–77 (175).

[45] Bellario proves to be a girl, thus invalidating claims of infidelity with Arethusa (*Philaster*, 1609); Vitelli is revealed to be a gentleman instead of a merchant, thus asserting his own rights to marriage (*The Renegado*, 1623); and Arbaces is revealed to be the son of Gobrius rather than of the king, thus licensing his marriage to his 'sister' Panthea, though this 'surprise' is hinted at throughout the play in the discussions of Gobrius and Arane (*A King and No King*, 1611). *Epicoene* (1609) uses the surprise revelation of a character's gender to more explicitly comic effect.

[46] See especially III.i, in which she uses 'Shepherd' in preference to 'Mucedorus' throughout.

it was made more explicitly a precursor of Shakespeare's plays of the same period with which it shares generic DNA, such as *The Winter's Tale* and *Cymbeline*. Barbara Mowat and David Frost both argue that these plays draw on old romance themes and plots to create a deliberately old-fashioned style – in the case of *Cymbeline*, even parodic – that allows the dramatist to blur the divide between tragedy and comedy.[47] For Frost, the revival of this 'primitive stage romance' was an act of penance for a recent offence, the company offering an old play 'clearly innocent of meaning' that made amends through nostalgic clowning.[48] In this final act, *Mucedorus* was perhaps deliberately cast as 'popular' in opposition to the play's artistic experiments, the removal of the surprise ending serving to associate the play more clearly with the company's nostalgic romances (typified by Shakespeare) and less with the newer tragicomedies emerging from the stable of Beaumont and Fletcher.

The popularity of *Mucedorus*, then, ultimately becomes an effect of the play's success in both elite and popular spheres. Its success cannot be attributed to a specific group or historical moment, for it is its versatility and appeal to all levels of society that perpetuated its appearances at court and in print. By turns ahead of its time and deliberately dated, socially transgressive yet politically apt, *Mucedorus*'s popularity needs to be located in its confluence of several spheres of activity at the end of the first decade of the seventeenth century, where an Elizabethan favourite became, for a short while, one of the most important items in the Jacobean repertory. We do not need to apologize for *Mucedorus*'s popularity; rather, *Mucedorus* alerts us to the importance of acknowledging that theatrical popularity cannot be quantified or objectively construed, but is itself an effect, a transitory and changing phenomenon that is partially reflected by, rather than entirely constructed within, the print market.

---

[47]   Barbara A. Mowat, '"What's in a Name?" Tragicomedy, Romance, or Late Comedy', in Richard Dutton and Jean E. Howard (eds), *A Companion to Shakespeare's Works Vol. IV: The Poems, Problem Comedies, Late Plays* (Oxford, 2003), pp. 129–49; David L. Frost, '"Mouldy Tales": The Context of Shakespeare's *Cymbeline*', *Essays and Studies* 39 (1986): 19–38. We might note that *The Winter's Tale* experiments with introducing a 'surprise ending', though one that is significantly more signposted than the other plays here mentioned.

[48]   Frost, 'Mouldy Tales', pp. 21–3. He conjectures that Shakespeare capitalized on the surprising success of *Mucedorus* by writing the deliberately old-fashioned *Cymbeline*.

Bibliography

Primary Text: Manuscripts

Bodleian: Bib. Eng. 1598.e.3.
Bodleian C.P. 1560.e.1.
Bodleian Library C.25.h.12.
Bodleian Library 6.d.9.
Bodleian 8° C 35 Th. Seld.
Bodleian Library C.P.1560.c.1.
Bodleian Library C.10.a.10(1).
Bodleian Library C.12.i.1.
Bodleian Library C.108.aaa.3.
Bodleian Library Lansdowne Vol. 83, f. 126.
British Library Additional Manuscript 37719, f. 5v.
British Library C.10.a.10.
British Library C.12.i.1.
British Library C.25.h.12.
British Library C.25.l.14.
British Library C.108.aaa.3.
British Library 6.d.9.
CSPD, 1649–50.
Durham University Library SB+ 0851/1.
Durham University Library SB 2186/1.
Folger A2254.5.
Folger V.a. 515.
Gloucester Record Office D 2375 / F10.
Houghton Library, Harvard University STC 2378.
Huntington Library 62273.
Lambeth Palace Library H5145.A4 1559.
The National Archives: SP 12/20 f. 1.
The National Archives: SP 12/27 f. 264.
The National Archives: SP 12/266 f. 120.
The National Archives: SP 12/287 f. 57.
The National Archives: SP 15/28/1 f. 98.
The National Archives: SP 63/212, f. 73r-v.
PC 2/26 f. 105.

Primary Texts: Print

Aduertisements from Brittany, And from the Lovv Countries, In September and October (London: John Wolfe, 1591).

Allison, Richard, *The Psalmes of Dauid in meter* (London: William Barley, 1599).

Allot, Robert, *England's Parnassus*, ed. Charles Crawford (Oxford: Clarendon Press, 1913).

——, *England's Parnassus: or the choysest Flowers of our Modern Poets* (London: for N. L[ing], C. B[urby] and T. H[ayes], 1600).

An answer to the vntruthes, published and printed in Spaine, in glorie of their supposed victorie atchieued against our English Nauie (London: John Jackson for Thomas Cadman, 1589).

The Ancient Historie of the Destruction of Troy (London: Bernard Alsop and Thomas Fawcett, 1636).

Andrewes, William, *The Celestial Observatory* (1655).

Anno Regni Caroli II (London: John Bill and Christopher Barker, 1662).

Ascham, Roger, *The Schoolmaster (1570)*, ed. Lawrence V. Ryan (Charlottesville: University Press of Virginia, 1967).

Bacon, Francis, *A Declaration of the Practices & Treasons Attempted and Committed by Robert late Earle of Essex* (London: Robert Barker, 1601).

Bandello, Matteo, *Certaine tragicall discourses*, trans. Geoffrey Fenton (London: Thomas Marshe, 1567).

Bayly, Lewis, *The practise of pietie* (London: T Snodham for John Hodgets, 1613).

Beaumont, Francis, *The Knight of the Burning Pestle*, ed. Sheldon P. Zitner (Manchester: Manchester University Press, 2004).

Bentley, Thomas, *The monument of matrones* (London: Henry Denham, 1582).

Birkenhead, John, *The assembly-man* (London, 1662 [1663]).

Blague, Thomas, *A schole of wise conceytes* (London: H. Binneman, 1569).

Bodenham, John, *Bel-vedére or the garden of the muses* (London: Hugh Astley, 1600).

Bodley, Thomas, *Letters of Sir Thomas Bodley*, ed. G.W. Wheeler (Oxford: Clarendon Press, 1926).

——, *The life of Sir Thomas Bodley* (Oxford: Henry Hall, 1647).

Bretnor, Thomas, *A newe almanacke and prognostication* (London: S.I., 1615).

Brooke, Robert, *Anni, regum, Edwardi Quinti, Richardi Tertii, Henrici Septimi, et Henrici Octaui omnes, qui antea impressi fuerunt, iam recens post priores editiones emendati & repurgati* (London: Jane Yetsweirt, 1597).

Browne, Thomas, *Christian Morals* [1761] (London, 1863).

Bullokar, John, *An English expositor* (London: John Legatt, 1616).

Burton, William, *Dauids euidenece* [sic] (London: R. Field, 1592).

Byron, George Gordon, *Byron's Letters and Journals*, vol. VII., ed. Leslie A. Marchand (London: John Murray, 1977).

C., H., *The forrest of fancy* (London: Thomas Purfoote, 1579).

Calendars of the State Papers, Domestic Series (London: HMSO, 1649–1650).

Caxton, William, *The booke of raynarde the foxe* (London: Thomas Gaultier, 1550).

Chamberlain, Robert, *A New Booke of Mistakes. Or, Bulls with Tales, and Buls Without Tales But No Lyes by any Meanes* (London: Nicholas Okes, 1637).

Cicero, *De Inventione, De Optimo Genere Oratorum, Topica*, trans. H.M. Hubbell (Cambridge, MA: Harvard University Press, 1949).

Cleaver, Robert, *A godly forme of household gouernment* (London: Felix Kingston for Thomas Man, 1598).

Concavum cappo-cloacorum (London: Printed for Benjamin Tooke, 1682).

Cooper, Thomas, *Thesaurus linguae Romanae & Britannicae* (London: Henry Denham, 1578).

Copie d'une lettre du prince de Parma, envoyée aux Estats Généraux des Païs Bas, assemblez en Anvers (Antwerp: C. Plantin, 1579).

Copley, Anthony, *Wits fittes and fancies* (London: Richard Jones, 1595).

Cornwallis, William, *Essayes* (London: S. Stafford and R. Read for Edmund Mattes, 1600–1601).

———, *Discourses upon Seneca the Tragedian* (London: S. Stafford for Edmund Mattes, 1601).

Credible reportes from France, and Flanders. In the moneth of May. 1590 (London: John Wolfe for William Wright, 1590).

D. Ioannis Chrysostomi Archiepiscopi Constantinopolitani, homiliae sex ex manuscriptis codicibus Noui Collegij, ed. *John Harmar* (Oxford: Joseph Barnes, 1586).

Daman, William, *The former booke of the musicke of M. William Damon and Cantus. The second booke* (London: Thomas Este, 1591).

———, *The psalmes of David in English meter* (London, 1579).

Darrel[l], John, *A Detection of that Sinnful, Shamful, Lying, and Ridiculous Discours, of Samuel Harshnet* (London, 1600).

Dekker, Thomas, *The Owles almanacke* (London: Edward Griffin for Laurence Lisle, 1618).

———, *The ravens almanacke* (London: E. Allde and Nicholas Okes for Thomas Archer, 1609).

———, *The Wonderfull Yeare. 1603* (London: Thomas Creede, 1603).

Dering, Sir Edward, 'A Booke of Expences for the Yeare 1619' (Maidstone: Centre for Kentish Studies), U350/E4.

The Destruction of Troy in Three Books (London: R.I. for S.S. to be sold by F. Coles, 1663).

Digges, Leonard, *A Prognostication of Right Good effect* (London: T. Gemini, 1555).

———, 'Upon Master William Shakespeare', in *Poems: written by Wil. Shakespeare. Gent.* (London: John Benson, 1640).

Dod, Henry, *Certaine Psalmes of David* (Edinburgh: Robert Waldgrave, 1603).

Dominicus (Nanus Mirabellius), *Polyanthea nova*, rev. Joseph Lang (Leiden: [n.pb.],1604).

Donne, John, *A sermon of commemoration of the Lady Da[n]uers* (London: I. Haviland for Philemon Stephens and Christopher Meredith, 1627).

Dove, Jonathan, *Speculum Anni* (1641).

East, Thomas, *The whole booke of Psalmes: with their wonted tunes* (London: Thomas Est, 1592; 2nd edn, 1594).

Eliot, John, *Ortho-epia Gallica Eliots fruits for the French* (London, 1593).

An Epistle in the Person of Christ to the Faithfull Soule (Antwerpe: [English Secret Press], 1595).

Euphues. The Anatomy of Wyt (London: [Thomas East] for Gabriel Cawood, 1578).

An example of Gods iudgement shew[n] vpon two children borne in high Dutch la[nd] in the citie of Lutssolof, the first day of Iulie (London: [J. Allde] for William Bartlet to be sold by Richard Ballard, [1582?]).

Fenner, Dudley, 'The Order of Houshold: Described Methodically out of the Word of God with the Contrary Abuses Found in the World', in *Certain godly and learned treatises written by that worthie minister of Christe, M. Dudley Fenner; for the behoofe and edification of al those, that desire to grovv and increase in true godlines. The titles whereof, are set downe in the page following* (Edinburgh: Robert Waldegraue, 1592).

The First Examination of the Worthy Seruant of God, Mystresse Anne Askew (London: Robert Waldegrave, [?1585]).

The First Part of the True and Honourable Historie, of the Life of Sir Iohn Old-castle, the Good Lord Cobham (London: V[alentine] S[immes] for Thomas Pavier, 1600).

Florio, John, *Florio his firste fruites* (London: Thomas Dawson for Thomas Woodcock, 1578).

————, *A letter lately written from Rome, by an Italian gentleman, to a freende of his in Lyons in Fraunce* (London: John Charlewood, 1585).

The Fourth Part of the True Watch Containing Prayers and Teares for the Churches (London: [?Isaac Jaggard] for Thomas Pavier, 1624).

Gallen, Thomas, *A new almanack for the said year 1668* (London: James Flesher, 1668).

Gouge, William, *Of Domesticall Duties Eight Treatises* (London: John Haviland for William Bladen, 1622).

Greene, Robert, *Greenes farewell to folly* (London: Thomas Scarlet for T. Gubbin and T. Newman, 1591).

————, *Greenes vision* (London: [E. Allde] for Thomas Newman, 1592).

Guevara, Antonio, *The familiar epistles* (London: Henry Bynneman for Raufe Newbery, 1575).

Hart, John, *A methode or comfortable beginning for all unlearned, whereby they may be taught to read English in a very short time, with pleasure* (London: Henrie Denham, 1570).

Harvey, Gabriel, *Gabriel Harvey's Marginalia*, ed. G.C. Moore (Stratford-upon-Avon: Shakespeare Head Press, 1913).

A helpe to discourse (London: Bernard Alsop for Leonard Becket, 1619).

Hereafter ensue the trewe encounter or ... batayle lately done between Engla[n]de and Scotlande (London: R. Faques, [?1513]).

Heylin, Peter, *Ecclesia restaurata* (London: Printed for H. Twyford, T. Dring, J. Place, W. Palmer, 1660–1661).

Hill, Thomas, *An almanack* (London: Henry Denham, 1571).

Hinde, William, *A faithfull remonstrance of the holy life and happy death of John Bruen of Bruen-Stapleford, in the county of Chester, Esquire* (London: R.B. for Philemon Stephens and Christopher Meredith, 1641).

The History of the Church of Englande. Compiled by Venerable Bede, Englishman (Antwerp: John Laet, 1565).

Hopton, Arthur, *New Almanacke* (1613), Bodleian Ash. 66, 'August'.

Incipit annus primus Ricardi tertii. De termino Michaelis anno primo Richardi tertii (London: Richard Tottel [?1559]).

Jones, John, *The Arte and Science of Preseruing Bodie and Soule in Healthe, Wisedome, and Catholike Religion* (London: Henrie Bynneman, 1579).

Jonson, Ben, *The nevv inne. Or, The light heart A comoedy. As it was neuer acted, but most negligently play'd, by some, the Kings Seruants. And more squeamishly beheld, and censured by others, the Kings subiects, 1629* (London: Thomas Alchorne, 1631).

———, *Sejanus His Fall*, ed. Philip J. Ayres (Manchester: Manchester University Press, 1990),

———, *The Staple of News*, ed. Anthony Parr (Manchester: Manchester University Press, 1988).

———, 'XCIIII. To Lvcy, Covntesse of Bedford, with Mr. Donne's Satyres', in *The workes of Benjamin Jonson* (London: William Stansby, 1616).

Keats, John, *Letters of John Keats, 1814–21*, ed. Hyder Rollins (Cambridge: Cambridge University Press, 1958).

Kirkham, Francis, *The English Rogue Continued* (London, 1668).

A letter lately written from Rome, by an Italian gentleman, to a freende of his in Lyons in Fraunce (London: John Charlewood, 1585).

The letters pattents of the Kings declaration for the referring of the generall assemblie of the princes, cardinals, dukes and peeres (London: Thomas Orwain for Augustine Lawton, 1590).

Lilly, William, *Anglicus, peace or no peace* (London: J.R. for John Partridge and Humphrey Blunden, 1645).

Marlowe, Christopher, *The Jew of Malta*, in *The Complete Works of Christopher Marlowe*, vol. IV, ed. Roma Gill (Oxford: Clarendon Press, 1995).

Maunsell, Andrew, *First part of the Catalogue of English printed books* (London: John Windet [and James Roberts] for Andrew Maunsell, 1595).

Middlesex county records: Volume 1: 1550-1603 ed. John Jefferson Cordy, A.T. Watson and Basil Woodd Smith (London: The Middlesex County Record Society, 1886), http://www.british-history.ac.uk/report.aspx?compid=65930& strquery=middlesex sessions rolls bible.

Middleton, Thomas, *The Collected Works*, ed. Gary Taylor and John Lavagnino (Oxford: Oxford University Press, 2007).

———, *No Wit, No Help Like a Woman* (1611).

Middleton, Thomas and Rowley, William, *A Fair Quarrel*, in *Thomas Middleton: The Collected Works*, ed. Gary Taylor and John Lavagnino (Oxford: Clarendon Press, 2007), pp. 1209–50.

Mirandula, Ottaviano, *Illustrium poearum flores* (Strasbourg: Wendelin Rihel, 1538).

Montaigne, Michel de, *The Essayes Or Morall, Politike and Millitarie Discourses*, trans. John Florio (London: Valentine Sims for Edward Blount, 1603).

A most pleasant comedie of Mucedorus the Kings sonne of Valentia, and Amadine the Kinges daughter of Aragon With the merry conceites of Mouse. Amplified with new additions, as it was acted before the Kings Maiestie at White-hall on Shroue-sunday night. By his Highnes Seruantes vsually playing at the Globe. Very delectable, and full of conceited mirth (London: William White, 1610).

A most pleasant comedie of Mucedorus the kings sonne of Valentia and Amadine the Kings daughter of Arragon with the merie conceites of Mouse. Newly set foorth, as it hath bin sundrie times plaide in the honorable cittie of London. Very delectable and full of mirth (London: Printed for William Jones, 1598).

A most strange and wonderfull herring, taken on the 26. day of Nouember 1597, neere vnto Drenton sometime the old and chiefe cittie of the kingdome of Norway (London: [J. Windet for] John Wolfe, 1598).

A Most straunge and wounderfull accident happened at Weersburch by Franckford, by a most fearefull earthquake and daknesse [sic], with a mighty tempest of thunder and lightning (London: William Barley, 1600).

A most straunge, rare, and horrible murther committed by a Frenchman of the age of too or three and twentie yeares (London: Thomas Purfoote, [1586]).

Munday, Anthony, *Bodenham's Belvedere, or The Garden of the Muses* (Manchester: C. Simms, 1875).

———, *Palmerin d'Oliva* [Part One] (London: John Charlewood for William Wright, 1588).

———, *Zelauto* (London: John Charlewood, 1580).

Nashe, Thomas, *Have With You To Saffron Walden* (London: J. Danter, 1596).

———, *The Works of Thomas Nashe*, ed. R.B. McKerrow, rev. F.P. Wilson (Oxford: Blackwell, 1958).

Newe Newes containing A shorte rehersall of the late enterprise of certaine fugytiue Rebelles ([London], [1579]).

Newes come latle frõ Pera ([London]: [W. Copland, 1561]).

Newes from Rome. Of two mightie armies, aswell footemen as horsmen: the first of the great Sophy ([London], [1606]).

Newes from Spayne and Holland conteyning. An information of Inglish affayres in Spayne (Antwerp: A. Conincx, 1593).

Newes out of France (London: John Wolfe for William Wright, 1592).

Norton, Thomas, *A Warning Agaynst the Dangerous Practises of Papistes and Specially the Parteners of the Late Rebellion* (London: John Daye, 1569).

Now, at last, set at liberty to the readers, his Maties seruants, and subiects, to be iudg'd (London: Thomas Harper, 1631).

Openshaw, Robert, *Short questions and answeares* (London: T. Dawson, 1579).

Overbury, Thomas, *Sir Thomas Ouerbury his Wife. With Additions of New Characters* (London: E. Griffin for L. Lisle, 1622).

Ovid, *Heroidum epistolae. Amorum, Libri III, De arte amandi, libri III, De remedio amoris, libri II Aliaq'[ue]huius generis, quæ sequens pagella indicabit. Omnia ex accuratiss. Andreæ Nauigerij castigatione. Guidonis Morilloni argumenta in epistolas* (London: Richard Field, 1594).

A packe of Spanish lyes, sent abroad in the vvorld (London: Christopher Barker, 1588).

Painter, William, *The Palace of Pleasure* (London: [John Kingston and] Henry Denham, 1566).

Perkins, William, *Christian oeconomie: or, A short survey of the right manner of erecting and ordering a familie according to the scriptures, trans. Tho. Pickering Bachelar of Diuinitie* (London: Felix Kingston, 1609).

Pettie, George, *A petite Pallace of Pettie his pleasure* (London: R. Watkins, 1576).

Phaedri Aug. Liberti Fabularum Æsopiarum libri V nunc primum in lucem editi (Augustobonæ Tricassium: J. Odotius, 1596).

Pollard, A.W. and G.R. Redgrave (eds), *A Short-Title Catalogue of Books Printed in England, Scotland, & Ireland and of English Books Printed Abroad, 1475– 1640*, 2nd edn, rev. W.A. Jackson, F.S. Ferguson, and Katharine F. Pantzer, 3 vols (London: Bibliographical Society, 1976–1991).

Poor Robin 1673 an almanack after a new fashion (London, 1673).

Positions ... necessarie for the training vp of children (London: Thomas Vautrollier for Thomas Chare, 1581).

Primary Sources of Copyright (1450–1900), http://copy.law.cam.ac.uk/cam/index. php.

Prynne, William, *Histrio-Mastix. The Player's Scourge* (London, 1633).

Purfoote, Thomas, *A blanke and perpetuall Almanacke* (London, 1566).

Regis Edvvardi tertii a primo ad decimum (inclusiue) anni omnes (London: Richard Tottel, 1562).

Rider, Cardanus, *British Merlin* (London: Thomas Newcomb, 1680).

———, *Merlinus, Cambro-Britannus* (London: John Field, 1654).

Rivington, Charles, *The Records of the Worshipful Company of Stationers* (London, 1883).

Rogers, Richard, *Seuen Treatises* (London: Felix Kingston for Thomas Man, 1603).

Salmon, William, *The London Almanack For the year of our Lord, 1697* (London: W. Horton, 1697).

A Sermon no Lesse Fruitfull then Famous (London: John Charlewood, 1582).

A Sermon no Lesse Fruteful then Famous ([?London: ? J. Maylor, ?1540]).

'Sessions, 1615: 28 and 29 March', in *County of Middlesex. Calendar to the sessions records: new series, volume 2: 1614–15* (1936), ed. William Le Hardy, pp. 220–56, http://www.british-history.ac.uk/report.aspx?compid=823 41&strquery=book.

Shakespeare, William, *The Complete Sonnets and Poems*, ed. Colin Burrow (Oxford: Oxford University Press, 2002).

———, *The Complete Works*, ed. Gary Taylor, Stanley Wells, John Jowett, and William Montgomery, 2nd edn (Oxford: Clarendon Press, 2005).

———, *An excellent conceited tragedie of Romeo and Iuliet As it hath been often (with great applause) plaid publiquely, by the right Honourable the L. of Hunsdon his Seruants* (London: John Danter [and Edward Allde?], 1597).

———, *Henry V, Prologue.15*, in *Mr. William Shakespeares Comedies, Histories, & Tragedies* (London, 1623), sig. h1r.

———, *The Norton Shakespeare based on the Oxford Edition*, ed. Stephen Greenblatt, Walter Cohen, Jean E. Howard, Katharine Eisaman Maus, and Andrew Gurr (New York: W.W. Norton, 2008).

———, *Romeo and Juliet*, ed. Rene Weis (London: Arden Shakespeare, 2012).

———, *Shakespeare's Poems,* ed. Katherine Duncan-Jones and H.R. Woudhuysen (London: Arden Shakespeare, 2007).

———, *Venus and Adonis* (London: Richard Field, 1593).

Smith, Henry, *The Trumpet of the Soule, Sounding to Judgement* (London, 1592).

Smith, Thomas, *De Republica Anglorum*, ed. Mary Dewar (Cambridge: Cambridge University Press, 1982).

Spenser, Edmund, *Edmund Spenser: The Shorter Poems*, ed. Richard A. McCabe (London: Penguin, 1999).

———, *The Faerie Queene*, ed. A.C. Hamilton (London: Longman, 1977).

——— 'Mother Hubberds Tale', in *Edmund Spenser: The Shorter Poems*, ed. Richard A. McCabe (London: Penguin, 1999), pp. 233–71.

———, 'The Shepheardes Calender', in *Edmund Spenser: The Shorter Poems,* ed. Richard A. McCabe (London: Penguin, 1999), pp. 23–156.

———, 'Three Proper and wittie, familiar Letters', in *The Works of Edmund Spenser: A Variorum Edition, The Prose Works*, ed. Edwin Greenlaw, Charles Grosvenor Osgood, Frederick Morgan Padelford, and Ray Heffner (Baltimore: John Hopkins Press, 1949).

Sportive Wit (1656).

Sternhold, Thomas and John Hopkins, *The Whole Booke of Psalmes* (London: Richard Day, 1584).

Stevenson, Matthew, *Norfolk Drollery* (London: Printed for R. Reynolds and John Lutton, 1673).

Stow, John, *A Survey of London* (London: R. Bradocke, 1598).

The New York Times Book Review, 16 March 2008.

The New York Times Book Review, 23 September 2007.

The strange and marueilous newes lately come from the great kingdome of Chyna, which adioyneth to the East Indya (London: Thomas Gardyner and Thomas Dawson, 1577).

The translation of a letter written by a Frenche gentilwoman to an other gentilwoman straunger, her frind, vpon the death of the most excellent and vertous ladye, Elenor of Roye, Princes of Conde, contaynyng her last wyll and testament (London: John Day for Humphrey Toye, 1564).

A true coppy of the admonitions sent by the subdued prouinces to the states of Holland (London: [John Windet for] John Wolfe, 1598).

A true copy of a letter sent by the Prince of Parma to the generall states of the lowe cuntries, assembled at Antwerpe (London: Richard Jones, [1579]).

A true discourse. Declaring the damnable life and death of one Stubbe Peeter, a most wicked sorcerer, who in the likenes of a woolfe committed many murders (London: [?R. Ward] for Edward Venge, [1590]).

A true discourse of a cruell fact committed by a gentlewoman towardes her husband, her father, her sister and two of her nephewes (London: [J. Windet for] John Wolfe, 1599).

A true discourse of an ouerthrow giuen to the armie of the Leaguers in Prouince: by Messieurs D'Esdiguieres and Lauallette. Translated verbatim out of the French copie, printed at Tours by Iamet Mettayer (London: Thomas Purfoot, [1591]).

The true discourse of the wonderfull victorie, obteined by Henrie the fourth, the French King, and King of Nauarre, in a battell against those of the League, neere the towne of Yurie (London: Thomas Orwin for Thomas Man, 1590).

A True relation of taking of Alba-Regalis in the German tongue, called Sfullweissenburgh [sic], the chiefe cittie in Nether-Hungarie, which was taken by the Christian armie, the twentith [sic] of September last past, 1601 (London: Ralph Blower for C.B., 1601).

Two right profitable and fruitfull Concordances (Christopher Barker, n.d.).

Vives, Juan Luis, *The Office and Duty of an Husband,* trans. William Whately (London, 1553).

Watson, Andrew, *Medieval Manuscripts in Post-Medieval England* (Aldershot: Ashgate, 2004).

Watson, Richard, *The Right Reverend Doctor John Cosin* (London: F. Leach for Nicholas Woolfe, 1684).

Webster, John, *The White Divel* (London: Nicholas Okes for Thomas Archer, 1612).

Wharton, George, *Calendarium Carolinum* (London: J. Grismond, 1664).

Whately, William, *A Bride-Bush or, A Direction for Married Persons. Plainely Describing the Duties common to both, and peculiar to each of them* (London: Felix Kingston for Thomas Man, 1619).

White, John, *Briefe and easie almanack for this yeare* (London: F.K., 1650).

Whitgift, John, *A Goodly Sermon* (London: Henry Bynneman for Humfrey Toy, 1574).

The whole booke of Psalmes ... composed into foure parts. Compiled by sundrie authors (London: William Barley, [1598?]).

Wilde, Oscar, *Essays and Lectures* (London: Methuen and Co., 1909).

Wilson, Thomas, 'The State of England, Anno Dom. 1600', ed. F.J. Fisher, in *Camden Miscellany* 16 (London, 1936), pp. 1–47.

Wither, George, *A Preparation to the Psalter* (London: Nicholas Okes, 1619).

Wood, Anthony, *Athenae Oxonienses: An Exact History of all the Writers and Bishops who have had their education in the most ancient and famous University of Oxford* (London: Thomas Bennet, 1691–2).

A Woorke of Ioannes Ferrarius Montanus, Touchynge the Good Orderynge of a Common Weale (London: John Kingston for John Whight, 1559).

The Works of our Ancient and Learned English Poet, Geffrey Chaucer, Newly Printed (London: Adam Islip, 1602).

Wren, Matthew, *Articles to be inquired of vvithin the dioces of Norwich in the first visitation* (London: Richard Badger, 1636).

Secondary Texts

Ackermann, P., *Wallpaper: Its History, Design and Use* (London: W. Heinemann, 1923).

Allison, A.F. and D.M. Rogers, *The Contemporary Printed Literature of the English Counter-Reformation Between 1558 and 1640: An Annotated Catalogue*, 2 vols (Aldershot: Scolar, 1989–1994).

Appadurai, Arjun (ed.), *The Social Life of Things: Commodities in Cultural Perspective* (Cambridge: Cambridge University Press, 1986).

Arber, Edward, An English Garner: *Ingatherings from our History and Literature*, 8 vols (London: E. Arber, 1877–1896).

———— (ed.), *A Transcript of the Registers of the Company of Stationers of London; 1554–1640 A.D.*, 5 vols (London: 1875–1894).

Armstrong, Guyda, *The English Boccaccio: A History in Books* (Toronto: University of Toronto Press, forthcoming).

Baker, J.H., 'English Law Books and Legal Publishing', in John Barnard and D.F. McKenzie (eds, with the assistance of Maureen Bell), *The Cambridge History of the Book in Britain* vol. IV (Cambridge: Cambridge University Press, 2002), pp. 474–503.

Barbarics-Hermanik, Zsuzsa, "Handwritten Newsletters as Interregional Information Sources in Central and Southeastern Europe", in Brendan Dooley (ed.), *The Dissemination of News and the Emergence of Contemporaneity in Early Modern Europe* (Farnham: Ashgate, 2010), pp. 155–78.

Barker, Nicolas, 'Editing the Past: Classical and Historical Scholarship', in John Barnard and D.F. McKenzie (eds, with the assistance of Maureen Bell), *The Cambridge History of the Book in Britain*, vol. IV (Cambridge: Cambridge University Press, 2002), pp. 206–27.

———— (ed.), *Treasures of the British Library* (London: British Library, 1996).

Barker, Nicholas and David Quentin, *The Library of Thomas Tresham & Thomas Brudenell* (London: Roxburghe Club, 2006).

Barker, S.K., 'Newes Lately Come: European News Books in English Translation', in S.K. Barker and Brenda M. Hosington (eds), *Renaissance Cultural Crossroads: Translation, Print and Culture in Britain, 1473–1640* (Leiden, forthcoming).

Barker, William, 'School Libraries (c. 1540 to 1640)', in Elisabeth Leedham-Green and Teresa Webber (eds), *The Cambridge History of Libraries in Britain and Ireland* (3 vols), *Volume I, to 1640* (Cambridge: Cambridge University Press, 2006), pp. 435–47.

Barnard, John, 'Politics, Profits and Idealism: John Norton, the Stationers' Company and Sir Thomas Bodley', *Bodleian Library Record* 17 (2002): 385–408.

———, 'The Stationers' Stock 1663/4 to 1705/6: Psalms, Psalters, Primers and ABCs,' *The Library*, 6th ser., 21 (1999): 370–75.

———, 'The Survival and Loss Rates of Psalms, ABCs, Psalters and Primers from the Stationers' Stock, 1660–1700', *The Library*, 6th ser., 21 (1999): 148–50.

Barnard, John and D.F. McKenzie (eds, with the assistance of Maureen Bell), *The Cambridge History of the Book in Britain*, vol. IV (Cambridge: Cambridge University Press, 2002).

Barry, Jonathan, 'Literacy and Literature in Popular Culture: Reading and Writing in Historical Perspective,' in Tim Harris (ed.), *Popular Culture in England, c. 1500–1850* (New York: St. Martin's Press, 1995), 69–94.

Barry, Jonathan and Christopher Brooks (eds), *The Middling Sort of People: Culture, Society and Politics in England, 1550–1800* (Basingstoke: Macmillan, 1994).

BBC News Entertainment & Arts, 'Ding Dong! The Witch is Dead enters chart at two', http://www.bbc.co.uk/news/entertainment-arts-22145306 (accessed 24.04.13).

Becher, Anne, 'Phaedrus, a New Found Yet Ancient Author: The Rise and Fall of Phaedrus as a Standard School Author, 1668–1828', *Paradigm: Journal of the Textbook Colloquium* 23 (July 1997), http://faculty.ed.uiuc.edu/westbury/paradigm/becher.html.

Belsey, Catherine, 'Historicizing New Historicism', in Hugh Grady and Terence Hawkes (eds), *Presentist Shakespeares* (London: Routledge, 2007), pp. 27–45.

Benjamin, Walter, 'Unpacking My Library', in *Illuminations*, trans. Hannah Arendt (New York: Schocken Books, 1968), pp. 49–68.

Bennett, H.S., *English Books and Readers, 1558–1603*, vol. II (Cambridge: Cambridge University Press, 1965).

Berkhout, Carl T. and Milton McCormick Gatch (eds), *Anglo-Saxon Scholarship: The First Three Centuries* (Boston: G.K. Hall, 1982).

Black, Joseph (ed.), *The Martin Marprelate Tracts: A Modernized and Annotated Edition* (Cambridge: Cambridge University Press, 2008).

Blagden, Cyprian, 'The Distribution of Almanacks in the Second Half of the Seventeenth Century', *Studies in Bibliography: Papers of the Bibliographical Society of the University of Virginia* 11 (1958): 107–16.

———, 'The English Stock of the Stationers' Company in the Time of the Stuarts', *The Library* 5th ser., 12 (1957): 167–86.

———, *The Stationers' Company: a History, 1403–1959* (Stanford: Stanford University Press, 1960).

Blair, Ann M., *Too Much to Know: Managing Scholarly Information before the Modern Age* (New Haven: Yale University Press, 2010).

Bland, Mark, 'The Appearance of the Text in Early Modern England', *Text: An Interdisciplinary Annual of Textual Studies* 11 (1998): 91–154.

———, 'The London Book-Trade in 1600,' in David Scott Kastan (ed.), *A Companion to Shakespeare* (Oxford: Blackwell, 1999), pp. 450–63.

Blayney, Peter, 'The Alleged Popularity of Playbooks', *Shakespeare Quarterly* 56. 1 (2005): 33–50.

———, *The Bookshops in Paul's Cross Churchyard* (London: Bibliographical Society, 1990).

———, 'The Publication of Playbooks', in John D. Cox and David Scott Kastan (eds), *A New History of Early English Drama* (New York: Columbia University Press, 1997), pp. 383–422.

———, *The Texts of King Lear and Their Origins, Volume 1: Nicholas Okes and the First Quarto* (Cambridge University Press, 1982).

Blench, J.W., *Preaching In England* (New York: Basil Blackwell, 1964).

Bloom, Clive (ed.), *Jacobean Poetry and Prose: Rhetoric, Representation and the Popular Imagination* (Basingstoke: Macmillan, 1988).

Boffey, Julia, 'Berners, Juliana (fl. 1460)', *Oxford Dictionary of National Biography*, http://0-www.oxforddnb.com.catalogue.ulrls.lon.ac.uk/view/article/2255.

Bosanquet, Eustace F., *English Printed Almanacks and Prognostications: A Bibliographical History to the Year 1600* (Chiswick Press: London, 1917).

Bowden, Caroline, 'The Library of Mildred Cooke Cecil, Lady Burghley', *The Library*, 7th ser., 6 (2005), pp. 3–29.

Bray, Alan, *The Friend* (Chicago and London: University of Chicago Press, 2003).

Brooke, C.F. Tucker (ed.), *The Shakespeare Apocrypha* (Oxford: Clarendon Press, 1908).

Bruster, Douglas, 'Deep Focus: Toward the Thin Description of Literary Culture', in *Shakespeare and the Question of Culture: Early Modern Literature and the Cultural Turn* (New York: Palgrave Macmillan, 2003), pp. 29–62.

Burke, Peter, *Popular Culture in Early Modern Europe*, 3rd edn (Farnham: Ashgate, 1978; 2009).

Butler, Martin, *Theatre and Crisis 1632–1642* (Cambridge: Cambridge University Press, 1984).

Cambers, Andrew, *Godly Reading: Print, Manuscript and Puritanism in England, 1580–1720* (Cambridge: Cambridge University Press, 2011).

Capp, Bernard, *Astrology and the Popular Press: English Almanacs 1500–1800* (London: Faber, 1979).

———, *English Almanacs 1500–1800: Astrology and the Popular Press* (Cornell: Ithaca and New York, 1979).

———, 'Popular literature', in Barry Reay (ed.), *Popular Culture in Seventeenth-Century England* (London & Sydney: Croom Helm, 1985), pp. 234–70.

Caraman, Philip, *Henry Garnet, 1555–1606, and the Gunpowder Plot* (London: Longmans, 1964).

Carley, James P., 'The Dispersal of the Monastic Libraries and the Salvaging of the Spoils', in Elisabeth Leedham-Green and Teresa Webber (eds), *The Cambridge History of Libraries in Britain and Ireland* (3 vols), *Volume I, to 1640* (Cambridge: Cambridge University Press, 2006), pp. 265–91.

Carpenter, Edward, *The Protestant Bishop: Being the Life of Henry Compton, 1632–1713* (London: Longmans, Green, 1956).

Case, Arthur E., *A Bibliography of English Poetical Miscellanies 1521–1750* (Oxford: The Bibliographical Society, 1935 [for 1929]).

Cerdeira, Christine, 'Early Modern English Medical Wills, Book Ownership, and Book Culture', *Canadian Bulletin of Medical History* 12 (1995): 427–39.

Certeau, Michel de, *The Practice of Everyday Life*, trans. Steven Rendall (Berkeley: University of California Press, 1984).

Chan, Mary, 'Music Books', in John Barnard and D.F. McKenzie (eds, with the assistance of Maureen Bell), *The Cambridge History of the Book in Britain*, vol. IV (Cambridge: Cambridge University Press, 2002), 127–37.

Chapman, Alison, 'Marking Time: Astrology, Almanacs, and English Protestantism', *Renaissance Quarterly* 60 (2007): 1257–90.

Chartier, Roger, *The Cultural Uses of Print in Early Modern France*, trans. Lydia G. Cochrane (Princeton: Princeton University Press, 1987).

———, 'Culture as Appropriation: Popular Cultural Uses in Early Modern France', in Steven Kaplan (ed.), *Understanding Popular Culture: Europe from the Middle Ages to the Nineteenth Century* (New York: Mouton, 1984), pp. 229–53.

———, *Forms and Meanings: Texts, Performances and Audiences from Codex to Computer* (Philadelphia: University of Pennsylvania Press, 1995).

———, 'Reading Matter and "Popular" Reading: From the Renaissance to the Seventeenth Century', in Guglielmo Cavallo and Roger Chartier, *A History of Reading in the West* (Cambridge: Cambridge University Press, 1999), pp. 269–83.

——— 'Texts, Printing, Readings', in Lynn Hunt (ed.), *The New Cultural History* (Berkeley: University of California Press, 1989), pp. 154–75.

Cheney, Patrick, *Shakespeare, National Poet-Playwright* (Cambridge: Cambridge University Press, 2004).

Chickera, Ernst de, 'The Theme of Revenge in Elizabethan Translations of Novelle', *The Review of English Studies* 11 (1960): 1–7.

Christ's College Magazine XXVI (Cambridge, 1911–1912).

Clark, Peter, 'The Ownership of Books in England, 1560–1640: the Example of Some Kentish Townsfolk', in Lawrence Stone (ed.), *Schooling and Society* (Baltimore: Johns Hopkins University Press, 1976), pp. 95–111.

Clegg, Cyndia Susan, *Press Censorship in Caroline England* (Cambridge, 2008).

———, *Press Censorship in Elizabethan England* (Cambridge, 1997; 2001; 2008).

———, *Press Censorship in Jacobean England* (Cambridge, 2001).

Clement, Richard W., 'The Beginnings of Printing in Anglo-Saxon, 1565–1630', *Papers of the Bibliographical Society of America* 91 (1997): *192–244*.

Cobbett, William, *Cobbett's Parliamentary History of England*, 36 vols (London: R. Bagshaw, 1806–1820).

Cogswell, Thomas, Richard Cust, and Peter Lake (eds), *Politics, Religion, and Popularity: Early Stuart Essays in Honour of Conrad Russell* (Cambridge: Cambridge University Press, 2002).

Cohen, Thomas V. and Warkentin, Germaine (eds), 'Things not easily believed: Introducing the Early Modern Relation', special issue of *Renaissance and Reformation* 34/12 (Winter-Spring 2011): 237–43.

Coletti, Theresa and Gail McMurray Gibson, 'The Tudor Origins of Medieval Drama', in Kent Cartwright (ed.), *A Companion to Tudor Literature* (Chichester: Wiley-Blackwell, 2010), pp. 228–45.

Collinson, Patrick, *Marking the Hours: English People and Their Prayers, 1240– 1570* (London: Yale University Press, 2006).

Cooper, Helen, *The English Romance in Time: Transforming Motifs from Geoffrey of Monmouth to the Death of Shakespeare* (Oxford: Oxford University Press, 2004).

———, 'Pursued by Bearists', *London Review of Books* 27.1 (6 January 2005), http://www.lrb.co.uk/v27/n01/letters#letter1.

Cormack, Bradin and Carla Mazzio (eds), *Book Use, Book Theory: 1500–1700* (Chicago: Chicago University Press, 2005).

Crane, Mary T., *Framing Authority: Sayings, Self, and Society in Sixteenth-Century England* (Princeton: Princeton University Press, 1993).

Crawford, Charles, 'Appendix D: J. Bodenham's *Belvedere*', in C.M. Ingleby, L. Toulmin Smith and F.J. Furnivall (eds), *The Shakespeare Allusion-Book*, vol. II, rev. J. Munro (London: Oxford University Press, 1932), pp. 489–518.

———, 'Belvedere, or The Garden of the Muses', *Englische Studien* 43 (1911): 198–228.

Cressy, David, *Birth, Marriage and Death: Ritual, Religion and the Life-Cycle in Tudor and Stuart England* (Oxford: Oxford University Press, 1997).

———, *Literacy and the Social Order: Reading and Writing in Tudor and Stuart England* (Cambridge: Cambridge University Press, 1980).

Croft, Pauline, 'Englishmen and the Spanish Inquisition 1558–1625', *English Historical Review* 87 (April 1972): 249–68.

Cross, Claire, 'A Medieval Yorkshire Library', *Northern History* XXV (1989): 281–90.

Cummings, Brian, 'Acts of Uniformity: Pluralization and the Vernacular in the First Book of Common Prayer', in Jan-Dirk Müller, Wulf Oesterreicher, and Friedrich Vollhardt (eds), *Pluralisierungen: Konzepte zur Erfassung der Frühen Neuzeit* (Berlin: Walter de Gruyter, 2010).

———, *The Book of Common Prayer: The Texts of 1549, 1559, and 1662* (Oxford: Oxford University Press, 2011).

Curth, Louis, *Almanacs, Astrology & Popular Medicine, 1550–1700* (Manchester: Manchester University Press, 2007).

Dahl, Folke, *A Bibliography of English Corantos and Periodical Newsbooks, 1620–1642* (London: Bibliographical Society, 1952).

Danner, Bruce, *Furious Muse: Edmund Spenser's War on Lord Burghley* (Basingstoke: 2011).

Das, Nandini, *Renaissance Romance: The Transformation of English Prose Fiction, 1570–1620* (Farnham: Ashgate, 2011).

Davis, Alex, *Chivalry and Romance in the English Renaissance* (Cambridge: Cambridge University Press, 2003).

———, *Renaissance Historical Fiction: Sidney, Deloney, Nashe* (Cambridge: D.S. Brewer, 2011).

Davis, Natalie Zemon, 'Towards Mixtures and Margins', *American Historical Review* 97 (1992): 1414–15.

Dickens, A.G., *The English Reformation* (London: Fontana/Collins, 1967).

Doty, Jeffrey S., 'Shakespeare's Richard II, "Popularity", and the Early Modern Public Sphere', *Shakespeare Quarterly* 61 (2010): 183–205.

Duffy, Eamon, 'Elite and Popular Religion: the Book of Hours and Lay Piety in the Later Middle Ages', in Kate Cooper and Jeremy Gregory (eds), *Elite and Popular Religion, Studies in Church History* 42 (2006): 140–61.

———, *Marking the Hours: English People and their Prayers, 1240–1570* (New Haven and London: Yale University Press, 2006).

Duncan-Jones, Katherine, *Shakespeare: Upstart Crow to Sweet Swan, 1592–1623* (London: Arden Shakespeare, 2011).

Dutton, Richard, *Ben Jonson, Volpone and the Gunpowder Plot* (Cambridge, 2008).

Early English Books Online (Chadwyck Healy, 1998–present), http://eebo.chadwyck.com.

East, Rev. John, 'The Treasure of Gladness', *The Cottager's Monthly Visitor* 28 (June 1848): 189–93.

Echard, Siân, *Printing the Middle Ages* (Philadelphia: University of Pennsylvania Press, 2008).

Eisenberg, Daniel, *Castilian Romances of Chivalry in the Sixteenth Century* (London: Grant and Cutler, 1979).

English Short Title Catalogue (British Library), http://estc.bl.uk.

Erne, Lukas, *Shakespeare as Literary Dramatist* (Cambridge: Cambridge University Press, 2003).

———, 'The Popularity of Shakespeare in Print', *Shakespeare Survey* 62 (2009): 12–29.

Farmer, Alan B. and Lesser, Zachary, 'Canons and Classics: Publishing Drama in Caroline England', in Adam Zucker and Alan B. Farmer (eds), *Localizing Caroline Drama: Politics and Economics of the Early Modern English Stage, 1625–1642* (New York: Palgrave Macmillan, 2006), pp. 17–41.

————, 'Playbooks, Ephemerality, and Loss Rates,' in Heidi Brayman Hackel, Jesse Lander, and Zachary Lesser (eds), *The Book in History, The Book as History*, forthcoming.

————, 'The Popularity of Playbooks Revisited', *Shakespeare Quarterly* 56.1 (2005): 1–32.

————, 'Structures of Popularity in the Early Modern Book Trade', *Shakespeare Quarterly* 56.2 (2005): 206–13.

Fehrenbach, R.J. and Leedham-Green, Elisabeth (eds), *Private Libraries in Renaissance England: a Collection and Catalogue of Tudor and Early Stuart Book-lists*, 6 vols to date (Binghamton, NY: Medieval and Renaissance Texts and Studies; Malborough: Adam Matthew, 1995–).

Ferguson, W.C., 'The Stationers' Company poor book, 1608–1700', *The Library*, 5th ser., 31 (1976): 37–51.

Ferrell, Lori Anne, 'Method as Knowledge: Scribal Theology, Protestantism, and the Reinvention of Shorthand in Sixteenth Century England', in Pamela H. Smith and Benjamin Schmidt (eds), *Making Knowledge in Early Modern England: Practices, Objects, and Texts, 1400–1800* (Chicago: University of Chicago Press, 2007), pp. 163–77.

Fleming, Juliet, 'Graffiti, Grammatology, and the Age of Shakespeare', in Patricia Fumerton and Simon Hunt (eds), *Renaissance Culture and the Everyday* (Philadelphia: University of Pennsylvania Press, 1999).

————, 'The Ladies' Man and the Age of Elizabeth', in James Grantham Turner (ed.), *Sexuality and Gender in Early Modern Europe* (Cambridge: Cambridge University Press, 1993), 158–81.

Fletcher, Anthony and Diarmaid MacCulloch, *Tudor Rebellions*, 5th edn (Harlow: Pearson/Longman, 2008).

Foakes, R.A. (ed.), *Henslowe's Diary*, 2nd edn (Cambridge: Cambridge University Press, 2002).

Foot, Mirjam, *The Henry Davis Gift: A Collection of Bookbindings*, vol. I (London: British Library, 1978).

Fowler, Elizabeth and Roland Greene, *The Project of Prose in Early Modern England and the New World* (Cambridge: Cambridge University Press, 1997).

Fox, Adam, *Oral and Literate Culture in England, 1500–1700* (Oxford: Clarendon Press, 2000).

————, 'Popular Verses and their Readership in the Early Seventeenth Century', in James Raven, Helen Small, and Naomi Tadmor (eds), *The Practice and Representation of Reading in England* (Cambridge: Cambridge University Press, 1996), pp. 125–37.

Frantzen, Allan J., *Desire for Origins: New Language, Old English, and Teaching the Tradition* (New Brunswick and London: Rutgers University Press, 1990).

Frere, W.H. and W.P.M. Kennedy (eds), *Visitation Articles and Injunctions of the Period of the Reformation 1536–1575* (London: Longmans, Green, 1910).

Frost, David L., '"Mouldy Tales": The Context of Shakespeare's *Cymbeline*', *Essays and Studies* 39 (1986): 19–38.

Fuchs, Barbara, *Romance* (London: Routledge, 2004).

Galbraith, Steven K., '"English" Black-Letter Type and Spenser's *Shepheardes Calender*', *Spenser Studies* 23 (2008): 13–40.

Gallagher, Catherine and Stephen Greenblatt, *Practicing New Historicism* (Chicago: University of Chicago Press, 2000).

Geertz, Clifford, 'Thick Description: Toward an Interpretive Theory of Culture', in *The Interpretation of Cultures: Selected Essays* (New York: Basic Books, 1973), pp. 3–30.

Gillespie, Stuart and Neil Rhodes (eds), *Shakespeare and Elizabethan Popular Culture* (London: Arden Critical Companions, 2006).

Goldschmidt, E.P., *Gothic and Renaissance Bookbindings* (London: Houghton Mifflin, 1928).

Graham, Timothy, 'Matthew Parker's Manuscripts: an Elizabethan Library and its Use', in Elisabeth Leedham-Green and Teresa Webber (eds), *The Cambridge History of Libraries in Britain and Ireland* (3 vols), *Volume I, to 1640* (Cambridge: Cambridge University Press, 2006) pp. 322–42.

————— (ed.), *The Recovery of Old English: Anglo-Saxon Studies in the Sixteenth and Seventeenth Centuries* (Kalamazoo, MI: Medieval Institute Publications, Western Michigan University, 2000).

Grant, Teresa, 'White Bears in Mucedorus, The Winter's Tale and Oberon, The FairyPrince', *Notes and Queries* 48.3 (2001): 311–13.

Gray, G. and W.M. Palmer, *Abstracts from the Wills and Testamentary Documents of Printers, Binders and Stationers of Cambridge from 1504 to 1699* (London: Blades, East and Blades, 1915).

Greaves, Richard L., *Society and Religion in Elizabethan England* (Minneapolis: University of Minnesota Press, 1981).

Green, Ian, *Print and Protestantism in Early Modern England* (Oxford: Oxford University Press, 2000).

—————, *The Christian's ABC: Catechisms and Catechizing in England, c. 1530–1740* (Oxford: Clarendon Press, 1996).

Green, Lawrence D. and James J. Murphy, *Renaissance Rhetoric Short-Title Catalogue 1460–1700*, 2nd edn (Burlington, VT: Ashgate, 2006).

Greenblatt, Stephen, *Renaissance Self-Fashioning: From More to Shakespeare* (London: University of Chicago Press, 1980).

Greening, Anna, 'Tottel, Richard (b. in or before 1528, d. 1593)', in *Oxford Dictionary of National Biography* (Oxford: Oxford University Press, 2004; online edn, May 2009), http://0-www.oxforddnb.com.catalogue.ulrls.lon.ac.uk/view/article/27573 (accessed 12 May 2012).

Greenlaw, Edwin, *Studies in Spenser's Historical Allegory* (New York: Octagon, 1967).

Greg, W.W., *A Companion to Arber: being a calendar of documents in Edward Arber's transcript of the Registers of the Company of Stationers of London 1554–1640* (Oxford: Clarendon, 1967).

—————, 'Elizabethan Book-Pirates', *Review of English Studies* 11: 44 (October 1935): 475–79.

————, '"The Spanish Tragedy": A Leading Case?', *The Library*, 4th ser., 7 (1926): 47–53.

Greg, W. W. and E. Boswell (eds), *Records of the Court of the Stationers' Company, 1576–1602: from Register B* (London: Bibliographical Society, 1930).

Griffiths, David N., *The Bibliography of the Book of Common Prayer 1549–1999* (London: British Library, 2002).

Gurr, Andrew, *The Shakespeare Company 1594–1642* (Cambridge: Cambridge University Press, 2004).

Hackel, Heidi Brayman, 'The Countess of Bridgewater's London Library', in Jennifer Andersen and Elizabeth Sauer (eds), *Books and Readers in Early Modern England* (Philadelphia: University of Pennsylvania Press, 2002), pp. 135-156.

————, 'Popular Literacy and Society', in Joad Raymond (ed.), *The Oxford History of Popular Print Culture, Vol 1: Cheap Print in Britain and Ireland to 1660* (Oxford: Oxford University Press, 2011), pp. 88–100.

————, *Reading Material in Early Modern England: Gender, Print, and Literacy* (Cambridge: Cambridge University Press, 2005).

Hackett, Helen, *Women and Romance Fiction in the English Renaissance* (Cambridge: Cambridge University Press, 2000).

Hadfield, Andrew, *Edmund Spenser: A Life* (Oxford: 2012).

Halasz, Alexandra, *The Marketplace of Print: Pamphlets and the Public Sphere in Early Modern England* (Cambridge: Cambridge University Press, 1997).

Hamilton, A.C., 'Elizabethan Romance: The Example of Prose Fiction', *ELH* 49 (1982): 287–99.

Hamilton, Donna B., *Anthony Munday and the Catholics, 1560–1633* (Aldershot: Ashgate, 2005).

Hamlin, Hannibal, *Psalm Culture in Early Modern England* (Cambridge: Cambridge University Press, 2004).

Hamling, Tara, *Decorating the 'Godly' Household: Religious Art in Post-Reformation Britain* (New Haven: Yale University Press, 2010).

Hammond, Gerald, 'Translations of the Bible,' in Michael Hattaway (ed.), *A Companion to English Renaissance Literature and Culture* (Oxford: Blackwell, 2003).

Harkness, Deborah, *The Jewel House: Elizabethan London and the Scientific Revolution* (New Haven, Conn.: Yale University Press, 2007).

Harris, Tim, 'Popular, Plebeian, Culture: Historical Definitions', in Joad Raymond (ed.), *The Oxford History of Popular Print Culture, Vol 1: Cheap Print in Britain and Ireland to 1660* (Oxford: Oxford University Press, 2011), pp. 50–58.

Harrison, G.B., 'Books and Readers, 1591–4,' *The Library*, 4th ser., 8 (1927): 273–301.

Harte, N.B., 'State Control of Dress and Social Change' in D.C. Coleman and A.H. John (eds), *Trade, Government and Economy in Pre-Industrial England* (London: Weidenfeld and Nicolson, 1976).

Hattaway, Michael, *Elizabethan Popular Theatre: Plays in Performance* (London: Routledge, 1982).

Hayes, Gerald R., 'Anthony Munday's Romances: A Postscript', *The Library*, 4th ser., 7 (1926): 31–8.

———, 'Anthony Munday's Romances of Chivalry', *The Library*, 4th ser., 6 (1926): 57–81.

Heal, Felicity, 'Appropriating History: Catholic and Protestant Polemics and the National Past', *Huntington Library Quarterly 68 (2005): 109–32.*

Herbert, A.S., *Historical Catalogue of Printed Editions of the English Bible 1525–1961* (London: British and Foreign Bible Society; New York: American Bible Society, 1968).

Herr, A.F., *The Elizabethan Sermon: A Survey and a Bibliography* (Philadelphia: University of Pennsylvania Press, 1940).

Herron, Thomas, 'Reforming the Fox: Spenser's "Mother Hubberds Tale", the Beast Fables of Barnarbe Riche, and Adam Loftus, Archbishop of Dublin', *Studies in Philology* 3 (2008): 336–87.

Highley, Christopher, *Catholics Writing the Nation in Early Modern Britain and Ireland* (Oxford: Oxford University Press, 2008).

Hill, Christopher, *Puritanism and Revolution: Studies in Interpretation of the English Revolution of the 17th Century* (London: Secker and Warburg, 1958).

Hill, Tracey, *Anthony Munday and Civic Culture: Theatre, history and power in early modern London 1580–1633* (Manchester: Manchester University Press, 2004).

Hobson, G.D., 'Et Amicorum', *Library*, 5th ser., 4 (1949): 87–99.

Holtcamp, Victor, 'A Fear of "Ould" Plays: How *Mucedorus* Brought down the House and Fought for Charles II in 1652', in Douglas A. Brooks (ed.), *The Shakespeare Apocrypha* (Lampeter: Edwin Mellin Press, 2007), pp. 141–66.

Hoppe, Harry R., 'John Wolfe, Printer and Publisher, 1579–1601', *The Library*, 4th ser., 14 (1933): 241–88.

Hughes, Paul L. and James Francis Larkin (eds), *Tudor Royal Proclamations* (New Haven: Yale University Press, 1964).

Hunt, Arnold, *The Art of Hearing: English Preachers and their Audiences, 1590–1640* (Cambridge: Cambridge University Press, 2010).

———, 'Clerical and Parish Libraries', in Elisabeth Leedham-Green and Teresa Webber, (eds), *The Cambridge History of Libraries in Britain and Ireland* (3 vols), *Volume I, to 1640* (Cambridge: Cambridge University Press, 2006), pp. 400–419.

———, 'The Lord's Supper in Early Modern England', *Past & Present* 161 (1998): 39–83.

Hunt, Maurice, '"Bearing Hence": Shakespeare's "The Winter's Tale"', *Studies in English Literature 1500–1900* 44.2 (2004): 33–46.

Hunter, Lynette, 'Books for daily life: household, husbandry, behaviour', in John Barnard and D.F. McKenzie (eds, with the assistance of Maureen Bell), *The Cambridge History of the Book in Britain*, vol. IV (Cambridge: Cambridge University Press, 2002), pp. 514–32.

Ivins, M., 'A Tudor paper Book Jacket,' *Bulletin of the Metropolitan Museum of Art* 22 (1927): 224–26.

Jackson, John, *A Treatise on Wood Engraving* (London: H.G. Bohn, 1839).

Jackson, Ken and Arthur F. Marotti, 'The Turn to Religion in Early Modern Studies', *Criticism* 46 (Winter 2004): 167–90.

Jackson, MacDonald P., 'Edward Archer's Ascription of *Mucedorus* to Shakespeare', *Journal of the Australasian Universities Language and Literature Association* 22 (1964): 233–48.

Jackson, William A., 'Printed Wrappers of the Fifteenth to the Eighteenth Centuries', *Harvard Library Bulletin* VI (1952): 313–21.

——— (ed.), *Records of the Court of the Stationers' Company 1602 to 1640* (London: The Bibliographical Society, 1957).

Jahn, Robert, 'Letters and Booklists of Thomas Chard (or Chare) of London, 1583-4', *The Library,* 4th ser., 4 (1923): 219–37.

Jardine, Lisa and Anthony Grafton, '"Studied for Action": How Gabriel Harvey Read his Livy', *Past and Present* 129 (1990): 30–78.

Jenkinson, Hilary, *English Wall-Papers of the Sixteenth and Seventeenth Centuries* (London: Society of Antiquaries of London, 1925).

Jenner, Mark, 'London', in Joad Raymond (ed.), *The Oxford History of Popular Print Culture, Vol 1: Cheap Print in Britain and Ireland to 1660* (Oxford: Oxford University Press, 2011) pp. 294–307.

Jensen, Kristian, 'Universities and Colleges', in Elisabeth Leedham-Green and Teresa Webber (eds), *The Cambridge History of Libraries in Britain and Ireland* (3 vols), *Volume I, to 1640* (Cambridge: Cambridge University Press, 2006), pp. 345–62.

Jones, Ann Rosalind and Peter Stallybrass, *Renaissance Clothing and the Materials of Memory* (Cambridge: Cambridge University Press, 2000).

Jones, Mike Rodman, *Radical Pastoral, 1381–1594: Appropriations and the Writing of Religious Controversy* (Farnham: Ashgate, 2011).

Johnson, Francis R., 'Notes on English Retail Book-Prices, 1550–1640', *The Library*, 5th ser., 5 (1950): 83–112.

Jowett, John, *Shakespeare and Text* (Oxford: Oxford University Press, 2007).

Judge, C.B., *Elizabethan Book Pirates* (Cambridge, MA: Harvard University Press, 1934).

Judson, A.C., 'Mother Hubberd's Ape', *Modern Language Notes* 63 (1948): 145–49.

Jupin, Arvin (ed.), *A Contextual Study and Modern-Spelling Edition of Mucedorus* (London: Garland, 1987).

Kassell, Lauren, 'Almanacs and Prognostications', in Joad Raymond (ed.), *The Oxford History of Popular Print Culture, Volume 1: Cheap Print in Britain and Ireland to 1660* (Oxford: Oxford University Press, 2011).

Kastan, David Scott, *Shakespeare and the Book* (Cambridge: Cambridge University Press, 2001).

Kesson, Andy, *John Lyly and Early Modern Authorship* (Manchester: Manchester University Press, 2013).

Kiessling, Nicolas K., *The Library of Robert Burton* (Oxford: Oxford Bibliographical Society, 1988).

King, Andrew, *The Faerie Queene and Middle English Romance: The Matter of Just Memory* (Oxford: Clarendon Press, 2000)

Kirkpatrick, Robin, *English and Italian Literature from Dante to Shakespeare* (London: Longman, 1995).

Kirwan, Peter, 'The First Collected "Shakespeare Apocrypha"', *Shakespeare Quarterly* 62.4 (2011): 594–601.

Klotz, Edith L., 'A Subject Analysis of English Imprints for Every Tenth Year from 1480 to 1640', *Huntington Library Quarterly* 1 (1938): 417–19.

Knapp, Jeffrey, *Shakespeare Only* (Chicago: University of Chicago Press, 2009).

Knight, Charles (ed.), *The Pictorial Edition of the Works of Shakspere: Doubtful Plays &c.* (London: Charles Knight and Co., 1841).

Knight, Jeffrey Todd, 'Fast Bind, Fast Find: The History of the Book and the Modern Collection', *Criticism* 51 (2009): 79–104.

———, 'Making Shakespeare's Books: Assembly and Intertextuality in the Archives', *Shakespeare Quarterly* 60 (2009): 304–40.

Knowles, James, 'Papering Rooms', *Notes and Queries*, 2nd series 27:2 (1856): 7–8.

Knutson, Roslyn Evander, *The Repertory of Shakespeare's Company 1594–1616* (Fayetteville: University of Arkansas Press, 1991).

Krause, Virginia, 'Serializing the French *Amadis* in the 1540s', in Marian Rothstein (ed.), *Charting Change in France around 1540* (Selinsgrove: Susquehanna University Press, 2006), pp. 40–62.

Krier, Theresa M. (ed.), Refiguring Chaucer in the Renaissance (Gainesville: University Press of Florida, 1998).

Kristeller, Paul, 'Woodcuts as Bindings', *Bibliographica* 1 (1895): 249–51.

Kummel, D.W., *English Music Printing 1553–1700* (London: Bibliographical Society, 1975).

Lake, Peter, 'Religion and Cheap Print', in Joad Raymond (ed.), *The Oxford History of Popular Print Culture, Vol 1: Cheap Print in Britain and Ireland to 1660* (Oxford: Oxford University Press, 2011), pp. 217–41.

Lamb, Mary Ellen, *The Popular Culture of Shakespeare, Spenser and Jonson* (London: Routledge, 2006).

Leedham-Green, Elisabeth, *Books in Cambridge Inventories: Book-lists from Vice-Chancellor's Court Probate Inventories in the Tudor and Stuart Periods*, 2 vols (Cambridge: Cambridge University Press, 1986).

———, 'Booksellers and Libraries in Sixteenth-Century Cambridge', in Robin Myers, Michael Harris and Giles Mandelbrote (eds), *Libraries and the Book Trade: the Formation of Collections from the Sixteenth to the Twentieth Century* (New Castle DE: Oak Knoll Press, 2000) pp. 1–14.

————, 'Perne's Wills', in David McKitterick (ed.), *Andrew Perne: Quatercentenary Studies* (Cambridge: Cambridge University Library, 1991), pp. 79–119.

Leedham-Green, Elisabeth and Webber, Teresa, (eds), *The Cambridge History of Libraries in Britain and Ireland* (3 vols), *Volume I, to 1640* (Cambridge: Cambridge University Press, 2006).

Le Huray, Peter, *Music and the Reformation in England 1549–1660* (New York: Oxford University Press, 1967).

Leinwand, Theodore B., 'Shakespeare and the Middling Sort', *Shakespeare Quarterly* 44 (1993): 284–303.

Lesser, Zachary, 'Typographic Nostalgia: Playreading, Popularity and the Meanings of Black Letter', in Marta Straznicky (ed.), *The Book of the Play: Playwrights, Stationers, and Readers in Early Modern England* (Amherst: University of Massachusetts Press, 2006), pp. 99–126.

Lesser, Zachary and Peter Stallybrass, 'The First Literary *Hamlet* and the Commonplacing of Professional Plays', *Shakespeare Quarterly* 59 (2008): 371–420.

Liddell, J.R., 'The Library of Corpus Christi College Oxford in the Sixteenth Century', *The Library,* 4th ser., 18 (1938): 385–416.

Liebler, Naomi Conn, 'Elizabethan Pulp Fiction: The Example of Richard Johnson', *Critical Survey* 12 (2000): 71–87.

Lievsay, John T., '"Silver-tongued Smith", paragon of Elizabethan preachers', *Huntington Library Quarterly* 11.1 (November 1947): 13–36.

Logan, Terence P., and Denzell S. Smith, eds. *The Predecessors of Shakespeare: A Survey and Bibliography of Recent Studies in English Renaissance Drama* (Lincoln: University of Nebraska Press, 1973).

Love, Harold, *The Culture and Commerce of Texts: Scribal Publication in Seventeenth-Century England* (Oxford, 1998).

Luborsky, Ruth Samson, 'The Illustrations to *The Shepheardes Calender*', *Spenser Studies* 2 (1981): 19–21.

Lucas, Caroline, *Writing for Women: The Example of Woman as Reader in Elizabethan Romance* (Milton Keynes: Open University Press, 1989).

Lucas, Peter J., 'From Politics to Practicalities: Printing Anglo-Saxon in the Context of Seventeenth-Century Scholarship', *The Library,* 7th ser. 4 (2003): 28–48.

Luders, Alexander, Sir T.E. Tomlins, John France, W.E. Taunton, and John Raithby (eds), *The Statutes of the Realm. Printed by Command of his Majesty King George the Third. In Pursuance of an Address of the House of Commons of Great Britain. From Original Records and Authentic Manuscripts*, 12 vols (London: George Eyre and Andrew Strahan, 1810–1828).

Mace, Nancy A., 'The History of the Grammar Patent, 1547–1602', *Papers of the Bibliographical Society of America* 87 (1993): 419–36.

————, 'The History of the Grammar Patent from 1620 to 1800 and the Forms of Lily's Latin Grammar', *Papers of the Bibliographical Society of America* 100 (2006): 177–225.

Machan, Tim William, 'Speght's Works and the Invention of Chaucer', *Text 8* (1995): 145–70.

MacLure, Millar, *The Paul's Cross Sermons* (Toronto: University of Toronto Press, 1958).

Malcolm, Noel, *Aspects of Hobbes* (Oxford: Oxford University Press, 2002).

Maltby, Judith, *Prayer Book and People in Elizabethan and Early Stuart England* (Cambridge: Cambridge University Press, 1998).

Mann, Jill, *From Aesop to Raynard: Beast Literature in Medieval Britain* (Oxford: Oxford University Press, 2009).

Marsh, Christopher, *Music and Society in Early Modern England* (Cambridge: Cambridge University Press, 2010).

Matthews, David, 'Public Ambition, Private Desire and the Last Tudor Chaucer', in Gordon McMullan and David Matthews, Reading the Medieval in Early Modern England (Cambridge: Cambridge University Press, 2007), pp. 74–88.

McClelland, Nancy, *Historic Wall-Papers* (Philadelphia: J.B. Lippincott Company, 1924).

McCullough, Peter, *Lancelot Andrewes: Selected Sermons and Lectures* (Oxford: Oxford University Press, 2005).

———, *Sermons at Court: Politics and Religion in Elizabethan and Jacobean Preaching* (Cambridge: Cambridge University Press, 1998).

McCullough, P., H. Adlington, and E. Rhatigan (eds), *The Oxford Handbook of the Early Modern Sermon* (Oxford: Oxford University Press, 2011).

McElligott, Jason, 'Edward Crouch (c. 1622–76), A Poor Printer in 17thc London', *Journal of the Printing Historical Society* (n.s.) 1 (2000): 49–73.

———, *Royalism, Print and Censorship in Revolutionary England* (Woodbridge: Boydell, 2007).

McKenzie, D.F., 'Stationers' Company "Liber A": An Apologia', in Robin Myers and Michael Harris (eds), *The Stationers' Company and the Book Trade, 1550–1990* (Winchester: St. Paul's Bibliographies, 1997), pp. 35–64

McKenzie, D.F. and Maureen Bell, *A Chronology and Calendar of Documents Relating to the London Book Trade 1641–1700*, 3 vols (Oxford, 2005).

McKitterick, David, *A History of Cambridge University Press, Volume 1: Printing and the Book Trade in Cambridge, 1534–1698* (Cambridge: Cambridge University Press, 1992), 118–19.

———, 'Libraries and the Organization of Knowledge', in Elisabeth Leedham-Green and Teresa Webber (eds), *The Cambridge History of Libraries in Britain and Ireland* (3 vols), *Volume I, to 1640* (Cambridge: Cambridge University Press, 2006), 592–615.

———, *The Library of Sir Thomas Knyvett of Ashwellthorpe, c. 1539–1618* (Cambridge: University of Cambridge Library, 1978).

McMullan, Gordon and David Matthews (eds), Reading the Medieval in Early Modern England (Cambridge: Cambridge University Press, 2007), pp. 74–88.

Mentz, Steve, *Romance for Sale in Early Modern England: The Rise of Prose Fiction* (Aldershot: Ashgate, 2006).

Metz, G. Harold (ed.), *Sources of Four Plays Ascribed to Shakespeare* (Columbia: University of Missouri Press, 1989).

'Middlesex Sessions Rolls: 1593', *Middlesex county records: Volume 1: 1550–1603* (1886), pp. 211–19. http://www.british-history.ac.uk/report.aspx?compi d=65962&strquery=middlesex sessions rolls book.

Mincoff, Marco, '*The Faithful Shepherdess*: A Fletcherian Experiment', *Renaissance Drama* 9 (1966): 163–77.

Mitchell, W. Fraser, *English Pulpit Oratory* (London: Macmillan, 1932).

Moore, Helen (ed.), *Amadis de Gaule, Translated by Anthony Munday* (Aldershot: Ashgate, 2004).

———, 'Anthony Munday', in Gordon Braden, Robert Cummings, and Stuart Gillespie (eds), *The Oxford History of Literary Translation in English: Volume 2 1550–1660* (Oxford: Oxford University Press, 2010), pp. 74–77.

———, 'Shakespeare and Popular Romance', in Stuart Gillespie and Neil Rhodes (eds), *Shakespeare and Elizabethan Popular Culture* (London: Arden Shakespeare, 2006), pp. 92–111.

Moretti, Franco, *Graphs, Maps, Trees: Abstract Models for Literary History* (London: Verso, 2005).

Morrissey, Mary, *Politics and the Pauls Cross Sermons, 1558–1642* (Oxford: Oxford University Press, 2011).

———, 'Sermons, Primers, and Prayer Books', in Joad Raymond (ed.), *The Oxford History of Popular Print Culture, Volume 1, Cheap Print in Britain and Ireland to 1660* (Oxford, 2011) pp. 491–509.

Moulton, Ian Frederick, *Before Pornography: Erotic Writing in Early Modern England* (Oxford: Oxford University Press, 2000).

Mowat, Barbara A., '"What's in a Name?" Tragicomedy, Romance, or Late Comedy', in Richard Dutton and Jean E. Howard (eds), *A Companion to Shakespeare's Works, Vol. IV: The Poems, Problem Comedies, Late Plays* (Oxford: Blackwell, 2003), pp. 129–49.

Murphy, Andrew, 'Configuring the Book', *EMLS* [forthcoming].

———, *Shakespeare in Print: A History and Chronology of Shakespeare Publishing* (Cambridge: Cambridge University Press, 2003).

Myers, Robin, (ed.), *Records of the Worshipful Company of Stationers, 1554–1920* (Teaneck, NJ: Chadwyck-Healey, c. 1985), microform reel 97, envelope 3.

——— *The Stationers' Company Archive: An Account of the records 1554–1984* (Winchester: St. Paul's Bibliographies, 1990).Newcomb, Lori Humphrey, *Reading Popular Romance in Early Modern England* (New York: Columbia University Press, 2002).

———, 'Romance', in Joad Raymond (ed.), *The Oxford History of Popular Print Culture, Volume 1, Cheap Print in Britain and Ireland to 1660* (Oxford, 2011), pp. 363–76.

Noble, Richmond, *Shakespeare's Biblical Knowledge and Use of the Book of Common Prayer* (London: SPCK, 1930).

Oliver, Leslie Mahin, 'A Bookseller's Account Book, 1545', *Harvard Library Bulletin* 16:2 (1968): 144–54.

Oman, C.C. and J.C. Hamilton, *Wallpapers: A History and Illustrated Catalogue of the Collection of the Victoria and Albert Museum* (London: Sotheby Publications, 1982).

Orgel, Stephen, 'Textual Icons: Reading Early Modern Illustrations', in Neil Rhodes and Jonathan Sawday (eds), *The Renaissance Computer: Knowledge Technology in the First Age of Print* (London, 2000), pp. 59–94.

Orlin, Lena Cowen, 'Fictions of the early modern English probate inventory', in Henry S. Turner (ed.), *The Culture of Capital* (New York: Routledge, 2002), pp. 51–83.

Ovenden, Richard, 'The Libraries of the Antiquaries (c. 1580–1640) and the Idea of a National Collection', in Elisabeth Leedham Green and Teresa Webber (eds), *The Cambridge History of Libraries in Britain and Ireland* (3 vols), *Volume I, to 1640* (Cambridge: Cambridge University Press, 2006), pp. 527–61.

Parker, Patricia A., *Inescapable Romance: Studies in the Poetics of a Mode* (Princeton: Princeton University Press, 1979).

Parmelee, Lisa Ferraro, *Good Newes From Fraunce: French Anti-League Propaganda in Late Elizabethan England* (Rochester, NY: University of Rochester Press, 1996).

Patchell, Mary, *The Palmerin Romances in Elizabethan Fiction* (New York: AMS Press, 1966).

Pearson, David, *Provenance Research in Book History: A Handbook* (London: British Library, 1994).

Peltonen, Markku, 'Rhetoric and Citizenship in the Monarchical Republic of Queen Elizabeth I', in John F. McDiarmid (ed.), *The Monarchical Republic of Early Modern England: Essays in Response to Patrick Collinson* (Aldershot: Ashgate, 2007), pp. 109–27.

Peterson, Richard S., 'Laurel Crown and Ape's Tail: New Light on Spenser's Career from Thomas Tresham', *Spenser Studies* 12 (1998): 1–35.

Pettegree, Andrew, *Reformation and the Culture of Persuasion* (Cambridge: Cambridge University Press, 2005).

———, 'Translation and the Migration of Texts', in *The French Book and the European Book World* (Leiden: Brill, 2007), pp. 203–18.

Pettegree, Andrew and Walsby, Malcolm (eds), *French Vernacular Books: Books Published in the French Language Before 1601* (Leiden: Brill, 2007).

Phillips, Joshua, *English Fictions of Communal Identity, 1485–1603* (Farnham: Ashgate, 2010).

Platt, C., *The Great Rebuildings of Tudor and Stuart England* (London: UCL Press, 1994).

Plett, Heinrich F., *English Renaissance Rhetoric and Poetics: A Systematic Bibliography of Primary and Secondary Sources* (New York: E.J. Brill, 1995).

Plomer, H.R., 'Some Elizabethan Book Sales', *The Library*, 3rd ser., 7 (1916): 318–29.

Pollman, K. and W. Otten (eds), *The Oxford Guide to the Historical Reception of Augustine* (Oxford: forthcoming, 2013).

Potter, Esther, 'Bookbinding for Libraries', in Robin Myers, Michael Harris, and Giles Mandelbrote (eds), *Libraries and the Book Trade* (New Castle, Delaware: Oak Knoll Press, 2000).

Preiss, Richard, 'A Play Finally Anonymous', in Douglas A. Brooks (ed.), in *The Shakespeare Apocrypha* (New York: Lampeter: Edwin Mellen Press), pp. 117–140.

Price, Leah, *How to Do Things with Books in Victorian Britain* (Princeton: Princeton University Press, 2012).

Proudfoot, Richard, '"Modernizing" the Printed Play-Text in Jacobean London: Some Early Reprints of *Mucedorus*', in Linda Anderson and Janis Lull (eds), *'A Certain Text': Close Readings and Textual Studies on Shakespeare and Others* (Newark: University of Delaware Press, 2002), pp. 18–28.

Purcell, Mark, 'The Library at Lanhydrock', *Book Collector* 54 (2005): 195–230.

Purcell, Stephen, *Popular Shakespeare: Simulation and Subversion on the Modern Stage* (Basingstoke: Palgrave Macmillan, 2009).

Quitslund, Beth, *The Reformation in Rhyme: Sternhold, Hopkins and the English Metrical Psalter, 1547–1603* (Aldershot: Ashgate, 2008).

———, 'Singing the Psalms for Fun and Profit', in Alec Ryrie and Jessica Martin (eds), *Private and Household Devotion in Early Modern Britain* (Aldershot: forthcoming).

Randall, David, *Credibility in Elizabethan and Early Stuart Military News* (London: Pickering and Chatto, 2008).

Rank: Picturing the Social Order, 1516–2009 (Sunderland: Art Editions North, 2009).

Raymond, Joad (ed.), *The Oxford History of Popular Print Culture, Vol 1: Cheap Print in Britain and Ireland to 1660* (Oxford: Oxford University Press, 2011).

Rees, Graham and Maria Wakeley, *Publishing, Politics, and Culture: The King's Printers in the Reign of James I and VI* (Oxford: Oxford University Press, 2009).

Remington, Preston, 'Elizabethan Wallpapers', *Bulletin of the Metropolitan Museum of Art* 22: 6 (June 1927): 168–70.

Reynolds, George F., '*Mucedorus*, Most Popular Elizabethan Play?', in Josephine W. Bennett, Oscar Cargill, and Vernon Hall, Jr. (eds), *Studies in the English Renaissance Drama* (London: P. Owen and Vision Press, 1961), pp. 248–68.

Rhodes, Neil, 'Articulate Networks: the Self, the Book and the World', in Jonathan Sawday and Neil Rhodes (eds), *The Renaissance Computer: Knowledge Technology in the First Age of Print* (London: Routledge, 2000), pp. 181–94.

———, *Shakespeare and the Origins of English* (Oxford: Oxford University Press, 2004).

Richardson, Catherine, *Domestic Life and Domestic Tragedy in Early Modern England: The Material Life of the Household* (Manchester: Manchester University Press, 2006).

Roberts, Julian, 'Extending the Frontiers: Scholar Collectors', in Elisabeth Leedham-Green and Teresa Webber (eds), *The Cambridge History of Libraries in Britain and Ireland* (3 vols), *Volume I, to 1640* (Cambridge: Cambridge University Press, 2006), pp. 292–321.

———, 'Importing Books for Oxford, 1500–1640', in James P. Carley and Colin G.C. Tite, *Books and Collectors, 1200–1700: Essays Presented to Andrew Watson* (London: British Library, 1997), pp. 317–33.

———, 'The Latin Trade,' in John Barnard and D. F. McKenzie (eds, with the assistance of Maureen Bell), *The Cambridge History of the Book in Britain*, vol. IV (Cambridge: Cambridge University Press, 2002), pp. 141–73.

Roberts, Julian and A.G. Watson (eds), *John Dee's Library Catalogue* (London: Bibliographical Society, 1990).

Robinson, Benedict S., 'John Foxe and the Anglo-Saxons', in Christopher Highley and John N. King (eds), *John Foxe and his World* (Aldershot: Ashgate, 2001), pp. 54–72.

Robinson, Hastings (ed.), *The Zurich Letters* (Cambridge: University Press, 1842).

Rodger, Alexander, 'Roger Ward's Shrewsbury Stock: an Inventory of 1585', *The Library*, 5th ser., 13 (1958): 247–68.

Rosenthal, Margaret F., 'Fashions of Friendship in an Early Modern Illustrated *Album Amicorum*: British Library, MS Egerton 1191', *Journal of Medieval and Early Modern Studies* 39 (2009): 619–41.

Salzman, Paul, *Literary Culture in Jacobean England: Reading 1621* (New York: Palgrave Macmillan, 2002).

Sargent, Clare, 'The Early Modern Library', in Elisabeth Leedham-Green and Teresa Webber (eds), *The Cambridge History of Libraries in Britain and Ireland* (3 vols), *Volume I, to 1640* (Cambridge: Cambridge University Press, 2006), pp. 51–65.

Saunders, J.W., 'The Stigma of Print: A Note on the Social Bases of Tudor Poetry', *Essays in Criticism* 1 (1951): 139–64.

Sayle, Charles, *Cambridge Fragments* (Cambridge, 1913).

Sayle, R.T.D., 'Annals of the Merchant Taylors' School Library', *The Library*, 4th ser., 15 (1935): 457–80.

Scanlon, Paul A., 'A Checklist of Prose Romances in English', *The Library*, 5th ser., 33 (1978): 143–52.

Scarisbrick, J.J., *The Reformation and the English People* (Oxford: Blackwell, 1984).

Schaffer, Simon, 'Science', in Joad Raymond (ed.), *The Oxford History of Popular Print Culture, Vol 1: Cheap Print in Britain and Ireland to 1660* (Oxford: Oxford University Press, 2011), 398–416.

Schalkwyk, David, 'What May Words Do? The Performative of Praise in Shakespeare's Sonnets', *Shakespeare Quarterly* 49 (1998): 251–68.

Scherer, Abigail, '*Mucedorus's* Wild Man: Disorderly Acts on the Early Modern Stage', in T.H. Howard-Hill and Philip Rollinson (eds), *Renaissance Papers 1999* (Rochester: Boydell and Brewer, 1999).

Schlueter, June, *The Album Amicorum and the London of Shakespeare's Time* (London: British Library, 2012).

Schmitt, Charles B., *John Case and Aristotelianism in Renaissance England* (Kingston and Montreal: McGill-Queen's University Press, 1983).

Schoenbaum, Samuel, *William Shakespeare: A Documentary Life* (Oxford: Clarendon Press, 1975).

Schurink, Fred, 'A Knowledge for Kings', in *The Origins of English Literature: Recovering Mid-Tudor Writing for a Modern Readership* (Sheffield: Humanities Research Institute, 2007–2008), http://www.hrionline.ac.uk/origins.

Schwegler, Robert A., 'Oral Tradition and Print: Domestic Performance in Renaissance England', *The Journal of American Folklore* 93 (1980): 435–49.

Scott-Warren, Jason, 'Books in the Bedchamber: Religion, Accounting and the Library of Richard Stonley', in John N. King (ed.), *Tudor Books and Readers: Materiality and the Construction of Meaning* (Cambridge: Cambridge University Press, 2010).

———, 'News, Sociability, and Bookbuying in Early Modern England: The Letters of Sir Thomas Cornwallis', *The Library*, 7th ser., 1 (2000): 381–402.

———, 'Reading Graffiti in the Early Modern Book', *Huntington Library Quarterly* 73 (2010): 363–81.

Scribner, Bob, 'Is a History of Popular Culture Possible?', *History of European Ideas* 10 (1989): 175–91.

Seaver, Paul, *The Puritan Lectureships* (Stanford: Stanford University Press, 1970).

———, *Wallington's World: A Puritan Artisan in Seventeenth-Century London* (London: Methuen, 1985).

Selwyn, David and Selwyn, Pamela, '"The Profession of a Gentleman": Books for the Gentry and the Nobility (*c.* 1560 to 1640)', in Elisabeth Leedham-Green and Teresa Webber (eds), *The Cambridge History of Libraries in Britain and Ireland* (3 vols), *Volume I, to 1640* (Cambridge: Cambridge University Press, 2006), pp. 489–519.

Selwyn, Pamela, 'Herald's Libraries', in Elisabeth Leedham-Green and Teresa Webber (eds), *The Cambridge History of Libraries in Britain and Ireland* (3 vols), *Volume I, to 1640* (Cambridge: Cambridge University Press, 2006), pp. 472–85.

Shaaber, Matthias A., *Some Forerunners of the Newspaper in England, 1476–1622* (Philadelphia: University of Pennsylvania Press, 1929).

Shagan, Ethan H., *Popular Politics and the English Reformation* (Cambridge: Cambridge University Press, 2003).

Shami, Jeanne, *John Donne and Conformity in Crisis in the Jacobean Pulpit* (Cambridge: Cambridge University Press, 2003).

Shapiro, James, *1599: A Year in the Life of William Shakespeare* (London: Faber and Faber, 2005).

Shell, Alison, *Catholicism, Controversy, and the English Literary Imagination, 1558–1660* (Cambridge: Cambridge University Press, 2004).

Shell, Alison and Alison Emblow, *Index to the Court Books of the Stationers' Company 1679–1717* (London: The Bibliographical Society, 2007).

Sherman, William H., *John Dee: The Politics of Reading and Writing in the English Renaissance* (Amherst: University of Massachusetts Press, 1995).

———, *Used Books: Marking Readers in Renaissance England* (Philadelphia: University of Pennsylvania Press, 2008).

———, 'The Social Life of Books', in Joad Raymond (ed.), *The Oxford History of Popular Print Culture*, 164–71.

Shinn, Abigail, '"Extaordinary discourses of vnnecessarie matter": Spenser's *Shepheardes Calender* and the Almanac Tradition', in Matthew Dimmock and Andrew Hadfield (eds), *Literature and Popular Culture in Early Modern Culture* (Farnham: Ashgate, 2009), pp. 135–49.

Simmons, Judith, 'Publications of 1623', *The Library*, 5th ser., 21 (1966): 207–22.

Simmons, R.C., 'ABCs, almanacs, ballads, chapbook, popular piety and textbooks', in John Barnard and D. F. McKenzie (eds, with the assistance of Maureen Bell), *The Cambridge History of the Book in Britain*, vol. IV (Cambridge: Cambridge University Press, 2002), pp. 504–13.

Simons, John, 'Open and closed books: a semiotic approach to the history of Elizabethan and Jacobean popular romance', in Clive Bloom (ed.), *Jacobean Poetry and Prose* (Basingstoke: Macmillan), pp. 8–24.

Slack, Paul, 'Mirrors of Health and Treasures of Poor Men: The Uses of the Vernacular Medical Literature of Tudor England', in Charles Webster (ed.), *Health, Medicine, and Mortality in the Sixteenth Century* (Cambridge: Cambridge University Press, 1979), 237–73.

Smyth, Adam, *Autobiography in Early Modern England* (Cambridge: Cambridge University Press, 2010).

———, '"Rend and teare in peeces": Textual Fragmentation in Seventeenth-Century England', *The Seventeenth Century* 19.1 (Autumn 2004): 36–52.

Spiller, Elizabeth, *Reading and the History of Race in the Renaissance* (Cambridge: Cambridge University Press, 2011).

Spufford, Margaret, 'Libraries of the "Common Sort"', in Elisabeth Leedham-Green and Teresa Webber (eds), *The Cambridge History of Libraries in Britain and Ireland* (3 vols), *Volume I, to 1640* (Cambridge: Cambridge University Press, 2006), pp. 520–26.

———, *Small Books and Pleasant Histories: Popular Fiction and Its Readership in Seventeenth-Century England* (London: Methuen, 1981).

———, 'The Importance of Religion in the Sixteenth and Seventeenth Centuries', in Margaret Spufford (ed.), *The World of Rural Dissenters, 1520–1725* (Cambridge: Cambridge University Press, 1995), pp. 1–102.

St. Clair, William, *The Reading Nation in the Romantic Period* (Cambridge: Cambridge University Press, 2004).

Stallybrass, Peter, '"Little Jobs": Broadsides and the Printing Revolution', in Sabrina Alcorn Baron, Eric N. Linquist, and Eleanor F. Shevlin (eds), *Agent of Change: Print Culture Studies after Elizabeth L. Eisenstein* (Amherst and Boston: University of Massachusetts Press, 2007) pp. 315–42.

Stallybrass, Peter, Roger Chartier, J. Franklin Mowery, and Heather Wolfe, 'Hamlet's Tables and the Technologies of Writing in Renaissance England', *Shakespeare Quarterly* 55 (2004): 379–419.

Starnes, DeWitt T., *Renaissance Dictionaries: English-Latin and Latin-English* (Austin: University of Texas Press, 1954).

Stern, Virginia F., *Gabriel Harvey: His Life, Marginalia and Library* (Oxford: Clarendon Press, 1979).

Stodder, Joseph H., 'Mucedorus and The Birth of Merlin at the Los Angeles Globe', *Shakespeare Quarterly* 41.3 (1990): 368–72.

Streckfuss, Richard, 'News Before Newspapers', *Journalism and Mass Communication Quarterly* 75/1 (1998): 84–97.

Stubbings, F.H., 'A Cambridge Pocket-Diary, 1587–92', *Transactions of the Cambridge Bibliographical Society*, v (1971): 191–202.

Sugden, A.V. and J.L. Edmondson, *A History of English Wallpaper 1509–1914* (London: B.T. Batsford, 1926).

Sullivan, Garret and Linda Woodbridge, 'Popular Culture in Print', in Arthur F. Kinney (ed.), *The Cambridge Companion to English Literature, 1500–1600* (Cambridge: Cambridge University Press, 2000), pp. 265–86.

Summit, Jennifer, *Memory's Library: Medieval Books in Early Modern England* (Chicago and London: University of Chicago Press, 2008).

Summit, Jennifer and David Wallace (eds), 'After Periodization', *Journal of Medieval and Early Modern Studies* 37 (2007).

Sutherland, John, *Bestsellers: A Very Short Introduction* (Oxford: Oxford University Press, 2007).

Tanselle, G. Thomas, 'The Bibliographical Concepts of *Issue* and *State*', *Papers of the Bibliographical Society of America* 69 (1975): 17–66.

Taylor, Gary, 'Thomas Middleton: Lives and Afterlives', in Gary Taylor and John Lavagnino (eds), *Thomas Middleton: Collected Works*, (Oxford: Oxford University Press, 2007).

Temperley, Nicholas, *Music of the English Parish Church* (Cambridge: Cambridge University Press, 1979).

Thomas, Henry, *Spanish and Portuguese Romances of Chivalry* (Cambridge: Cambridge University Press, 1920).

Thomas, Keith, 'The Meaning of Literacy in Early Modern England', in Gerd Baumann (ed.), *The Written Word: Literacy in Transition* (Oxford: Clarendon Press, 1986), pp. 97–132.

Thornberry, Richard T., 'A Seventeenth-Century Revival of *Mucedorus* in London before 1610', *Shakespeare Quarterly* 28.3 (1977): 362–64.

Tite, Colin G.C., *The Manuscript Library of Sir Robert Cotton*, Panizzi lectures, 1993 (London: British Library, 1994).

Treadwell, Michael, 'The Stationers and the printing acts at the end of the seventeenth century', in John Barnard and D.F. McKenzie (eds, with the assistance of Maureen Bell), *The Cambridge History of the Book in Britain*, vol. IV (Cambridge: Cambridge University Press, 2002), pp. 755–76.

Trigg, Stephanie, *Congenial Souls: Reading Chaucer from Medieval to Postmodern* (Minneapolis: University of Minnesota Press, 2001).

Urry, William, *Christopher Marlowe and Canterbury* (London: Faber, 1988).

Varty, Kenneth, *Reynard, Renart, Reinaert and other Foxes in Medieval England: The Iconographic Evidence* (Amsterdam: Amsterdam University Press, 1999).

Wall, Wendy, 'Disclosures in Print: The "Violent Enlargement" of the Renaissance Voyeuristic Text', *Studies in English Literature* 29 (1989): 35–59.

Walsham, Alexandra, *Church Papists: Catholicism, Conformity and Confessional Polemic in Early Modern England* (Woodbridge: Boydell Press, 1999).

Watson, Andrew, *Medieval Manuscripts in Post-Medieval England* (Aldershot: Ashgate, 2004).

Watt, Tessa, *Cheap Print and Popular Piety, 1550–1640* (Cambridge: Cambridge University Press, 1991).

Werstine, Paul, 'The Science of Editing,' in Andrew Murphy (ed.), *A Concise Companion to Shakespeare and the Text* (Oxford: Blackwell, 2007), 109–27.

Wilkinson, Alexander S., 'Lost Books Printed in French before 1601', *The Library: The Transactions of the Bibliographical Society 10* (2009), 188–205.

Willard, Oliver M., 'The Survival of English Books Printed before 1640: A Theory and Some Illustrations', *The Library,* 4th ser., 23 (1942): 171–90.

Williams, Deanne, 'Medievalism in English Renaissance Literature', in Kent Cartwright (ed.), *A Companion to Tudor Literature* (Oxford: 2010), pp. 213–27.

———, 'Shakespearean Medievalism and the Limits of Periodization in *Cymbeline*', *Literature Compass* 8/6 (2011): 390–403.

Williams, Franklin B. Jr, 'Lost Books of Tudor England', *The Library*, 7th ser. 33 (1978), 1–14.

Williams, Raymond, *The Long Revolution* (London: Chatto and Windus, 1961).

Willis, Jonathan, *Church Music and Protestantism in Post-Reformation England: Discourses, Sites and Identities* (Aldershot: Ashgate, 2010).

Wilson, Katherine, 'Revenge and Romance: George Pettie's *Palace of Pleasure* and Robert Greene's *Pandosto*', in Mike Pincombe and Cathy Shrank (eds), *The Oxford Handbook of Tudor Literature 1485–1603* (Oxford: Oxford University Press, 2009), 687–703.

Wiseman, Susan, 'Popular Culture: A Category for Analysis?', in Matthew Dimmock and Andrew Hadfield (eds), *Literature and Popular Culture in Early Modern England* (Farnham: Ashgate, 2009).

Woolf, Daniel R., *Reading History in Early Modern England* (Cambridge: Cambridge University Press, 2000).

Woudhuysen, Henry, *Sir Philip Sidney and the Circulation of Manuscripts, 1558–1640* (Oxford: Oxford University Press, 1996).

Wright, Christopher J. (ed.), *Sir Robert Cotton as Collector: Essays on an Early Stuart Courtier and his Legacy* (London and Toronto: British Library, 1997).

Wright, Herbert G., *The First English Translation of 'Decameron'* (Upsala: Harvard University Press, 1953).

Wrightson, Keith, 'Estates, Degrees, and Sorts: Changing Perceptions of Society in Tudor and Stuart England', in P.J. Corfield (ed.), *Language, History and Class* (Oxford: 1991), pp. 30–52.

Zim, Rivkah, 'Batman, Stephan (*c.* 1542–1584)', *Oxford Dictionary of National Biography*, Oxford University Press, 2004; online edn, May 2011, http://www.oxforddnbe.com/view/article/1704.

Zunshine, Lisa (ed.), *Acting Theory and the English Stage, 1700–1830*, vol. I (London: Pickering and Chatto, 2009).

Zurcher, Andrew, *Shakespeare and Law* (London: Arden Shakespeare, 2010).

Index